LAN Times Guide to Interoperability

Edited by Tom Sheldon

Osborne **McGraw-Hill**

Berkeley New York St. Louis San Francisco
Auckland Bogotá Hamburg London Madrid
Mexico City Milan Montreal New Delhi Panama City
Paris São Paulo Singapore Sydney
Tokyo Toronto

Osborne **McGraw-Hill**
2600 Tenth Street
Berkeley, California 94710
U.S.A.

LAN Times Guide to Interoperability

1234567890 DOC 9987654

ISBN 0-07-882043-X

Publisher
Lawrence Levitsky

Acquisitions Editor
Jeff Pepper

Project Editor
Nancy McLaughlin

Copy Editor
Jan Jue

Proofreader
Stefany Otis

Indexer
Matthew Spence

Computer Designer
Peter F. Hancik

Quality Control Specialist
Joe Scuderi

Illustrator
Marla Shelasky

Cover Design
John Nedwidek

About the Authors

In the early stages of this book it became clear that there was no way one person could put together what we were trying to accomplish. We decided to gather a group of industry experts to write about their respective areas of expertise. We thank each of these authors for a fine job, and for their patience during the process of bringing this project together.

Tom Sheldon has worked in the computer industry for fifteen years, and is a fully authorized Novell service and support technician and Novel Certified Network Engineer (CNE). He is the author of eighteen books, including *Novell NetWare 386: The Complete Reference, Novell NetWare 4: The Complete Reference, Windows NT Inside and Out,* and the *LAN Times Encyclopedia of Networking.*

Bradley F. Shimmin is an associate reviews editor for McGraw-Hill's *LAN Times* magazine, and a former local area network administrator. He has had extensive experience with, and written many articles about, personal computer hardware and software. Brad's areas of expertise include the Macintosh, OS/2, Ethernet standards, Hub architecture, cabling systems, and internetworking strategies. He lives in Salt Lake City, Utah.

James Pringle is a consulting systems engineer for CompuCom Systems in the Seattle area. He has been in the computer industry for fifteen years. He has designed, installed, and maintained numerous and diverse wide area networks for numerous Fortune 500 companies. In addition to telecommunications, Jim supports multihost, multiprotocol environments over various topologies.

Joseph Radin, co-author of *X Window Inside and Out* and the *Unix System Administration Guide,* is a software specialist at the Canadian division of Digital Equipment Corporation. He holds a Masters of Science degree from the Technion, Israel Institute of Technology, which he received after completing his thesis at the University of California, Berkeley.

Levi Reiss, co-author of *X Window Inside and Out* and the *Unix System Administration Guide,* has been working with computers since 1972. He has served as a consultant at the Ottawa Heart Institute, where he set up microcomputer databases. Levi has published several text books, and holds a Master's degree in Computer Science from the University of Paris. Currently he is an instructor at La Cité Collégiale in Ottawa, Ontario.

Gary Burnette joined IBM's Networking Systems Division in 1983 as a VTAM development programmer. He has worked on numerous SNA enhancements to VTAM, both as a designer on the APPN S/390 implementation and managing APPC/mVS development in IBM's Enterprise Systems Division. He currently manages the VTAM Strategy and Requirements group, setting the direction for technical production, and has spoken at a number of industry tradeshows and user groups.

Mary Morris has worked in various MIS positions for 13 years. Her experience includes mixing Novell and TCP/IP at Hunter Systems, and mixing LAN Manager and TCP/IP at Grid Systems. Currently she is a Systems Administrator at Sun Microsystems, where the network is everything.

Ken Neff has been working with and writing about NetWare since 1986, when he started as a product documentation writer for Novell, Inc. He has been a technical editor for *NetWare Technical Journal* and a reviews editor for *LAN TIMES*. He is currently the managing editor of *Novell Application Notes,* a monthly technical journal published by Novell's Systems Research Department.

J. D. Marymee has worked in the networking industry since 1983. An Enterprise Certified Network Engineer and a current Certified NetWare Instructor, Marymee has experience in consulting, programming, network design, and implementation. Currently, he is employed by Novell as a Corporate Integration Manager responsible for pre-sales technical briefings, end-user seminars, and network design, as well as for knowing everything else (when technically possible).

Mary Hubley is Datapro Information Services Group's senior analyst, responsible for analyzing open systems markets and technologies. She has been published in several magazines, including *Computerworld* and *BYTE,* and is frequently quoted in trade publications. Prior to her six years with Datapro, Mary spent eight years at RCA, where she developed engineering courses and evaluated and wrote software applications. She has also served as a technical representative and systems manager for a medical software developer.

Joe Salemi is a freelance writer and computer consultant, and a contributing editor to *PC Magazine,* specializing in databases, networks, and communications. He is also the author of three books on Client/Server computing: *PC Magazine Guide to Client/Server Databases, Client/Server Computing with ORACLE,* and *Client/Server Computing with SYBASE SQL Server.* Joe lives in Alexandria, Virginia with his wife Nancy, Max the dog, a parakeet, and two gerbils.

Irving Robinson is a Chief Technical Officer for the Decision Enabling Systems Division of AT&T Global Information Solutions (formerly NCR Corporation). His work with AT&T has included designing architecture for massively parallel-processing computer systems, developing database management strategy, and enterprise-wide information management. Irv has also served as a database management systems developer for Cincom Systems Inc.

Larry Joseph's area of expertise is visualizing how to improve data-based business processes with new information technologies. Periodically, he emerges from his imagination to check reality, explain his visions to business and government clients, and listen to his voice mail at Virtual Firmware, the Austin, Texas-based company he founded, which specializes in creating rapid development methodologies, tools, and systems for business managers, end-users, and database developers.

Barbara R. Hume is a partner with Network Technical Services, a Provo, Utah-based consultancy. Co-author of *The Small Business Guide to Networking* from M&T Books and author of the long-running *LAN Times* column "LAN'guage," she has written about networking in books and trade publications since 1985. Barbara specializes in writing for the end-user and network administrator audiences.

Barbara Bochenski is President of the Bolden Group in Bellevue, Washington. A 32-year IS veteran, she has worked as an Integration Specialist at Rockwell International, manager of Integration Technology at General Dynamics, and a team member in the international interoperability standards work at Boeing. She has also performed general computer services for IBM, Bell Labs, the Federal Reserve Banking System, the Executive Office of the President of the United States, and The White House in Washington D.C., among other enterprises. Barbara has written many articles in *Computerworld* and *Software Magazine*, and currently has a column in *Client/Server Computing* called "Client/Server 101." She is author of the John Wiley & Sons book, *Implementing Production-Quality Client/Server Systems*.

Raymond C. Williams is a Senior Technical staff member at IBM's Networking Software Division, currently working on Systems and Network Management Strategy including Heterogeneous Network Management involving SNA, OSI and TCP/IP protocols. Ray is a frequent speaker on Network Management at industry conferences and forums in the U.S. and overseas. He was named one of the "Top 25 Industry Visionaries for 1991" by *Communications Week*, and is listed in *Who's Who in Registry of Global Industry Leaders*.

Mark Pielocik is a Senior Network/Systems Analysis working for BOSE Corporation. He has 13 years experience designing, installing and managing local and wide area networks

Contents

Part II

Transport Services

Part III

Application-Level Technologies and Services

Acknowledgments

An undertaking such as this one is a lot of work for a lot of people. In order to do the job well, we enlisted the support of some of the best people in the industry. Our thanks go out to all of you. Hopefully we haven't forgotten anyone.

The project was masterminded and organized by Jeff Pepper at Osborne/McGraw-Hill, who acted as talent agent and editor. His associate, Ann Wilson, did an admirable job of keeping the project in focus while maintaining her good humor. Cleaning up the manuscript was ably managed by Nancy McLaughlin, also at Osborne.

There were also a number of people who critiqued the book or helped locate authors. Since this is a *LAN Times* book, we'll start with the people at *LAN Times*: Michela O'Connor Abrams, Susan Breidenbach, Eric Harper, Eric Boden, Thom Duncan, and Laura Moorhead. We also got help from Mike Nadeau and Ben Smith at *BYTE*, David Flack at *Open Computing*, and Joe Braue at *Data Communications*.

Aside from the magazines, the companies that are striving to make interoperability work have provided tremendous support for this project, and we owe them a debt of gratitude. We hope that this book will help their customers become better acquainted with the field.

Our friends at Oracle Corporation, Matt Bennett and David Michaud, provided much necessary technical information. IBM marched out the troops for this one; we'd like to thank Melissa Robertson, Gail Ostrow, Diane Walewski, Mary Wright, Joanne Perry, Cheryl Milton, and Luther Griffin.

Randy Smerik of AT&T, Nan Borreson at Borland, Jim McGuinness at DEC, Greg Lobdell and David Seres at Microsoft, Chris Germann and Rose Kearsley at Novell, Richard Soley of the Object Management Group, Dave Doring at Network Technical Services, Vivian Hannon of Dalhousie University, and Kevin Marinelli at UCONN all lent their support, ideas or recommendations to this project. Special thanks to Karin Ellison at SunSoft for her always cordial assistance and fine recommendations.

Finally, thanks to the following writers, whose ideas and participation helped shape the book: Jed Harris, David McClanahan, James Keogh, John Hedtke, Ed Jones, Werner Feibel, Frank Hayes, T. K. Nelson, Daniel Kelly, and Tom Rutt.

Introduction

*I*nteroperability is the ability of different computer systems, networks, operating systems, and applications to work together and share information. Of course, there are many levels of interoperability. We can get two different systems to exchange files, but we may not be able to open and read those files unless they undergo some alteration. Computers, networks, and the computer industry in general will gain a high level of interoperability in the 1990s. The *LAN Times Guide to Interoperability* will help you evaluate current technologies and future interoperability trends. It has been written for network managers, administrators, planners, technicians, and just about anyone else involved in the integration of computer systems, applications, and data. In particular, it provides information that can help you accomplish the following:

- Build a network platform for your organization that serves as a "plug-and-play" communication system, onto which you can attach a variety of computer systems and resources

- Connect networks and computing resources that currently exist as "islands" in departments and workgroups

- Interconnect systems that use a variety of different communication protocols, such as Novell's IPX and the Internet's TCP/IP protocol suite

■ Take advantage of new high-speed communications services for wide area networks (WANs) that give remote users the same speed and access to data as locally connected users

■ Provide users with easy access to mainframe and minicomputer systems and the data that resides on those systems

■ Provide users with access to data at a variety of dispersed locations, while maintaining the accuracy and timeliness of the data

■ Incorporate client/server applications and technologies into your organization

■ Allow users within your organization to share electronic mail and documents

■ Enable users anywhere in your organization to work on group projects, and automate the flow of paperwork throughout the organization

■ Create a common network management system

These are only a few of the topics covered in this book. We have gathered some of the best writers and professionals in the industry to address issues related to building interoperable systems and company-wide networks. We start at the hardware level by discussing the components, wiring systems, and architectures you need for integrating systems. We then discuss common industry-standard network communication protocols, and how to work with one or more of these protocols at a time. We move on to the application level by discussing tools and techniques that allow users in your organization to share data and resources, and to communicate with one another. You'll learn about emerging technologies that take advantage of enterprise networks, such as the following.

Client/Server Computing   Defines an architecture for network computing in which users running applications at network-attached computers (clients) interact with applications running at server systems.

Compound Documents   Documents containing text and multimedia information that can be edited by anyone on the network.

Electronic Mail   A system that allows users to communicate via messages over a network. Messages are stored and forwarded, and the recipients can read them and reply at their convenience.

Groupware Applications   Applications that let users work on group projects and share information. Electronic mail forms the delivery system for groupware applications.

Middleware Products   Programs that help network designers and administrators link a diversity of computer systems and data by providing a "middle layer" of software that serves as an interface.

Object-Oriented Data Storage   Software technologies for storing data in many forms (text, graphics, multimedia) that can be accessed by many different applications and systems.

Workflow Software   Programs that help automate paper processes and the flow of documents through an organizations by providing document management systems for computer networks.

This book can be approached in two ways. Each chapter can be read on its own, or you can start with Chapter 1 and read progressively to the end. Most of the topics presented here are relevant in a variety of situations, and different authors sometimes offer differing strategies or opinions about the topic at hand. I have not tried to sway the opinions of the authors in any one direction, especially in discussions of which standard is better than another. Each chapter reflects the author's unique and valuable networking experience.

What Is an Enterprise Network?

When we talk about _enterprise networks,_ we are referring to a network that has been created by linking existing computer resources within an organization. These resources are typically located in separate departments or workgroups, and often use a variety of network topologies and communication protocols. At higher levels, these systems typically run different operating systems and applications. The goal of an enterprise network administrator is to integrate these systems so that anyone in the organization can communicate, share information, and share resources. An enterprise network provides interoperability among autonomous and heterogeneous systems. The goals of building an enterprise network include the following:

- Integrating incompatible communication systems
- Reducing the number of communication protocols in use throughout the organization
- Increasing network throughput to handle more users and larger data files (multimedia files)
- Allowing users of diverse applications to share information in a variety of formats and standards, without their having know about those differences
- Maintaining reasonable levels of security without encumbering the use of the system
- Quickly adapting the system to changing needs

Enterprise networking is an evolutionary step beyond the departmental networks and workgroup computing strategies of the 1980s, which were concerned with integrating small groups of personal and desktop computers. Enterprise networking is both local and wide area in scope. It integrates all the systems within an organization, whether they are DOS-based computers, Apple Macintoshes, UNIX workstations, minicomputers, or mainframes. Many companies have revolted against the proprietary interfaces of the so-called "big-iron" vendors like IBM and DEC, and have moved to systems that use open networking standards or that operate with a variety of *de facto* industry standards. IBM and DEC have followed the trend toward interoperable systems, and now support non-proprietary networking schemes.

An enterprise network can be viewed as a "plug-and-play" platform on which a variety of systems will connect, as shown in Figure A. Bridges, routers, and wide area telecommunication links are used to interconnect the once isolated networks in different departments and workgroups. In this scheme, no system is an island.

There are two scenarios for building enterprise networks:

■ Using operating systems, applications, and hardware products that support a variety of networking protocols

■ Creating a network platform with underlying communication standards that allow hardware and software products to work together

Interestingly, both strategies are being implemented as computer processing power improves and equipment costs drop. Vendors are no longer focusing on a single standard or protocol architectures, but instead are providing support for a variety of

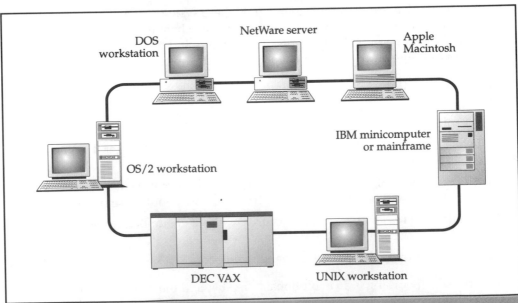

Figure A.   *An enterprise network is a platform that allows for the connection of a variety of systems.*

protocols. It is not uncommon to find a network that simultaneously transports IPX, TCP/IP, and AppleTalk protocol packets for attached DOS, Unix, and Windows NT, and Macintosh workstations. Servers run multiple protocol stacks to communicate with a variety of systems. Chapter 9 of this book discusses multiprotocol strategies in the network environment.

But a multiprotocol strategy only provides links at the network level. Just because a Unix workstation can communicate with a NetWare server using the TCP/IP protocol does not mean that it can run applications or access files on that system. Higher levels of interoperability are required in order to let users open files on other systems and display those files in their native formats. For example, a user at a UNIX workstation might want to open a file created by a user at a DOS workstation, without losing the formats applied to that document. Software vendors who provide applications for multiple platforms are making this type of access possible. For example, a user of Microsoft Excel on a Windows workstation can open an Excel file created in the Apple Macintosh environment without losing any of the formatting information. In Chapter 10 of this book, we begin our discussion of application-level integration.

Client/Server Computing and Middleware

Fortunately, high levels of interoperability are emerging in the '90s with the growth of client/server computing, middleware products, interplatform messaging services, and vendor strategies that support other vendors' products. Client/server computing provides a way for desktop system users to access a server and then to open and save files or run processes on that server. In most cases, the same or compatible operating systems and computer platforms are used, but current trends give the client the ability to access data on a variety of back-end systems. We examine client/server computing in Chapter 12.

The industry is firmly set on providing client/server computing and enterprise network capabilities. Consider the following vendor or industry strategies, which are detailed in this book.

- Microsoft's *Windows Open Service Architecture (WOSA)* is a strategy to build middleware directly into its operating systems so that information flows more easily throughout the enterprise. WOSA includes Open Database Connectivity (ODBC), which is a standard for interfacing many different types of databases.

- Apple Computer's *Apple Open Collaborative Environment (AOCE)* is a development environment for consolidating workgroups and workflow within an enterprise.

- The Open Software Foundation's (OSF's) *Distributed Computing Environment (DCE)* is a set of "enabling" software that hides the difference between multivendor products, technologies, and standards by providing tools for the development and maintenance of distributed applications.

■ *SQL Access Group (SAG)* and the *X/Open* group comprise a consortium of database vendors that are enforcing SQL (Structured Query Language) standards for accessing databases across multivendor systems.

■ *Distributed Relation Database Access (DRDA)* is an IBM standard for accessing database information across IBM platforms that follows SQL standards.

■ *The Object Management Group (OMG)* is providing standards for implementing cross-platform object-oriented environments. *Common Object Request Broker Architecture (CORBA)* is part of OMG's Object Management Architecture (OMA).

■ The *Common Open Software Environment (COSE)* is a consortium of vendors, including IBM, Hewlett Packard, SunSoft, and Novell, that are cooperating to deliver a common environment for UNIX.

In the IBM environment, APPC (Advanced Program-to-Program Communication) and APPN (Advanced Peer-to-Peer Networking) are providing a way to implement decentralized computing environments that support cooperative, peer-to-peer networking. IBM's *Networking Blueprint* defines support for industry standard communication protocols, such as TCP/IP and the OSI protocols. APPN allows each workstation to initiate its own communication session over the network, thus allowing for client/server computing, distributed databases, and remote procedure calls between multivendor products in traditionally IBM environments. Distributed database technologies are presented in Chapter 13, and object technologies are discussed in Chapter 14.

An emerging trend is toward making desktop and network operating systems interoperable right out of the box. For example, Microsoft Windows NT provides support for multiple protocols, such as TCP/IP and NetBIOS. The Open Software Foundation's (OSF's) Distributed Computing Environment (DCE) provides an environment that any vendor can use to develop applications with built-in, multivendor-distributed processing capabilities, including directory services, authentication, public key encryption, and more. DCE is basically the common infrastructure on which an organization can build its enterprise system.

Messaging, Workflow, and Workgroups

Enterprise networking is getting a boost at the application level as software suites, groupware, and workflow software gain popularity. This category of software uses electronic messaging as a vehicle for user interaction. Messaging systems provide communication tools that allow network users to collaborate on projects, work in diverse groups, and electronically automate paper processes, such as the flow of business documents, through an organization. To streamline the development of these products, the industry has developed the following messaging standards, which are covered further in Chapters 15 and 16.

Common Mail Calls   An industry supported specification that will allow applications to access messaging services on a variety of supported platforms. The X.400 API Association is supporting and improving the standard.

Apple Open Collaboration Environment   An Apple Computer-specific architecture that defines how to create applications in a distributed Macintosh, and multivendor environment.

Messaging API (MAPI)   A Windows-specific messaging interface that is part of Microsoft's Windows Open Services Architecture (WOSA).

Vendor-Independent Messaging (VIM)   A Lotus-specific interface that lets applications communicate with a variety of application, including Lotus cc:Mail and Lotus Notes. It is supported by a number of other vendors.

The Future of Interoperability

Current trends point to increased client/server computing in distributed computing environments. Users will require faster links to back-end services, including database management systems running on different platforms. High-speed, wide area network communication strategies such as Frame Relay, SMDS (Switched Multimegabit Data Service), and the emerging ATM (Asynchronous Transfer Mode) standard allow organizations to link people at widely dispersed locations while maintaining a high level of throughput. High throughput is required for such applications as on-line transactions, groupware, and video conferencing. High-speed local and wide area networking technologies are discussed in Chapters 1 through 3.

Graphical user interfaces like Microsoft Windows now support multimedia right out of the box. However, the new voice e-mail, video, and other multimedia features require increasingly large storage devices, as well as high-bandwidth connections. Technologies like switched Ethernet LANs and Fast Ethernet can provide this bandwidth in the local environment. For example, Switched Ethernet supports *microsegmentation*, which places as few as one workstation on a LAN segment and reduces contention for the media. *Prioritization* methods provide a way to deliver real-time video by setting aside a number of packets in the communication stream, thus ensuring that video information has enough bandwidth to arrive on time and in order. Chapters 1 through 3 cover these technologies as well.

Vendors are now providing hubs that support a number of different LAN and media types and that allow communication between those LANs. It is now possible to create "virtual LANs" that connect groups of users over any type of hardware platform. For example, a user on a token ring segment and a user on an Ethernet segment can now become part of the same workgroup. ATM switching hubs can provide the bandwidth and connectivity necessary for linking any user with any other user or device, over a virtual circuit that can eliminate the need for routing devices.

PART ONE

The Network Platform

Chapter One

Networks—Today and Tomorrow

by Tom Sheldon

Acomputer network is a data communication system that links two or more computers and peripheral devices. As shown in Figure 1-1, a network consists of network interface cards (NICs), cables, and software. An NIC is installed in each system, and systems are interconnected with cable. The logical configuration of a network communication system is pictured in Figure 1-2. In each system, network communication software is installed, allowing users and applications to access the network and exchange information with other systems attached to the network.

Why Establish a Network?

The growth of local area network (LAN) technology has, for the most part, taken place at the departmental level. During the 1980s, personal computers began to invade the desktop. Individual users collected and stored their own programs and data and broke free from the control of central information systems such as mainframes. Eventually, department managers turned to LAN technology as a way to share data resources among departmental users. Each department typically followed its own selection criteria when purchasing hardware and software. Consequently, organizations that are faced with the task of integrating departmental LANs into enterprise-wide networks must find ways to get dissimilar systems to interoperate.

The basic departmental LAN is pictured on the left in Figure 1-3. On the right, several departmental LANs are connected together to form an *internetwork,* which allows more users in an organization to communicate and share resources with one another. The internetwork in the picture is still a LAN because it occupies a local area. In fact, the term "internetwork" is very loosely defined. It could describe the interconnection of two LANs that use different network operating systems and communication protocols, or it could describe the interconnection of LANs that are separated by buildings or a large geographic area. This latter category is usually referred to as a wide area network (WAN), and is pictured in Figure 1-4. A WAN is an

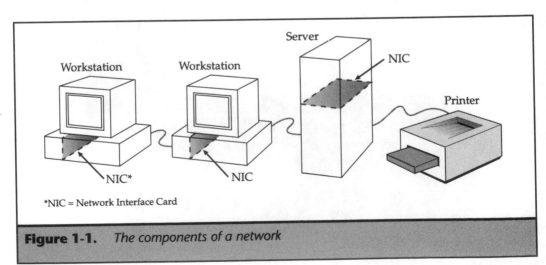

Figure 1-1.   *The components of a network*

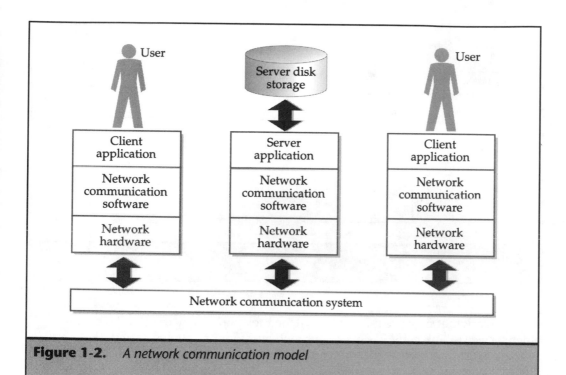

Figure 1-2.   *A network communication model*

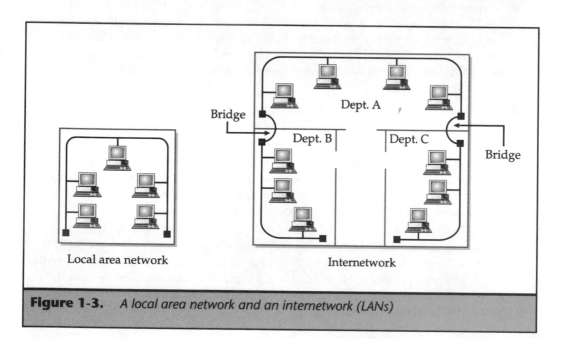

Figure 1-3.   *A local area network and an internetwork (LANs)*

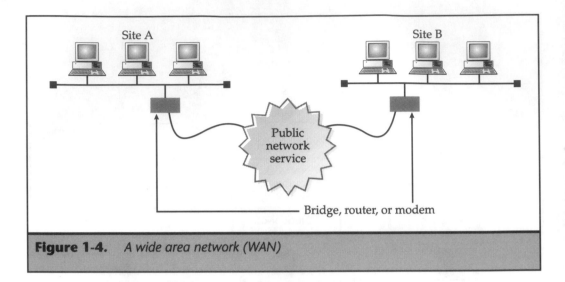

Figure 1-4. *A wide area network (WAN)*

internetwork that may use the public switched-telephone network (PSTN) or some other service to link networks over metropolitan, state, or national boundaries.

A network can start small, and then grow with an organization. Here is a list of the different types of networks available:

■ *Network segment or subnetwork*   A network segment is typically defined by hardware or a specific network address. For example, in the Novell NetWare environment, a network segment includes all the workstations attached to a network interface card in a server; each segment has its own network address. In the Ethernet environment, all computers attached to a segment receive the same signal broadcasts.

■ *Local area network (LAN)*   A LAN is a network segment with attached workstations and servers, or a collection of interconnected network segments, generally within the same area, such as a building.

■ *Campus network*   A campus network extends to other buildings within a campus or industrial park. The various segments or LANs within each building are typically connected with backbone cables. The organization usually owns the grounds and is free to lay cable as required.

■ *Metropolitan area network (MAN)*   A MAN network is a network that spans cities or counties, and is interconnected using various public or private facilities, such as the public telephone system or providers of microwave or optical media communication systems. Note that the organization does not usually own the interconnection facilities, which span public space and are subject to various local or federal restrictions.

- *Wide area network (WAN) and global networks*   WANs and global networks span intercity, interstate, or international borders. Links are made with public and private telecommunications facilities, as well as microwave and satellite links.

- *Enterprise network*   An enterprise network interconnects all the computer systems within an organization, regardless of operating system, communication protocols, application differences, or geographic location. It may therefore be a LAN, MAN, or WAN. The network itself is viewed as a platform onto which many different types of devices are connected. Various techniques are employed to hide the differences among systems so users can access any resources in a transparent way. For example, middleware products hide communication protocols and differences in applications.

The enterprise network is typically a *distributed computing system*, one in which resources and data are located throughout the organization. In this environment, directory services are required to help users locate other users, resources, and data. Security is also an issue. Once a network connects an entire company, department and workgroup managers need to restrict access to the data they own through various security techniques. In addition, some databases are copied to remote locations to make data more readily available to users at those sites and to reduce costs associated with accessing that data over expensive WAN links.

Why establish a computer network? That may seem obvious, but the reasons for doing so, as outlined next, shed light on what a network is and what it can do for an organization.

Program and File Sharing   Networkable versions of many popular software packages are available at considerable cost savings compared with buying individually licensed copies. The program and its data files are stored on a file server and accessed by many network users.

Network Resource Sharing   Network resources include printers, plotters, and storage devices. The network provides a communication link that lets users share these devices.

Database Sharing   A database management system is an ideal application for a network. A network feature called *record-locking* lets multiple users simultaneously access a file without corrupting the data. Record-locking ensures that no two users edit the same record at the same time.

Economical Expansion of the PC Base   Networks provide an economical way to expand the number of computers in an organization. You can attach to a network inexpensive diskless workstations that use the server's hard drive for booting and storage.

Workgroups   A network provides a way to create groups of users that are not necessarily located within the same department. Workgroups facilitate new "flat" corporate structures in which people from diverse and remote departments belong to special group projects.

Electronic Mail   Electronic mail (e-mail) lets users easily communicate with one another. Messages are dropped in "mailboxes" for the recipients to read at a convenient time.

Groupware and Workflow Software   Groupware and workflow software are designed specifically for networks and take advantage of e-mail systems to help users collaborate on projects, schedules, and document processing.

Centralized Management   A network provides a way to centralize servers and their data, along with other resources. Hardware upgrades, software backups, system maintenance, and system protection are much easier to handle when devices are located in one place.

Enhancement of the Corporate Structure   Networks can change the structure of an organization and the way it is managed. Users who work in a specific department and for a specific manager no longer need to be in the same physical area. Their offices can be located in areas where their expertise is most needed. The network ties them to their department managers and peers. This arrangement is useful for special projects in which individuals from different departments, such as research, production, and marketing, need to work closely with each other.

Network Environments

The environment of a network is defined by the network operating system and the protocols that provide communication and network services. There are two basic types of network operating systems: peer-to-peer systems and dedicated server systems.

Peer-to-peer   This type of network operating system allows users to share the resources on their computers and to access shared resources on other computers. The term *peer-to-peer* indicates that all systems have the same status on the network. No system is subordinate to another.

Dedicated-server   In a dedicated-server operating system, such as Novell NetWare, one or more computers perform the task of storing shared files and making network resources available to network users. Each server may have its own administrator or supervisor who manages security, data protection (for example, backups), and other required tasks.

Some common network operating system environments are listed next, but keep in mind that most vendors now offer a variety of operating system and communication protocol options that allow organizations to build heterogeneous networks.

- IBM peer-to-peer SNA networks running APPC/APPN protocols
- UNIX peer-to-peer operating systems running TCP/IP protocols
- Novell NetWare dedicated server operating systems running SPX/IPX communication protocols
- Windows NT and Windows for Workgroups peer-to-peer environments running NetBIOS/NetBEUI or TCP/IP communication protocols

To understand network operating environments, it's useful to compare them to the centralized minicomputer and mainframe processing environments. In the centralized processing environments that were dominant before desktop computers and local area networks, a central processing system performed all the processing tasks for the terminals attached to it. Terminals are often called *dumb* devices because they have no processor or memory of their own. They simply provide output on the screen and accept input from the user via the keyboard. The central processor allocates a share of its processing power to every user who is accessing the system through a terminal. Performance of central processing systems drops as more users log on.

In the network environment, desktop computer systems attached to the network have their own processors and memory, and can run programs on their own. Because each system performs its own processing, the network as a whole can scale up to higher levels of performance. When performance degradations occur, it is usually due to excessive network traffic or overworked servers. But since each computer attached to the network can handle many processing and storage tasks (using local disk storage) on its own, network traffic and loads on network servers are minimal compared to loads placed on centralized processing systems by dumb terminals.

Since, in a distributed computing environment, each system performs some processing on its own, we can view the entire network as a collection of processing devices. In some cases, a task might be processed by several computers simultaneously, with the network providing a way to communicate the exchange of information and to coordinate events. Servers are often the most powerful processing devices on the network. Networks and applications that split processing between a "front-end" workstation and a "back-end" server are engaged in *client/server relationships*. The server provides tasks such as file storage and retrieval, management, printer sharing, and security.

In a distributed computing environment, a wide variety of servers may be used. These servers can be used at one centralized site to simplify management and backups, or be used at individual department or workgroup sites where local managers maintain control over data. Data is often duplicated or replicated to multiple sites to reduce loss from downed systems, keep the data available, and make it more easily accessible to users at remote sites. For example, it makes sense to copy data to a server at a remote site, rather than have remote users access the data over expensive WAN links at a central site. In this scenario, synchronization of data is an issue. Managers need to evaluate whether users accessing replicated data need immediate access to changes in the master database. In some cases, timely updates are not an issue.

Components of a Network

A computer network consists of both hardware and software. The hardware includes network interface cards and the cable that ties them together. The software components include server operating systems, communication protocols, and network interface card drivers.

Network Operating System

In a peer-to-peer network, each node on the network runs an operating system with built-in networking support that allows users to share files and peripherals with other network users. Some security and management features may be built into the software. Microsoft Windows for Workgroups, Microsoft Windows NT, Novell Personal NetWare, and Artisoft LANtastic are examples of peer-to-peer network operating systems, These operating systems support the most common network interface cards and communication protocols. As few as two systems can be interconnected to allow users to exchange files, electronic messages, and run programs located on other systems.

The network operating system for a dedicated network operating system runs on stand-alone servers. The advanced versions of Novell NetWare run on stand-alone systems and provide high levels of performance and security. Workstations run client software that provides the communication protocols and network interface card support.

Servers

A server provides the following capabilities to users on the network. Modular network operating systems like Novell NetWare can provide some or all of these services in one or more servers, depending on which modular components the administrator chooses to load.

- *File server*   This server provides file storage and retrieval services, including security features that control file access rights.

- *E-mail server or gateway*   An e-mail server or gateway provides local or enterprise-wide electronic mail services and translation between different mail systems.

- *Communications server*   This server provides connection services to mainframe or minicomputer systems, or to remote computer systems and networks via wide area links.

- *Database server*   This server is a dedicated system that handles user database requests and responses.

- *Backup and archive server*   This system is dedicated to backing up and archiving files on the network.

- *Fax server*   This server manages incoming and outgoing faxes for network users. Users can send faxes from their desktop to the fax server, which forwards them over the telecommunication system, or to other network users.

- *Print server*   This server provides user access to printers attached to the network and manages print jobs through a print queue system.

- *Directory services server*   This server provides a way for users to look up information about users and resources on the network. The server tracks network users, servers, and resources in a database.

Client Systems (Nodes or Workstations)

Client systems attach to the network via network interface cards. Client software is required in each system to support the specific type of interface card attached and the routines the card uses to access the network. Client software is typically loaded when the network-attached system is started. The client software directs service requests made by users or applications to either the local operating system or to remote servers and resources.

A specific protocol allows clients to communicate with servers. In the NetWare environment, this protocol is Internetwork Packet Exchange (IPX). Other common protocols include Transmission Control Protocol/Internet Protocol (TCP/IP), DECnet, and AppleTalk. As organizations connect their diverse networks into enterprise systems, there has been a need for individual systems to support more than one protocol. For example, a user might need to run IPX to communicate with a NetWare server and TCP/IP to communicate with a UNIX system.

Two major network driver standards have been developed to support these multiprotocol requirements: Microsoft Network Driver Interface Specification (NDIS) and Novell Open Data-link Interface (ODI). Both provide a way to load multiple protocol stacks into the memory of a computer to support multiple network protocols on one or more network interface cards.

Network Interface Cards (NICs)

Network interface cards (NICs) are adapters installed in a computer that provide the connection point to a network. Each NIC is designed for a specific type of network, for example, Ethernet, token ring, FDDI, or ARCNET. NICs operate at the physical layer relative to the Open Systems Interconnection (OSI) protocol stack and provide an attachment point for a specific type of cable, such as coaxial cable, twisted-pair cable, or fiber-optic cable. NICs for wireless LANs have an antenna for communication with a base station.

Network interface cards have specific mechanical and electrical interface characteristics. The mechanical specifications define the physical connection methods for cable. The electrical specifications define the methods for transmitting bit streams across the cable and the control signals that provide the timing of data transfers across the network. The network interface card also defines cable access methods in accordance with IEEE 802.*x* standards or other standards. The IEEE 802.*x* standards define CSMA/CD (carrier sense multiple access/collision detection), token passing, and other access methods. IEEE 802.*x* networks including Ethernet, token ring, and FDDI use these access methods.

Circuitry on the card handles many of the network communication functions. To prepare for data transmission, a *handshaking* process takes place between two stations. This handshaking establishes communication parameters, such as the transmission speed, packet size, time-out parameters, and buffer size. Once the communication parameters are established, transmission of data packets begins. Data is converted in two ways before it is placed on the cable for transmission. First, a parallel-to-serial conversion transforms data for transport as electrical signals (a bit stream) over a cable. Second, data is encoded and compressed to improve transmission speed in some cases.

Global addressing ensures that every network interface card has a unique identifying node address. Token ring and Ethernet card addresses are hard-wired on the card. ARCNET addresses are switch-selectable by the end user. The IEEE (Institute of Electrical and Electronics Engineers) committee is in charge of assigning addresses to Token ring and Ethernet cards. Each manufacturer is given a unique code and a block of addresses. When you install a card, it is a good idea to determine the card address and write it down for future reference. You can also use a diagnostics utility supplied with the card to determine its address after you've installed the card in a system. You might also find the address on a label attached to the card.

Most network cards come with a socket for a remote-boot PROM (programmable read-only memory). You use remote-boot PROMs on diskless workstations that can't boot on their own, but instead boot from the network server. A diskless workstation is less expensive than a system with floppy disk and hard disk drives. It is also more secure because users can't download valuable data to floppy disks or upload viruses and other unauthorized software.

Cabling

Managers who need to install cable for networks face critical decisions. Cable and cable equipment must meet current and future transmission requirements, electrical characteristics, and topology. Fortunately, manufacturers have boosted data transfer rates on relatively inexpensive copper twisted-pair wire so that it should meet future demands for high-bandwidth to the desktop. Fiber-optic cable is a good choice for backbones. To help managers make informed decisions and design workable cable systems, a new wiring standard has emerged from the EIA/TIA (Electronic Industries Association/Telecommunications Industries Association) called the EIA/TIA-568 Commercial Building Wiring Standard. This standard is discussed further in Chapter 2 of this book.

There are two types of media for data transmission:

- *Guided media* includes metal wire (copper, aluminum, and so on) and fiber-optic cable. Cable is normally installed within buildings or underground conduit. Metal wires include twisted-pair wire and coaxial cable, with copper being the preferred core transmission material for networks. Fiber-optic cable is available with either single or multiple strands of plastic or glass fiber.

- *Unguided media* represents the techniques used to transmit signals through air and space from transmitter to receiver, such as infrared and microwave.

Copper cable is a relatively inexpensive, well-understood technology that is easy to install. It is the cable of choice for most network installations. However, copper cable suffers from various electrical characteristics that impose transmission limits. For example, it is resistant to the flow of electrons, which limits its transmission distance. It also radiates signals that can be monitored and is susceptible to external radiation that can distort signals. However, current products support Ethernet transmission speeds up to 100 megabits per second (Mbps), and AT&T is reportedly working on technology that will boost twisted-pair transmission rates above 500 Mbps.

In contrast, fiber cable transmits light signals (photons) through a core of pure silicon dioxide that is so clear, a three-mile thick window of it would not distort the view. Photonic transmissions produce no emissions outside the cable and are not affected by external radiation. Fiber cable is preferred where security is an issue. Computer signals are transmitted through fiber-optic cable by converting electronic 1's and 0's to light flashes. A light-emitting diode at one end flashes light through the cable that is collected at the other end with a simple photodetector and converted back to electrical signals. Because signals encounter virtually no resistance and because there are no emissions, fiber cable transmission rates are limited only by the purity of the glass core, the quality of equipment, and the speed of light.

One other overall characteristic of cable has to do with where it gets installed. To comply with the National Electrical Code (NEC), all cable installed in the *plenum space*, which is the airspace between the ceiling and the next floor or roof, must be installed in metal conduit, or must meet local fire codes. If the cable burns, it must not produce noxious or hazardous gases that are pumped to other parts of a structure through the plenum. Consequently, there are normal cable types that are insulated with PVC (polyvinyl chloride) materials and plenum-rated cables that are insulated with fluoropolymers such as DuPont's Teflon.

Copper Cable Characteristics

Binary data is transmitted over copper cable by applying a voltage at one end and receiving it at the other. Typically, a voltage of +V volts represents a digital 1, and a voltage of –V represents a digital 0. The three primary types of copper cable used to transmit digital signals are discussed next.

Straight Cable   Straight copper cable consists of copper wires surrounded by an insulator. It is used to connect various peripheral devices over short distances and at low bit rates. Serial cables that connect modems or serial printers use this type of wire. Straight cable suffers from crosstalk over long distances, so it is not suitable for networks.

Twisted-Pair   Twisted-pair cable consists of copper core wires surrounded by an insulator. Two wires are twisted together to form a pair, and the pair forms a circuit that can transmit data. A cable is a bundle of one or more twisted pairs surrounded by an insulator. Unshielded twisted-pair (UTP) is common in the telephone network. Shielded twisted-pair (STP) provides protection against interference. The twisting prevents interference problems. High data rates (100 Mbps) are possible if data-grade cable (Category 5) is installed and if the twists are maintained all the way to the connection points. Twisted-pair cable is used in Ethernet, token ring, and other network topologies.

Coaxial Cable   Coaxial cable consists of a solid copper core surrounded by an insulator, a combination shield and ground wire, and an outer protective jacket. Coaxial cable traditionally has higher bit rates (10 Mbps) than twisted-pair, but newer transmission techniques for twisted-pair equal or surpass coaxial cable rates. However, coaxial cable has greater distance potential than twisted-pair. While coaxial cable is the traditional media for Ethernet and ARCNET networks, twisted-pair and fiber-optic cable are common today. New structured wiring system standards call for data-grade twisted-pair wire that transmits at 100 Mbps, ten times the speed of coaxial cable. Coaxial cable is most likely a dead-end cabling scheme for large office environments and is being supplanted by twisted-pair and/or fiber-optic cabling schemes.

Twisted-Pair Cable

As mentioned earlier, twisted-pair cable is available as unshielded twisted-pair (UTP) or shielded twisted-pair (STP). UTP is the most commonly used twisted-pair cable, and it is specified in the EIA/TIA 568 Commercial Building Wiring Standard. The EIA/TIA 568 standard defines premises wiring. It applies to all UTP (unshielded twisted-pair) wiring schemes that work with Ethernet 10Base-T, token ring, PBX, ISDN, and twisted-pair-physical media-dependent (TP-PMD). EIA/TIA-568 has benefits for customers because it standardizes network cabling and installation, opening the market for competing products and services such as design, installation, and management of premises wiring.

EIA/TIA-568 defines the following cable categories:

- *Category 1*   This is traditional unshielded twisted-pair telephone cable that is suited for voice but not data. Most telephone cable installed before 1983 is Category 1 cable.

- *Category 2*   This is unshielded twisted-pair cable certified for data transmissions up to 4 Mbps. Similar to IBM Cabling System Type 3. This cable has four twisted pairs and costs less than 10 cents per foot. Plenum cable costs about 30 to 40 cents per foot.

- *Category 3*   This supports 10 Mbps transmission rates and is required for token ring (4 Mbps) and 10 Mbps Ethernet 10Base-T topologies. The cable has 4 pairs and three twists per foot. Costs are around 7 cents per foot. Plenum cable costs about 50 cents per foot.

- *Category 4*   This is certified for 16 Mbps transmission rates and is the lowest grade acceptable for 16 Mbps token ring topologies. The cable has four pairs and costs around 11 cents per foot. Plenum cable costs about 60 cents per foot.

- *Category 5*   This is 100-ohm, four-wire, twisted-pair copper cable that can transmit data at 100 Mbps to support emerging technologies like Fast Ethernet and ATM. The cable is low-capacitance and exhibits low cross talk. It costs about 16 cents per foot. Plenum cable costs about 60 cents per foot.

The high transmission rates of Category 5 (and other standards in the works) that deliver hundreds of megabits per second are attributable to tighter twisting of copper pairs, better materials, improved hardware designs, and new access methods. All cables, patch panels, and terminations must conform to the specifications to eliminate cross talk between wire pairs. Older modular connectors and jacks are not suitable for Category 5 installations. In addition, the twists in the wire must be maintained all the way up to the connection point.

The performance characteristics of Category 5 cabling and connections can provide 100 Mbps network connections. Any network that operates at this rate can take advantage of the cabling scheme. The standard is designed to support current and future networking needs. Recent studies by AT&T Paradyne indicate that Category 5 UTP cable can transmit up to 950 Mbps over 100-meter distances.

If an organization expects to need such high data rates, it would seem that Category 5 UTP is the most logical cable to install, preferable even to optical cable for horizontal runs. Though many organizations can't afford to pay now for what might be needed in the future, installing lower-grade cable will limit future growth. Managers will need to carefully evaluate current and future needs and the requirements of emerging high-bandwidth multimedia, videoconferencing, and imaging applications.

Network Connection Methods

To connect a network, you need network interface cards and cable (unless you're going wireless). There are several types of interface cards and cabling schemes.

Networks are defined by the type of cable used, the cable layout or topology, data transfer rates, communications protocols, and the method used by nodes to access and use the network (access methods). It's possible to build an internetwork that connects a variety of networks using bridges and routers.

The most popular network types are Ethernet (coaxial cable or twisted-pair cable), token ring, ARCNET, and FDDI (Fiber Distributed Data Interface). The data transfer rate of a network type is usually a deciding factor. ARCNET operates at 2 Mbps, token ring operates at 4 and 16 Mbps, Ethernet operates at 10 or 100 Mbps, and FDDI operates at 100 Mbps. In the past, the cable type used by a network was a factor, but today, most operate over inexpensive and adaptable twisted-pair cable. FDDI uses fiber-optic cable that provides a growth path to even faster network throughput.

Bridges and routers provide a way to join network segments of similar and dissimilar network types. A *bridge* only lets you interconnect similar network types, for example, Ethernet to Ethernet, or token ring to token ring, but a *router* lets you interconnect dissimilar network types, such as Ethernet to token ring. Novell NetWare, Windows NT, Banyan VINES, and other server operating systems have built-in bridging and routing. Each NIC installed in the server creates a separate network segment, and the operating system handles internetwork traffic.

Network Architecture

The architecture of a network is defined by its topology and the cable access method and communications protocols it uses. Before any workstation can access the cable, it must establish communication sessions with other nodes on the network. The cable access method in a network specification defines how a workstation gains access to the shared media so it can transmit information. Protocols are the rules and procedures that systems use to communicate with one another over the network.

Topology

You can think of a network's *topology* as a map of its cable layout. Topology defines how you run the cable to individual workstations and plays an important part in the decision you make about cable. As illustrated in Figure 1-5, a network can have a linear, ring, or star topology. You must consider the topology of a network when making decisions about which network type to install. Topology corresponds to how you will run the cable through the walls, floors, and ceilings of your building, as described next.

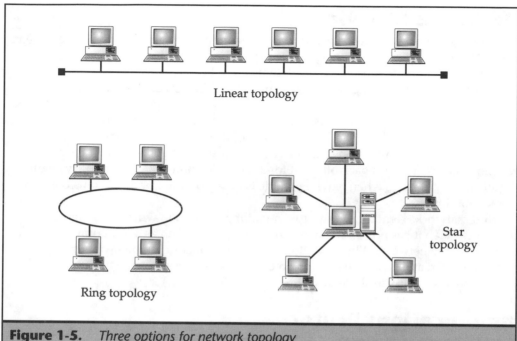

Linear topology

Ring topology

Star topology

Figure 1-5. *Three options for network topology*

Linear Topology   A linear topology consists of a single cable that extends from one computer to the next in a daisy-chain fashion. The ends of the cable are terminated with a resistor. Ethernet coaxial networks use linear topologies. While the single cable is easy to install, a break anywhere in the cable disables the entire network.

Star Topology   In a star topology, all wires branch from a single location, such as a file server or a central wiring closet. Star topologies require a cable to each workstation, but a broken cable only disconnects the workstation attached to it. Ethernet 10Base-T and token ring networks use star topologies.

Ring Topology   In a ring topology, the network cable connects back to itself and signals travel in a ring. Today, physical ring topologies are rare; however, token ring and ARCNET networks transfer packets in logical rings.

NOTE: *Token ring topology is wired in a star configuration, but forms a logical ring configuration—signals are passed from one station to the next, and eventually loop back to the beginning.*

Cable Access Method

The cable access method describes how a workstation gains access to the cable system. When the network interface card gains access to the cable, it begins sending packets of information in a framed format as bit streams over the network.

Linear cable systems such as Ethernet use a CSMA/CD (carrier sense multiple access/collision detection) method in which a workstation accesses the cable but backs off if another workstation attempts to access it at the same time. A workstation broadcasts a signal and every other node on the network hears it, but only the addressed node pays attention to it. If two nodes broadcast at the same time, a collision occurs and both back off, wait for a random amount of time, and try again. Performance degrades when network traffic is heavy because of these collisions and retransmissions.

Ring networks commonly use a token-passing method in which a station only transmits when it has possession of a token. Think of a token as a temporary ticket or pass to use the network. When a station is ready to transmit, it must wait for an available token and then take possession of the token. This prevents two machines from using the cable simultaneously.

Communications Protocols

Communications protocols are the rules and procedures used on a network to communicate among nodes that have access to the cable system. Protocols govern two levels of communications. High-level protocols define how applications communicate, and lower-level protocols define how signals are transmitted over a cable. There are protocols between these levels that establish and maintain communication sessions between computers and monitor traffic for errors. Communications protocols can be compared to diplomatic protocols, in which diplomats at different ranks negotiate with peer diplomats at other embassies. When network protocols are defined and published, vendors can easily design and manufacture network products that work on multivendor systems. Common communication protocols are discussed in Part II of this book.

Networking Devices

Network cabling systems have distance limitations due to signal loss and other electrical characteristics. You can extend the distance of network segments by adding a *repeater*, which regenerates the electrical signal and doubles the allowable length of the cable. A repeater may not let you add more workstations to the extended network than defined in the network's specification. A repeater is often used to connect workstations in a back office or warehouse with a front office.

To increase the distance of a network and add more stations, you can add another network segment and link them with a bridge. Bridges can be stand-alone devices, or may exist in network servers. For example, you can create a bridge in a NetWare server by installing two network cards. Bridges have the capability of keeping local traffic local and transferring only packets destined for other segments over the link. This helps reduce excess network traffic.

Routers provide a level of interconnectivity a step above bridges. A router can read addressing information in a packet that helps it determine the best possible path that will get it to its destination when a network has many different links, or pathways.

Hubs and wiring centers are used to build structured cabling systems. A *hub* is a concentrator that forms the center of a star-configured wiring scheme. The hub has a bus that typically accepts plug-in Ethernet, FDDI, token ring, or other types of modules. These modules have multiple ports for network workstations. Hubs are typically installed in a department and connect all the computers in that department to one another. Enterprise hubs interconnect each of the departmental hubs to form a hierarchical wiring scheme.

MAN and WAN Connection Methods

Metropolitan area networks (MANs) and wide area networks (WANs) provide connections between geographically diverse networks. *MANs* are usually high-speed fiber-optic networks that connect LAN segments within a metropolitan area. An alternative method is to use private networking schemes such as microwave systems. Microwave dishes are mounted on top of buildings and pointed at each other to establish an internetwork link.

WANs provide countrywide or global connections via telephone lines and satellites. Large corporations that have regional or worldwide offices use WANs to interconnect networks. Dedicated circuits are leased from long-distance carriers to provide full-time connections between systems. Alternatively, circuit-switched or packet-switched connections are available that operate at lower cost and provide more flexibility as far as usage and connection points.

Networking in the '90s

The current network paradigm is a multivendor, multiprotocol (heterogeneous) network, rather than the long-envisioned open systems environment in which all vendors create compatible equipment. Heterogeneous networks are built on an enterprise-wide level and connect a diverse range of systems, including department and workgroup LANs, as well as corporate mainframe and minicomputer systems. In this environment, network administrators are faced with the task of making diverse systems interoperate. This is accomplished by supporting a number of communications protocols, or using middleware products that hide protocols from users and applications.

While the physical computing resources of the network are distributed among departments and divisions of a company, responsibility and management of those resources is often handled by an enterprise network manager. This is because the enterprise network is designed to help the whole organization reach its goals, which include sharing of data and resources by any user anywhere within the organization. Departmental LANs can still maintain autonomy so that local managers can define security rights and protect local data from unauthorized users. However, the enterprise manager guides departments toward the common goal of companywide integration.

The new network is built with hubs, structured wiring systems, collapsed multiprotocol backbones, and high-speed wide area connections that let users at remote sites access corporate networks with little delay. Workstations will use RISC (reduced instruction set computer) processors that provide performance levels of 100 MIPS (millions of instructions per second) with hundreds of megabytes of RAM and gigabytes of disk storage space. Server throughput is increasing to meet the high demands of users. Ultrahigh-speed servers use multiple processors running at up to 200 MHz and providing 300 million instructions per second and higher. Mainframe and minicomputer systems are now viewed as powerful servers that attach directly to the network.

Many of the lower-level communication differences have been solved by supporting multiple communication protocols in every computer attached to the network. Administrators are now concerned with raising the level of interoperability to the application layer. The goal is to allow users running a variety of applications on a variety of platforms to access data throughout an enterprise network without worrying about interface, translation, and conversion issues. *Middleware* makes it easier for application developers to create software for these new environments. Middleware provides a standard programming layer that hides the complexity of networks and multivendor protocols from the programmer. The layers provide high-level APIs.

The Distributed Computing Environment (DCE) developed by the Open Software Foundation is providing tools that help administrators integrate heterogeneous environments. Apple's Open Collaborative Environment and Microsoft's Windows Open Services Architecture are strategies for building enterprise networks. Object-oriented environments like Microsoft's Cairo are in the works with the goal of providing data access through object technologies. In an object-oriented environment, data and the methods for working on that data are combined into a single object. Objects are important because they can be used across software and hardware platforms. Users can access objects on other systems at other locations using a variety of application interfaces. This global approach lets developers more easily create applications for accessing distributed databases.

Centralized management platforms are necessary in these computing environments. They reduce the number of management utilities and packages that must be learned, and centralize management, which helps reduce the number of required administrators. The next few chapters discuss these important trends in more detail.

Chapter Two

Network Technologies for the '90s

by Bradley F. Shimmin, *LAN Times*

Ahas technology progresses toward the end of the 20th century, both hardware and software approach one goal: complete interoperability between networks, between applications, and between users. Where there once were numerous, isolated workgroups, there will be a thriving metropolis of interconnected networks where individuals and companies can share information.

We are already nearing this goal. Consider the Internet, a rapidly growing, globe-spanning web of over 7500 networks with over a million host systems supporting 25 million users (and these numbers are expected to double by 1995).

Moving in tandem with this need to interconnect are a number of relatively new networking technologies that have previously been the subject of science fiction. For example, through videoconferencing, users are able to hold face-to-face electronic meetings over vast distances. Through powerful client/server database applications, companies can coordinate the simultaneous access of data by many users. And through multimedia applications, users are able to bring sound and animation from the network to the desktop.

To support these applications and their associated working environments, today's networks rely upon a heterogeneous mix of hardware and software. Driven by user choice and technical requirements, a network utilizing these features can consist of UNIX, DOS, OS/2, and Macintosh workstations operating over many different networking systems such as Ethernet, token ring, FDDI, and so on. Additionally, to connect these workstations, many different hardware products like repeaters, bridges, and routers must be used.

The Challenges of Networking in the '90s

Those responsible for building this network of the '90s have discovered that these applications and networking technologies bring, in addition to their inherent benefits, many challenges:

- Interoperability
- Manageability
- Security
- Capacity

Interoperability

The network of the '90s must be able to bring a large number of heterogeneous technologies together in a seamless manner. For example, in some enterprises, users of UNIX, Macintosh, and DOS workstations have a need to communicate with IBM mainframe systems and Novell NetWare file servers at the same time. These enterprise network configurations, as pictured in Figure 2-1, are basically the outgrowth of an emerging need for companies to connect their isolated departmental or workgroup

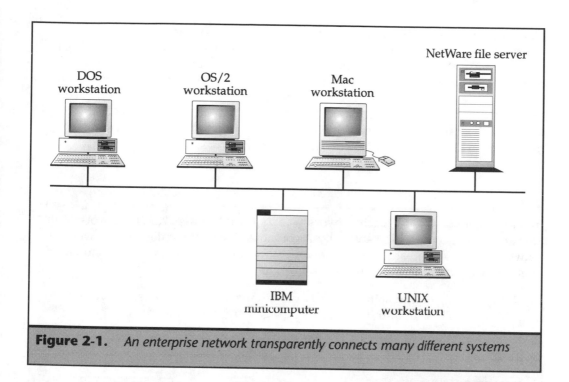

Figure 2-1.   *An enterprise network transparently connects many different systems*

networks into an encompassing, company-wide network that provides users with unlimited access to all company resources.

The road to such interoperability, however, is fraught with obstacles. For example, *bridges* are required to interconnect client workstations running token ring with client workstations running Ethernet. A bridge converts the frames of information transmitted on one network into a frame type that is required for transmission over another network. Bridges have several benefits, and some limitations. They can help administrators expand the distance limitations of a network, add more nodes to the network, reduce the amount of traffic, and link disparate protocols on a network. However, bridges are incapable of determining optimal pathways for data, and they lack any sort of network congestion control. These higher-level functions are handled by routing devices, which cost more money, but are well worth the expense on large, busy networks.

Manageability

A large problem with interoperable networks concerns their chaotic and complex nature. The numerous protocol suites such as TCP/IP, IPX/SPX, and DecLAT require hardware devices, such as multiprotocol routers, that demand higher management skills. To simplify this complexity, networks of the '90s will support management platforms that are capable of drawing status, configuration, and performance information from different hardware devices in a passive manner (see Figure 2-2). In this way, the managed hardware provides information that is passed on to management systems. Network managers can then view this information in various forms and use statistical methods to evaluate network performance and bottlenecks. In addition, management systems can help network managers handle software upgrades, licensing, and security. One thing to keep in mind, however, is that management systems can add excess traffic to the network, depending on the management features that are enabled.

Security

In the old network model, each network was confined to a department or workgroup area and managed by a local authority. As organizations build enterprise networks, network resources and stored information become more widely available, and become likely prey to security threats like the following:

■ Monitoring of transmitted data by unauthorized users with network monitoring devices. These unauthorized users may gather information directly by

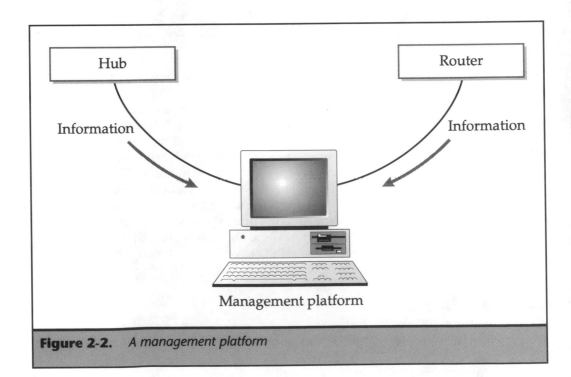

Figure 2-2. *A management platform*

capturing transmitted data, or seek to obtain security access information, such as user logon passwords.

- The masquerading of a user by an unauthorized person who has obtained the password or other information required to logon as the user.
- The modification and/or theft of information by unauthorized users.

Key encryption techniques are available that can make information confidential during transmissions. This is essential if logon information traverses the network. A key is a software algorithm or hardware device that encrypts and locks information so that it can't be easily deciphered. Only the same key, or an associated key, can decrypt the information. For example, consider the process of sending confidential data to another user over a telephone link. Encryption techniques can be used to make the data confidential, but if a key is used to encrypt the data, the recipient must also have a copy of the key to decrypt the data. How do you get a key to the recipient without compromising security? Sending the key over the line is not the answer, since anyone with a monitoring device could capture the key codes during transmission. You could try manual deliver methods such as an express delivery service, but can you be sure that the key was properly delivered? In highly secure environments, these are very important questions.

Fortunately, *public key encryption* methods have been developed that allow users to safely exchange information. Every network user owns a private key and a public key that operate together to allow encryption and decryption of messages. The public key is placed on a common security server that other users can access. If someone wants to send you a confidential message, they encrypt it with your public key. Upon receipt of the messages, you decrypt it with your private key. Only your private key can decrypt messages encrypted with your public key.

The following services are required in distributed computing environments in which many users from many locations are accessing information on a variety of servers.

Authentication Services

These services identify users as they log into the network and provide proof of their authenticity to other devices on the network. As a result, a user only needs to log in once, rather than log into every device (such as file servers) that he or she must access.

Authorization Services

These services provide authenticated users with access to services on the network through access rights.

Confidentiality Services

These services hide data from unauthorized access and assure sender and receiver that information has not been viewed by "network snoopers."

Integrity Services

These services are particularly important for business transactions; they provide assurance that messages are authentic and unaltered.

Nonrepudiation Services

These services can provide proof that messages were sent by the specified sender, and can prevent the sender from disowning the message once it is sent.

Capacity

The network of the '90s suffers from one major affliction in response to the ever-increasing demands that interoperability, management, and multimedia applications place upon available network bandwidth. Quite simply, as companies grow in size and complexity, and as users add emerging applications that support such features as sound and video in electronic mail, the amount of bandwidth required on the network naturally increases. In an Ethernet environment, where each logical network can only provide 10 Mbps (megabits per second) throughput, increasing the number of users from five to ten effectively reduces by half the amount of information that the network can transmit. Effective bridging and routing can help alleviate some of the bandwidth problems by eliminating unwanted traffic on various branches of the network. In other words, local traffic stays local instead of being transmitted over the entire network. But there is still a need to increase network bandwidth as more users come online and use even more sophisticated applications.

Technologies That Will Take You There

Emerging local and wide area network technologies are providing organizations with solutions today and for the future. These technologies will allow users to transmit the information they need and allow managers to integrate sophisticated network management tools without degrading network performance. In addition, emerging technologies like the following provide better security and scalability:

- FDDI (Fiber Distributed Data Interface)
- Fast Ethernet (100VG-AnyLAN and 100Base-X)
- Switching technologies
- ATM (Asynchronous Transfer Mode)
- Structured cabling
- Hub technologies

Fiber Distributed Data Interface (FDDI)

FDDI is a fiber-optic cable standard developed by the American National Standards Institute (ANSI) X3T9.5 committee. It transmits data at 100 Mbps over a dual-ring topology that supports 500 nodes across a distance of 100 kilometers (62 miles). The dual-ring provides redundancy in the transmission systems that protects against cuts or faults in the cable system. Information is transmitted by light pulsing through the pure glass or plastic media. The sending device translates electronic 1's and 0's into optically coded 1's and 0's and transmits them across a fiber strand to a photodetector at the other end.

An interesting feature of FDDI is its built-in redundancy. Since FDDI functions as a token passing ring (much like token ring), an interruption in the ring can affect all connected workstations. However, because FDDI uses a counter-rotating ring design, it can maintain connections for workstations if the ring is broken. The ring automatically reconfigures itself to operate with a loopback configuration, as shown in Figure 2-3, in which signals are redirected back in the opposite direction on a redundant set of wires.

Because of its high speed, security, adaptability, and ability to span large distances, FDDI has enjoyed, despite its high cost, tremendous acceptance. For example, with FDDI, you do not have to worry about such copper-wire problems as attenuation, capacitance, and crosstalk.

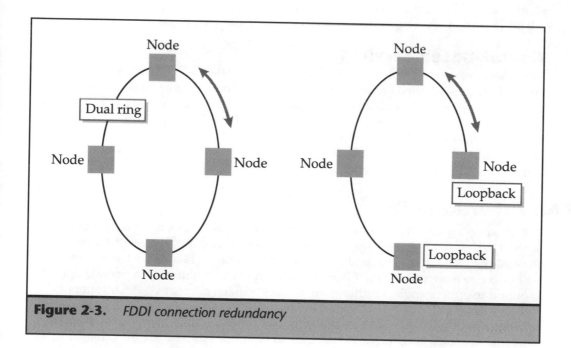

Figure 2-3.   *FDDI connection redundancy*

- *Attenuation*   The loss of signal strength or amplitude as distance increases
- *Capacitance*   A natural distortion worsened by cabling distance and insulator thickness
- *Crosstalk*   A leakage of signal from adjacent cables in a twisted-pair configuration, which causes line noise

A copper wire version of the FDDI standard is called CDDI (Copper Distributed Data Interface). While it is more cost-effective, its cable distances are limited due to the attenuation, capacitance, and crosstalk problems mentioned above. Copper wire can only reach 100 meters (109 yards), and it emits a signal outside of the cable that can be easily monitored, adding to security risks. FDDI, on the other hand, does not emit external signals and is immune to the resulting security problem.

Cabling a network with FDDI does have its limitations. The token-passing nature of the standard does not easily accommodate video transmissions. Video images may appear jumpy if the transmitting workstation is not given enough time to get its signals on the network. To eliminate this problem, FDDI now has two new standards in addition to the traditional Asynchronous Services: Synchronous Services and Circuit-Based Services.

Synchronous Services

These are priority-based services that allow a network manager to specify which stations function synchronously and thereby receive priority when the token is passed. All other stations operate under the standard asynchronous mode.

Circuit-Based Services

These services are available in a new FDDI standard called FDDI-II. Here a virtual connection is established between selected stations. These circuits (16 in all) are created by means of multiplexing techniques that divide up the 100 Mbps bandwidth of FDDI. Each circuit receives a dedicated amount of bandwidth, which can range from 6.144 Mbps to 99.072 Mbps. In addition, each of the 16 available channels can be divided into a total of 96 64-Kbps circuits. In this way, video traffic between two stations does not have to contend with any other traffic.

The Future of FDDI

FDDI's speed, security, and robustness make it an excellent choice for connecting file servers to desktop workstations, and from desktop to desktop. However, based upon the cost of FDDI hubs, NICs, and cable, such a proposition takes a backseat to more cost-effective alternatives like 10Base-T, which in many situations can operate upon standard telephone cable. Furthermore, as a high-speed alternative FDDI suffers from the same affliction as 10 Mbps Ethernet and 4/16 Mbps token ring. As you add additional workstations onto an FDDI, Ethernet, or token ring network, the amount of available bandwidth decreases, since all workstations must share the same communications pipe.

In accordance with these factors, FDDI will play an interesting role in the network of the '90s. There are basically three configurations in which you will find FDDI: workgroups, server connections, and backbones.

Workgroups

An FDDI workgroup can be found in environments requiring dedicated video and voice conferencing. In this scenario, FDDI is used to connect a number of users that share the same applications. For example, a campus may use an FDDI workgroup to broadcast video classroom discussions.

Server Connections

Since today's networks are able to take advantage of high performance server hardware (90 MHz, Intel Pentium microprocessors, 64MB of RAM, and so on), FDDI is able to provide an excellent file server access point. By placing an FDDI NIC into a Novell file server, for example, you can dramatically increase the amount of information processing power within your server tenfold over a single 10 Mbps NIC. By routing ten Ethernet 10 Mbps lines through a switching hub that contains an FDDI connection, you can guarantee full bandwidth for each workstation (see Figure 2-4).

Backbones

An FDDI backbone can take many forms. It can be a router-based backbone in which two or more network segments are attached to an FDDI ring through routers. It can be

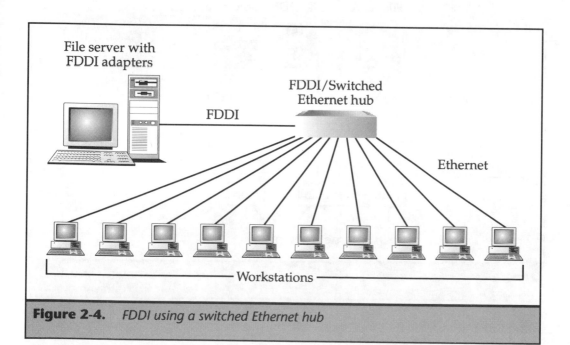

Figure 2-4. *FDDI using a switched Ethernet hub*

a collapsed backbone in which a similar ring exists not across the enterprise, but within the confines of a single hub, to which all subnetworks are attached. It can also be a centralized backbone, which provides a central point of service for numerous network peripherals. For example, a series of file servers, a management platform, numerous workstation hubs, and a public data network connection can connect to a single hub across FDDI cables (see Figure 2-5).

Fast Ethernet

Fast Ethernet is a recent innovation that appeared in response to emerging limitations in the standard Ethernet networking system. Ethernet was originally created by Xerox, and was formalized in 1980 by Digital Equipment Corporation, Intel, and Xerox. It was then adopted by the IEEE (Institute of Electrical and Electronics Engineers) as the 802.3 standard.

Since its inception, Ethernet (particularly the 10Base-T standard) has enjoyed a great deal of success. The flexibility and fault tolerance of the standard has helped to make it successful.

With Ethernet, there are a number of different topologies and wiring standards available, as listed on the following page.

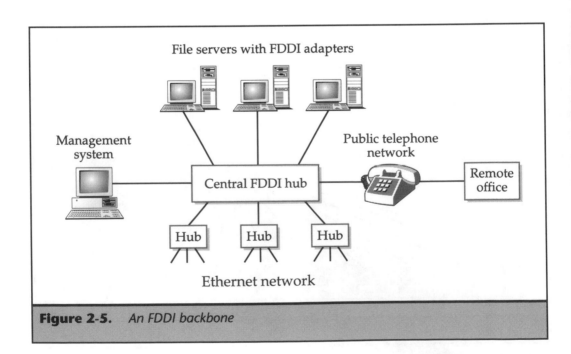

Figure 2-5. *An FDDI backbone*

- **10Base-5**   Coaxial cable with a maximum length of 500 meters (547 yards)

- **10Base-2**   Coaxial cable (RG 58 A/U) with a maximum length of 185 meters (202 yards)

- **10Base-T**   Twisted-pair cable with a maximum length of 100 meters (109 yards)

- **1Base-5**   Twisted-pair cable with a maximum length of 500 meters (547 yards)

- **10Base-F**   Fiber-optic cable backbones of up to 4 kilometers (2.5 miles)

Each standard has its own assets and limitations. 10Base-5 and 10Base-2 provide greater distances than 10Base-T, but they must be wired in a bus topology, which falls prey to the same cable failure problems as token ring. 10Base-T provides high data-transfer rates over a fault-tolerant topology; however, it has distance limitations. 1Base-5 can be wired over great distances using inexpensive twisted-pair cable, but its data transfer rate is limited to 1 Mbps. 10Base-F is an excellent choice for traversing long distances at high speed, as with campus wiring schemes, but it is expensive in comparison with its counterparts.

Overcoming Ethernet Access Methods

Networking standards like Ethernet and token ring use a shared access method in which each station on a logical network is connected to the same cable segment. With token ring, when a station wants to send a message to a network device, it must wait for a token that travels from station to station. If able, that station takes control of the token and releases its packet. This technology ensures that stations do not have to compete for access to the network. But it also makes room for failure. If the token ring network is not wired with a redundant set of cables, any break in the main ring will immediately stop all communication between workstations.

Ethernet 10Base-T does not suffer from such an affliction. Its cabling topology consists of a star structure in which each workstation and device is attached to a central hub with its own length of cable, as shown in Figure 2-6. Traditional Ethernet uses a shared access scheme called CSMA/CD (Carrier Sense Multiple Access/Collision Detection), in which multiple workstations can attach to and access the same cabling system, although only one workstation at a time can transmit over that cabling system.

Collision detection methods ensure that only one station is transmitting on the cable. If two stations attempt to access the cable and transmit at exactly the same time, it is said that a "collision" occurs, and both stations are notified of the error. They will then "back off" for a short time before attempting the transmission again. When there are few users on the network, traffic is light and few collisions occur. Under these circumstances, the collision detection method works well. As network traffic increases, collisions also increase, and network throughput can slow down dramatically. As

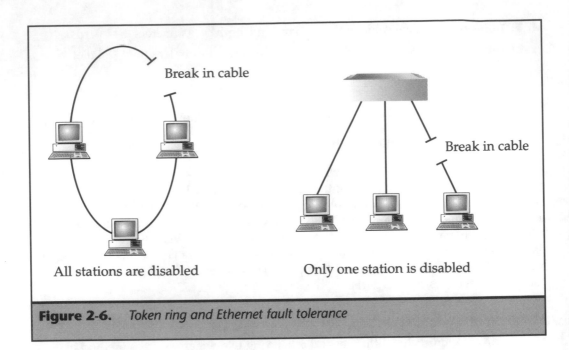

Break in cable

Break in cable

All stations are disabled

Only one station is disabled

Figure 2-6. *Token ring and Ethernet fault tolerance*

traffic increases, workstations that have to back off and retransmit may have to back off the retransmissions in an ever-escalating manner.

One way to solve this problem is to reduce the number of workstations attached to each LAN segment. For example, reducing the number of workstations on a segment from 20 to 5 or even 2 workstations will drastically reduce the number of collisions and maintain throughput. However, this requires increasing the number of segments, then using bridges to attach each segment so network users can still communicate with one another. A number of vendors are working on Ethernet switching technologies that provide just this type of microsegmentation, at an affordable price, in hub-like devices. (Ethernet switching is discussed later in this chapter, under "Switching Technologies.")

Two new Ethernet standards, 100Base-X and 100VG-AnyLAN, are boosting the Ethernet data transfer rate from 10 Mbps to 100 Mbps.

Ethernet 100Base-X

100Base-X was originally developed by Grand Junction Networks, 3Com, SynOptics, Intel, and other vendors, and is an extension of the IEEE 802.3 standard. It uses the CSMA/CD access method, standard Ethernet twisted-pair cabling (EIA/TIA Category 5, as discussed later), and a star configuration topology.

100Base-X has many features that make it a desirable option. By extending the scaleable CSMA/CD access method, the developers of 100Base-X were able to ensure compatibility between 100Base-X and existing Ethernet topologies. In this way hardware manufacturers like Intel and SynOptics have been able to create hardware that can operate at either 100 Mbps or 10 Mbps. If you purchase a 10/100-capable hub from SynOptics, you can upgrade individual workstations on an incremental basis. Likewise, you can purchase Intel's 10/100 capable NICs and utilize 10Base-T until 100 Mbps hubs become available (see Figure 2-7). This is possible because 100Base-X fits into the IEEE Media Access Control (MAC) sub layer. Therefore, these hubs and NICs need only match speeds when switching between 10Base-T and 100Base-X.

This technology does have one limitation for those thinking of upgrading their legacy networks. 100Base-X must run on top of four-pair Category 5 cable. If your building uses any other cabling system, you will have to rewire. As you may have guessed, 100Base-X fits into the network of the '90s in a similar fashion to standard 10Base-T Ethernet. Utilizing a hierarchical cable configuration, 100Base-X interconnects outlying hubs, which fits perfectly into the EIA/TIA 568 Commercial Building Wiring Standard (see Figure 2-8).

Ethernet 100VG-AnyLAN

In contrast, 100VG-AnyLAN departs from IEEE 802.3 by abandoning the CSMA/CD access method in lieu of an access method called *Demand Priority*. This method places the decision making power in the hub instead of in the adapter. Hubs are smart devices that give each workstation the go-ahead to transmit, based on a first-come, first-serve basis or a predetermined priority value. Where standard 10Base-T cable utilizes two-pair wiring (one to receive and one to send), 100VG-AnyLAN uses four

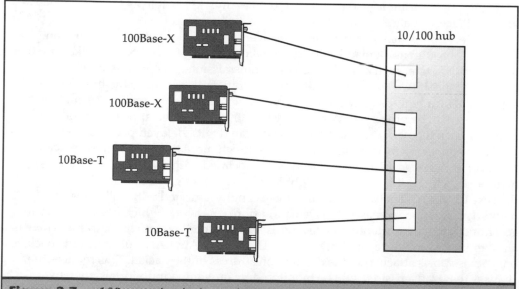

Figure 2-7.   *10Base technologies and 100Base-X working from a 10/100 hub*

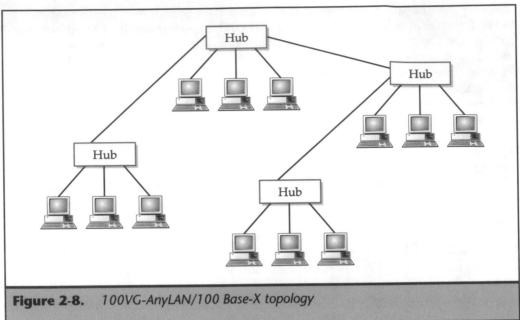

Figure 2-8.   *100VG-AnyLAN/100 Base-X topology*

pairs. It sends out 25 MHz signals over each of the four pairs. This keeps radio
frequencies within required standards and allows the use of voice-grade cable
(Category 3). By using four-pair wiring, 100VG-AnyLAN is able to simultaneously
send and receive data.

This technology has many advantages over traditional Ethernet transmission
methods. Through its Demand Priority signaling, 100VG-AnyLAN can make sure that
time-sensitive data, such as real-time video transmission, gets priority over other
types of traffic. If two stations simultaneously transmit requests to the hub, and one
happens to be a high-priority packet, that packet is processed first. The second packet
merely waits to be processed. With timely transmission, video appears smooth and
does not have the "jerky" picture quality associated with delayed packets.

This sequencing methodology helps with much more than just video applications,
however. It removes the network overhead associated with the CSMA/CD access
method, in which all workstations fight for access to a single network segment.
Because CSMA/CD networks become increasingly saturated with collisions as
network utilization increases, the Demand Priority network, which does not have to
accommodate wire contention collisions, is able to accommodate more traffic. There is
another benefit to this technology as well. The 100VG-AnyLAN hub transmits packets
only across ports attached to the destination address of the packet. This reduces the
chances that transmissions will be monitored by unwanted individuals, thereby
ensuring privacy.

The cabling distances defined in the 100VG-AnyLAN standard are somewhat different than those used with traditional Ethernet. Normal UPT/STP cabling can extend up to 200 meters (218 yards) in comparison to the 100 meters (109 yards) of standard Ethernet. The hubs and workstations are wired just like 10Base-T and 100Base-X (see Figure 2-8).

With either technology, your network can enjoy 100 Mbps at the desktop and at the backbone. Although these technologies are usually depicted as workgroup solutions, they, like FDDI, can be used to take advantage of high-speed server front-ends. For example, you can plug a 100 Mbps NIC, which will most likely be either an EISA (Extended Industry Standard Architecture) or PCI (Peripheral Component Interface) NIC, into a server and connect it to a 100 Mbps hub just as you would an FDDI hub and NIC (see Figure 2-4).

Switching Technologies

If you decide to support the shared network topology of Ethernet, you will, even with 100 Mbps 100Base-X, eventually run into the problem of degraded network throughput. It is simple. As you increase the number of workstations on an Ethernet segment, the number of collisions also increases. The more collisions, the more wasted bandwidth you experience. In the past, to solve this problem, network administrators have subdivided network segments into segments with fewer attached workstations, then connected the segments with bridges or routers. But it also decreased the performance of the network as a whole because each time a workstation's network request crossed a bridge, it was slowed down by the inherent latency within bridging technology.

Giving this idea a new twist, a company called Kalpana, Inc. introduced the first switching hub, which it called the EtherSwitch. This hub reduced contention on a shared network by reducing the number of nodes on a logical segment using micro-segmentation techniques. In essence, it reduced the number of workstations on each segment to two: the workstation initiating the request and the workstation responding to that request. No other workstation sees the information being passed between the two workstations. It is almost as if a network were no longer subject to the CSMA/CD access method's collision degradation. Packets are passed between workstation level segments as though they were passing through a bridge, but without the bridge's latency.

On a switched Ethernet network, a workgroup of ten individuals can be guaranteed simultaneous 10 Mbps availability. To understand how a hub can do this, try to imagine a switching hub as an old-style telephone switchboard—the one with coaxial-like cables connecting parties wishing to speak on the telephone. When you call the switchboard and ask to be connected with Redwood City 419, the operator checks to see if that line is open, and if no one else is currently speaking with the party at Redwood City 419, you are connected directly to the party via a private cable. No other parties are then able to hear your conversation. When you are finished and hang

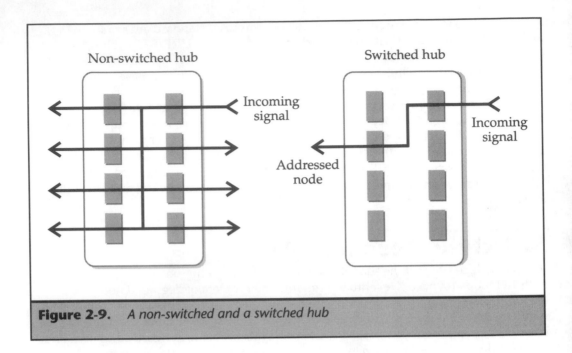

Figure 2-9. *A non-switched and a switched hub*

up the phone, the operator, seeing that both ports are now free, disconnects the cable from each and awaits the next call (see Figure 2-9).

Switching hubs accomplish this feat in a similar, albeit quicker, manner by passing packets from the entry port to the exit port through an internal matrix switch. When a packet enters the entry port, its MAC (Media Access Control) layer address is read (switches are OSI layer 2 sensitive), and it is immediately routed to the port that is connected with that address. (See Chapter 4 for more on OSI layers.) If the port is busy, the packet is placed in a queue, which is actually a memory buffer at the entry port, where it awaits the availability of its destination port. This may sound fairly straightforward, but the way switching hubs handle this falls into two slightly more complex categories: cut-through and store-and-forward.

Cut-Through

When a packet enters a switching hub using this technique, its address is read. Regardless of whether the packet is badly formed, it is transmitted. This provides stellar switching times, as only the first few bytes of a packet are read. However, all packets are transmitted, even those that might be corrupted. It is up to the receiving station to detect these corrupted packets and request a retransmission from the sender. Modern cabling systems are relatively error-free, which minimizes retransmissions. However, errors might be frequent if a network interface card is failing, the cable is defective, or there is an external signal source causing packet corruptions.

Store-and-Forward

When a packet enters a switching hub under this technique, enough information is read to enable the hub to decide not only which port to pass the packet along to, but also whether to pass the packet along at all. This effectively isolates defective network segments attached to the hub. Although this technique cannot match the switching speed found in cut-through products, it can remove the often hazardous consequences caused by corrupted packets. For example, with cut-through, if your coaxial network contains a bad cable, you may experience a barrage of corrupted packets that bring your network throughput to its knees.

As vendors improve switching techniques, the need for cut-through switching should evaporate. Currently, companies like Cisco are developing switching hubs that not only read the physical MAC layer of the protocol stack, but that actually read three layers above that, into layer 5 (the Session layer). These hubs will be able to add an unprecedented level of security by allowing administrative personnel to monitor and control not only workstation access, but application access as well. For example, on a Novell and UNIX network, you may want to allow FTP (File Transfer Protocol) sessions while blocking transmissions from IPX/SPX workstations.

Asynchronous Transfer Mode (ATM)

ATM functions in much the same way as switched Ethernet. However, whereas Ethernet switching operates on a packet level in which each packet may be a different size, ATM switches information on a cell level, in which each cell is exactly the same size (53 bytes). Switched Ethernet networks must contend with packets ranging in size from 56 bytes to 1514 bytes, which means that an Ethernet switching hub must contend with an ever-changing level of bandwidth utilization from each workstation. Since all ATM cells are the same size, they flow steadily through switching hubs—no single node can tie up the hub with long packets. With ATM, you can allocate specific amounts of bandwidth for each workstation.

Because each cell is the same size, a stream of cells entering a hub can expect a predictable amount of delay. This ability to predict the length of a transmission is ATM's strength. The ATM interface takes the packet information from a transmitting device and breaks it up into a number of cells suitable for transmission over the network. At the receiving end, the cell contents are recombined into the original packet.

ATM, as a data transmission technology, has the potential to revolutionize the way networks are built and utilized. First, it is able to integrate equally well into both WANs and LANs. Second, it is able to transmit data at a very high speed (155 Mbps to 622 Mbps). And third, it is able to communicate varied types of data, such as voice, facsimile, real-time video, CD-quality audio, and imaging. These attributes alone make ATM the perfect medium for the network of the '90s. And yet this technology is only now beginning to emerge:

■ Public telephone vendors like AT&T and US Sprint are already deploying ATM support, but hardware vendors are only beginning to announce ATM products. Leading the way in this regard is Fore Systems Inc. with their ForeView, an ATM switch, and adapter products.

■ IBM has entered the LAN ATM market with a hub and adapter set that switches ATM at 25 Mbps.

■ ATM routers and ATM switches are appearing that connect to carrier ATM services in order to build global networks.

■ ATM devices are appearing for building private backbone networks to connect LANs.

■ ATM adapters and workgroup switches are appearing that will bringing ATM to the desktop.

ATM transmissions are able to reach such high speeds by traveling across fiber-optic cables. Currently ATM is able to utilize the SONET (Synchronous Optical Network), which is implemented on optical cable and provides a common, global communication standard. SONET will allow the "internationalization" of the independent phone systems that exist around the world. It is a broadband technology that relies upon cell relay operations.

Another aspect of ATM that is appealing is its similarity to Ethernet switching. When an ATM packet enters an ATM hub, that packet leaves only on the port directly connected to the destination device. And what's more, ATM workstations, servers, hubs, routers, and so on, can transmit simultaneously. They do not need to wait for a token, as with token ring, or risk data loss due to a collision, as with Ethernet (see Figure 2-10). This type of connection is called any-to-any communication.

In the 90's, ATM will help remove the barrier between LANs and WANs. Currently, networks must rely upon slow transmission speeds, unreliable services, and a certain amount of latency in data transmission. With ATM, corporations will no longer be limited by the poor price-to-speed ratio of ISDN (Integrated Services Digital Network), T1, and other networking schemes. Also, if a telephone carrier's central office experiences a line failure, ATM packets will be able to reroute around the troubled area. The slow throughput associated with store-and-forward as well as dial-up routers will disappear.

Along the way to this perfect world, ATM will most likely be implemented in a gradual manner. For example, using a hierarchical wiring system (like Fast Ethernet), you could begin by installing ATM switches as backbone links regardless of the connection type (FDDI, Ethernet, and so on). In the next phase, you could use ATM switches to connect high-powered servers. Then, in the final phase, you could fortify each workstation with an ATM card and distribute data solely within an ATM network.

Based upon the current prices associated with ATM hardware and telephone carrier ATM services, a more likely scenario will include the high-speed capabilities of FDDI or 100VG-AnyLAN coupled with the high-speed switching capabilities of switched 100 Mbps Ethernet. Other technologies will coexist as well: 10 Mbps Ethernet

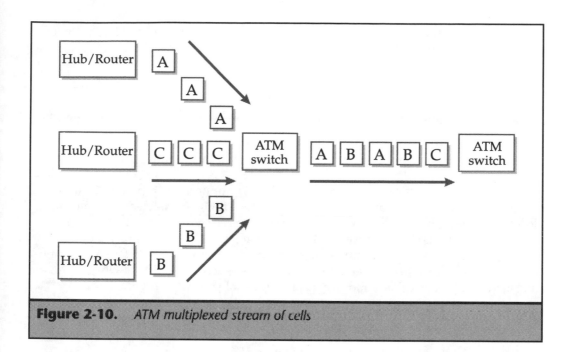

Figure 2-10.   *ATM multiplexed stream of cells*

and token ring (both 4 Mbps and 16 Mbps), as well as the new switched token ring currently under development.

Structured Cabling

Regardless of your network choice (FDDI, Fast Ethernet, ATM, and so on), you should implement a cabling plan that is easy to manage and that supports future growth. The Commercial Building Wiring Standard put forward jointly by the Electronic Industries Association and the Telecommunications Industries Association (EIA/TIA), known as EIA/TIA 568, is such a cabling system. It basically provides guidance for all communications wiring. The EIA/TIA standard was specifically designed to work with Ethernet 10Base-T, token ring, PBX, ISDN, as well as other networks. Its features and functions include:

- A generic telecommunication wiring system for commercial buildings
- Defined media, topology, termination and connection points, and administration
- Support for multiproduct, multivendor environments
- Direction for future design of telecommunication products for commercial enterprises
- The ability to plan and install the telecommunication wiring for a commercial building without prior knowledge of the products that will use the wiring

The first step toward fulfilling these goals includes a set of wire standards. To this end, the EIA/TIA has defined five categories of twisted-pair cable standards:

- Traditional telephone cable
- Cable certified for data transmissions up to 4 Mbps
- Cable to support token ring (4 Mbps) and 10 Mbps Ethernet 10Base-T networks
- Cable to support 16 Mbps token ring networks
- Cable to support 100 Mbps or greater technologies like 100Base-X

The EIA/TIA specification defines a hierarchical physical star topology, as shown in Figure 2-11. Here cables are pulled in a star configuration from telecommunications closets to outlets on the wall where computer devices connect into the network. The telecommunications closet(s) on each floor are then joined in an equipment room. These equipment rooms are in turn connected to a main cross-connect and an entrance facility that provide central access to remote services such as an ATM, ISDN, or T1 link, as well as to any other buildings. Each of these elements is explained next.

Work Area

This subsystem encompasses the communication outlets (wall boxes and faceplates), wiring, and connectors that allow the connection of computers, printers, and so on.

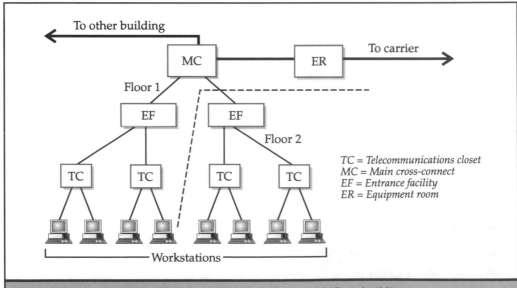

Figure 2-11.   *EIA/TIA 586 wiring standard for a multifloor building*

This structure, under the EIA/TIA 568, always constitutes a horizontal wiring scheme, for example, a single floor. The object of this system is to provide a single point of access for disparate communication devices. Through a single faceplate, you can connect a telephone, workstation, video monitor, dumb terminal, and so on.

Horizontal Wiring

This subsystem includes the requirements for the actual wiring from the workstation faceplate to the telecommunications closet. The EIA/TIA states that the distance between the two elements should not exceed 90 meters (98 yards). The wiring itself can consist of the following:

Four-pair 100-ohm unshielded twisted-pair (UTP) cables

Two-pair 150-ohm shielded twisted-pair (STP) cables

50-ohm coaxial cables

Fiber-optic cable with a core diameter of 62.5 microns

Telecommunications Closet

The telecommunications closet can include all equipment required to connect workstations to the equipment room, such as hubs, repeaters, concentrators, and so on. This general-purpose room can also contain entrance facility hardware. Each floor can have a number of these closets.

Equipment Room

The equipment room provides a central location from which the vertically wired backbone equipment may connect to the telecommunications closets.

Backbone Wiring

The backbone wiring incorporates all hardware needed to provide a building-wide access point for each floor's equipment room. This hardware runs vertically through each floor and terminates in the main cross-connect. The cable used for this backbone can consist of the following types:

Four-pair 100-ohm UTP cables

Two-pair 150-ohm STP cables

50-ohm coaxial cables

Fiber-optic cable with a core diameter of 62.5 microns

Main Cross-Connect

This facility includes all hardware required to connect the building's backbone to other buildings' backbones.

Entrance Facilities

These provide an access point for external telecommunications services such as ISDN, T1, and so on. Entrance facilities can also contain an access point for other campus-wide buildings.

Structured wiring is critical for future expansion of networks, and should be implemented in all new building construction. While structured wiring is expensive, its implementation supports future growth not only of the physical cabling plant, but also of technologies that support higher data transfer rates and the simultaneous transmission of voice, video, and data.

Hub Technology

The single theme running through all the previously discussed technologies is the hub-centric architecture. The hub evolved out of the limitations associated with early wiring topologies, in which a network consisted of a number of workstations daisy-chained together by a single cable. For small networks, this arrangement worked just fine, because if the entire network failed to operate, which was usually caused by a single point failure such as a loose connector or bad cable, the problem was easy to locate and fix. Even on small networks, however, such a process was not easy. You needed special equipment to evaluate the cable and return the exact distance to the break.

As networks grew larger, installing and maintaining linear networks became, as you may imagine, far too cumbersome and counterproductive. In response to this, hubs were introduced. At first, hubs functioned as simple repeaters. They took a signal from one cable and repeated it over another, thereby extending the possible length of the network. Hubs became popular with the introduction of 10Base-T cabling because they allowed network administrators to easily extend and expand networks by connecting hubs together in a hierarchical star configuration (see Figure 2-9). For example, on an Ethernet 10Base-T network, you can have a workstation connected at the end of a chain of up to four hubs.

In networks of the '90s, hubs are taking on a much larger role by providing the following:

- Easy additions, changes, and moves within a structured wiring system
- Networks that can expand incrementally
- Accommodation for many disparate LAN and WAN networks, including Ethernet, token ring, FDDI, Frame Relay, SMDS, ATM, and so on
- Centralized management capabilities as well as the automatic collection of network events and statistics
- Fault-tolerant features, which are able to maintain network integrity

Hubs reside within a wide range of hub generations and types, as discussed next.

First-Generation Hubs

This is the simplest of hubs. Usually made up of eight ports, these hubs merely repeat any incoming signal over all active ports. There are no management features whatsoever. These are still quite viable within small networks at the workgroup level.

Second-Generation Hubs

These hubs offer the same basic service as first-generation hubs, but they include management features. They are generally intelligent in that they collect management information from each port, translate that information into a standardized format like SNMP (Simple Network Management Protocol), and then make the information available to a management system.

Second-generation hubs also contain multiple buses, which allow them to accommodate different media like Ethernet, token ring, and FDDI. Associated with these buses is a high-performance backplane, usually powered by a high-performance RISC (Reduced Instruction Set Computer) processor. Also, second-generation hubs are able to create virtual LAN segments. This comes as a boon to network administrators, for it allows them to make adds, moves, and changes electronically from a remote console. If one segment becomes overwhelmed, you can simply reassign one or more ports (affecting workstations or other hubs) from the busy segment to one that is less inundated.

Third-Generation Hubs

These hubs are called enterprise hubs because they are designed specifically to handle all of the cabling and internetworking requirements of an organization. Third-generation hubs typically contain intelligence and a high-speed backplane, and are extremely modular. For example, faulty components can be "hot-swapped" without any need for bringing down the whole hub device. These hubs, in addition to providing all of the features found in the previous two generations, provide built-in redundancy through dual power supplies, busses, and wide area links. Many of these hubs utilize ATM as a cell-switching backplane medium because of its speed and ability to work with different network types (see Figure 2-12).

In today's network, all three generation hubs can be found acting in different capacities. In this regard there are three hub categories that correlate with the three generations of hubs: workgroup hubs, intermediate hubs, and enterprise hubs.

Workgroup Hubs

A workgroup hub connects a limited number of workstations, generally within a limited radius. For example, it could be used to connect 8 or 12 editorial personnel in a single room. A first- or second-generation hub works best in this sort of situation.

Intermediate Hubs

This type of hub is usually found in the wiring closet, telecommunications closet or equipment room. It is used to connect workgroup hubs to a vertical backbone that

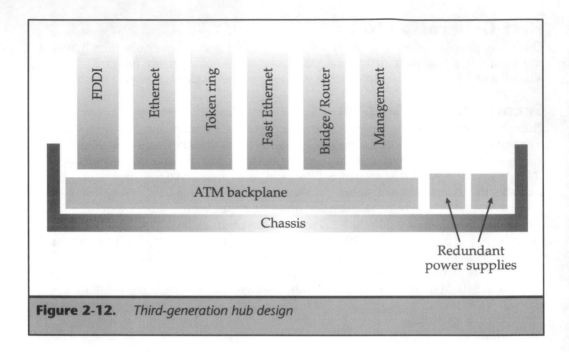

Figure 2-12. *Third-generation hub design*

spans floors or rooms. For example, the editorial, art, and copy desk workgroups can all connect into this hub.

Enterprise Hubs

The Enterprise hub acts as the central connecting point for all intermediate hubs and subsequent workgroup hubs. They can function as either a collapsed backbone, in which all intermediate hubs connect directly, or as a connecting point to the backbone. As a collapsed backbone, they will be found in either the entrance facility or the main cross-link subsystems of the EIA/TIA Commercial Building Wiring Standard (see Figure 2-13). Some of the features found in enterprise hubs include:

- Integration of many different network components in one location
- Reliability through redundant (fault-tolerant) components
- A central connecting point for intermediate and workgroup hubs
- High-speed connections
- Virtual segmentation (electronically dividing ports into different network segments)
- Advanced management features

And yet the evolution of hub design is not complete. The network of the '90s will push these "superhubs" to a new level of performance by necessitating the incorporation of two additional technologies. First, packet-switching technologies

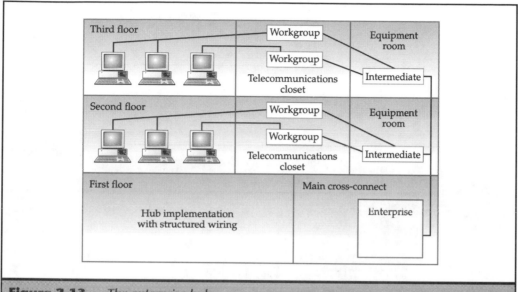

Figure 2-13. *The enterprise hub*

will be implemented in all three types of hubs. Workgroup hubs from Grand Junction, intermediate hubs from Kalpana, and enterprise hubs from LANNET are already available with switching technologies. Grand Junction and Kalpana also offer what is called "full duplexed Ethernet" in their switching hubs, which allows you to create a 20 Mbps connection between hub and hub, or hub and server.

The second technology to push these hubs to the next level is ATM. SynOptics, Fore Systems, Cabletron, and Ungermann-Bass have announced enterprise hubs that incorporate ATM cell-switching technology. Currently, there are plans for ATM to move from enterprise hubs to intermediate and workgroup hubs. Now available are ATM EISA and PCI adapters for servers and high-powered workstations. However, due to the high price of this emerging technology, ATM at the intermediate and workgroup level will not appear for some time.

Summary

Regardless of the time frame involved in the blossoming of these technologies, one thing is certain, the zenith of networks in the '90s is on its way. Through technologies such as FDDI, Fast Ethernet, ATM, structured cabling, and hub technology, network designers, integrators, and administrators will find that their concerns of interoperability, manageability, security, and capacity will, for now, be fulfilled.

Chapter Three

Wide Area Networking Technologies

**by James Pringle,
CompuCom Systems**

This chapter is geared toward identifying wide area network solutions in the United States. Some European standards will be mentioned where it might be useful. General explanations are provided for each type of connectivity option. The goal is to leave you, the reader, with a good understanding of the WAN transports available today, without exposure to minute details. A wide area network can be a VAX cluster, networks comprised of UNIX platforms, PCs, or any combination of computer equipment. However, the solutions detailed in this chapter are directed toward the homogenous network addressing most computer systems. In our discussion, a *local area network* (LAN) is two or more computers connected through a network interface card (NIC). A *wide area network* (WAN) is two or more LANs connected by a bridge or router spanning a telecommunications line. A subset of a WAN is a *metropolitan area network* (MAN). A MAN is a network spanning 50 miles or less. Larger networks are often called *enterprise networks*.

A *bridge* is a device that connects onto the LAN and passes data to and from another segment of the LAN or WAN. Transparent bridging allows all traffic on both sides of the bridge connections to merge as if they were a single LAN. Thus, a LAN consisting of transparent bridges is basically viewed as a large integrated LAN. Some bridges are able to route traffic. These bridges are more commonly referred to as *brouters* or bridge/routers. Companies such as IBM and Crosscom Corp. apply proprietary technology to "route" SNA, NetBIOS, and other protocols considered nonroutable. A *router* is a device that passes routable protocols. Examples of these protocols are TCP/IP and IPX. A router looks at network traffic and allows only selected protocols to pass on a particular LAN segment. This is sometimes referred to as setting up a *fire wall*. Most routers are also capable of transparent bridging. Routers are not only black boxes; they also can be file servers, minicomputers, and even mainframes. For example, IBM's AS/400 does APPN (Advanced Peer-to-Peer Networking) routing. We will be limiting our discussion of bridges and routers in this chapter to how they relate to WAN connectivity.

There are two basic types of WAN configurations, hub and spoked hub. Figure 3-1 depicts a spoked hub. The *hub* consists of a central location with remote offices connecting through the central point. It is equivalent to a star configuration. A *spoked hub* is made up of groups of hubs with some form of connection to each central location of each hub. In Figure 3-1, for instance, the United Kingdom is the central location of a hub that has connections throughout Europe. The United Kingdom is connected to the central point of another hub located in the northeastern United States.

Wide area connectivity has advanced significantly in the last few years. Until the late 1980s, most connections were either point-to-point or asynchronous in nature. The majority of point-to-point line connections were used for cluster controllers, mainframes, minicomputers, and terminal emulation to mainframes and minicomputers. Although these applications still exist, they are rapidly being replaced with peer-to-peer connectivity over a variety of telecommunication links. Today, corporate America has a wide range of telecommunications options in formulating WANs. They include asynchronous, synchronous, switched 56, ISDN, dedicated digital point-to-point (9600-T3), X.25, Frame Relay, switched multimegabit data service

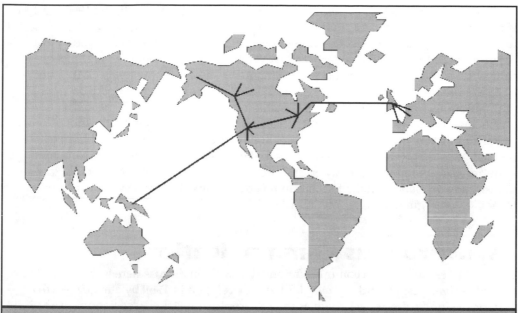

Figure 3-1.   *A spoked hub configuration for a wide area network*

(SMDS), and asynchronous transfer mode (ATM) in the future. All of these methods have their niche in today's WAN environment.

The implementation of these connectivity solutions can be divided into three categories:

■ Asynchronous communications

■ Digital point-to-point networks

■ Digital packet-switching networks

Asynchronous communication has the highest error rate with the lowest throughput, but allows the greatest mobility. Recognizing that X.25 is used in a variety of manners, I have grouped X.25 as an asynchronous solution, because it is probably the most common usage today and will continue to be in the future. However, unlike direct dial-up solutions, X.25 is considered one of the most reliable connection methods in the world. The weak point is from the users' equipment to the local link. For a further discussion of X.25, refer to the X.25 section of this chapter.

Digital point-to-point networks allow high transfer rates with minimal errors and are available at nearly all U.S. locations. Nearly all carriers offer this service. On point-to-point connections, all data travels the same route between the two linked locations. All carriers involved program a permanent switched link. These circuits generally are the fractional-T1, T1, and T3 lines.

Digital packet-switching technology was introduced to the public in the 1990s and is not available in most areas in the United States. Even if one of these digital technologies is available, most equipment vendors are in the process of stabilizing errors and conforming to standards. However, these services offer the high-speed connectivity that today's networks are demanding. ISDN, Frame Relay, SMDS, and ATM are the response to meet the new multimedia requirements that are becoming popular on networks. Digital packet switching is able to attain high speeds by sacrificing error correction and using newer technology for physical transport. Error correction techniques used in X.25, Frame Relay, and ATM are listed in Table 3-1. The perception is that technological advances make data delivery so reliable, compared with previous methods, that any error correction can be done on a higher OSI layer. Expect radical changes in the telecommunications market in the 1990s as the technologies begin to gain momentum.

Asynchronous Communications

The type of asynchronous communications that we will discuss here is the RS-232-C and its derivatives. The RS-232 standard was developed in 1969 by a major North American standards group known as the Electronic Industries Association (EIA) to bring coherence to the interconnectivity world. Most of today's microcomputers are standardly equipped with one or more RS-232-C-compliant ports. The advantage of asynchronous communications is that they can use standard telephone lines. You can connect to numerous locations merely by disconnecting and redialing different locations, being charged only by distance and length of call, using standard analog lines supplied by the local exchange. These connections are also referred to as POTS (plain old telephone system).

Laptop computers have made our society more mobile. Telecommuting from any location is a requirement for many Information Systems departments. Users are requesting 24-hour, seven-day-a-week availability of data, which is often distributed in the many locations where an organization maintains offices. The best solution for

Error Correction Features	X.25	Frame Relay	ATM
Frame boundary recognition flags	X	X	
Bit stuffing	X	X	
CRC checking	X	X	
ARQ (automatic repeat request)	X		
Flow control	X		
Multiplexing of logical channels	X		

Table 3-1.   *Error Correction Techniques Used by Three Modes of Telecommunication*

giving users access to enterprise data has been and will continue to be the analog phone line. Since analog lines are available nearly everywhere, asynchronous connectivity is probably the most common connectivity method available in the world. With the increasing need for computer resources, electronic mail, and other electronic data, the call for asynchronous solutions has skyrocketed.

For small or infrequently accessed PC networks, one solution is to load software such as Microcom's Carbon Copy or Symantec's PC Anywhere. This "remote control" software allows users to dial in and connect with a network, then control a computer on that network as if they were physically sitting at the computer (see Figure 3-2, segment A). Such remote connections dramatically reduce throughput requirements across the analog line, since only keyboard commands and screen updates are transferred. The advantage of this solution is that the host computer does the processing. The client computer merely receives the incoming data and presents it to the user. This solution requires that host software be running on the remote computer, and that the remote computer be turned on. The dial-up user connects to the host computer by using client software. The actual network connections and applications reside on the host computer. The client PC can run local or network applications on the host PC; it merely mimics the host's screens and keystrokes. File copies sent to the client PC require that a file-transfer utility be included with the software.

Another solution is to install *protocol-dependent* bridges and routers or asynchronous *multiprotocol* bridges and routers (see Figure 3-2, segment B). These allow a user to connect to a network over a dial-up line and connect as a node to a specific network. Novell's Network Connect, Shiva's NetModem family, Microsoft's Remote Access Server (RAS), and Telebit's ACS are examples of products that provide these services.

Protocol-dependent bridges only service a particular protocol. Novell's Network Connect permits a client PC, with special software, to dial up a network and become a NetWare client. Microsoft's RAS permits a Microsoft NT, Windows for Workgroups, or DOS client to connect with a Microsoft LAN Manager server or Microsoft Windows NT Advanced Server.

Multiprotocol offerings such as those from Shiva, DCA, and Telebit offer a wider range of connectivity. A Shiva NetModem supports AppleTalk, IPX, and Microsoft's Windows for Workgroups Protocols. DCA's RLN and Telebit's ACS offer AppleTalk, TCP/IP, IPX, and NetBIOS connectivity with supplied software. These connections support not only PC connectivity, but also peer-to-peer connectivity on the LAN. Thus, a user has access to all the services as if he or she were directly connected to the network.

Additionally, there are asynchronous bridges and routers available. These bridges connect onto the network itself (see Figure 3-2, segment C). When a bridge determines that a remote connection is needed, the bridge or router dials up the remote site. The bridges maintain a table for connection locations. Typically, the bridges support only specific protocols and easily become congested with traffic, while a dial-up router "fire walls" traffic. One such router is the Telebit Netblazer.

In addition to dial-in capabilities, another asynchronous demand has arisen: *modem pooling*. LAN users are requesting connectivity with outside services such

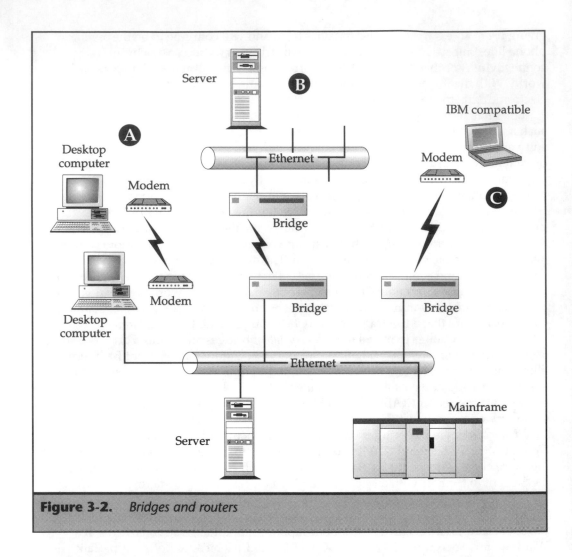

Figure 3-2. *Bridges and routers*

as bulletin boards, informational services such as CompuServe, America OnLine, and the Internet. Modem pooling allows users to share modems on the WAN.
Thus, users who do have modems or analog lines at their desks can dial out using network connected modem pools. Shiva, Telebit, DCA, Novell, and Microsoft all have such solutions.

Although we typically only think of local area networks consisting of PC servers and clients, networks also can consist of VAXes, UNIX OS systems, HPs, IBMs, and other mainframes and minicomputers. These systems support direct dial-up from serial ports or terminal servers. Asynchronous implementations are no longer married to direct-connect, proprietary connectivity solutions. Terminal servers are popular because they support dial-up TCP/IP or short-haul modem-connected terminals and

PCs, and convert them to Ethernet or token ring with full telnet and FTP capabilities. Users are no longer limited by the number of serial ports on a given box or the distance from the LAN cabling. Many IBM systems will support ASCII workstation controllers, asynchronous FEPs (front-end processors), protocol converters that will allow multidrop asynchronous connections from SDLC (synchronous data link control), and asynchronous gateways.

With our growing dependence on electronic information, the need for asynchronous network connectivity is now a necessity whether those connections are to mainframes, minicomputers, or PC LANs. However asynchronous connections do have certain limitations:

- Slow transmission speeds, usually ranging from 2400 to 19,200 bits per second (bps)
- Likelihood of overruns at speeds higher than 9600 bps
- Disconnections attributed to line noise or bad connections
- Extremely slow transmission of graphical applications
- Limited data integrity checks (performed only by endpoints)

Although vendors may represent themselves as supporting speeds of up to 57.6 kilobits per second (Kbps), both endpoints must be able to support that speed. It's the age-old argument of the fast UART (universal asynchronous receiver transmitter) versus the standard UART (16550 versus 8550) chips on PCs. As depicted in Figure 3-2, an asynchronous connection consists of the serial interface speed between the computer and the modem and the transmission speed between the two modems. The serial interface speed depends on the serial chip in the computer. The modem takes the data and usually compresses it to give high throughput speeds. This is why manufacturers claim connection speeds of 38.4 to 57.6 Kbps. However, the serial interface speeds must be able to support these high speeds. Traditionally, terminal emulation programs such as Procomm, Kermit, and Qmodem, take advantage of high-speed connections, but most network node connections are unable to process data at those speeds.

Synchronous Communications

Synchronous communications was the wide area network connectivity transport of choice from the late '70s until the late '80s. Although HDLC (high-level data link control) is the ISO standard, the U.S. standard synchronous protocol is SDLC. IBM supports HDLC, but SDLC was IBM's implementation of the HDLC standard and is not 100 percent compatible. Connection speeds range from 2400 to 56,000 bps. Typically, connect speeds of 9600 bps or less are dial-up, while higher speeds use digital Switched 56 or point-to-point. These connections were used for cluster controllers (coaxial or twin axial) and gateways to connect terminals and PCs into the mainframe and minicomputer network. Once considered to be the future of data communications, this connection type has actually been replaced by more common asynchronous connection methods.

The advantage of synchronous versus asynchronous connections is the throughput. Until the late 1980s, reliable asynchronous communications throughput was limited to the range of 2400 bps (uncompressed) to 19.2 Kbps (compressed). Coupled with the inefficiency of the asynchronous protocol, this meant slower throughput speeds compared with synchronous communications.

The asynchronous data format consists of each byte of data sandwiched by stop and start bits (see Figure 3-3). The stop-and-start-bit sequence is mutually agreed upon by the two connecting devices. The header and trailer of each byte transmitted consist of at least 25 percent of the data traffic. The stop and start bits alert the receiver of incoming data and give the receiver adequate time to perform certain timing functions before the next byte of data arrives.

The synchronous data formats consist of fixed-length data packets sandwiched by synchronization or sync bytes. The sync bytes alert the receiver of incoming data. In synchronous communications, the overhead of the synchronization bits is significantly

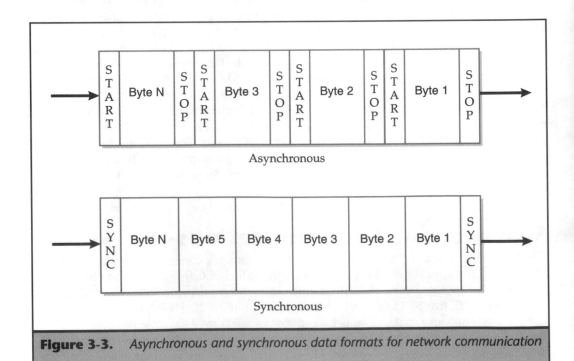

Figure 3-3. *Asynchronous and synchronous data formats for network communication*

less than it is in asynchronous. One major drawback, however, is that should an error occur, more data will need to be retranslated. Additional packet information is required, such as identification information for both the receiver and transmitter, control information that defines the protocol implementation, and frame check sequence (FCS) information that is used to perform a cyclic redundancy check (CRC).

Although synchronous communications is still widely used today in the IBM world, it is rapidly being replaced by LAN connectivity products such as bridges and routers. As WAN connection methods become cheaper to implement, a greater number of remote offices are connecting with and sharing network services. Synchronous communications is now used primarily to implement IBM-to-IBM connectivity or gateway services.

Switched Multimegabit Data Service (SMDS)

Early in the chapter we briefly touched upon metropolitan area networks (MANs). The LAN-to-MAN connectivity is described by the IEEE (Institute of Electrical and Electronics Engineers) 802.6 standard. SMDS is a by-product of the 802.6 standard. Supported by the Regional Bell Operating Companies (RBOC), ANSI, and the IEEE standards committee, SMDS is perceived as the technology for providing LAN interconnectivity to the local carrier's central office (also known as CO, local exchange, or end office). Every telephone service is connected from a local carrier's central office to the customer's premises. The local carrier then provides services to the central office. There are over 18,000 COs in the United States.

SMDS is based on a dual queue dual bus (DQDB) topology. DQDB consists of two buses. Each bus transmits data in only one direction. Two types of services are provided by the DQDB topology:

- Voice and video
- Access on demand

The voice and data services use preassigned bandwidths. The access-on-demand service accommodates bursts in traffic, which can give customers more bandwidth than they normally require without first contacting the carrier.

SMDS implementations support transfer rates from 34 Mbps to 150 Mbps, depending on the implementation. Access, where available, is offered for T1 and T3 services. Like most of the digital packet-switching technology, SMDS access is offered on a limited basis, depending on the carrier and the metropolitan area. The RBOCs are slowly implementing this technology as needed. Whether they will embrace SMDS or just skip to full ATM implementation remains to be seen.

Integrated Services Digital Network (ISDN)

Much attention has been given recently to the emerging Integrated Services Digital Network (ISDN). IEEE and CCITT (Consultive Committee for International Telegraph and Telephone) standards are being proposed to facilitate digital network compatibility. Driving these standards are three basic goals:

- To make services compatible across international borders
- To standardize user-to-network interfaces, thus encouraging independent terminal and network equipment
- To advance network communications

ISDN implementation is currently in its infancy. Most local carriers began offering limited ISDN service around July, 1993. Charges by each local exchange carrier (LEC) vary from being a fixed cost to a nominal fee plus a per-packet charge. Major long-distance carriers will support limited service to specific locations and LECs. Average installation time is 30 to 90 days in large metropolitan areas.

Generally, there are only two ISDN implementations being offered in the United States; both are depicted in Figure 3-4. The first implementation, known as the basic rate interface (BRI), is the most common. The BRI was designed to support telephonic and computer interfaces. This implementation is a 144 Kbps interface that breaks down into two 64 Kbps channels, known as B channels, and one 16 Kbps channel, referred to as a D channel (2B+D). Although each B channel is capable of voice transmission, the B channels are typically combined for a data throughput rate of 128 Kbps. The D channel is intended to carry control and signaling information.

The second implementation is the primary rate interface (PRI). This implementation delivers a data rate of 1.544 Mbps and breaks down into 23 B channels and one D channel (23B+D). The European offering is 30B+D. Other interfaces are currently under study.

Videoconferencing, full-motion videophones, and high-speed network connectivity on demand are just a few of the uses of ISDN. A few companies, such as Microsoft, Boeing, and IBM, are beginning to implement ISDN solutions. For our purposes, we are focusing on wide area network solutions.

At the time of this writing, only transparent bridging was offered for most ISDN solutions. Some vendors offer compression for which they claim BRI connection throughput speeds of up to 500 Kbps. Most ISDN schemes do not offer compression. There are also some primary rate hubs and bridges available. All ISDN networks require an NT1, NT2, or NT12 device.

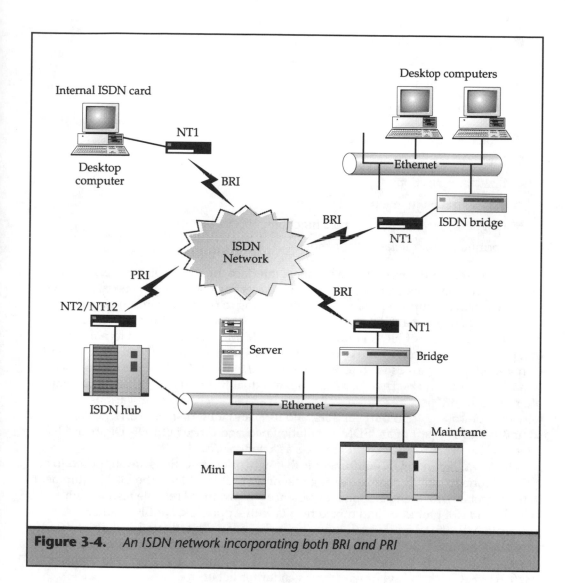

Figure 3-4.   *An ISDN network incorporating both BRI and PRI*

The NT1 device provides these features:

- Termination of the line
- Layer 1 line maintenance
- Transmission signaling and timing

- Capability of providing power to the channel
- Possible multiplexing at the layer-1 level
- Interface termination, including multidrop terminations if necessary

The NT2 and NT12 devices provide the following:

- Protocol handling for layers 2 and 3
- Multiplexing for layers 2 and 3
- Switching functions
- Concentration functions
- Ongoing network maintenance functions
- Termination of the layer 1 functions

Overall, the NT devices allow a seamless interface into the ISDN network while providing certain services depending on the connecting equipment's needs. It allows manufacturers to supply equipment without having to concern themselves with varying types of internal ISDN implementations that each carrier has provided.

There is a variety of ISDN equipment available. Most devices are external boxes that provide connections to a network. Companies such as DigiBoard, Combinet, and Gandalf offer—or are close to offering—single BRI external ISDN boxes that connect two local area networks. DigiBoard also offers a dual BRI port bridge, while Gandalf offers a multi-BRI port ISDN hub. NT devices can be purchased from various telecommunications (telecom) vendors, and local and long-distance carriers, and sometimes can be part of an ISDN installation package. Since fall 1993, DigiBoard has offered an internal PC ISDN card that acts as a network card.

The advantage of ISDN equipment is that network connections are supposed to be quick to connect and disconnect during idle time. You should test the ISDN equipment in the target environment. Personal experience has produced reliable results with TCP/IP and IPX protocols, and mixed results with AppleTalk, NetBIOS, and SNA protocols. Most ISDN equipment today has to be manually activated and deactivated when using SNA, NetBIOS-oriented, AppleTalk, and other protocols. Since some carriers charge by packet or connect time, this can be quite expensive if the connection is left active. Check with your hardware vendor for details.

Due to the rapid growth of ISDN technology, check with your local or long-distance carrier for other ISDN equipment vendors and services not mentioned.

Point-to-Point Digital Circuits

The most widely used WAN connection today are point-to-point digital circuits, also known as private lines or leased lines. A *point-to-point connection* is a dedicated circuit provided by one or more telecommunication carriers. The carriers set up a permanent link from each endpoint, guaranteeing a specific full duplex bandwidth. Local area networks become interconnected through these circuits with bridges/routers. The type of circuits generally available are listed in Table 3-2. We will be limiting our discussion to the DS0, multi-DS0, T1, T2, and T3 circuits, as those are the fastest telecom links most bridges and routers support.

Most carriers offer leased lines, but some only offer a service called Switched 56, which is a dial-out/dial-in digital connection. The bridge/router dials out for a connection and disconnects during long idle times, similar to ISDN. However, if it is used as a leased line (maintaining connections over a long period), the costs can be exorbitant. Unless speed and absolute integrity are required, most users implement an asynchronous solution. Switched 56 lines enable the local carriers to leverage their limited digital resources. We will limit our discussion to the dedicated digital point-to-point connections, since they are the most widely implemented point-to-point connections.

The DSO circuit is the prevalent circuit today. This is basically a standard conditioned line. This circuit is the smallest data line that most LECs will support. The multi-DSO line is relatively new, and the main reason this service is being offered is to support Frame Relay. Although the offering is actually two to 23 circuits, the user will discover that a T1 circuit is typically four times the monthly cost of a DSO. T1 circuits are the backbone of most high-speed WANs.

Until ATM becomes generally available and affordable (probably in the next 10 to 15 years), dedicated circuits will continue to play an important role. However, many WANs are converting to Frame Relay services, and many customers are using

Circuit	Channels	Bit Rate*	Bit Rate**
DSO	1	56	64
Multi-DSO	-4	224	256
T1	24	1344	1544
T1C	48	2688	3152
T2***	96	5376	6312
T3	672	37,632	44,736
T4M	4032	225,792	274,176
FT3C	1344	75,264	90,524
FT-4E-144	2016	112,896	140,000
FT-4E-432	6048	338,688	432,000

* Some carriers use one byte out of every bit for network signaling.
** The non-conformity of the bit rate is due to the use of additional framing bits.
*** Used internally by the carriers.

Table 3-2.   *Types of Point-to-Point Digital Circuits*

dedicated circuits as pipelines to send their data to carrier-provided Frame Relay networks (sometimes called a "clouds"). For more details, see the "Frame Relay" section later in this chapter.

Traditional X.25 Packet-Switching Services

As previously mentioned, X.25 was the first widespread implementation of packet switching. The first publicly available implementations occurred in the 1960s. X.25 and its international cousin, X.75, are the most widely used communication transports in the world. X.25 is considered one of the most reliable asynchronous connections, and it is often used today in third-world countries that have unreliable telephone service. The reason for its reliability is also the reason for its low throughput rate. Error checking is performed by each receiving and transmitting node (see Table 3-1). The maximum throughput rate on most X.25 networks is 56 Kbps. Some service providers such as CompuServe offer connection speeds of 256 Kbps. Although perceived as infeasible for high-speed traffic requirements, it still services a large population and will continue to do so in the foreseeable future.

X.25 supports four basic categories:

■ Permanent virtual circuits (PVC)

■ Virtual circuits (VC)

■ Fast-select call

■ Fast-select call with immediate clear

A PVC is equivalent to the point-to-point connection previously discussed. With a PVC setup, no call setup or negotiation is necessary. With a VC, a call is made into the X.25 network, and a request is made to connect to the destination node. A circuit is then maintained until the session ends. The premise of the fast-select services is for point-of-sale transactions, credit checks, funds transfers, and other activities that constitute small transactions in which a switched virtual call is not really needed.

Most long-distance carriers have an X.25 presence in nearly all the countries in the world. Where they do not, they are tied into X.75 gateways. Some examples of how we use the X.25 network are automatic tellers, credit card verification machines, cash registers, CompuServe services, and private and public WANs. As we become increasingly global in our economy, we need to have reliable connectivity into our data. Direct asynchronous dial-up from some countries is likely to end in frustration. Because X.25 is so prevalent, it allows users to reliably reconnect into their home networks from anywhere in the world.

Normally, an X.25 network is accessed locally, via synchronous dial-up (see Figure 3-5). The user connects to a packet assembler/disassembler (PAD). Once the connection has been established, the user usually enters an account code and an X.25 destination

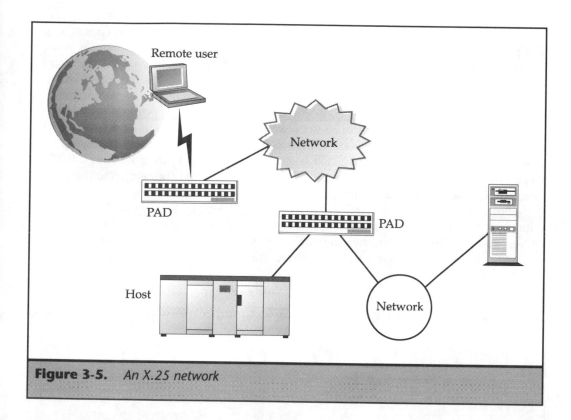

Figure 3-5.   *An X.25 network*

address. The destination address is the PAD port on the remote end that connects to the desired services.

Frame Relay

As mentioned earlier in this chapter, Frame Relay is part of the packet-switching family. Differing from other packet-switching methods, Frame Relay supports variable-length packet sizes. This allows applications to use the best packet sizes for optimal performance. Frame relay was designed to operate over more reliable communication channels and equipment, and so eliminates some of the error checking used in X.25, which thus increases throughput. Frame Relay is rapidly becoming the WAN network transport of choice. Frame Relay service was not generally available until late 1993, and is still in its infancy. Currently, point-to-point T1 connections are required for transferring data from a customer site into a Frame Relay network, but other methods are under consideration. Feasibility studies have determined that Frame Relay technology is capable of 140 Mbps. Note also that few carrier implementations are compatible with each other and many LECs do not have an offering yet.

Each desired connection into the Frame Relay network requires a port connection. The port speed determines the throughput into the Frame Relay network and is known as the port interface speed. Each network interface into the Frame Relay cloud has a virtual connection set up between the desired remote network interfaces. These virtual connections are called PVCs (permanent virtual circuits). Unlike most digital packet-switching networks, a PVC is likened to a permanent connection, much like a point-to-point connection. In Figure 3-6, network D has PVCs to A, B, and C. Network C has PVCs to B and D. Notice that the interface speed of network D is 256 Kbps, while the interface speed of C is 128 Kbps. The maximum data rate from D to C is 128 Kbps as that is the bandwidth of the pipe (the circuit-switched connection to the Frame Relay cloud) into the C network.

Additionally, the pipe on the D network is simultaneously sending and receiving data from A and B, while C is sending and receiving data from D and B. If the interface speeds greatly differ between two networks, severe degradation could occur as packets will be lost. For example, let's assume that Network D's interface speed was

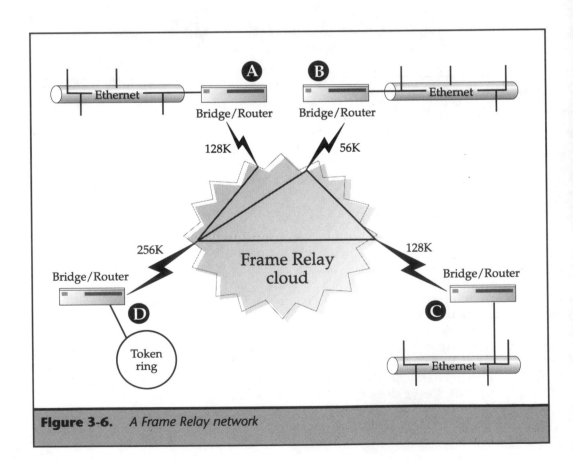

Figure 3-6. *A Frame Relay network*

1.544 Mbps and you tried to send a large file to network C. Packets are likely to be lost because network D is sending packets into the Frame Relay cloud at T1 speeds, while network C can only accept them at 128 Kbps. Due to the lack of error correction (refer back to Table 3-1), the Frame Relay cloud will discard those packets that it has not buffered; the lost data will then have to be retransmitted. Carriers do buffer short traffic bursts, but the buffers are simply not that large.

There are many advantages to Frame Relay:

- Equipment costs are less than with point-to-point connections, since only one connection is required into a carrier's Frame Relay network from each site.

- Customers get similar data throughput for similar prices.

- Multiple connections to the same site are easy, and relatively inexpensive, to implement.

- Frame Relay supports connectivity into the ATM world.

Equipment costs are reduced as the multiple PVCs share the same port. For example, connection D supports three PVCs on a single port. This means one WAN port on the bridge/router. Additionally, any PVC CIR (committed information rate) can be increased on D for faster throughput speeds without the need for increasing bandwidth on the port interfaces. For instance, if the PVC speed between D and C were 56 Kbps, it could be increased to 128 Kbps without the purchase of additional bandwidth for the port interfaces. With Frame Relay, additional PVCs can be set up to support redundant or alternate paths to locations to minimize downtime. In Figure 3-6, C has two paths it can travel to B: C to B, or C to D to B. Lastly, Frame Relay, with its packet-switching format, will be an integral part of the ATM solution (discussed next) throughout the 1990s.

Unlike the other digital packet-switching methods, ISDN Frame Relay is very much connection oriented. To identify the PVC, each packet uses a data link connection identifier (DLCI), rather than source and destination addresses. Data passing through a Frame Relay network specify a DLCI rather than a destination address. Additionally, Frame Relay enforces PVC rates. Each connection has a committed information rate (CIR). Frame relay supports higher traffic rates than the CIR only if bandwidth is available. Remember that Frame Relay is a packet-switching network; if bandwidth is available on the Frame Relay network, the network will attempt to queue the data. If a packet cannot be delivered based on the CIR, the packet will be discarded.

When setting up a WAN with Frame Relay, research the offerings of various carriers, along with the bridge/router equipment available. Some equipment, like CrossCom's bridge/router line, supports automatic recognition of PVCs and their interface speeds. Some carriers allow different send and receive speeds between each PVC, while others do not. A good rule of thumb is five PVCs per bridge/router port. More or fewer PVCs can be assigned depending on the result of traffic analysis.

Asynchronous Transfer Mode (ATM)

Asynchronous transfer mode (ATM) is the current craze in the networking community. Although ATM is commonly referenced, few understand what the technology is. Asynchronous transfer mode, also known as ATD (asynchronous time division) is a fast packet-switching technology. The IEEE and CCITT, in conjunction with the ATM Forum (a group of ATM service and equipment vendors and potential ATM users) are developing standards. ATM was chosen the preferred transport method of BISDN (broadband integrated services digital network), servicing multimedia and other high-speed data requirements. ATM standards are being developed to be flexible, make efficient use of available resources, and support the evolution of one universal network.

ATM will be introduced in phases. Currently, ATM interfaces are offered by most equipment vendors. What does this mean to the user? In reality, true ATM is offered on a limited basis. Many vendors have implemented ATM-like fast packet switching internally. As the physical links (such as FDDI-II), become affordable, reliable, and more mainstream, UNIs (universal network interfaces) will link the vendors' equipment with the physical link. Vendors such as Cisco Systems, WellFleet, Cabletron, Optical Data Systems, and others already have such interfaces. Major carriers such as Sprint and AT&T currently offer ATM WAN connections at the T3 level and above. The carriers only offer this service on a limited basis.

The following characteristics make ATM a powerful connectivity option for a wide range of organizations:

- Error handling on a link-by-link basis is eliminated, thus increasing throughput.
- Transactions occur in a connectionless mode, and any-to-any connections are provided.
- The amount of header information required to transport a packet is reduced.
- Data packets are relatively small and consistent in size, thus reducing the type of delays that large packets can cause at switches in the network. (Think of the time it takes to get a small car through an intersection, as opposed to a semi truck.)

ATM was designed to operate on relatively error-free physical connections, such as fiberoptic media and silicon-based (integrated circuit) switching devices. As integrated circuitry becomes increasingly fast and more reliable, higher throughput speeds are attainable. The bit error rate (BER) of ATM is at minimum 10^{-12}, while X.25 is 10^{-6} and point-to-point is 10^{-7}. This means that in ATM circuits, one in a trillion packets will have an error compared to one in ten million for point-to-point. Because errors are considered so rare, ATM does relatively no error checking. Error checking in an ATM network is performed by the sending and receiving devices.

ATM operates in a true connectionless environment. Under this mode, resources are dynamically allocated. There are two types of data transfer methodologies currently being utilized: permanent virtual circuits (PVC) and switched virtual circuits (SVC). Like Frame Relay, the PVC connection has a fixed allocated bandwidth that delivers data between specific end-points. The SVC methodology creates a virtual circuit as needed, and then when the transfer is finished, the bandwidth of the circuit is relinquished to the overall resource pool. As in Frame Relay, virtual circuits are used. ATM is based on statistical modeling of various types of data. Unlike X.25, data has to arrive in the order sent. This means if a cell is dropped, retransmission will have to occur. This makes congestion a real concern in an ATM network, and various methods of dealing with it are still being investigated. Until a reliable congestion management system is developed, the PVC method will likely be prevalent.

The cell consists of 53 bytes, with 48 bytes reserved for data and 5 for the header, of which 3 are the ATM routing address. These 3 bytes are called the virtual path identifier/virtual circuit identifier (VPI/VCI), comparable to the DCLI in Frame Relay. Overall, the main function of the header is the identification of the virtual connection in which the packet is to be routed. Once a circuit is established, data transfer is very efficient. ATM's fixed-size cells are easily managed at switches. With all cells the same size, no particular data transmission can place an excessive load on the network that delays other transmissions. An ATM network can guarantee the delivery of time-sensitive information like video, assuming the proper priorities have been assigned. Transmission that involve variable-length data packets like that used in Frame Relay cannot gaurantee timely delivery, because one large data packet might tie up a switch for an extraordinary amount of time. As mentioned earlier, using the analogy of a city intersection is helpful. A network that uses variable-length frames is like a city intersection that allows many different sizes of vehicles to pass through. Delays occur when long semi trucks pass through the intersection. Switching in a fixed-size cell network like ATM can be compared to a city intersection through which only Porsche 911s are allowed to pass.

How can ATM technology fit into today's WANs? Through 1995, ATM technology will be limited to fast packet switching on hubs, with an ATM backbone between the hubs and bridge/routers (see Figure 3-7) in all but the largest networks. Frame relay is becoming the WAN transport mode of choice. Starting in late 1995, long-distance carriers should be introducing true ATM solutions on a limited basis at less than T3 speeds. This will change Figure 3-7 from a Frame Relay cloud to an ATM cloud with possible ATM telecommunication connections.

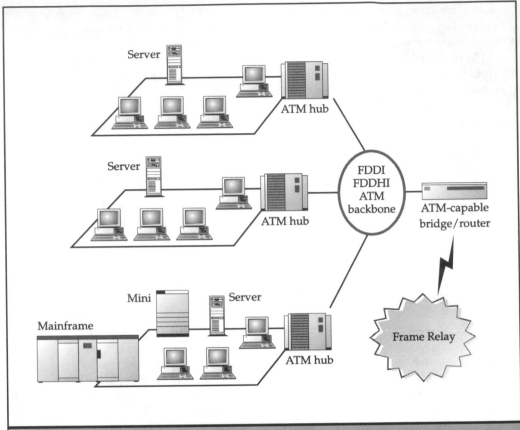

Figure 3-7. *With ATM solutions still in early development, Frame Relay remains the WAN transport mode of choice*

Summary

The WAN solutions discussed in this chapter include current or soon-to-be-offered services. Options such as microwave, VSAT (satellite), infrared, and others do exist, but generally are used for extraordinary needs. Networking schemes vary by necessity. It is not uncommon to see one solution for the metropolitan area network and another for the remainder of the wide area network. Local carriers also play a role in determining what offerings are available. However, compared to the 1980s, our options have increased tremendously, and wide area network solutions are becoming economically feasible.

PART TWO

Transport Services

Chapter Four

Network Communication and Protocols

by Levi Reiss, La Cité Collégiale, Ottawa
and Joseph Radin,
Digital Equipment Corporation

C omputer network communication relies on protocols—sets of rules and procedures that allow network components to exchange information. This chapter introduces the most common communications protocols, many of which will be examined in greater detail in forthcoming chapters.

Communication protocols are designed around an architectural model that is layered or stacked, somewhat like layers in a wedding cake. Each layer is self-contained, and deals only with the interface of the layer immediately above it and the layer immediately below it. This layered approach divides communication protocols into manageable areas of functionality that allow software and hardware vendors to design products that will interoperate with other vendors' products at any desired level. For example, manufacturers of modems and network interface cards need only design products that integrate at the lowest hardware-level layers of a protocol stack in order to ensure interoperability with other vendors' hardware.

Communications protocols, whether proprietary or not, can be divided into two classes: connection-oriented protocols and connectionless protocols. These two classes differ in their functionality and consequently in performance. *Connection-oriented protocols* assure that the packets composing a message are delivered from Point X to Point Y in order, and over a defined path to improve throughput and reduce errors. *Connectionless protocols* deliver the packets from Point X to Point Y over any path that the network might have available or deem most efficient. The sender and receiver are responsible for packet sequencing (in case packets arrive out of order) and for error detection. A single protocol suite, such as the OSI Reference Model, is likely to include both connection-oriented protocols and connectionless protocols. (It would be very wasteful for each protocol layer to be responsible for message reliability.)

This chapter introduces the OSI Reference Model, which we use to compare proprietary protocol suites. Major proprietary protocol suites are then examined. These suites are presented in the following order: IBM's Systems Network Architecture (SNA), Digital Equipment Corporation's Digital Network Architecture (DNA), the Transmission Control Protocol/Internet Protocol (TCP/IP) associated with UNIX systems, Novell's NetWare, AppleTalk, and Microsoft's LAN Manager. Many of these protocol suites and their underlying network architecture are discussed in detail in the next chapters.

The OSI Reference Model

The open computing environment is a multivendor environment where hardware, software, and communications equipment supplied by different vendors work together. Such an environment does not occur by chance. The International Standards Organization (ISO) has developed a seven-layer protocol known as the Open System Interconnection (OSI) Model, shown in Figure 4-1. The bottom four layers are hardware and software oriented, while the top three layers are software only. An OSI network consists of end systems (ES) and intermediate systems (IS). *Intermediate systems* connect two or more subnetworks and perform routing functions by directing

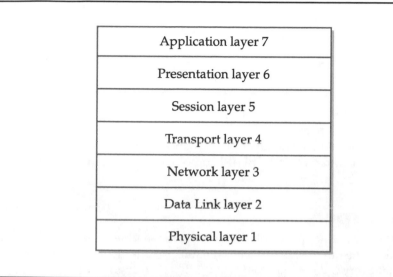

Figure 4-1.   *The Open Systems Interconnection (OSI) Reference Model*

packets among the varous subnetworks that form a network. *End systems* are attached to subnetworks and do not have routing functions. An ES is basically a user's workstation, a server, or some other network attached node or device.

Layer 1: Physical

The Physical layer defines the information transmission to and from the physical components of the network. Its functions include establishing and terminating a communications link such as on the public telephone system, synchronizing data transfer, transferring bits of data, reporting on errors, and monitoring layer performance. Commonly used local area network (LAN) systems defined at the Physical layer are Ethernet, token ring, and Fiber Distributed Data Interface (FDDI).

Layer 2: Data Link

The Data Link layer defines protocols for sending and receiving information between units that are directly connected to each other. Its functions include establishing and terminating a communications link, assembling bits received from the Physical layer into blocks and transferring them, controlling the sequence of data blocks, detecting and perhaps correcting errors, and monitoring layer performance. Ethernet and token ring standards are also defined at the Data Link layer. Other data link protocols include the frame relay and Asynchronous Transfer Mode (ATM) transmission used in wide area network (WAN) systems.

Layer 3: Network

The Network layer defines connectionless protocols that dynamically route user data between systems in the network. Its functions include routing data blocks, segmenting and subsequently reassembling data blocks when required, monitoring data blocks to ensure rapid transmission, maintaining a routing database, detecting and perhaps correcting errors, and monitoring layer performance. Commonly used Network layer protocols include the Internet Protocol (IP) and Novell's Internetwork Packet Exchange (IPX).

Layer 4: Transport

The Transport layer defines protocols responsible for sending messages from one end of the network to the other. This service is reliable; in other words, the system guarantees that every byte transmitted will reach its destination in the order it was sent, or it notifies the destination. The Transport layer provides either connection-oriented or connectionless functions. If the underlying protocol does not perform error checking and ensure packet ordering, the Transport layer does. Additional Transport layer services include assuring equality between the transmission rate and the reception rate; managing network traffic to avoid congestion while assuring a reasonable transmission time; and processing user messages to overcome size limitations imposed by the network. Commonly used Transport layer protocols include the Internet Transmission Control Protocol (TCP), Novell's Sequenced Packet Exchange (SPX), and Microsoft NetBIOS/NetBEUI.

Layer 5: Session

The Session layer enables the dialog between users at separate locations. For example, it manages data transport requests during a communication session.

Layer 6: Presentation

The Presentation layer assures that information is delivered in understandable form. For example, it manages file transfers, translates data from one code to another, and formats the video screen. The Presentation layer is concerned with the form of the data, but not its meaning.

Layer 7: Application

The Application layer supports the actual end-user application. This layer is concerned with the data's meaning. For example, it may provide utilities to assist users with file access or to generate network usage statistics.

Protocol Layer Interaction

Layered architectures provide a way for vendors to design software and hardware that is interoperable with other vendors' products. Without open, standardized protocols, you would need to obtain all your networking equipment from one vendor. Layering specifies different functions and services at levels in the protocol stack. The protocol stack defines how to create hardware and software components that operate at each level of the stack. So if you wanted to create a network interface card that would interoperate with other vendors cards, you would conform to standards defined in the lower layers of the stack. At lower levels, the process of actually transmitting bit- streams of data is separated from the task of managing the communication session between systems. At the upper levels, layering separates the user applications from the underlying communication services.

Note the following:

- Lower layers provide services to upper layers.
- Each layer has a set of services.
- Services are defined by protocols.
- Product designers and programmers only need to be concerned with the protocols in the layer they are working with, the services provided to upper layers, and the services provided by lower layers.

When systems communicate, peer protocols at each level of each system coordinate the communication process. For example, the Transport layer processes in one system coordinate communication activities with Transport layer processes in the other system. As an analogy, imagine the creation of a formal agreement between two embassies. At the top, formal negotiations take place between ambassadors, but in the background, diplomats and officers work on documents, define procedures, and perform other activities. The ambassador at the highest level passes orders down to a lower-level diplomat and uses services provided by that diplomat. At the same time, the diplomat below the ambassador in rank is coordinating his or her activities with a diplomat of equal rank at the other embassy. Each diplomat follows established diplomatic procedures defined at their level of operation. For example, an officer at one level may provide language translation services or technical documentation. This officer communicates with a peer at the other embassy to coordinate the translation of documents they are exchanging.

In the diplomatic world, a diplomat at one embassy simply picks up the phone and calls a peer at another embassy. In the world of network communication, entities in each protocol layer communicate with peer entities by attaching messages to packets that are sent to other systems. As information (such as data or user commands) is passed down through the protocol stack, entities (communication processes) in each layer add their own information to the PDU in the form of messages called *protocol control information* (PCI). PCIs are destined for peer entities in the other system. As shown in Figure 4-2, each layer adds a PCI to the data packet. This package of information that passes between layers is called a *protocol data unit* (PDU). the PDU eventually reaches the lowest Physical (hardware) layer, where it is "framed" into a stream of data bits and transmitted to the other system. When the packet reaches its destination, it is passed up through the protocol stack, and PCI information destined for each layer is stripped off and passed to the entity at that layer.

Entities, like diplomats with various ranks, reside at each layer of the protocol stack and provide services to upper layers. Entities in one computer communicate with peer entities in the other computer. Protocols at each layer define the syntax and semantics of peer communication between the entities. Some of the information added and actions taken at each level are listed here:

- *Application* Destination node address information
- *Presentation* Code-set information added
- *Session* Communication session information added
- *Transport* Checksum header added
- *Network* Packet quantity/sequence information added
- *Data Link* Packet checksum trailer/message end added
- *Physical* Message converted to bit- stream and transmitted

Although entities communicate with their peers, they must utilize the services of lower layers to get those messages across. *Service Access Points* (SAPs) are the connections that entities in adjacent layers use for communicating messages. Multiple SAPs are allowed between layers to support a number of communication processes.

A *packet* is a package of information that is exchanged between devices over a data communication link. The data being exchanged may take any of the following forms:

- Messages and commands, such as a request for service
- Control codes for managing the session, such as codes that indicate communication errors and the need for retransmission
- Data, such as the contents of a file

For example, the Transport layer protocol of System A in Figure 4-2 adds a sequence number to the PDU. This sequence number is read by the Transport protocol in System B to ensure that the packets have arrived in order. One of the main reasons for packeting and framing information is that once this is done, any errors on the communication link only affect a small, discernible part of the transmission, which can then be easily retransmitted.

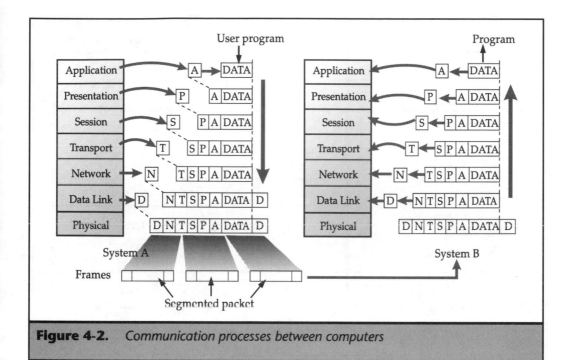

Figure 4-2.   *Communication processes between computers*

While the communication protocol defines the packet structure, the networking system defines the frame structure for bit stream transmission. As shown in Figure 4-2, when the PDU reaches the Physical layer, it is transmitted as a stream of bits. On copper wire, the bit streams takes the form of voltage level changes that represent binary 1s and 0s. The Data Link layer frames the packet into a bit stream and uses a media access method (e.g., CSMA/CD, token) to get it on the transmission media. The PDU might be subdivided into a number of separately addressed frames, a process called *blocking* or *framing*. The frame format is defined by the network in use. For example, Ethernet defines frames that can hold up to 1500 bytes of packet data.

Systems Network Architecture (SNA)

Systems Network Architecture (SNA) is IBM's proprietary networking architecture, shown in Figure 4-3. This widely used network architecture was first introduced in 1974 and provided the primary basis for the OSI Reference Model. SNA was originally designed to connect mainframe computers and nonprogrammable terminals. SNA has developed over the years, in line with the evolution in computers and networking. Chapter 5 presents the Systems Network Architecture and its protocols in great detail.

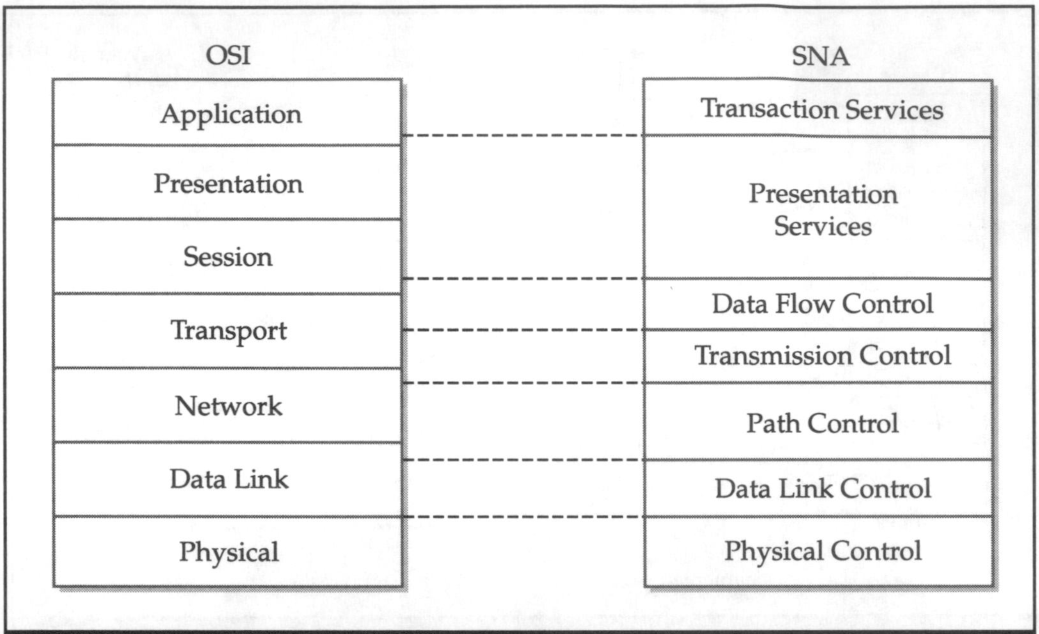

OSI		SNA
Application		Transaction Services
Presentation		Presentation Services
Session		
Transport		Data Flow Control
		Transmission Control
Network		Path Control
Data Link		Data Link Control
Physical		Physical Control

Figure 4-3.   *A comparison of SNA and OSI layering*

The SNA Protocol Suite

The proprietary SNA network architecture model, also called the SNA Protocol Suite, consists of seven layers, as does the industry standard OSI Reference Model. These seven layers are Physical Control, Data Link Control, Path Control, Transmission Control, Data Flow Control, Presentation Services, and Transaction Services. These layers are described next, and then compared with layers in the OSI Reference Model.

Physical Control Layer

The SNA Physical Control layer describes the electrical and mechanical properties of the physical media and its interfaces. This layer closely corresponds to the OSI Physical layer.

Data Link Control Layer

The SNA Data Link Control layer builds data link headers and trailers, transfers data frames over the data link, performs error checking, and retransmits frames that were in error. This layer closely corresponds to the OSI Data Link layer and provides support for the widely used Token Ring protocol for local area networks. Recently, support has been added for Ethernet and the Fiber Distributed Data Interface (FDDI) for LANs and frame relay for WANs.

Path Control Layer

The SNA Path Control layer performs the routing and datagram assembly/disassembly functions associated with the OSI Network layer. It also performs flow control functions associated with the OSI Data Link layer.

Transmission Control Layer

The SNA Transmission Control layer assures reliable message transmission across the network, as does the OSI Transport layer. It also encrypts and decrypts messages, a function of the OSI Presentation layer.

Data Flow Control Layer

The SNA Data Flow Control layer batches data requests, determines whose turn it is to transmit, groups messages, and interrupts data flow when so requested. It is similar to the OSI Session layer.

Presentation Services Layer

The SNA Presentation Services layer specifies the way in which the data format is translated, the major function of the OSI Presentation layer. It also synchronizes operations and coordinates resource sharing.

Transaction Services Layer

The SNA Transaction Services layer provides applications services such as distributed processing via system programs. This layer is somewhat similar to the OSI Application layer.

> NOTE: *While there are seven layers in the SNA model, the central functions are handled by layers 2 to 6. It is customary to regroup these layers into two categories, Path Control Network (layers 2 and 3) and Network Addressable Units (layers 4-6).*

Software Implementation

The basic SNA protocol consists of the seven layers just described. Five of these functions are consolidated in two packages: Path Control Network and Network Addressable Units.

The Path Control Network

The Path Control Network consists of layers 2 and 3 of the SNA model; namely Data Link Control and Path Control. These two layers control the routing and flow of data throughout the network and manage the physical transmission of data from one SNA node to another. These functions are assumed by the mainframe software Advanced Communications Function/Network Control Program (NCP).

Network Addressable Units

The Network Addressable Units consist of layers 4, 5, and 6 of the SNA model: Transmission Control, Data Flow Control, and Presentation Services. These three layers provide network control and management, moving data from one user to another. These functions are assumed by the mainframe software Advanced Communications Function/Virtual Telecommunications Access Method (VTAM).

Extensions to the Basic Protocol

SNA has evolved over the years to service LANs and WANs. However, the basic SNA protocol still relies on mainframe computers. IBM markets the Advanced Program-to-Program Communications (APPC) and Advanced Peer-to-Peer Networking (APPN) for installations requiring program-to-program communication or those considering TCP/IP. A peer-to-peer mode is one in which each computer controls its own session. This is in contrast to centralized systems in which a mainframe computer is responsible for communication sessions.

Advanced Program-to-Program Communications (APPC)   Advanced Program-to-Program Communications (APPC) is a Session layer protocol allowing separate programs running on different computers in an SNA-based network to communicate in a peer-to-peer mode.

Advanced Peer-to-Peer Networking (APPN)   Advanced Peer-to-Peer Networking (APPN) furnishes peer-to-peer networking services in an SNA-based network. This product is positioned to compete with the Transmission Control Protocol/Internet Protocol (TCP/IP).

DIGITAL Network Architecture (DNA)

DIGITAL Network Architecture (DNA) is a model of the structures and functions that underlie all DEC networking implementations. The DNA model includes proprietary protocols and interfaces, and Open System Interconnection (OSI) protocols and services defined by the International Standards Organization. Chapter 6 presents the DIGITAL Network Architecture and its protocols in great detail.

The DNA Protocol Suite

Figure 4-4 shows the seven DNA layers. There are two complementary choices, described next.

The OSI Application   This application generally conforms to the OSI specifications at all seven layers of the OSI Reference Model.

The DNA Application This application consists of proprietary DNA functions built on the first four (hardware) layers of the OSI Reference Model.

DNA Physical Layer

The Physical layer defines information transmission to and from the Physical components of the network. DNA fully conforms to OSI Physical layer standards that describe, for example, how data is converted to and from electrical signals.

DNA Data Link Layer

The Data Link layer provides a dependable communication path between units that are directly connected to each other. DNA may use several protocols for this layer, some of which conform to the OSI Reference Model. The DNA Data Link layer supports Ethernet, which is widely used on local area networks.

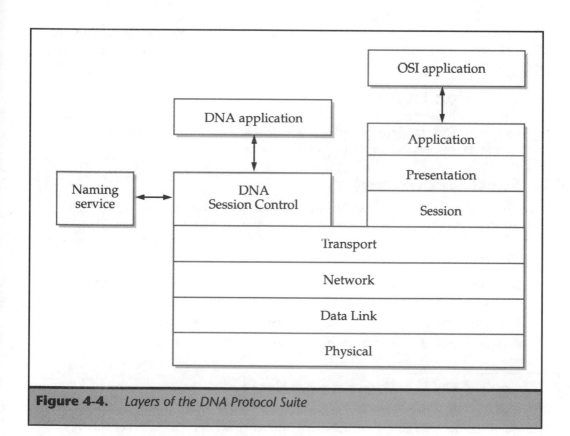

Figure 4-4. *Layers of the DNA Protocol Suite*

DNA Network Layer

The Network layer dynamically routes user data between systems in the network. DNA supports OSI standards associated with this level for a variety of topologies.

DNA Transport Layer

The Transport layer is responsible for sending messages from one end of the network to the other. DNA supports OSI standards associated with this level and applies functions associated with this level in the upper layer protocols.

Session Layer

The Session layer enables the dialog between users at separate locations. The OSI application supports OSI standards associated with this level, while the DNA application replaces it with DNA Session Control (described shortly).

Presentation Layer

The Presentation layer assures that information is delivered in understandable form. The OSI application supports OSI standards associated with this level, while the DNA application replaces it with DNA Session Control.

Application Layer

The Application layer supports the actual end-user application. The OSI Application layer supports OSI standards associated with this level, while the DNA Application layer replaces it with DNA Session Control.

DNA Session Control

DNA Session Control is proprietary DNA software providing the link from DNA Transport level functions to the application. It replaces the three OSI levels: Session level, Presentation level, and Application level. Among the communication functions it provides are:

- *Name-to-address translation*   This feature allows users to refer to remote objects by name, increasing network transparency.
- *Protocol selection*   This feature increases network flexibility.
- *Access control*   This feature may increase network security.

The TCP/IP Protocol Suite

TCP/IP is an abbreviation for the Transmission Control Protocol/Internet Protocol. Figure 4-5 compares TCP/IP with the OSI Reference Model. The Internet network, which connects millions of computers around the globe, relies on TCP/IP. This protocol was originally developed for the ARPA (Advanced Research Projects Agency)

OSI	TCP/IP
Application (Presents user's application)	File Transfer Protocol (FTP), Simple Mail Transfer Protocol (SMTP)
Presentation (Translates data)	Network Filing System (NFS), Domain Name Service (DNS)
Session (Controls dialog)	TELNET
Transport (Ensures message integrity)	Transport Control Protocol (TCP), User Datagram Protocol (UDP)
Network (Routes transmissions)	Internet Protocol (IP), Address Resolution Protocol (ARP)
Data Link (Detects errors)	
Physical (Connects devices to network)	

Figure 4-5.   *The TCP/IP protocol suite, as compared with the OSI Model*

associated with the U.S. Department of Defense. TCP/IP is composed of two interrelated protocols, the connection-oriented Transmission Control Protocol and the connectionless Internet Protocol, described shortly. In addition, it contains multiple applications protocols, some of which are described later in this chapter. Chapter 7 presents the TCP/IP protocols in great detail.

The Transmission Control Protocol (TCP)

The Transmission Control Protocol (TCP) is connection-oriented; it assures that the packets composing a message are delivered from Point X to Point Y in order, and have been transmitted without error. In particular, TCP performs the following services:

- *Acknowledgment*   TCP informs the senders that the proposed recipient has, in fact, received the packet.

- *Checksumming*   TCP calculates a control total known as a checksum to detect transmission errors.

- *Flow Control*   TCP flow control reduces the frequency of lost packets.
- *Retransmission*   TCP automatically retransmits lost or erroneous packets.
- *Sequencing*   TCP uses packet numbers to verify that they are received in the order sent.

The Internet Protocol (IP)

The Internet Protocol is connectionless. It delivers packets from Point X to Point Y without any guarantees—the sender and receiver are responsible for packet sequencing and error detection. IP provides a datagram service; a datagram is a self-contained packet routed to single or multiple nodes, without services such as acknowledgment, checksumming, flow control, retransmission, or sequencing. Because it does not include these services, IP is faster and more efficient than TCP.

Applications Protocols

The TCP/IP protocol suite includes multiple applications protocols. The File Transfer Protocol (FTP), Network File System (NFS), Simple Mail Transfer Protocol (SMTP), Simple Network Management Protocol (SNMP), and Telnet are described next.

File Transfer Protocol (FTP)

The File Transfer Protocol (FTP) is a commonly used program for transferring files between the TCP/IP environment and another environment, not necessarily TCP/IP. It is typically used to download files to the client from a remote server. FTP is implemented at the Applications level of the OSI Reference Model. It supports ASCII (microcomputer standard format), EBCDIC (IBM mainframe standard format), and formatted files, and provides optional password protection and data compression. Anonymous FTP is used to access data from public servers on the Internet without a password. The Trivial File Transfer Protocol (TFTP) is a limited version of FTP.

Network File System (NFS)

Sun Microsystems is one of the major manufacturers of engineering workstations running under UNIX. It developed the Network File System (NFS) and the associated Network Information Services (NIS), previously called the Yellow Pages, that rely on the UDP/IP protocol, with its own method for assuring reliability. The Network File System allows users to access disks independently of their physical location. The Network Information Services aids system administrators in configuring a network-based system. These two products are available on all UNIX systems and on the major non-UNIX systems.

Simple Mail Transfer Protocol (SMTP)

The Simple Mail Transfer Protocol (SMTP) provides a store-and-forward mail processing between host computers on TCP/IP networks. It handles both client and server functions. SMTP verifies the connection, identifies the sender, applies the parameters, and handles the actual message transmission. It works with the Internet Domain Naming Services that converts numeric addresses to standard Internet address names.

Simple Network Management Protocol (SNMP)

The Simple Network Management Protocol (SNMP) is the most commonly used protocol for collecting management information from network devices, such as data throughput, error frequency, and historical record management and trend analysis. It is often used to manage wiring centers known as hubs. For example, it can automatically disconnect malfunctioning equipment and connect or disconnect workstations based on the time of day.

Telnet

The Telnet protocol, which is part of the TCP/IP suite, enables users to log into a remote computer as if they were sitting at a directly attached terminal. Logging into a remote Internet computer via Telnet requires only that you know its name.

UDP/IP

UDP/IP is an abbreviation for User Datagram Protocol/Internet Protocol. It is a fast way to transmit data packets between two or more applications. However, it is unreliable; it does not guarantee that every byte transmitted will reach its destination in the order that it was sent. Because it performs less verification and monitoring than TCP/IP, it can generate much greater throughput. UDP/IP is often used with NFS and NIS, described next.

Novell NetWare

The term NetWare signifies a series of local area network operating systems, ranging from NetWare Lite, an operating system for peer-to-peer networks with two to about two dozen users; NetWare 3.*x*, an operating system for single-server LANs supporting hundreds of users; and NetWare 4.*x*, an enterprise network operating system. NetWare provides support to hosts running multiple operating systems including DOS, MS-Windows, OS/2, and UNIX. Chapter 8 presents the NetWare protocols in great detail.

The NetWare Protocol Suite

The NetWare protocol suite is divided into six layers as shown in Figure 4-6. LAN Manager layers correspond closely to one or two layers in the seven-layer industry standard OSI Reference Model. These six layers are Physical layer, Open Data Link Interface (ODI) and Network Driver Interface Specification (NDIS), Internetwork Packet Exchange (IPX), Sequenced Packet Exchange (SPX), Network Basic Input-Output System (NetBIOS) or Named Pipes, and NetWare Core Protocol (NCP).

Physical Layer

The Physical layer defines the information transmission to and from the physical components of the network. NetWare supports commonly used Ethernet, Token Ring, and ARCNET technologies.

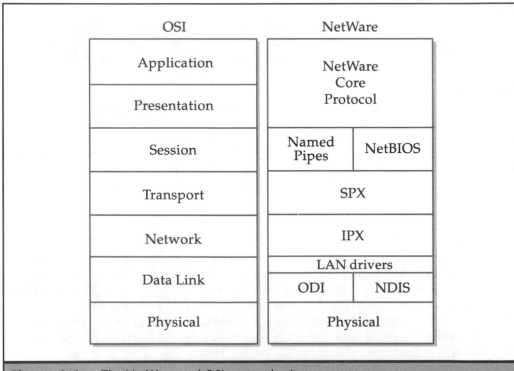

Figure 4-6. *The NetWare and OSI protocol suites*

Open Data Link Interface and Network Driver Interface Specifications

The ODI and NDIS specifications correspond to the Data Link layer of the OSI Reference Model, which defines protocols for sending and receiving information between units that are directly connected to each other. ODI provides support for multiple Transport layer protocols including NetWare's IPX (described next), TCP/IP, and AppleTalk. The Network Driver Interface Specification (NDIS) can serve as a link to LAN Manager, TCP/IP, and Windows NT protocols simultaneously.

Internetwork Packet Exchange (IPX)

IPX is a peer-to-peer networking protocol that operates at the Network layer of the OSI Reference Model. This layer defines connectionless protocols that dynamically route user data between systems in the network.

Sequenced Packet Exchange (SPX)

SPX is a connection-oriented network communication protocol that operates at the Transport layer of the OSI Reference Model. This layer defines protocols responsible for sending messages from one end of the network to the other and guarantees that every byte transmitted will reach its destination in the order it was sent, or it notifies the destination.

Named Pipes and NetBIOS

The Session layer of the OSI Reference Model enables the dialog between users at separate locations. For example, it provides log-in services, manages data transport requests during the entire session, and provides log-out services. NetWare implements Session layer functions with two products: Named Pipes and NetBIOS.

Named Pipes execute Session layer services on NetWare networks. They provide an interface between processes running on separate computers. While named pipes are more sophisticated and perhaps more efficient than NetBIOS, they do not support NetBIOS node naming and connectionless datagram services.

The Network Basic Input Output System, commonly called NetBIOS, is an application program interface (API) for LAN applications running in the NetWare, LAN Manager, and OS/2 environments. NetBIOS services include communications session management, naming of nodes, broadcasting server names and locations, and transmitting connectionless datagrams.

NetWare Core Protocol (NCP)

The NetWare Core Protocol (NCP) is the most commonly used protocol for transmitting information to a server and its clients on a NetWare local area network. It corresponds to the Presentation and Session layer functions of the OSI Reference

Model. Among the functions provided are: file access, printing services, resource allocation, network management and security, and inter-server communications.

AppleTalk

AppleTalk is a series of specifications describing the connections between Apple Macintosh hardware (computers and peripherals) to computer networks, as shown in Figure 4-7. At its inception, AppleTalk applied the proprietary LocalTalk cabling system, but it now supports industry standard Ethernet and Token Ring networks.

The AppleTalk Protocol Suite

The AppleTalk protocol suite is divided into seven layers, as is the industry standard OSI Reference Model. These seven layers are Physical layer, Data Link layer, Network layer, Transport layer, Session layer, Presentation layer, and Application layer—the same names as in the OSI Reference Model. Multiple protocols are defined for several layers.

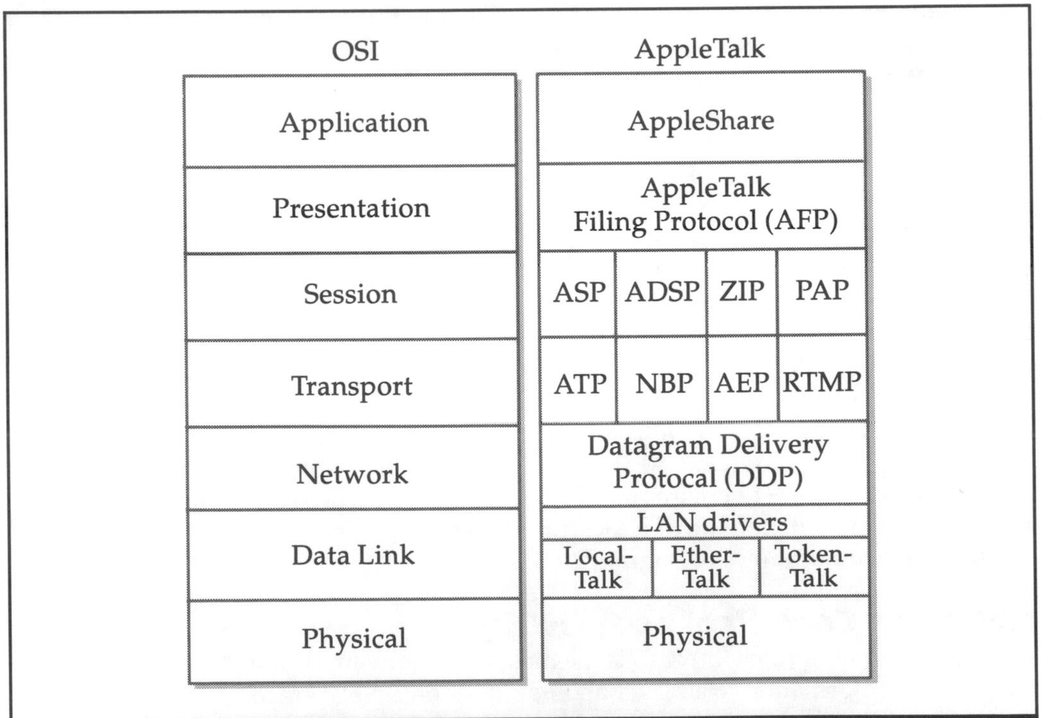

OSI	AppleTalk			
Application	AppleShare			
Presentation	AppleTalk Filing Protocol (AFP)			
Session	ASP	ADSP	ZIP	PAP
Transport	ATP	NBP	AEP	RTMP
Network	Datagram Delivery Protocal (DDP)			
Data Link	LAN drivers			
	Local-Talk	Ether-Talk		Token-Talk
Physical	Physical			

Figure 4-7.   *The AppleTalk and OSI protocol suites*

Layer 1: Physical

The Physical layer defines the information transmission to and from the physical components of the network. AppleTalk supports commonly used Ethernet and Token Ring technologies, as well as the proprietary LocalTalk.

Layer 2: Data Link

The Data Link layer defines protocols for sending and receiving information between units that are directly connected to each other. AppleTalk calls these protocols link access protocols (LAP). AppleTalk calls the Ethernet version EtherTalk, the Token Ring version, TokenTalk. It also provides the proprietary LocalTalk for Data Link communications.

Layer 3: Network

The Network layer defines connectionless protocols that dynamically route user data between systems in the network. AppleTalk supports the datagram delivery protocol (DDP) with a maximum packet size of 586 bytes. DDP places the destination address and error-checking information in the packet header, and then transmits it to the appropriate link access protocol.

Layer 4: Transport

The Transport layer defines protocols responsible for sending messages from one end of the network to the other. This service is reliable, in other words, the system guarantees that every byte transmitted will reach its destination in the order it was sent, or it notifies the destination. AppleTalk defines the following four Transport layer protocols.

AppleTalk Transaction Protocol (ATP)   The AppleTalk Transaction protocol handles transaction requests, transaction responses, and transaction releases.

Name Binding Protocol (NBP)   The Name Binding protocol translates a node's numeric internet address into a named address.

AppleTalk Echo Protocol (AEP)   The AppleTalk Echo protocol determines whether a destination node will be available for communication.

Routing Table Maintenance Protocol (RTMP)   The Routing Table Maintenance protocol maintains address tables and communicates with other routers to determine network status.

Layer 5: Session

The Session layer enables the dialog between users at separate locations. AppleTalk defines four Session layer protocols, discussed next.

AppleTalk Session Protocol (ASP)   The AppleTalk Session protocol initiates and terminates sessions between two nodes.

AppleTalk Data Stream Protocol (ADSP)   The AppleTalk Data Stream protocol manages data transmission between two computers. It supports full-duplex transmission, enabling both computers to transmit simultaneously.

Zone Information Protocol (ZIP)   The Zone Information protocol maintains the network map for routing and control purposes.

Printer Access Protocol (PAP)   The Printer Access protocol maintains communication between a user's workstation and a printer.

Layer 6: Presentation

The Presentation layer assures that information is delivered in understandable form. The AppleTalk Filing Protocol (AFP) provides access to remote files on network servers.

Layer 7: Application

The Application layer supports the actual end-user application. AppleTalk does not define any proprietary Application layer protocols.

LAN Manager

Microsoft LAN Manager is a network management and file system layered upon the OS/2 operating system. This product was jointly developed by Microsoft and IBM, but IBM is no longer associated with this product. The LAN Manager protocol suite is divided into five layers, as shown in Figure 4-8. LAN Manager layers correspond closely to one or two layers in the seven-layer industry standard OSI Reference Model. These five layers are Physical layer, NDIS, NetBEUI, NetBIOS or Named Pipes, and Server Message Blocks.

Physical Layer

The Physical layer defines the information transmission to and from the physical components of the network. LAN Manager supports commonly used Ethernet and Token Ring technologies.

Network Driver Interface Specification (NDIS)

The Network Driver Interface Specification (NDIS) corresponds to the Data Link layer of the OSI Reference Model. It defines protocols for sending and receiving information between units that are directly connected to each other. The NDIS protocol is not restricted to LAN Manager. It can also serve as a link to NetWare, TCP/IP, and Windows NT protocols simultaneously.

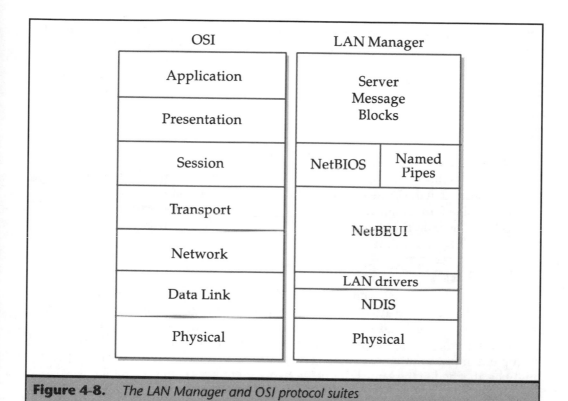

Figure 4-8.   *The LAN Manager and OSI protocol suites*

NetBIOS Extended User Interface (NetBEUI)

The NetBIOS Extended User Interface, commonly called NetBEUI, corresponds to the Network and Transport layers of the OSI Reference Model. Recall that the Network layer defines connectionless protocols that dynamically route user data between systems in the network, and the Transport layer defines protocols responsible for sending messages from one end of the network to the other. NetBEUI is highly integrated with NetBIOS, described next.

NetBIOS and Named Pipes

The Session layer of the OSI Reference Model enables the dialog between users at separate locations. For example, it provides log-in services, manages data transport requests during the entire session, and provides log-out services. LAN Manager implements Session layer functions with two products: NetBIOS and Named Pipes.

The Network Basic Input Output System (NetBIOS) is an application program interface (API) for LAN applications running in the LAN Manager, NetWare, and

OS/2 environments. NetBIOS services include communications session management, naming of nodes, broadcasting server names and locations, and transmitting connectionless datagrams.

Named Pipes execute Session layer services on LAN Manager networks. They provide an interface between processes running on separate computers. While named pipes are more sophisticated and perhaps more efficient than NetBIOS, they do not support NetBIOS node naming and connectionless datagram services.

Server Message Blocks (SMB)

Server Message Blocks (SMB) carry out Presentation layer and Application layer services. Recall that the Presentation layer assures that information is delivered in understandable form and that the Application layer supports the actual end-user application. The SMB protocol is also employed in peer-to-peer networks.

Summary

Interoperability can be achieved among networks that use different protocols by the implementation of gateways and routers that perform protocol conversions. First, the level at which conversion is necessary must be determined. It is helpful to place the protocol stack diagrams side-by-side, as shown in Figure 4-9, to determine this. For example, computer systems running Novell IPX/SPX and TCP/IP protocol stacks might be attached to the same Ethernet network. In this case, interoperability is already achieved at the physical layer. What is needed is a way for TCP/IP users to access files on IPX/SPX systems, and vice-versa. Novell NetWare and Microsoft Windows NT Advanced Server are examples of network operating systems that provide multiprotocol routing functions and the ability to load multiple file systems. For example, Novell's Open Data-link Interface (ODI) allows administrators to load both IPX/SPX and TCP/IP protocol stacks and use those stacks to send and receive packets on the same network interface card. In this way, network operating systems are providing the services required to link enterprise networks.

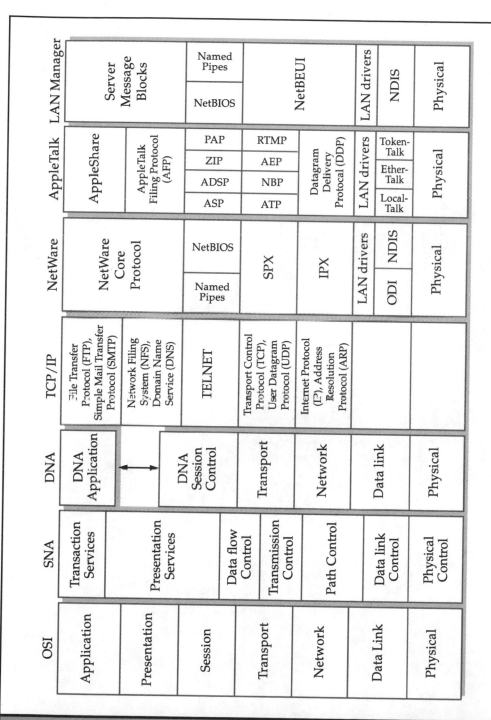

Figure 4-9. *Popular protocol suites discussed in this chapter, compared with the OSI reference model*

Chapter Five

SNA and the Networking Blueprint

by Gary Burnette, IBM

IBM's Systems Network Architecture (SNA) is an extensively used protocol for today's wide area networks. All facets of industry, including banking and finance, manufacturing, and retail, use SNA, and these companies rely on its "industrial strength" nature to manage and run their networks. This chapter addresses several aspects of SNA interoperability. First, the protocol within SNA networks has been enhanced to support today's dynamic, peer-oriented networks. These "new SNA" protocols and architectures have been made available to other vendors, opening up new possibilities for multivendor SNA networking.

Second, the Networking Blueprint, introduced by IBM, addresses another aspect of interoperability. Through it, SNA applications may have their data carried over various nonnative transports. Likewise, applications not written to SNA interfaces may have their traffic transported over the SNA network. By enabling like-to-like application traffic independent of the transport network, the Blueprint offers a unique set of multivendor possibilities.

Many companies have installed wide area networks that implement multiprotocol routing. SNA traffic has not always been easy to converge into such networks. An open, standards-based technique for doing this will be discussed.

Finally, SNA continues evolving to address the changing needs of networks. Future trends in the evolution of SNA are discussed later in this chapter.

SNA: The Basics of Data Transport

In general, network protocols fall into two categories—*connection-oriented* and *connectionless*. These network methods determine how packets flow from one end-point to another. The connection-oriented method transmits information as a steady and orderly stream of packets over an established route that requires some setup time. The connectionless method uses the "shotgun" approach—packets may be sent over multiple routes to the destination, some faster than others, and packets may arrive out of sequence, so the destination may need to reorder them upon arrival. Suppose that two riders must travel the New York City subways from the World Trade Center to Rockefeller Center. The first rider boards her train immediately. The second rider boards the next train because he has paused to buy a newspaper. Both trains make the same stops and follows the same track to Rockefeller Center, and the riders arrive in the same order in which they departed.

For the connectionless protocol, suppose that the same two riders return to the World Trade Center by taxi. They hail separate taxis, and each takes a different route to the World Trade Center. One taxi may arrive before the other, but there is no guarantee which will arrive first because either one might experience traffic congestion along the way. Connection-oriented network protocols provide superior performance because routes are established that help eliminate congestion and manage network utilization.

SNA is a connection-oriented protocol, and the connections are referred to as *sessions*. Sessions are established as users log on to access network resources, run network applications, and access network data. The session path is established at session startup, and all data over the session traverses the same route. The connection-oriented nature of SNA has made it the choice for many corporate networks primarily because of the following characteristics:

- Cost-effective utilization of network resources
- High reliability—predictable response times and guaranteed data delivery
- Security

Cost-Effective Utilization of Network Resources

Much of the total cost of a network is tied up in line costs, especially if the lines are expensive wide area links between remote locations. A goal of SNA is to maintain very high utilization rates for lines in order to give the network owners a good return on their investment.

The first mechanism employed to meet this goal is a scheme for congestion control. Congestion control (or *pacing*) algorithms are designed to monitor network traffic and adjust data rates accordingly. A well-behaved network carries data at consistent rates without the threat of packet loss and retransmission of data. Without controls, traffic such as bulk file transfers may flood and even overrun the network. During an overrun, data packets may be lost and require retransmission, adding to an overall loss of performance on the network.

The number of messages that can be sent before confirmation is received is called a *pacing window*. For example, the pacing window may be set to ten. In this case, a resource can send ten messages to its session partner before receiving confirmation in the form of a pacing response. On the tenth message, the first resource will request a pacing response and must receive one before messaging can continue. In the interim, data is held.

There are multiple levels of pacing within SNA. Pacing may occur at the session level, thereby controlling the data flow on a given session, it may occur on a logical network pipe over which many sessions are multiplexed. Pacing algorithms in SNA may be *fixed*, meaning the window size never adjusts, or *adaptable*, meaning the window size dynamically increases and decreases as network capabilities change.

Pacing algorithms ensure that SNA networks remain well-behaved and all bandwidth is utilized to the fullest extent possible. It is estimated that SNA can drive network links at utilization rates exceeding 80 percent. In fact, many SNA customers have network links utilized at sustained rates in excess of 95 percent.

Reliability

SNA networks provide a high level of reliability in the local and wide-area environment. These networks offer the ability to predict network response time due to the connection-oriented design and pacing features, the ability to prioritize data to guarantee timely delivery, and the ability to implement security features.

Predictable Response Times

A key property of a highly reliable network is predictable response times. The pacing described previously is one element of SNA's ability to meet this requirement.

A second basic element is data prioritization. As sessions are established in the SNA network, users or applications may specify a *class of service*. Class of service defines such characteristics as level of security required and data priority. Sessions are established over lines that best match these class of service requirements. Figure 5-1 illustrates data prioritization at work in the network.

In this figure, box N represents a routing point in the network. Assume that an interactive session has been established between Resource A and Resource C. As described earlier, now assume that Resource B establishes a session with Resource D and begins a file transfer through the network. Recall that pacing will be managing the data flow on these sessions, but even so, the file transfer has the tendency to monopolize the bandwidth within its pacing window.

This is where prioritization is useful. As usual, the owners of the network in this example have determined that interactive traffic will be routed at a higher priority than file transfer data. Therefore, as data for the interactive A-D session arrives at routing point N, it will be processed at a higher priority than the file transfer data associated with the B-C session. Even though the file transfer has begun in the network, the interactive session continues with its users seeing the same predictable response time.

A second kind of prioritization establishes certain flow control messages as having network priority. This ensures data such as pacing responses can flow through the network quickly, and in our example means that even the pacing responses on the interactive session are not hindered in any way by the file transfer.

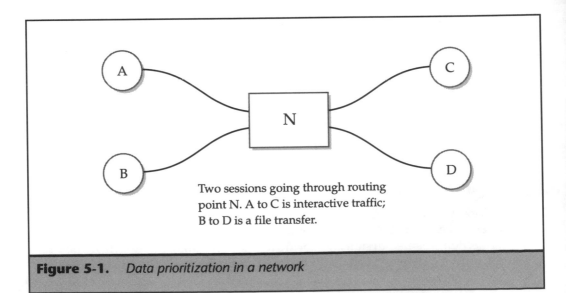

Two sessions going through routing point N. A to C is interactive traffic; B to D is a file transfer.

Figure 5-1. *Data prioritization in a network*

Guaranteed Data Delivery

As a connection-oriented protocol, SNA is aware of the data path for session traffic from endpoint to endpoint. At each intermediate routing point, a confirmation scheme is employed to ensure that data sent is received. Any data not received by the next routing point is retransmitted (up to a specified retry limit) until confirmed.

The recovery algorithms are at the link level and are managed on a hop-by-hop basis. If the data cannot be transmitted, or if a physical outage occurs in the network, the session endpoints are notified of the failure and must react.

Security

A fundamental requirement on corporate networks today is secured data transmission. This is particularly true of networks that carry sensitive data such as those in the finance or banking industry. SNA provides owners of networks various means for maintaining security.

For traffic to/from mainframe applications, security techniques may be initiated at session startup to grant or restrict access from the network. Advanced Communication Function/Virtual Telecommunications Access Method (ACF/VTAM) provides user exit call points enabling system programmers to create installation-specific security controls. SNA session initiation may also be governed by security packages on the mainframe such as RACF.

Applications may also utilize underlying services of SNA for session-level security. In addition, traffic flowing through an SNA network may use cryptography algorithms to restrict unauthorized access to data as it travels through the network.

Advanced Peer-to-Peer Networking (APPN)

Traditionally, SNA networks have been hierarchical. Mainframes were in control of the network, and network resources such as terminals and printers required the services of the mainframe to send or receive data from their applications. The characteristics of SNA, as described here, have worked well in this kind of network. Over time, however, requirements in the network have changed.

One fundamental change has involved the emergence of personal computers and midrange processors. These devices have their own processing capabilities and storage space, and their owners expect to utilize these features. Local area networks require communication among workstations; they cannot rely on a mainframe to provide the networking.

The trend for client/server or distributed applications has resulted in a need for changes in the way SNA manages applications and end stations (called Logical Units or LUs in SNA). Client/server programming cannot be effective if all communication must terminate or route through a mainframe computer. And so, despite the high reliability and cost-effectiveness of SNA networking, changes in the fundamental way companies want to utilize their networks have driven changes in the SNA network.

Advanced Peer-to-Peer Networking (APPN) is a variation of SNA that has evolved to address the following requirements:

- Peer-to-peer networking
- Dynamic networking
- Multivendor networking

Evolution is a key concept here, because APPN builds on the reliability, security, and other properties offered by SNA. APPN has been designed to address these new requirements, and to allow system administrators and users to get the most out of network resources.

Advanced Peer-to-Peer Communications (APPC)

An IBM SNA network consists of *Logical Units,* or *LUs.* These are ports through which a user accesses a network resource, or through which one program communicates with another. Before peer-to-peer support in SNA, there were three key methods by which SNA Logical Units (LUs) communicated over their sessions:

- *LU Type 0 (LU0) Protocols*   This set of protocols provides a customized "roll your own" interface in which the application and its session partners adhere to a unique set of interfaces and protocols.

- *LU Type 2 (LU2) Protocols*   This is a defined set of interfaces and protocols typically used by 3270-type terminals or emulators to communicate with their applications.

- *LU Type 3 (LU3) Protocols*   This is a defined set of interfaces and protocols typically used by applications to communicate with printers.

For each of these sets of protocols, the LUs were dependent upon the mainframe for such services as transmittal of application sign-on screens, and processing of logon and logoff requests.

Peer-to-peer networking defines a new LU protocol (LU type 6.2), which can operate independently of any controlling function or device. LU type 6.2 is also known as Advanced Peer-to-Peer Communication (APPC). APPC is a conversational model that incorporates many services which can be utilized by its applications. Examples include security and synchronization. The APPC protocols may be accessed via a common, portable interface called CPI-C (Common Programming Interface for Communications), which makes it a good choice for client/server or distributed programming. Both APPC and CPI-C are open architectures. Both are enhanced via open forums, and specifications are available to software vendors for implementation. IBM and approximately 40 other vendors provide APPC platforms, along with over 400 off-the-shelf APPC application products, solving such core business requirements as code distribution, remote console access, file transfer, the choice of many vendor workstation platforms, and distributed database capabilities. The combination of APPC services, a portable interface, and the high-performance characteristics of SNA described earlier make it a good choice for local area network or client/server implementations.

Participatory Network Control

There are two types of nodes in the APPN network, as described here:

■ *End Nodes* are users of the network. Examples include workstations that support end users, or even mainframe computers whose primary function is to run network-accessible applications.

■ *Network Nodes* provide the services for the network, such as tracking the connectivity of the network, maintaining information about other Network Nodes, maintaining information about network links, and providing directory services to end users (such as the location of an application or resource).

Each APPN node contains a Control Point (CP). An End Node establishes a session between its Control Point and an adjacent Network Node's Control Point. This CP-CP connection is used by the End Node to request network services on behalf of its users and applications. Network Nodes maintain CP-CP sessions with adjacent Network Nodes, which are used in directory services and network maintenance.

> *NOTE: It is not necessary for CP-CP sessions to be fully meshed throughout the network. They need only be established to provide a full view of the network connectivity.*

In the SNA hierarchical networking scheme, the mainframe established control sessions between itself and the resources it owned. CP-CP sessions differ in that they are peer-oriented, meaning that nodes do not have control over other nodes, so neither partner is the controlling partner in the communication. Interestingly, a mainframe in an APPN network has a Control Point and establishes CP-CP sessions just as any other node in an APPN network. The mainframe is a peer alongside other APPN nodes.

Topology

Topology defines the layout of a network, how nodes on that network are connected, and in an indirect way, how information flows through that network. Information about the topology of the network and the location of Network Nodes is periodically exchanged between routing devices. This information is used to route traffic through the network. APPN uses an algorithm that exchanges information about the network only when something changes (e.g., when a new network link becomes active or an existing one becomes inoperable). Information about the event is all that is exchanged; there is no exchange of data pertaining to unaffected areas of the topology.

This algorithm reduces the amount of traffic on the network. Each APPN Network Node maintains topology information for the entire network. This information is stored in tree format and depicts how the nodes are connected, the status of the connection (that is, active or inactive) and the characteristics of the link (that is, bandwidth capabilities, secured or not, and so on). This information is used when End-Nodes need to establish a path through the network for the exchange of information.

The link-state algorithms help establish the optimal path through the network. Definitions exist at each Network Node to indicate adjacent connections, but no other definitions are required. Any given Network Node can interrogate its topology database and calculate a route to any other Network Node without any sort of topology-oriented definition work on the part of a system administrator. This topology mapping enables dynamic growth and change in the APPN network. Nodes can be added or moved in the network without the added task of system definition. The network simply discovers the change.

Topology information is exchanged and maintained by Network Nodes—End Nodes have no need for this information. If connectivity is lost, the entire topology need not be recalculated. Network Nodes retain their topology databases, and when they return on-line, they are updated with information about events that occurred while they were down.

Directory

APPN provides dynamic directory flows to locate SNA Logical Units (LUs). SNA LUs include applications, terminals, and printers. Directory flows are initiated by session requests. When a given end user or application requests a session, the network steps in to locate the partner resource.

Network Nodes bear the responsibility for finding resources in the network. An End Node participates by first reporting its resources to its Network Node. Later, an End Node may request that a Network Node set up a session triggering the search for the partner resource.

The directory is a cache implemented in each Network Node. This cache contains the information reported by the End Nodes, as well as any learned information about the location of other resources attached to other Network Nodes.

If a Network Node has cached information about a requested resource, it will send a "directed" locate request to confirm its location. If it does not have information, it will initiate a "broadcast" search through the network to find the requested resource. Once the location is known, the requesting Network Node caches the information.

Central Directory Server

In a network where all parameters are defined there is little chitchat or overhead. APPN utilizes several key elements to minimize the amount of bandwidth used by directory flows; in particular, it tries to minimize the number of broadcast searches that occur. The primary function is called Central Directory Server (CDS).

One or more Network Nodes may establish themselves as a Central Directory Server. A CDS advertises itself through the topology flows discussed in the "Topology" section of this chapter.

A CDS maintains a *super cache,* which is a compilation of the caches of all the Network Nodes. A Network Node will interrogate this cache before initiating any broadcast searches. In most cases, the CDS super cache will know the location, so only a confirmation is required.

The APPN directory maintained by Network Nodes as well as by the CDS is a fully dynamic directory. APPN LUs are addressed by their names, which eliminates the need for network administrator intervention should a resource move in the network. In APPN, if an LU moves, the network simply finds it again and remembers the change in the information so it can be found.

The dynamic directory and topology features of APPN create a "plug and go" environment for the end user. Applications may be moved without changes by the end user looking for that application. The Network Node providing services will locate the relocated LU.

End users' workstations may be added or moved through the network with no definition work on the part of network administrators. The users at the workstation have minimal changes in their definition, and with that, become participants in the network.

Current implementations of APPN in workstation products require the end user to define the address of his Network Node server. New applications now emerging employ discovery techniques so that even this level of definition can be eliminated.

Establishing a Session in the APPN Network

At session establishment time, the dynamic nature of topology and directory come together. Topology flows have ensured that any given APPN Network Node has a full view of the network's connectivity. When any given end user or application requests a session partner, dynamic directory flows ensue to locate the resource.

The end user or application has provided a third piece of information: class of service. Class of service is an important concept in APPN networking, as it defines the requirements the session will have on the network. Examples include secured data transmission and link capacity.

With a completed directory flow, the Network Node server acting on behalf of the requesting user can construct the optimal path through the network based on location of the target and the requested class of service.

IBM APPN Platforms

IBM has announced a large number of APPN-compatible products in the last few years. A number of these platforms are listed here:

- Communications Manager/2
- AIX/SNA Server (Advanced Interactive Executive/SNA Server), IBM's version of UNIX
- IBM 3174, a cluster controller that provides mainframe attachment points for SDLC, X.25, and token ring networks
- AS/400, an IBM midrange system
- DPPX, an operating system on the IBM 8100 computer
- ACF/VTAM (Advanced Communication Function/Virtual Telecommunication Access Method), software products that support mainframe computer networking for IBM systems
- IBM 6611 Network Processor, an IBM LAN and WAN integration router
- IBM 8250 Multiprotocol Intelligent Hub, a product that provides connection for Ethernet, Token Ring, and FDDI networks
- IBM System/36 midrange system
- NS/DOS (Networking Services/DOS), an IBM program that provides APPC connections for DOS-based systems and computers running Microsoft Windows

APPN in a Multivendor Environment

APPN, like APPC and CPI-C, is developed by an open forum, called the APPN Implementor's Workshop (AIW). Nearly 40 software and hardware vendors participate in this forum along with IBM. Many of these vendors have shipped APPN implementations, and many others have announced an intent to provide these products. Licensed APPN code is available from at least two vendors other than IBM for porting to other platforms, such as network routers or UNIX workstations.

APPN interoperability showcases have been demonstrated at various industry trade shows and have included IBM products along with those of other key software, hardware, and router vendors. A complete up-to-date listing of available (or soon to be available) APPN products can be obtained by request via the Internet to:

appnmkt@vnet.ibm.com

Examples of these products include Cisco, Wellfleet, and 3Com routers, as well as a variety of APPN offering for such platforms as Sun, Hewlett Packard, and SynOptics.

Interoperability and the Networking Blueprint

Earlier networks tended to be single-protocol, and thus were reasonably easy to manage. However, recent years have brought considerable change. The need for computing power has increased at the departmental level, and many such groups have made computer choices and networking choices independent of the corporate Information Technology (IT) shops. Also, business mergers and acquisitions have resulted in the need for connecting disparate networks, creating interoperability problems for the companies involved.

In general, multiple protocols are required within a network to allow for multiple applications. Unique application needs have driven the need for a variety of network protocols. In turn, routing complexities have increased in shops where the LAN protocols differ from the WAN protocols. The emerging multiprotocol environment has posed significant challenges for owners and operators of SNA/APPN networks.

Multiprotocol Transport Networking

In March 1992, IBM introduced the Networking Blueprint, illustrated in Figure 5-2. The primary goal of the Networking Blueprint is to offer network owners a means to simplify the challenges they face in managing the network. The chief way this is accomplished is by making the application choice independent of the underlying network. By uncoupling the application decisions from the network transport, the Blueprint can reduce complexity by reducing the numbers of protocols that must be handled.

The Networking Blueprint divides a typical communication stack into layers—application interfaces, application services, networking transports, subnetworks, and finally, the physical services underneath. It also introduces a layer in the center of that stack called Common Transport Semantics (CTS).

The APIs and application services are above the CTS layer and are referred to as the A-Stack. The network transports, subnetworks, and physical layers are below CTS and are referred to as the B-Stack. CTS allows network administrators to make selections from the A-Stack independent of the selections made from the B-Stack.

A second key theme of the Networking Blueprint is interoperability. For this reason, the Blueprint embraces industry standards at all layers, including CTS. CTS implementation is defined by an architecture called Multiprotocol Transport Networking, or MPTN. The standards have been embraced by X/Open. MPTN decouples an application from its native networking scheme and allows it to run on other networking schemes, such as TCP/IP, OSI, or SNA. It can perform protocol conversion on the fly, allowing client-server applications to operate across a variety of protocols. MPTN-compatible products are collectively called AnyNet by IBM.

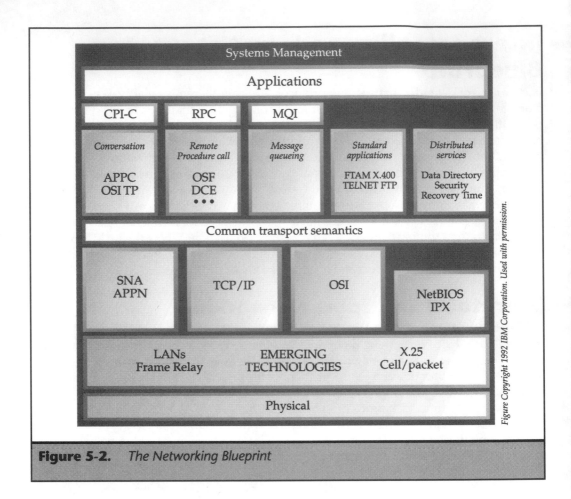

Systems Management

Applications

CPI-C	RPC	MQI		
Conversation	*Remote Procedure call*	*Message queueing*	*Standard applications*	*Distributed services*
APPC OSI TP	OSF DCE •••		FTAM X.400 TELNET FTP	Data Directory Security Recovery Time

Common transport semantics

SNA APPN	TCP/IP	OSI	NetBIOS IPX
LANs Frame Relay	EMERGING TECHNOLOGIES	X.25 Cell/packet	

Physical

Figure Copyright 1992 IBM Corporation. Used with permission.

Figure 5-2. *The Networking Blueprint*

Figure 5-3 illustrates the case for routing application traffic of several well-known protocols over various network transports.

If the application is utilizing its native transport, then CTS is essentially a pass-through. If, as described earlier, industry standards exist for transporting nonnative application traffic, CTS will utilize them. If no such standards exist, the MPTN architecture provides the necessary logic to transport the nonnative application traffic. This is the case for transporting TCP/IP application traffic over the SNA/APPN network or SNA/APPN application traffic over the TCP/IP network. It should be noted that MPTN provides "like-to-like" support, meaning the application partners must utilize the same protocol. For example, there is no mechanism provided for a TCP/IP application to converse with an SNA partner.

Techniques for routing non-native traffic exist today. One example is encapsulation. *Encapsulation* means that the data from one protocol is "tunneled," or routed inside packets of a different protocol. The data traverses all layers of its native

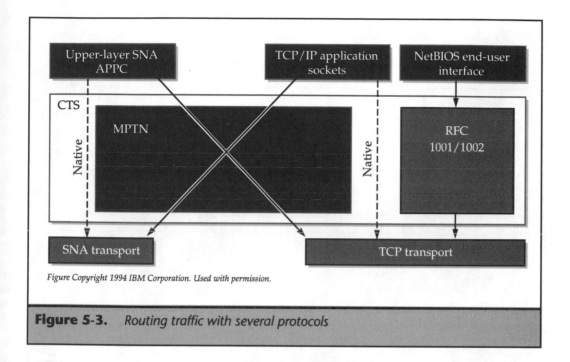

Figure Copyright 1994 IBM Corporation. Used with permission.

Figure 5-3.   *Routing traffic with several protocols*

stack before being packaged inside the transport protocol. Then, the data must traverse the relevant layers of the transport protocol stack.

Full stacks for both protocols exist, and from a network management perspective, awareness of both kinds of networking is maintained. MPTN's method for routing non-native traffic differs from encapsulation. It's goal is to reduce the number of protocols in the network. MPTN does this by merging the information needed for managing the application data with that needed by the transport. CTS is then able to route and deliver the resulting packet.

Multiprotocol Transport Networking Nodes

Figure 5-4 illustrates two types of MPTN nodes. The first, an MPTN access node, defines a station on which an MPTN implementation exists. A good example of an MPTN access node would be the case where a company has an established SNA/APPN backbone network, but needs to introduce a TCP/IP application. Rather than implement an entire TCP/IP network, MPTN could be used to transport the TCP/IP traffic over SNA/APPN.

Network owners often find themselves with a multitude of local area network protocols and a need to route them over the wide area. It may not be possible for any number of reasons, such as product availability, to have MPTN access nodes at every end station in the network. For this reason, MPTN gateways may be employed.

In Figure 5-4, assume that applications such as those written to the TCP/IP socket interface are to be used in a local area network. If that traffic must then be transported

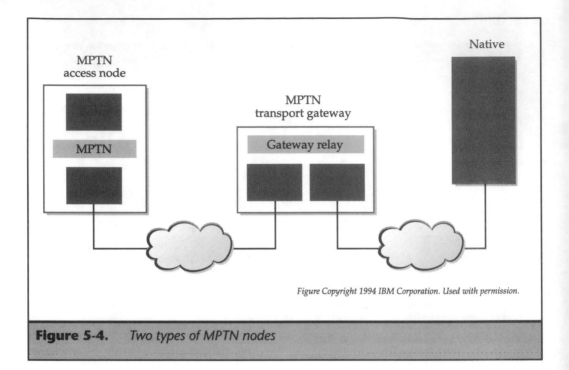

Figure Copyright 1994 IBM Corporation. Used with permission.

Figure 5-4.   *Two types of MPTN nodes*

over the SNA/APPN wide area network, an MPTN gateway offers a translation point at the edge of the wide area network. The traffic may be destined for a TCP/IP application residing on an MPTN access node or on a native TCP/IP platform. In the latter case, an MPTN gateway could be employed to translate the application traffic back to native TCP/IP before reentering the local area network. MPTN offers a unique way to join dissimilar networks through the use of gateways.

AnyNet Offerings

As mentioned earlier, IBM's AnyNet is a product implementation of Multiprotocol Transport Networking that offers a solution for SNA/APPN interoperability. Companies may retain their SNA/APPN wide area networks while introducing application or local area network traffic that utilizes other protocols. The result is a simpler, easier-to-manage network configuration.

A good LAN-to-SNA/APPN WAN example might be the case where a company has employed applications such as Lotus Notes in the local area that use NetBEUI or NetBIOS. For them, AnyNet offers a good alternative to routing local area traffic over the SNA/APPN backbone.

For those companies who have chosen other backbones, AnyNet gives them the chance to retain their SNA/APPN applications but route them over nonnative transports.

In either case, through MPTN access nodes and MPTN gateways, companies have new options for multivendor interoperability in their SNA/APPN networks. Figure 5-5 illustrates the protocol combinations and platforms offered. As was mentioned earlier, MPTN is an open technology and as such, other vendors have announced MPTN solutions within their product lines. These are also illustrated in Figure 5-5.

SNA/APPN in a Multiprotocol Router Network

Another means for incorporating SNA/APPN into a multivendor, multiprotocol environment is by bridging or routing the traffic through a router network. The goal is

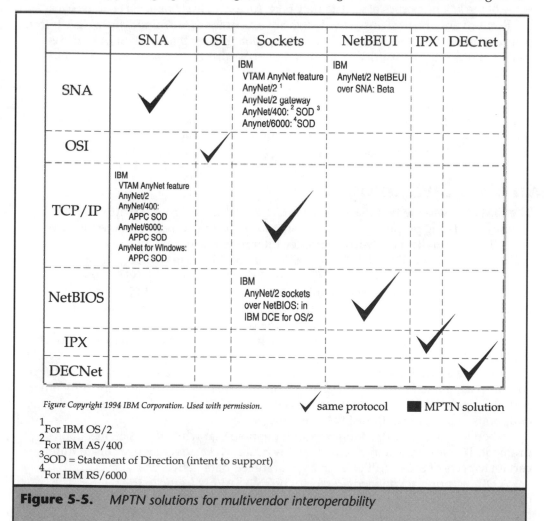

Figure Copyright 1994 IBM Corporation. Used with permission.

✓ same protocol ■ MPTN solution

[1] For IBM OS/2
[2] For IBM AS/400
[3] SOD = Statement of Direction (intent to support)
[4] For IBM RS/6000

Figure 5-5. *MPTN solutions for multivendor interoperability*

typically to collapse the SNA/APPN traffic over an existing router backbone, thereby reducing physical lines and resources in the network while preserving the well-behaved nature of SNA transport. SNA/APPN traffic is *encapsulated*, or *tunneled*, inside the routing protocol, and routed or bridged alongside other LAN protocols in the WAN.

In general, this approach has been difficult to implement. The fundamental characteristics of SNA/APPN for reliable data transport are functions of its being a connection-oriented protocol. And, because of these features, SNA is a well-behaved protocol on the wide area network.

The local area network protocols, as well as most routing protocols, are usually connectionless. Routing or bridging SNA/APPN across a connectionless backbone tends to create problems for its network administrators. For one, SNA/APPN begins to lose some of the key properties of its data transport. An example is link-level error recovery.

Router vendors have implemented various techniques for mimicking SNA's traffic prioritization. However, these tend to be on a global basis; that is, all SNA traffic is routed at one relative priority or another. But no prioritization is attempted within SNA traffic, including that requested by SNA class of service.

One result of this inability to prioritize individual SNA transmissions is that SNA traffic, some of which is interactive, receives treatment much the same as that given a large file transfer over the same lines. The results can include unreliable response times and sporadic session loss. Various techniques have been invented to address this problem, including Data Link Switching (DLSw), which is described next.

Data Link Switching

The IBM 6611 was the first to ship Data Link Switching on a router platform. The technique is being proposed as an open standard for multivendor SNA/APPN over TCP/IP connectivity. This helps guarantee interoperability between various router platforms in routing SNA/APPN over a TCP/IP backbone network.

First and foremost, a DLSw router can be an APPN Network Node. It may maintain Control Point-to-Control Point sessions with adjacent APPN nodes, and it fully supports the dynamic topology and directory features. However, rather than routing SNA/APPN traffic natively across the wide area network, DLSw nodes encapsulate the traffic within TCP. As shown in Figure 5-6, this switch takes place at the bottom of the SNA transport stack in the Networking Blueprint.

Since the entire SNA transport stack is traversed before the switch, SNA functions such as pacing and prioritization occur before entering the DLSw network. Any other APPN-capable DLSw nodes that see the traffic (that is, intermediate routing nodes or endpoints) also perform these SNA functions.

When looking at TCP/IP, it is important to note that while IP is a connectionless protocol, TCP is connection-oriented. DLSw routers take advantage of this to mimic certain aspects of SNA/APPN, such as guaranteed data delivery.

A DLSw router acknowledges receipt of SNA/APPN traffic to the sender. This eliminates the time-out problems traditionally found when bridging or routing SNA.

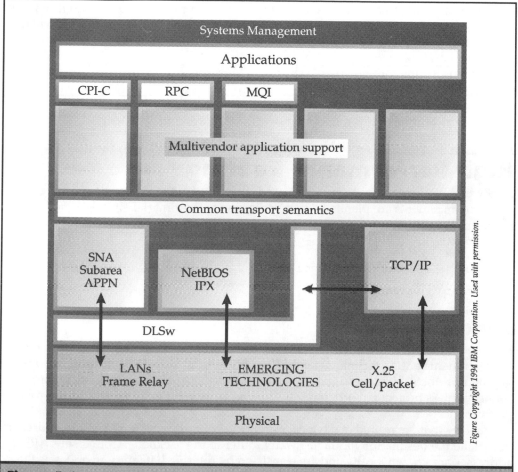

Figure 5-6. *DLSw in the Networking Blueprint*

The data is encapsulated within TCP and routed toward its destination. Even though the traffic is acknowledged to the sender before it actually gets to the receiver, the connection-oriented nature of TCP serves to guarantee delivery.

Data Link Switching also provides for some support of traffic prioritization. DLSw traffic can be configured with a priority that defines how it is to be treated relative to other protocols being routed in the network. This option can help with the fairness issue of SNA versus other transports. Again, this is not an SNA class of service routing; rather it sets a global priority for all SNA traffic flowing through the network. The IBM 6611 is enhancing its APPN support when used in conjunction with DLSw to provide a more granular level priority.

DLSw supports traditional SNA routing in addition to APPN routing. In fact, it can be viewed as a migration step toward a meshed APPN network. Although we will not discuss the details here, DLSw is also a technique for routing NetBIOS traffic across a wide area network.

APPN is a superior way to fully support a high-speed, dynamic, peer-oriented network. DLSw offers companies with multiprotocol router strategies a way to tap into this network. In addition, by working through standards bodies, it helps guarantee a solution that is interoperable with other vendors' products.

High Performance Routing

As SNA/APPN continues to evolve toward support of higher-speed networking, more enhancements are planned. High Performance Routing (HPR) is designed to build upon the reliable aspects of SNA, the dynamics of APPN, and provide two key elements:

- Higher-speed network routing
- Improved availability

Routing Functions

HPR networks make use of APPN Control Points and can be thought of as providing a replacement routing technique for APPN. HPR, like SNA/APPN, is a connection-oriented protocol. However, it takes on some of the beneficial characteristics of a connectionless protocol in order to solve key networking requirements and improve performance.

Packets that are routed in a typical multiprotocol router network contain addresses that make the destination locatable by any router in the backbone. Conversely, APPN addresses are known locally and are translated by intermediate routing nodes as the session traffic travels the network. This type of routing requires session awareness in the intermediate nodes so that the mapping of local address-to-local address can occur.

HPR routing is called Automatic Network Routing (ANR), and it routes information by means of a labeling scheme. Packets entering the HPR network have headers that contain labels representing each hop along the connection. As an intermediate box receives the packet, it removes the leading label and routes the traffic over the link associated with that label.

Routing done in this manner can be handled very quickly and requires no intermediate session awareness, as each packet has the information required to route through the entire network. It requires no table lookups or address translation and as such provides a routing scheme that should be superior not only to current APPN routing, but also to other network routing methods.

Improved Availability and High-Speed Networking

HPR networks are overlaid with logical connections called Rapid Transport Protocol (RTP) pipes. RTP endpoints define the edges of the HPR and are responsible for building the ANR labels described previously. HPR utilizes APPN Control Points, dynamic topology, and directory flows. As with APPN, the class of service dictates the path through the network for a particular session. The first session request to use the HPR network determines the RTP. Further session requests with equivalent class-of-service requirements will be mapped over the same RTP.

RTPs are optimized for today's reliable networks and have the option to handle recovery at the endpoints rather than at each intermediate hop. This makes HPR an ideal fit for high-speed physical networks such as Frame Relay or networks that operate over optical fiber cable.

HPR traffic is acknowledged by the RTP endpoints, and they are responsible for retransmission should any packets be lost. However, RTP retransmission is selective: only individual packets that are lost are retransmitted, as opposed to all packets sent since the last acknowledgment.

Also, the RTP endpoints are responsible for detecting any loss of connection, as well as for reconstructing the path, altering the packets' ANR labels, and retransmitting any lost data. Since failure is often a stress point in a network, selective retransmission is essential in order to reduce its impact. Session endpoints do not see this non-disruptive rerouting around the failure.

HPR is intended to be a software upgrade and will be fully compatible with APPN networking. A session path may travel any combination of HPR and APPN subnetworks from one end to the other. Interoperability will be further enhanced for SNA/APPN as HPR specifications are made available to requesting vendors. This is a subject of discussion in the aforementioned APPN Implementor's Workshop. The techniques employed by HPR will make SNA/APPN routable in a router network. When combined with the expected availability of HPR routers, these techniques should mean more options for network owners as they evolve their mission-critical SNA/APPN networks toward higher-speed networks.

Chapter Six

DEC Networking Concepts and Products

by Levi Reiss, La Cité Collégiale, Ottawa

and Joseph Radin,

Digital Equipment Corporation

This chapter presents networking and operability as practiced by a major player, Digital Equipment Corporation, commonly known as DEC. First it considers DEC's theoretical model, the DIGITAL Network Architecture (DNA). Then it ex1amines four complementary product lines, DECnet, PATHWORKS, ADVANTAGE-NETWORKS, and DECadvantage. Before starting, let's take a brief look at the history of DEC networking.

DEC introduced DNA in 1975. Today this architecture is still flourishing, and products developed two decades ago can be linked to those developed yesterday. In 1980, DEC, Intel, and Xerox codeveloped the very widely used Ethernet protocol for local area networks. In 1987, DEC announced DECnet OSI Phase V, which integrated proprietary DEC networks with the industry standard OSI Reference Model. DEC announced the ADVANTAGE-NETWORKS family in 1991.

DIGITAL Network Architecture (DNA)

DIGITAL Network Architecture (DNA) is a model of the structures and functions that underlie all DEC networking implementations. Just as a serious programmer should not consider writing even moderately complicated programs without applying a formal programming methodology, real-world networks require a networking methodology.

The DNA Model includes proprietary protocols and interfaces, and Open System Interconnection (OSI) protocols and services, defined by the International Standards Organization. This section presents Phase V of DNA, which maintains compatibility with Phase IV.

DNA Design Goals

DNA was designed to meet the following major goals:

Transparency   Users must be shielded from network complexity. They should access the network as if it were a stand-alone microcomputer.

Support for Multiple Applications   A network architecture unable to support a full range of MS-DOS, Windows, and UNIX applications cannot survive in today's competitive marketplace.

Support for Numerous Protocols   Users and administrators alike often complain about the alphabet soup that describes networking products. DNA must be able to deal with all the common protocols and several of those less frequently encountered.

Conformance to Standards   DEC has made a specific commitment to follow OSI standards, instead of creating a proprietary network architecture. This philosophy distinguishes DNA from many competitive architectures.

Growth and Migration   Networks are nothing if they are not dynamic. It is not unusual for networks to expand by one or more orders of magnitude within a few months. Sometimes this growth necessitates integrating presently existing networks, whether based on DNA or not.

Various Levels of Functionality   Many installations choose to implement only selected network features with the ability to implement additional features as required.

Maximum Availability   Organizations cannot afford downtime. The network must be highly redundant, rerouting messages automatically in case of hardware, line, or software failure.

Extensive Security   At the same time that networks extend computer resources to a wide range of individuals, they must resist unauthorized access.

DNA Structure

DNA is a layered architecture; its functions are built on one another similar to layers in a wedding cake. Each layer processes a message consisting of user data with a header containing control information such as a sequence number and the type of communication service requested. The seven layers are independent; a given layer need not concern itself with the details of the higher or lower layers. This layer philosophy did not originate with DEC. It is a key aspect of the OSI Reference Model described in Chapter 4. Figure 6-1 shows the DNA layers. There are two complementary choices: the OSI Application, generally conforming to the OSI specifications at all seven layers of the OSI Reference Model, and the DNA Application, consisting of proprietary DNA functions built on the first four (hardware) layers of the OSI Reference Model.

The DNA Physical Layer

The Physical layer defines information transmission to and from the Physical components of the network. DNA fully conforms to OSI Physical layer standards that describe, for example, how data is converted to and from electrical signals.

The DNA Data Link Layer

The Data Link layer provides a dependable communication path between units that are directly connected to each other. DNA may use several protocols for this layer, some of which conform to the OSI Reference Model. The DNA Data Link layer supports Ethernet, which is widely used on local area networks.

NOTE: This support should come as no surprise; DEC was a developer of Ethernet.

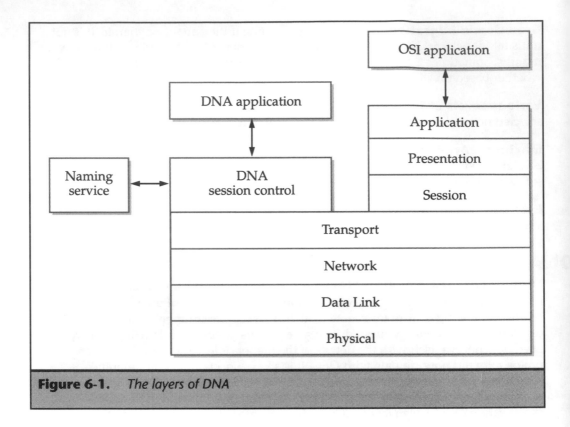

Figure 6-1.   *The layers of DNA*

The DNA Network Layer

The Network layer dynamically routes user data between systems in the network. DNA supports OSI standards associated with this level for a variety of topologies.

The DNA Transport Layer

The Transport layer is responsible for sending messages from one end of the network to the other. DNA supports OSI standards associated with this level and applies functions associated with this level in the upper layer protocols.

The DNA Session Layer

The Session layer enables the dialog between users at separate locations. The OSI Application supports OSI standards associated with this level, while the DNA Application replaces it with DNA Session Control (described later in this section).

DNA Presentation Layer

The Presentation layer assures that information is delivered in understandable form. The OSI Application supports OSI standards associated with this level, while the DNA Application replaces it with DNA Session Control.

DNA Application Layer

The Application layer supports the actual end-user application. The OSI Application layer supports OSI standards associated with this level, while the DNA Application layer replaces it with DNA Session Control.

DNA Session Control   DNA Session Control is proprietary DNA software providing the link from DNA Transport level functions to the application. It replaces the three OSI levels: Session level, Presentation level, and Application level. Among the communication functions it provides are:

■ Name-to-address translation, which allows users to refer to remote objects by name

☐ Increasing network transparency

☐ Protocol selection, which increases network flexibility

☐ Access control, which may increase network security

> *NOTE: DNA Session Control provides compatibility with versions of DNA predating Phase V, for example, the still widely used Phase IV, which does not support the OSI Reference Model.*

A major component of DNA Session Control is the Naming Service, a database containing names defined throughout the network. While this database is mostly used by Session Control, it is available to all applications that require names defined across the network.

DNA Network Management

DNA provides multiple distributed network management facilities. These services include:

☐ Physical configuration, for maximum performance

☐ Setting and examining parameters such as resource limits

☐ Analyzing performance statistics

☐ Running diagnostics to help locate errors

DNA is designed around the Enterprise Management Architecture, DEC's proprietary architecture for enterprise networks. Enterprise networks integrate all systems within an organization, including PCs, mini- and mainframe computers, and local area and wide area networks as shown in Figure 6-2. Successful enterprise networking relies on networking, operating system, and applications interoperability. As the "ADVANTAGE-NETWORKS" section later in this chapter indicates, DEC products aid the network management process.

DECnet Products

DECnet is a family of communications software and hardware that enable DIGITAL operating systems and computers to network to additional DIGITAL systems and to non-DIGITAL systems.

TCP/IP Software

DECnet products supporting the TCP/IP protocol suite commonly encountered with UNIX systems include TCP/IP Services for OpenVMS and TCP/IP Services for OpenVMS AXP. Because these two products are quite similar, only the first is discussed in detail.

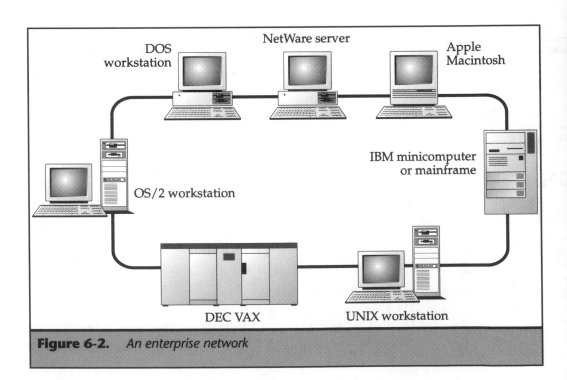

Figure 6-2. *An enterprise network*

TCP/IP Services for OpenVMS

TCP/IP Services for OpenVMS is a layered software product providing interoperability and resource sharing between OpenVMS systems, UNIX systems, and other systems that support the TCP/IP Protocol Suite. It features network file access, remote terminal access, remote command execution, remote printing, mail, and application development.

Communications are based on the 4.3 Berkeley Software Distribution (BSD) UNIX, and implement the following protocols and features: Transmission Control Protocol (TCP), Internet Protocol (IP), Internet Control Message Protocol (ICMP), User Datagram Protocol (UDP), Ethernet support, and Fiber Distributed Data Interface (FDDI) support, plus enhancements such as security and event logging. Other features include DCL-style commands to control and monitor software components, applying the Simple Network Management Protocol (the Internet standard protocol for network management) to generate information about network activity, and applying network security features to control the accessibility to OpenVMS systems from remote Internet hosts.

TCP/IP Services for OpenVMS includes multiple application programming interfaces, such as the C Socket programming interface, a Berkeley UNIX Socket programming interface to develop TCP/IP networking applications. It contains the C language and the SunRPC library, which includes the widespread end-user protocols for file transfer, remote log-in, remote command processing, remote printing, and mail exchange. Other protocols supported include File Transfer Protocol (FTP), Telnet, (including Telnet 3270), and the Network File System (NFS) presented in Chapter 4. The product supports both BSD UNIX and System V UNIX remote commands such as remote log-in and remote printing. Users can send and receive electronic mail to and from remote hosts.

> **NOTE:** *The TCP/IP Services for OpenVMS AXP product is similar to the TCP/IP Services for OpenVMS product just described. However, it supports additional features such as remote booting for diskless clients, client/server licensing, and both remote and local TELNET printing.*

OSI Software

DEC has made a major commitment to the industry standard OSI Reference Model presented in Chapter 4. DECnet products supporting this model include:

- DECnet/OSI for ULTRIX, a DEC UNIX-based proprietary operating system
- DECnet/OSI for OpenVMS VAX, a DEC proprietary operating system
- DECnet/OSI for DEC OSF/1 AXP, an open operating system defined by an industry consortium, the Open Software Foundation
- DECnet/OSI for OpenVMS AXP

The first two products are discussed next in detail. See the DEC documentation for enhancements available on the two AXP (64-bit alpha processor) products.

DECnet/OSI for ULTRIX

DECnet/OSI for ULTRIX is an implementation of the Digital Network Architecture (DNA) for the ULTRIX Operating System and ULTRIX Worksystem Software (UWS) for VAX and RISC systems. As a Phase V product, it provides interoperability with multivendor networks adhering to the Open Systems Interconnection (OSI) specifications as defined by the International Standards Organization (ISO). DECnet/OSI for ULTRIX is available in two forms: End System and Extended Function. Extended Function provides all the features of the End System, plus FTAM-FTP gateway, Virtual Terminal gateways (VT/Telnet, VT/CTERM, LAT/VT), and the DECdns Server. DECnet/OSI and TCP/IP can also share the same system resources, such as LAN interfaces. In general, existing programs running over TCP/IP can be easily modified to run with DECnet/OSI. DECnet programs can run on TCP/IP, provided they do not apply DECnet-specific operations.

DECnet/OSI for ULTRIX software offers the following features:

- Client server communications
- Network virtual terminal
- Remote file transfer
- Mail
- Coexistence with Internet protocols (TCP/IP-based)
- Network-wide resource sharing and management, as defined by the DNA protocols

DECnet/OSI for ULTRIX can communicate with OSI conforming systems and other Digital DECnet products. Depending on the system configuration, networks combining DECnet/OSI for ULTRIX systems with other OSI and DECnet products may limit the functions available if all products do not support equal features.

Among the features provided are:

- Digital Distributed Time Service (DECdts), a software-based service that provides precise, fault-tolerant clock synchronization for systems in LANs and WANs
- Remote File Transfer via the FTAM (OSI) protocol and the DNA-based Data Access Protocol (DAP)
- The "dcp" utility for network file transfers using the DAP protocol
- Network File Access remote file access from other Digital systems
- Sending mail to and receiving mail from users on other DECnet/OSI-conformant systems

DECnet/OSI for OpenVMS VAX

DECnet/OSI for OpenVMS VAX is an implementation of Phase V of the Digital
Network Architecture (DNA) for the OpenVMS Operating System for VAX hardware.
It integrates DECnet and OSI network protocols allowing shared network functions
up to the Transport layer, and supports existing DECnet Phase IV and new DECnet
and OSI applications. In combination with the optional TCP/IP Services for OpenVMS
products, OpenVMS systems can participate in multivendor, multiprotocol networks
adhering to Open Networking standards.

DEC TCP/IP Services for OpenVMS is a VMS-layered software product that
promotes interoperability and resource sharing between VMS systems, UNIX systems,
and other systems that support the TCP/IP and NFS protocol suites. The product
provides easy to use tools for file access, remote terminal access, remote command
execution, remote printing, mail, and application development.

DECnet SNA Products

A wide variety of DECnet products assures communication between DEC networks
and networks based on IBM's proprietary System Network Architecture, presented in
Chapter 5. These products are discussed next.

VMS SNA   This product provides a system-to-network connection between DEC's
proprietary VMS architecture and SNA networks.

DECnet SNA Gateway-ST and DECnet SNA Gateway-CT   These offer a
medium-speed or a high-speed network-to-network connection between DEC's
proprietary VMS and ULTRIX (UNIX-based) networks and SNA networks.

DEC SNA Domain Gateway   This product enables users to exchange information
and share resources between Digital and IBM networked systems in a bidirectional
manner. The Domain Gateway is part of both the DECnet network and the SNA
network. Suitably configured Digital-based applications can be interactively accessed
from IBM SNA networked 3270 devices and PCs. This Ethernet-based product
supports over a thousand concurrent sessions.

PATHWORKS

The PATHWORKS family of PC networking and multivendor network operating
system integration products is designed to facilitate the participation of PC users in
open enterprise networks. PATHWORKS is based on the client/server architecture
discussed in Chapters 10 and 12. Table 6-1 lists components that ensure PATHWORKS
client/server interoperability.

Server	Transport	File Protocol	Clients
PATHWORKS for DEC OSF/1 AXP (LAN Manager)	IPX TCP/IP DECnet	NetWare	PATHWORKS for DOS and Windows (NetWare) or NetWare
PATHWORKS for Open VMS (LAN Manager)	NetBEUI TCP/IP DECnet	LAN Manager	PATHWORKS for DOS and Windows PATHWORKS for OS/2 PATHWORKS for Windows NT or LAN Manager
PATHWORKS for Open VMS (Macintosh)	NetBEUI TCP/IP DECnet	LAN Manager	PATHWORKS for Macintosh*
Pacer for ULTRIX	AppleTalk	AFP	PATHWORKS for Macintosh
PATHWORKS for Windows NT	NetBEUI TCP/IP DECnet	AFP	PATHWORKS for DOS and Windows PATHWORKS for OS/2 PATHWORKS for Windows NT or LAN Manager
PATHWORKS for SCO UNIX	NetBEUI TCP/IP DECnet	LAN Manager	PATHWORKS for DOS and Windows PATHWORKS for OS/2 PATHWORKS for Windows NT or LAN Manager
PATHWORKS for OS/2	NetBEUI TCP/IP DECnet	LAN Manager	PATHWORKS for DOS and Windows PATHWORKS for OS/2 PATHWORKS for Windows NT or LAN Manager

*This software supports DECnet and AppleTalk communications, as well as TCP/IP with MacX. The file and print services run over AppleTalk.

Table 6-1. *PATHWORKS Client/Server Interoperability*

PATHWORKS Client Software

PATHWORKS client software runs on standard 286, 386, 486, and Pentium hardware in a DOS (2MB suggested minimum memory) or a Windows (4MB suggested minimum memory) environment. Also required are a network interface card with a network driver. (See DEC for a list of acceptable cards and drivers.) Among the facilities supported are:

■ NetWare or LAN Manager local area network operating systems (according to the license), including their print and file utilities

- A Windows-based graphical user interface
- Management of multivendor PC networks via a local or remote PC running Windows
- An X Window System (via PC DECwindows Motif), bringing the power of the standard UNIX windowing system to PCs
- Remote booting, especially useful for diskless PCs
- Simultaneous multiple transport protocols including NetBEUI (MS-DOS), IPX/SPX (NetWare), TCP/IP (UNIX), and DECnet
- Other PATHWORKS client software is designed to link to Windows NT, OS/2, and Macintosh systems.

PATHWORKS Client Software Products

PATHWORKS client software products currently available include: PATHWORKS for DOS and Windows (LAN Manager and NetWare), PATHWORKS X.25 (DOS and Windows), PATHWORKS ISDN (DOS), PATHWORKS for Windows NT, PATHWORKS for OS/2, PATHWORKS TCP/IP (OS/2), and PATHWORKS for Macintosh.

PATHWORKS Server Software

PATHWORKS server software provides a variety of networking services to PC clients. These clients can concurrently access OS/2, UNIX, Windows NT, and OpenVMS server systems. Among the facilities supported, depending on the specific PATHWORKS server version are:

- File and print services
- LAN and WAN features using the DECnet and TCP/IP protocols
- Electronic mail
- LAN administration via a graphical user interface on a Windows PC running PATHWORKS client software
- Date and time services

Different PATHWORKS server software versions run on OpenVMS (connecting to LAN Manager, NetWare, or Macintosh networks), OSF/1 AXP, ULTRIX, SCO UNIX, Windows NT, and OS/2 systems.

PATHWORKS Server Software Products

PATHWORKS server software products currently available include PATHWORKS for OpenVMS (LAN Manager, Macintosh, and NetWare), PATHWORKS Desktop Backup, PATHWORKS for DES OSF/1 AXP (LAN Manager), PATHWORKS for Windows NT, PATHWORKS for OS/2, and PATHWORKS for SCO UNIX.

ADVANTAGE-NETWORKS

The ADVANTAGE-NETWORKS set of products brings the standards set by the OSI Reference Model into the Digital Network Architecture. It presently includes DECnet, OSI, TCP/IP, and SNA protocols, with plans for additional protocols.

Multiprotocol Network Software

The ADVANTAGE-NETWORKS software products include DECnet/OSI for ULTRIX and DECnet/OSI for VMS, TCP/IP Services for OpenVMS, and TCP/IP Services for OpenVMS AXP discussed in the DECnet section, and ULTRIX TCP/IP, which has not been included because of its similarity to the DECnet/OSI for ULTRIX software. The OSI Applications Developer's Toolkit is discussed next.

OSI Applications Developer's Toolkit

The OSI Applications Developer's Toolkit enables users to write distributed applications that communicate over open networks and use the OSI services provided by DECnet/OSI for OpenVMS, DEC OSF/1, and ULTRIX. This environment permits application writers to use the services of the OSI upper layers in their applications. The Application Programming Interfaces (APIs) provide access to the OSI services supported by the underlying DECnet/OSI system. The resulting application can run on any DECnet/OSI system with the appropriate operating system. The Toolkit is not required on these target systems unless the application is using OSI TP.

Multiprotocol Network Hardware

The ADVANTAGE-NETWORKS hardware products include the DEC WANrouter 100/500 and the DEC Network Integration Server (DECNIS 500/600), discussed next.

DEC WANrouter 100/500

The DEC WANrouter 100/500 provides a wide area network (WAN) routing service for nodes on a local area network (LAN). These packages are known as the DEC WANrouter 100 when running on a DEC MicroServer-SP (DEMSB) and DEC WANrouter 500 when running on a DEC MicroServer (DEMSA). The DEC WANrouter 100/500 software provides a network routing service for DECnet/OSI Phase V nodes, DECnet Phase IV nodes, TCP/IP hosts, and OSI-compatible end systems. The DEC WANrouter 100/500 software can be managed from any VMS or ULTRIX end system using the DECnet Network Command Language (NCL). Management of its Internet functions can be performed from any end system supporting the Simple Network Management Protocol (SNMP). A separate data tracing utility, available on VMS end systems, assists problem solving by tracing data packets as routed by the DEC WAN router 100/500 software.

DEC Network Integration Server (DECNIS) 500/600

The DEC Network Integration Server (DECNIS) 500/600 product provides multiprotocol routing, bridging, and X.25 gateway services to host systems on local area networks (LANs) or wide area networks (WANs) connected to the DECNIS. The DECNIS 500/600 software runs on any DECNIS 500 or 600 hardware unit. This software provides a routing service for: TCP/IP hosts, DECnet Phase IV nodes, DECnet/OSI Phase V nodes, OSI-compatible systems, Novell NetWare nodes, and AppleTalk nodes.

The DECNIS software is managed from any MS-DOS, DEC OSF/1, Open VMS or ULTRIX system using the Network Command Language (NCL) command-line interface. Event logging and data tracing utilities are also available on DEC OSF/1 AXP, OpenVMS, or ULTRIX systems to assist problem solving by logging network events and by tracing control messages received or sent by the DECNIS software.

BM Interconnectivity Software

The ADVANTAGE-NETWORKS IBM interconnectivity software includes the DECnet SNA Domain Gateway discussed in the DECnet SNA products section.

Multiprotocol Network Management

The ADVANTAGE-NETWORKS POLYCENTER Network Manager, described next, can be an active partner in network management.

POLYCENTER Network Manager

The POLYCENTER Network Manager, one version of which was known as the DECmcc Basic Management System (BMS) is a complete network management system, designed to support ADVANTAGE-NETWORKS and open system environments. Network management can start with a minimum package configuration and select options to build management systems for their specific environments. It provides a graphical user interface (GUI) with pull-down and pop-up menus, enabling users to select and display real-time or historical information. Versions of this product are available on the Digital OpenVMS VAX and ULTRIX operating systems.

DECadvantage

DECadvantage is the family name for a unified set of products and related services that upgrade a basic Intel/SCO system to the level required for mission-critical business computing. Interfacing DECadvantage products with a basic Intel/SCO system generates an open system with UNIX servers and Microsoft Windows clients, on Intel-based hardware. Doing so adds pre-integrated local and wide area networking capabilities, IBM interworking, PC integration, and enhanced system management functionality in a simple, cost-effective way.

OSI Products

Many networks rely on the OSI reference model. Such networks can increase their functionality by applying the DECadvantage OSI products—namely, OSI TP4 for DECadvantage and OSI for DOS.

OSI TP4 for DECadvantage

OSI TP4 (Transport Protocol class 4) implements communication services via standard UNIX program interfaces. OSI TP4 is used for communications with MS-DOS PCs, other UNIX systems, or other systems using OSI. The product links MS-DOS PCs processing applications to a server over a local area network (LAN).

OSI TP4 for DECadvantage can operate on several types of networks, including:

- Ethernet, accessed using the Enhanced LAN Processor (ELP)
- Ethernet, accessed using a dumb Ethernet controller via a Logical Link Interface (LLI) driver
- Token ring, X.25, accessed using the Network Processor (NWP)
- Asynchronous connection with Point-to-Point Protocol (PPP)
- IBM's System Network Architecture (SNA)

It allows networks to communicate via a third network, instead of communicating directly. Transport Components OSI TP4 for DECadvantage contains numerous transport components, each with particular functions. One or more components can be installed, depending on needs. The main distinction between the components is the routing capability.

OSI for DOS

OSI for DOS implements the OSI transport and network layers. It provides a low-cost, low-memory, high-performance solution for connecting PCs to OSI servers. OSI for DOS is an integral part of the client/server communications services provided by DECadvantage and can run on several major network types: Ethernet, token ring, X.25, and asynchronous connection with Point-to-Point Protocol (PPP). OSI for DOS is compatible with both MS-DOS and Microsoft Windows. It provides ISO standard implementation of NetBIOS Transport, Network, and Data Link layers, and supports additional industry standards.

TCP Products

As discussed in Chapters 4 and 5, TCP/IP (Transmission Control Protocol/Internet Protocol) is a major networking protocol, in particular for UNIX systems. Such networks can increase their functionality by applying the DECadvantage TCP products—namely, TCP for DECadvantage and TCP for DOS.

TCP for DECadvantage

TCP for DECadvantage provides a transport mechanism, with standard UNIX program interfaces, for communications with MS-DOS PCs, other UNIX systems, or other systems using TCP. It is compliant with industry standard TCP/IP protocols, implemented according to U.S. Department of Defense standards.

TCP for DECadvantage supports both single- and multiclient/server applications and provides distributed NetBIOS name services. In star-shaped configurations where many servers are connected to an IBM mainframe, TCP transport connections can be made using SNA as a subnetwork.

TCP for DECadvantage provides TLI and Socket interfaces for application programs. Its NetBIOS component for support of communications with PCs is implemented in STREAMS and accessible using TLI. As well as Ethernet, TCP for DECadvantage can run with several other types of network, including token ring, X.25 accessed using the Network Processor (NWP), asynchronous connection with Point-to-Point Protocol (PPP), and IBM's System Network Architecture (SNA). In addition to the basic Transport and Network protocols, it includes standard applications such as accessing remote hosts via Telnet, file transfer (FTP and TFTP), and electronic mail (STMP), and can access both local and remote printers.

TCP for DOS

TCP for DOS provides a complete TCP/IP protocol implementation for MS-DOS. It supports TCP/IP-related standard applications including virtual terminal service (Telnet), file transfer (FTP), and electronic mail (SMTP). TCP for DOS can run on several major network types including Ethernet, token ring, X.25, and asynchronous connection with Point-to-Point Protocol (PPP).

TCP for DOS is MS-DOS and Microsoft Windows compatible, provides ISO standard implementation of NetBIOS Transport, Network, and Data Link layers, and supports additional industry standards. It allows PC users to access remote hosts via Telnet and emulates the popular VT100 and VT220 terminals. It enables file transfer, electronic mail, and execution of commands on remote UNIX servers.

Server Products

DECadvantage server products include SMB Server for DECadvantage and the SNA Server.

SMB Server for DECadvantage

The SMB Server for DECadvantage provides file and printer services to personal computer users, enabling them to share applications, data, and valuable computing resources, whether local or remote. This product is based on the LAN Manager-compatible SMB core protocols and is associated with both OSI and TCP/IP protocol stacks. The SMB Server for DECadvantage runs on a UNIX server.

The SMB Server for DECadvantage File Services provides DOS users with a transparent remote file system accessed using standard DOS commands. The UNIX file system stores applications and data, which may be shared among network users. The SMB Server for DECadvantage Print Services provides access to shared UNIX printing facilities by issuing standard commands to DOS printers. The SMB Server for DECadvantage Remote Execution allows DOS users access to native UNIX software, and furnishes file system information in a UNIX format. The product includes a menu-driven user interface for system administrators to display server statistics, modify server configuration parameters, and ensure numerous security options.

SNA Server

SNA Server allows a stand-alone or a networked SCO UNIX system to act as one or more nodes in an SNA network. The product interface is implemented according to the client-server architecture. Client applications can reside on the same system as the server or on any other networked SCO UNIX system or MS-DOS PC. The software, offers standard Microsoft Windows functions such as mouse support, pull-down menus, cut and paste to clipboard, and the ability to customize using the graphics interface.

3270 Products

DECadvantage 3270 products enable a PC to emulate (behave and work like) an IBM 3278/79 or 3178 Display Station. They allow PC users to access interactively IBM host-based applications developed for IBM 3270 Display Stations in a Systems Network Architecture (SNA) networking environment. They require an SNA Server product for accessing the SNA environment. These products include 3270 for DECadvantage WIN, 3270 Emulator for UNIX and 3270 for DECadvantage DOS.

3270 for DECadvantage WIN

The 3270 for DECadvantage WIN accesses the SNA Server using the Microsoft NetBIOS interface for communication. It offers several options for transferring ASCII and binary files to and from IBM hosts. It includes a Terminal Definition Utility that redefines keys to meet specific user needs. Code translation tables enable international communication. The software offers standard Microsoft Windows functions, such as mouse support, pull-down menus, cut and paste to clipboard, and the ability to customize using the graphics interface.

3270 Emulator for UNIX

The 3270 Emulator for UNIX can be used as a native display emulator or from a user-written C language application program. It offers several options for transferring ASCII and binary files to and from IBM hosts. It includes a Terminal Definition Utility that redefines keys to meet specific user needs. Code translation tables provide for international communication. The server may run on the same system as the 3270 Emulator for UNIX or on an SCO UNIX system networked to the emulator.

3270 for DECadvantage DOS

The 3270 for DECadvantage DOS can be used as a native display emulator or from user-written C language application programs. It offers several options for transferring ASCII and binary files to and from IBM hosts. It includes a Terminal Definition Utility that redefines keys to meet specific user needs. Code translation tables enable international communication.

Summary

DIGITAL Network Architecture (DNA)

DIGITAL Network Architecture (DNA) is a model of the structures and functions that underlie all DEC networking implementations. The DNA Model includes proprietary protocols and interfaces, and Open System Interconnection (OSI) protocols and services, defined by the International Standards Organization.

DNA was designed to meet the following major goals: transparency, support for multiple applications, support for numerous protocols, conformance to standards, growth and migration, various levels of functionality, maximum availability, and extensive security.

DNA Structure

DNA is a layered architecture similar to the OSI Reference Model. In addition, DNA Session Control is proprietary DNA software providing the link from DNA Transport level functions to the application. It replaces the three OSI levels: Session level, Presentation level, and Application level. A major component of DNA Session Control is the Naming Service, a database containing names defined throughout the network.

DNA provides multiple distributed network management facilities. These services include physical configuration for maximum performance, setting and examining parameters such as resource limits, analyzing performance statistics, and running diagnostics to help locate errors. It is designed around the Enterprise Management Architecture (EMA), DEC's proprietary architecture for enterprise networks.

DECnet Products

DECnet is a family of communications software and hardware that enable DIGITAL operating systems and computers to network to additional DIGITAL systems and to non-DIGITAL systems. DECnet products supporting the TCP/IP protocol suite commonly encountered with UNIX systems include TCP/IP Services for OpenVMS, and TCP/IP Services for OpenVMS AXP. DECnet products supporting the OSI

Reference Model include DECnet/OSI for ULTRIX, DECnet/OSI for OpenVMS VAX, DECnet/OSI for DEC OSF/1 AXP, and DECnet/OSI for OpenVMS AXP. A wide variety of DECnet products assure communication between DEC networks and networks based on IBM's proprietary System Network Architecture, presented in Chapter 5. These products include VMS SNA, DECnet SNA Gateway-ST and DECnet SNA Gateway-CT, and the DEC SNA Domain Gateway.

PATHWORKS

The PATHWORKS family of PC networking and multivendor network operating system integration products is designed to facilitate the participation of PC users in open enterprise networks. PATHWORKS is based on the client/server architecture discussed in Chapters 10 and 12. PATHWORKS client software runs on standard 286, 386, 486, and Pentium hardware in a DOS (2MB suggested minimum memory) or a Windows (4MB suggested minimum memory) environment. Also required are a network interface card with a network driver. PATHWORKS server software provides a variety of networking services to PC clients. These clients can concurrently access OS/2, UNIX, Windows NT, and OpenVMS server systems.

ADVANTAGE-NETWORKS

The ADVANTAGE-NETWORKS set of products brings the standards set by the OSI Reference Model into the Digital Network Architecture. It presently includes DECnet, OSI, TCP/IP, and SNA protocols, with plans for additional protocols. The ADVANTAGE-NETWORKS software products include DECnet/OSI for ULTRIX and DECnet/OSI for VMS, TCP/IP Services for OpenVMS, and TCP/IP Services for OpenVMS AXP and ULTRIX TCP/IP, and the OSI Applications Developer's Toolkit. The ADVANTAGE-NETWORKS hardware products include the DEC WANrouter 100/500 and the DEC Network Integration Server (DECNIS) 500/600. The ADVANTAGE-NETWORKS IBM interconnectivity software includes the DECnet SNA Domain Gateway. The ADVANTAGE-NETWORKS POLYCENTER Network Manager can be an active partner in network management.

DECadvantage

DECadvantage is the family name for a unified set of products and related services that upgrade a basic Intel/SCO system to the level required for mission-critical business computing. Interfacing DECadvantage products with a basic Intel/SCO system generates an open system with UNIX servers and Microsoft Windows clients, on Intel-based hardware. Doing so adds pre-integrated local and wide area networking capabilities, IBM Interworking, PC Integration, and enhanced System Management functionality in a simple, cost-effective way. Networks relying on the OSI Reference Model can increase their functionality by applying the DECadvantage OSI products (OSI TP4 for DECadvantage and OSI for DOS). TCP/IP networks can increase their functionality by applying the DECadvantage TCP products (TCP for DECadvantage and TCP for DOS). DECadvantage server products include SMB Server for DECadvantage and the SNA Server. DECadvantage 3270 products enable a PC to emulate (behave and work like) an IBM 3278 /79 or 3178 Display Station. These products include 3270 for DECadvantage WIN, 3270 Emulator for UNIX, and 3270 for DECadvantage DOS.

Chapter Seven

TCP/IP and the Internet

by Mary Morris, Sun Microsystems

"Much of the success of the TCP/IP protocols lies in their ability to accommodate almost any underlying communications technology."

—Douglas Comer

For many years Transmission Control Protocol/Internet Protocol (TCP/IP) and the Internet have been effectively synonymous. If a system was connected to the Internet, it used TCP/IP. Conversely, if a system used TCP/IP, it could easily connect to the Internet. As the primary operating system using TCP/IP, UNIX became commercialized. TCP/IP spread into companies that couldn't justify or afford an Internet connection, but TCP/IP was still the only networking option available for UNIX systems. Then came the PC LANs. With the connection of PCs together, products began appearing that could connect those PCs to the TCP/IP networks already in existence. Sun Microsystems Inc. created PC-NFS. Wollongong created the Pathway product series. Microsoft bought into the Santa Cruz Operations Xenix project. For Microsoft circa 1991, TCP/IP had to coexist with their NetBIOS networking because their network used Xenix systems to back up clients worldwide. The final integrating factor was when the X Window product was brought to the PC. A full X Window system operates equally well locally or remotely. In fact, many applications may only be available for specific platforms or operating systems. X Window transparently displays windowed applications onto X-servers, regardless of vendor.

TCP/IP has become the most versatile set of network protocols available. It can operate on almost any network medium, hardware, and operating system in existence. It can be used for anything from a small workgroup LAN, to connecting the over two million systems that make up the Internet itself. TCP/IP is still required for operating on the Internet. Until recently, TCP/IP has also been synonymous with the UNIX operating system. With the recent advent of the full range of TCP/IP capabilities appearing on DOS-based PCs, there are as many TCP/IP-based PCs on the Internet as UNIX systems. TCP/IP has gone into the corporate world on the back of UNIX and returns to the Internet leading a vast hoard of networked PC and Macintosh systems back to the largest network in the world. With these additions, the Internet has been growing recently at about 10 percent a month.

UNIX systems have typically relied heavily on network services. This heavy reliance on networking has caused an explosion of services that can be provided by TCP/IP protocols. Networked UNIX systems can use the network for mail delivery, file transfer, obtaining name service information, network management, time synchronization, remote execution of both character- and window-based applications, and obtaining data with new hypertext applications. This is by no means a comprehensive list. All these capabilities and more have been built into the TCP/IP protocol suite.

This is not to say that all systems using TCP/IP have the complete suite of protocols. In most cases, there is a standard list of basic services that are provided with the base networking software. Additional protocol-handling software is usually bundled with the application that will serve that service. The basic TCP/IP services also vary, based upon the operating system that TCP/IP will be running on. For example, a standard UNIX system may provide between 50 and 70 basic services, whereas a standard Microsoft (MS) Windows system may only provide about five to ten of the most common TCP/IP services. As the non-UNIX systems become more common on the Internet, they will have more of the functionality of their UNIX cousins. However, because of the non-multiprocessing nature of the DOS systems, complete TCP/IP suite functionality will probably never be added to them.

Where Did TCP/IP Come From?

In 1969, the Defense Advanced Research Projects Agency (DARPA) sponsored an experiment which linked three computers. The goal of this project was to provide reliable networking technology that could recover from problems and errors. Originally, three systems were tied together with leased lines from the phone company. These systems used a protocol called NCP (Network Control Protocol). Remember that in the late 1960s and through most of the 1970s, most engineering/computer science departments had only one computer. Many universities had only one or two computers for the entire university to use. Therefore, when NCP was built in the late 1960s, the NCP developers couldn't imagine developing a product anywhere near the scope of the current Internet.

By about 1974, it was obvious that a new networking scheme was needed that could handle more systems. The wish list had virtually unlimited growth potential with the four billion uniquely addressable systems that TCP/IP offered. DARPA was also interested in expanding networking from the leased lines to packet switching via radio and satellites. This became a second criteria for the new networking scheme on the drawing board. By 1978, TCP/IP was the preferred method for ARPANET traffic. The complete conversion of the ARPANET to TCP/IP was accomplished in 1983. Throughout the 1980s the ARPANET became the DARPANET, added the NSFNET, and gradually evolved into the Internet of today. Table 7-1 shows the Internet's rate of growth over time.

Features of TCP/IP

TCP/IP wasn't developed to provide solutions for modern networks. It was created to solve network problems that were occurring in the late 1970s and early 1980s. However, it has withstood the test of time and evolved to keep pace with the needs of its user community. Many of the features of TCP/IP went into the design specifications of the International Standards Organization's Open Systems Interconnection (OSI) specifications.

Date	Number of Hosts
August, 1981	213
August, 1983	562
October, 1985	1,961
December, 1987	28,174
October, 1989	159,000
October, 1990	313,000
October, 1991	617,000
October, 1992	1,136,000
October, 1993	2,056,000
January, 1994	2,217,000

Table 7-1.   *Historical Growth Rate of the Internet*

Packet Switching

Many of the original features of TCP/IP are now incorporated into almost every network used today. This doesn't change the fact that many of these concepts originated with TCP/IP and its ancestor, NCP. TCP/IP can be characterized as a network that can recover from host component failures. This is because TCP/IP uses packet switching. Packet switching was tried as an alternative to circuit switching in the original NCP experiment. If you used circuit switching, you would establish a connection-oriented link or circuit between two systems. They would have a conversation and then disconnect. One problem with this setup is that you need to have a specific circuit to connect each system to every other system. This method is fine for two or three systems, as shown in Figure 7-1, but when the count goes to ten or 100 systems, the result is a rat's nest of wires. Another problem results when the connection between two systems is broken. Those systems can talk to all of the other systems, but not to each other. The government wanted a network that could handle downed connections, and funded ARPANET to research networking methods including connectionless packet switching to create a more consistent and reliable network.

Connectionless transmissions can follow many routes between the source and the destination system. The data to be exchanged is put into a packet and labeled with the destination system's address. This packet of data is then transmitted to the next system in line. If this system isn't the one on the address, that system will forward the packet to the next most likely destination.

In the example shown here, if Apple sent a message to Pineapple, the message could go to Orange, then to Grape, and finally to Pineapple. If the connection between Orange and Grape were down for some reason, the message could be rerouted from Apple to Pear to Grape to Pineapple.

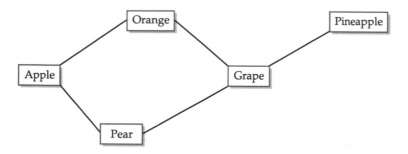

Notice that in this setup, the connection most at risk is that between Grape and Pineapple. If this connection were down, Pineapple would be cut off. To prevent this sort of risk, most networks have at least two major connections between hosts. This redundancy is currently a normal part of most network planning for critical resources.

The TCP/IP Standardization Process

TCP/IP is based upon a set of standards. There is a standard for most protocols in the TCP/IP protocol suite. The original protocol standards were developed in a set of meetings of the Internet Engineering Task Force (IETF) and published as a Request for Comments (RFC). RFCs continue to be one method for developing the standards for the new protocols that are evolving to this day. It is important to note here that RFCs are not just for the specification of new protocols. They are the archives of important information. This information can be new protocol specifications, a writing of the oral

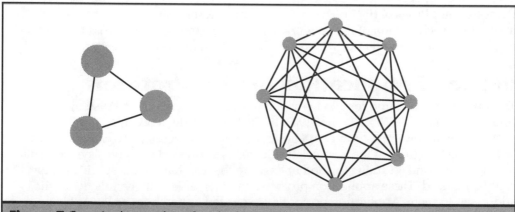

Figure 7-1. *As the number of nodes increase, so does a network's complexity.*

traditions of the Internet, or something cute such as *'Twas the Night Before Startup* (see poem at the end of this chapter).

TCP/IP as an Open Standard

The TCP/IP protocols were not only standardized, they were also made publicly available. This was and continues to be a significant variation on the government's practice toward new technology. In addition, the government funded the effort to incorporate the TCP/IP protocol suite into the Berkeley Standard Distribution (BSD) variation of the UNIX operating system. At the time when TCP/IP was incorporated into BSD, BSD was widely distributed to colleges and universities around the country in source code format. The ability to view the source code accelerated development of additional protocols for specific use. As PCs began connecting into networks, these open standards were used to integrate the systems into larger networks.

TCP/IP as a Modular Standard

The most significant feature of TCP/IP is the modularity of the protocol suite. Suppose you have a network configuration of Fiber Distributed Data Interface (FDDI) between buildings on your local campus, twisted-pair Ethernet between the systems in each building, and a T1 link to the Internet. TCP/IP has the capability to handle all of these diverse hardware and media. TCP/IP is a stack of protocols, not just a single protocol. Each layer of the stack fulfills a different function in the job of getting the data from the source to the destination. For example, at the bottom of the protocol stack, the hardware medium can be chosen independently of the method of transmission.

With TCP/IP, fiber optic cable can be used with Ethernet, or twisted-pair can be used with Copper Distributed Data Interface (CDDI), or modems can be used with Point-to-Point Protocol (PPP). This independence means that you can use the best method for each portion of the network. Almost any combination is possible, and there will usually be a vendor who offers the implementation you need.

A Wealth of Application-Specific Protocols

TCP/IP has been around for a long time. It has been required of any system connecting to the ARPANET since 1983. In the first decade of use, many application protocols were developed. On UNIX systems, there is a process, or a *daemon*, called *inetd* that listens to all of the network traffic that is addressed to a given system. This daemon will hand off traffic to another daemon that can handle the specific protocol type being used. These application protocols can then efficiently handle the traffic addressed to them. Application protocols are needed as much as the lower-level medium-specific interfaces are. The reason is that a single protocol would need to understand hundreds of different formats for each type of information that it handles. Then the program would have to know all of the routines that this protocol could invoke, and how to deal with them. This would make the program large and slow. By having small modular protocols that connect to specific addresses, the protocol type identification is only done once, and the size is kept to a minimum. On DOS-based systems, the number of application-specific protocols that the software can handle has been very limited. Thus, an inetd-style handling program hasn't yet evolved for them.

The TCP/IP Protocol Stack

TCP/IP was developed as a layered architecture. It was designed to be able to interchange the pieces at each level for the type of connection that was used. Since it was designed to operate on several different technologies, the parts needed to be structured much like Tinkertoys, where only one piece needed to change for use on a different medium. For example, a WAN connection using PPP will have a different physical layer and a different network interface layer than Ethernet would.

The International Standards Organization has developed OSI (Open System Interconnection), the most widely used model for describing layered networking technology. This model was developed several years after TCP/IP. Figure 7-2 shows the relationship between TCP/IP and OSI layering.

The Hardware and Network Interface Layers

At the bottom of each stack in Figure 7-2 is the physical hardware. This may be coaxial cable, twisted-pair cable, fiber optic cable, or a phone line. The OSI model includes this part of networking in its design. The TCP/IP model doesn't officially consider the hardware medium as a specific component in its model. TCP/IP tends to lump the hardware interfacing into the network interface layer.

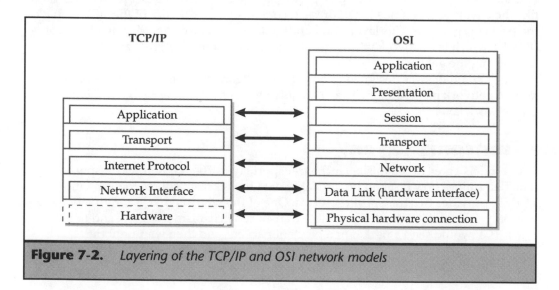

Figure 7-2.   *Layering of the TCP/IP and OSI network models*

Regardless of which hardware medium is used, it will require a specific network interface card. These network interface devices are specific to the hardware media that the signals are transmitted on. Each of these devices requires a software component called a device driver. For most network operating systems, the device driver should be included with the base operating system or provided from the hardware manufacturer.

There are hardware-specific and transmission-specific protocols. The most notable of these are:

- *ARP and RARP*   These are Ethernet-specific protocols that deal with translating Ethernet addresses into IP (Internet protocol) addresses. They are also used when booting systems across the net instead of from the local disk.

- *SLIP and PPP*   Serial line IP (SLIP) and Point-to-Point Protocol (PPP) are used across serial or phone lines. PPP is a relative newcomer and is gaining quickly in popularity. These protocols allow a much wider range of connectivity between systems. There are some Internet providers teaming up with DOS and Macintosh TCP/IP vendors to produce direct Internet connectivity products. We expect that 1994 will see the largest explosion of the Internet users from these connectivity products.

The Internet Protocol (IP) Layer

The next layer up is the Internet Protocol (IP) layer, also known as the Internet layer. This layer deals with the addressing and routing of data to the target system. This layer would be where packet switching would happen if a bridge were used to change from TCP/IP to DECnet. A gateway which routes data from one subnet to another also operates at this layer. All of the other protocols ride upon the Internet protocol. IP is like the envelope that holds the address. It contains the IP number of the system that the packet is going to. This layer also handles the Internet Control Message Protocol (ICMP), which is a network maintenance/management protocol that assists in monitoring the network.

The OSI model was designed to be generic instead of specific to TCP/IP or any known network methodology. The OSI equivalent of the IP layer in TCP/IP is called the network layer.

The Transport Layer

Both models agree to call this layer the transport layer. The method of transporting data determines how fast and how reliably data travels from source to destination. TCP/IP provides two transport protocols. One of them is called TCP. Originally there was only TCP, and it provided a reliable transport mechanism from one end to the other. TCP would send a packet or a block of packets, and then wait until the destination system had acknowledged that it received the data, and that the data was OK, before the sending system sent any more data. This was a specification of the DoD when TCP/IP was developed in 1976. At that time, today's error-correcting technology wasn't available. The current hardware is vastly more reliable than the original satellite and long-distance phone connections. WAN communication is better than a decade ago; however, it still isn't up to the standards of LAN communication. The reliability of TCP was needed for quality communications.

Now TCP/IP tends to be as much a LAN network product as a WAN network product. The reliability problems of long-distance communication and older technology don't plague the LAN networks. Consequently, gaining faster data communication throughput has emerged as a primary issue. In response, the User Datagram Protocol (UDP) was developed. This protocol doesn't wait for an acknowledgment. It will send data continuously as long as it can transmit on the network. It will respond to problems that are reported by the receiving system, but to this protocol, no news is good news.

All of the application-specific protocols use one of these two protocols for transporting data from point A to point B. Many of the application protocols have the capability of using either TCP or UDP for transmission.

Application-Specific Protocols

This is the point where the OSI model and the TCP/IP model go their separate ways. TCP/IP recognizes anything from this point on as an application protocol. The OSI model further breaks down the descriptions.

There are hundreds of application protocols in use today. Some are still experimental. Others are awaiting formal recognition. Some of the most common protocols and their uses are discussed next.

> **NOTE:** On UNIX systems, the configuration information about the application-specific protocols can be found in /etc/services for outgoing protocols and /etc/inetd.conf for incoming protocols. Non-UNIX systems will usually call the outgoing configuration information services if the TCP/IP variant can configure this information. There isn't any standard inetd style daemon on non-UNIX systems, so there isn't any inetd.conf naming convention.

FTP and Telnet   These are the oldest application protocols in existence. The first systems used only FTP and Telnet to transfer data from system to system and execute things on a remote system. Client-side FTP and Telnet are offered for every implementation of TCP/IP regardless of platform. FTP still produces the most traffic on the Internet.

HTTP   This is one of the newer protocols. It is used for handling hypertext lookup and data access with World Wide Web (WWW). HTTP traffic recently has become a significant portion of the traffic on the Internet because of the exponential growth of WWW servers and users. HTTP traffic doesn't load a network any more than FTP traffic does. The problem with HTTP is that the programs that use it are able to request data from all over, almost instantaneously. In the same time that an FTP user can download 100K of data, a Mosaic user can request about 2MB.

NNTP   Net News Transfer Protocol was developed to transfer Net News across the Internet without using the cumbersome UUCP (UNIX to UNIX copy) transfer method. Net News wasn't always on the Internet. Originally, the UUCP program was used to produce a bulletin board which became known as Net News. As the Internet spread, the NNTP protocol was developed to use the Internet to transmit these postings instead of using expensive phone connections.

NTP   Network Time Protocol allows all of the systems to synchronize time with a system designated to serve "time."

SNMP   Simple Network Management Protocol is a network administration protocol that is used to administer systems remotely. It has previously been used heavily to monitor network traffic and system availability. However, this robust protocol can actually be used to issue many routine administration duties, such as unsticking a problem printer.

SMTP, X.400, UUCP, and POP3   Mail has been transmitted with UUCP since UUCP was developed. However, UUCP has an obtuse and cryptic syntax. X.400, SMTP, and POP3 are newer mail-transfer protocols that have more versatility than the original UUCP.

RIP, EGP, OSPF, IGP, and HELLO   Getting data from point A to point B is a primary function of TCP/IP. Routing has evolved to be a very dynamic process to deal with the complexity of the Internet itself. These are some of the protocols that broadcast and track route information.

SUN-NFS and SUN-RPC   Sun Microsystems pioneered the use of virtual disks on TCP/IP when it developed NFS. Sun found that they needed a protocol specifically for this purpose. Later, Remote Procedure Calls (RPCs) were developed. (See Chapter 10 for information on RPCs.) Most NFS traffic is now a special case of the RPC protocol.

NVP-II and PVP   Network Voice Protocol (NVP-II) and Packet Video Protocol (PVP) are still in the experimental stage. They will be the basis for the expansion into videoconferencing over the Internet.

Domain   This protocol is the basis for Domain Name System (DNS), the primary name service for locating domains and systems on the Internet.

TCP/IP Network Components

TCP/IP networks are simple beasts. The smallest recognizable unit is the network interface device. For PCs and Macintoshes the network interface device is actually a card that is added to the system. For many UNIX systems, the system usually comes network-ready with the first network interface built onto the motherboard.

The next largest component is the host itself. A host can have one or more network interface devices.

Host   Network interface device

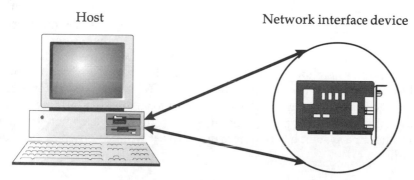

The host is known by many different names. It will have a host name, an IP number, and if it is on an Ethernet system, it will have an Ethernet address. The host may have more than one of any of these names.

Hosts connected together make up a small network called a *subnet*. This is the smallest network component of a TCP/IP network. The subnets are connected together with gateways (the Internet term for routers) to form networks, as shown in Figure 7-3. Networks are connected together to form *internets*, the most renowned being the Internet itself. In addition to IP addresses, networks have names of their own. Network names are usually called domain names.

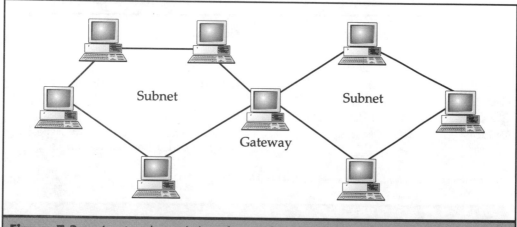

Figure 7-3. *A network consisting of two subnets joined by a gateway*

Hosts and Their Many Names

TCP/IP was designed to use host names that are normal words. This is because it isn't easy to remember a long string of numbers for each system that you need to access. However, the systems themselves do not use the host name when communicating with another system. They use numbers instead of names because the numbers are easier to manipulate. When a system communicates with another system, it may use different numbers. The first number, and the one that is always used, will be the IP number. This is the system identifier at the IP level. Most LANs are based upon Ethernet. Ethernet communications requires a unique Ethernet number for each network interface that a system has. This is referred to as the MAC address. (Note that this isn't one Ethernet number per system. It is one address for each network device that a system has. If a system has two network cards, it will be known by two different Ethernet addresses.)

IP Names and Where They Come From

The IP address is composed of four fields of numbers separated by periods or *dots*. This is also known as dotted decimal notation. The number in each field can go as high as 255. This is because each of these numbers uses a byte, or 8 bits, for each section of the address. Each of these fields is also called an *octet*. An example of an IP address would be 129.192.84.10.

A portion of each address is devoted to the network ID number, and the rest goes toward identifying the specific host within that network. Ranges of addresses are segregated into classes based upon how much of the address refers to the network ID and how much is reserved for identifying specific hosts. The ranges are listed in Table 7-2.

Type	Range*	Network ID
Reserved	0.*xx.xx.xx*	
Class A	1.0.0.0 - 126.255.255.255	First octet.
Reserved	127.0.0.*xx*	Loopback or local host address.
Class B	128.0.0.0 - 191.255.255.255	First two octets.
Class C	192.0.0.0 - 223.255.255.255	First three octets.
Multicast	224.0.0.0 and up	These addresses are reserved for a special type of broadcasting called *multicast*.

*In format *nnn.hhh.hhh.hhh*, *nnn* is the network ID and *hhh* is the host ID.

Table 7-2.   *Internet Protocol Address Ranges*

For example, it is common to hear a reference to the "192.28.44 net." In this case, 192.28.44 is the network portion. The host ID portion is left off when referring to the network as a whole. A class B network would be referred to as the "129.144 net."

> *NOTE:* *This information is maintained in /etc/hosts or obtained from a name service such as NIS, NIS+, or DNS for UNIX systems. Non-UNIX systems refer to this information as hosts information as well.*

Special IP Addresses

The network as a whole is addressed by making the host ID portion of the IP address all 0's. 129.188.0.0 would be an example of this. This is used when defining routing information.

There is a second special type of IP address called broadcasting. *Broadcasting* is sending a message to a group of systems instead of to a single system. In BSD convention, the all-zeros addressing was also used for broadcasting. System V and newer versions of the UNIX operating system use the host ID 255 for broadcasting to the entire network. Every system uses this when receiving routing and Ethernet name information. The host ID numbers 0 and 255 are reserved for broadcasting depending on the network's standards. This is usually configurable when installing the network software. Ideally, each system will actually listen for both the 0 and 255 broadcast messages. In reality, if a system is loaded, it may never respond to a broadcast other than the one that it is configured with.

There is a new type of broadcast being used now. Called *multicasting,* it is used for broadcasting to select systems on various networks. The Internet uses the Multicast BackBone (MBONE) for transmitting several types of multicast data. One notable use of multicast includes video and sound from several space shuttle missions being broadcast live. Locally, a few corporations are experimenting with videoconferencing via multicast. This technology does take up a lot of the bandwidth of a network. On a standard 10 Mbps Ethernet network, it is recommended that each multicast traffic utility keep its refresh and transmit and receive rates around 100 Kbps to prevent network degradation.

The network portion of the address is primarily used for routing data to the specific subnet where the host resides. A class B network could in theory support about 65,000 hosts. Unfortunately, the Ethernet media can't support 65,000+ hosts on the same logical division of wire. Therefore, on LANs it is also common to route as a class C network regardless of the official network classification. The only time that this would get confusing is when someone refers to the "129.88.42 net." When you hear a class A or B network referred to in class C terms, keep in mind that at that computer site, this is probably the logical way that the network is laid out for routing.

Host Names and Domains

Systems have normal names like "peach" or "sea," so that people aren't forced to use long and obnoxious number systems. Each system is known by a regular host name.

Many systems are known by more than one host name. A system will always have a primary host name. A system can have secondary names if:

■ The system has multiple interfaces. If a system is attached to two or more networks, it has a name for the specific network interface that touches each net.

■ The system uses alias names. These names can be used to indicate services that it provides. For example, *sendmail*, the standard UNIX mail processor, uses the name "mailhost" as its default name for the mail routing hub. You may want the system trash can to be your mail hub. By giving this system the secondary name of mailhost, the *sendmail.cf* on each client system doesn't need to be modified.

A system may also have a domain name. If the system is attached to the Internet, it will *always* have a domain name. A domain name is a name to uniquely describe your system in the vast expanse of the Internet. You might describe yourself as Joe Doe, from Los Angeles, California, Accountant. On the Internet, systems are identified in a similar fashion. A system might have the name snoopy.mfg.bigco.com. This name will tell everyone that the system's host name is Snoopy, that it lives in the manufacturing domain at Bigco, and that Bigco is a commercial establishment. Domain names are hierarchical; for example, bigco.com is a domain; mfg.bigco.com is a subdomain of bigco.com. Domains can be nested several levels deep as in epctestlab.sound.software.eng.bigco.com.

Ethernet Names and Their Use

IP addresses are used for routing data between subnets. The sending system needs to contact the receiving system and obtain its Ethernet address to actually send data. The receiving system won't be listening for its IP number. Instead, it listens for its Ethernet address. This can be done on the network interface device. Once data has come in that matches the Ethernet address, it will be forwarded to the CPU for decoding and processing.

Routers and Routing

Routing is moving data from one subnet to another, to get that data closer to its destination. Most routers don't know where every system is located. Each router will only know about the specific subnets that it can talk to, and the accessible subnets of the routers that are directly connected to that router. A router will have a table of network numbers and which path to take to get to each network. If the specific network number doesn't match the address that the data is going to, the data will be sent to the default router.

In Figure 7-4, John works at Bigco, a large company on a campus of several buildings. Their network is composed of one or more subnets in each building; there are subnets used for connecting desktop systems together, and other subnets used for testing and lab experiments. All of these subnets are tied together with routers so that each individual lab can have access to all the resources of the network at large,

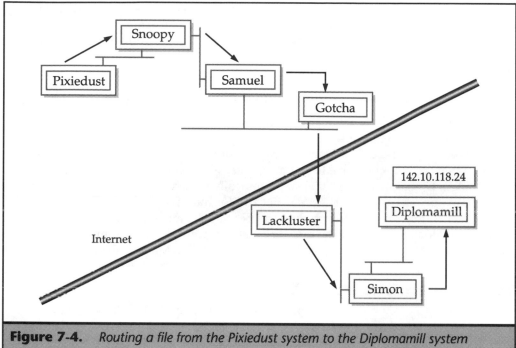

Figure 7-4.   *Routing a file from the Pixiedust system to the Diplomamill system*

including the Internet itself. John needs to get from his system, Pixiedust, to Diplomamill, a system at Sheepskin University.

First, Pixiedust obtains the IP address for Diplomamill. Then, Pixiedust sends out a request to connect to the system 142.10.118.24. Snoopy, the router which connects John's lab to the subnets in his building, examines the packet and finds that the net 142.10 is not in its route table. So Snoopy transfers John's message to the network where Snoopy's default router, Samuel, exists. Samuel connects all of the building subnets to the Bigco campus backbone. Samuel gets the packet and repeats the process. This time, the packet is passed on to Samuel's default router, Gotcha, which connects the campus backbone to the Internet. The transferral process is repeated. Gotcha's default route is the Internet itself, so the packet is placed onto the Internet.

At Sheepskin University, Lackluster is the router that connects the campus backbone to the Internet, so John's packet is received by Lackluster, which finds 142.10 in its route table. Lackluster passes the data on to Simon, the router that connects campus backbone to the 142.10.118 subnet, which Diplomamill is on. Simon echoes the data onto the appropriate net, and Diplomamill receives and responds to John's file. Each of these network changes is called a *hop* so there are seven hops between Pixiedust and Diplomamill.

Routers keep track of each other's routes by periodically broadcasting their routes. When a router hears the broadcast of another router, it updates its routing tables with this information. When the number of hops to a specific net is known, it is included in this broadcast. There may be more than one path from Pixiedust to Diplomamill. Usually the shortest path, or fewest hops, is the fastest route. Where there is more than one route, most routing will go according to the smallest hop count. There is one routing protocol, Open Shortest Path First (OSPF), which actually keeps track of time as well as hop counts. In cases where the time is shorter on a route that has more hops, the shorter time route can be taken.

The method just described is called *dynamic routing*. Originally, routing was static. That is, a person hard-coded routes for networks. When systems went down, static routes failed. Dynamic routing that can periodically update what routes are available is the most efficient method for the Internet and for most networks that have redundant routing. This routing method can be used for much of the UNIX community. However, it is not the case for most of the non-UNIX community. A default gateway needs to be hard-coded on most DOS and Macintosh systems.

Netmask and Broadcast

Only one computer should be talking on a network at a time. On Ethernet, if more than one system is talking, a collision occurs and each system must wait a little bit and start over. Token ring-type systems don't allow more than one system to talk at a time at all. Systems must wait their turn to talk. The more systems on the network, the longer a system must wait for its turn. The amount of time that the network is busy transmitting data is the level of traffic that is on the system. To control the amount of traffic that occurs, networks can be broken up into subnets. By breaking a network up into smaller pieces, or subnetting, the traffic for one subnet will stay within that subnet. Only the data that needs to go to a system on another subnet will leave the current subnet.

The gateway or router system will examine each packet of data and decide which subnet the packet should go to, based upon the net ID portion of the IP address. Since the ~65,000 hosts that a Class B network is capable of addressing are definitely too many hosts for one network to handle, the netid portion is changed with a netmask. The netmask will have a portion of the address that must match if that data is to go to that network. A netmask looks like an IP address, and it defines what is the host part of the address by using a masking procedure.

TCP/IP Security Features

Security is an important concern when you hook up your network with the outside world. The best security is to remain isolated. Unfortunately, this method doesn't promote efficient communications. A balance must be struck between securing the network and letting users get work done. The worst problem that you will find is that few applications use any method of encryption. Basic TCP/IP software doesn't encrypt things by itself; the application must do this. There is a kerberos protocol for carrying encrypted transactions, but not for encrypting specifically. Without encryption, if you telnet or rsh to another system and log in, the password that you type is sent in clear text. Any person with the know-how and ability to see the actual packets on the network can read your password. This isn't a common occurrence, but one that every network manager should be aware of.

It is one thing to keep people from watching your traffic. It is another to keep them out of your systems. If you need to connect to another network or to the Internet itself, create a fire-wall system. This system will function as a gateway or router, with one exception—you select the protocols that will be passed. For example, if you need to receive e-mail and provide basic Telnet and FTP, you still don't need to service requests for information about users. Whatever you don't need, turn off. There are also one-way FTP and Telnet utilities available. These are utilities that will allow someone on your side of the fire wall to go out, but users on the outside cannot come in.

Troubleshooting TCP/IP Installations

Networks sometimes become *notworks*. TCP/IP has developed a well-rounded network tool kit of its own. Some of these tools only exist on UNIX systems. Others, like ping, have been a part of every TCP/IP software package ever made.

Ping

Ping is usually the first tool used to test connectivity between systems. With ping you can tell if the system is responding to the network. It is important to remember at this point that the system may not be responding to protocols because ping only talks to the network interface. Ping doesn't test whether the network utilities on the system itself are responding. Using ping is like asking to a network interface, "Are you there?" As soon as the system has initialized its network interface, that network interface can respond independent of the CPU, "Yes, I am here." That system may not yet have started decoding traffic and responding to requests for NFS or Telnet, but the physical end of the troubleshooting can be isolated quickly with this utility.

Rup

Rup, like ping, is almost a universal command. Rup simply probes a remote system to see if it is alive and answering network traffic. After ping verifies that there is connectivity from source to destination, rup can be used to verify that the destination is alive and responding.

```
snoopy% rup terminal
  terminal     up 22 days,  6:21,    load average: 0.12, 0.14, 0.13
```

Traceroute

Traceroute is used when there are routers or gateways between the source and destination, and the message isn't getting across. This would be used in a case where ping fails. Traceroute shows the route that it takes to get to the destination, and how long it takes for each hop.

```
snoopy# traceroute terminal
traceroute to terminal (129.188.1.125), 30 hops max, 40 byte packets
 1   snoopy-239 (129.188.239.1)    2 ms   2 ms   2 ms
 2   dmv1a-60   (129.188.60.210)   2 ms   2 ms   2 ms
 3   terminal   (129.188.1.125)   76 ms   4 ms   3 ms
```

Netstat

Netstat is the Swiss Army knife of TCP/IP. With different options, netstat can list the routers, the types of traffic and traffic problems, and the types of services that the system is listening for. The following is a sample route table listing from netstat:

```
snoopy% netstat -rn

Routing Table:
  Destination       Gateway          Flags  Ref   Use    Interface
  -------------     --------         -----  ----  ----   ----------
  127.0.0.1         127.0.0.1        UH     0        0   lo0
  129.188.22.23     129.188.60.210   UGH    0        0
  129.158.0.0       129.188.60.201   UG     0        0
  192.99.55.0       192.99.55.1      U      2      173   le0
  129.188.60.0      129.188.60.135   U      3     2273   le1
  129.188.239.0     129.188.239.1    U      2      231   le2
  224.0.0.0         129.188.60.135   U      3        0   le1
default             129.188.60.210   UG     0        0
```

A network interface listing from netstat is shown here:

```
snoopy% netstat -I
Name  Mtu    Net/Dest      Address     Ipkts  Ierrs  Opkts  Oerrs  Collis Queue
lo0   8232   loopback      localhost   10573   0     10573   0       0     0
le0   1500   dmv1-lab1     snoopy-55    5520   0      2368   1       0     0
le1   1500   dmv01-060-n   snoopy      57656   0      7332   3      813    0
le2   1500   dmv01-239-n   snoopy-239   5147   4      2602   91      2     0
```

config

Ifconfig is a UNIX command that lists the basic statistics of the network interface devices. This program can change the parameters that an interface is operating with as well. This utility isn't usually ported to non-UNIX packages.

```
# ifconfig -a
lo0: flags=849<UP,LOOPBACK,RUNNING,MULTICAST> mtu 8232
        inet 127.0.0.1 netmask ff000000
le0: flags=863<UP,BROADCAST,NOTRAILERS,RUNNING,MULTICAST> mtu 1500
        inet 192.99.55.1 netmask ffffff00 broadcast 192.99.55.255
        ether 8:0:20:11:fc:44
le1: flags=863<UP,BROADCAST,NOTRAILERS,RUNNING,MULTICAST> mtu 1500
        inet 129.188.60.135 netmask ffffff00 broadcast 129.188.60.255
        ether 8:0:20:11:fc:44
le2: flags=863<UP,BROADCAST,NOTRAILERS,RUNNING,MULTICAST> mtu 1500
        inet 129.188.239.1 netmask ffffff00 broadcast 129.188.239.255
        ether 8:0:20:11:fc:44
```

niffing the Network

Some flavors of UNIX offer tools that will listen to the network for you. Etherfind from Sun Microsystems is a good example of this. If there aren't any tools available locally, you can get a *network sniffer,* which is a device that tracks network communications and can report on activities that might be causing problems. This type of device is usually used when you know that there is a problem on the network, but it cannot be isolated. A sniffer is actually a system dedicated to listening to the network, and tracking activity.

 CAUTION: Network sniffers are expensive, so it's best to purchase one—or rent one—only if your network is large enough to justify the cost.

TCP/IP on Specific Platforms and Networks

TCP/IP can be found for most operating systems. TCP/IP does have some limitations on some platforms. This is primarily due to the fact that the operating system cannot handle the multitasking nature of full networking. TCP/IP can coexist on the same hardware medium with other network protocols. TCP/IP can encapsulate other protocols and be encapsulated.

TCP/IP and DOS

There are dozens of vendors offering their version of TCP/IP for the DOS system. The biggest problem is that with DOS itself, the full range of TCP/IP functions cannot be used. This is primarily because DOS is a single-user operating system. It has no concept of users, user names, and logging on to a system. It lacks the multitasking capabilities that it would need for listening to the network and performing local tasks at the same time. Terminate-and-stay-resident (TSR) products can handle some of this responsibility, but they use significant memory resources on a limited memory system, and they cannot replace a real multitasking operating system.

The lack of full TCP/IP functionality is quickly being resolved by the latest crop of MS Windows TCP/IP applications. They can do a reasonably good job of managing multiple tasks. There are even systems that can create a mock user name table to enable FTP. Most of these applications offer full TCP/IP functionality only when MS Windows is running.

These DOS and MS Windows TCP/IP products offer a wide range of features, listed here:

- *NFS client capabilities*   These are usually offered on about 75–80 percent of the DOS TCP/IP packages. In fact, the original reason that TCP/IP came to the DOS world was for the file-sharing capabilities.

- *NFS server capabilities*   These are usually offered only on MS Windows-based TCP/IP packages. Having a system that acts as a server and runs MS Windows is a good environment for a small localized workgroup. However, the combination of MS Windows and file-serving is not very efficient when it comes to serving many users or handling large quantities of data.

- *FTP and Telnet client capabilities*   All TCP/IP packages offer these.

- *FTP server capabilities*   There are a couple of MS Windows-based packages that offer the ability to FTP files. This feature isn't a real necessity. NFS serves files to other clients with less work. The security of authenticating a user isn't real security when the password is still sent clear text on the network, even if it isn't displayed on the screen.

- *X Window software*   This is the newest feature of TCP/IP on MS Windows, and on DOS with QEMM systems. X Window software allows the MS Windows systems to execute X Window applications. There was a significant market in the X-terminal business before the introduction of PC X Window software. The market still appears strong, but combining X Window with the full range of PC applications offers the best of both worlds.

- *WWW and Gopher software*   This software provides access to much of the data on the Internet, and offers an intuitive, user-friendly interface. It is usually shareware that can be downloaded from the Internet itself.

Dual Protocol Stacks

TCP/IP peacefully coexists with other network protocols. There are several vendors who offer dual- or multiple-protocol stack capabilities. A multiple-protocol stack is primarily used on systems that connect with Ethernet. The Ethernet card will catch any data that is addressed to its Ethernet address. This data is then passed to the primary protocol. If that protocol determines that the data is not in a format that it can read, it will then pass the data to the secondary protocol.

TCP/IP is able to share the wire with other Network Operating Systems (NOSs). In many cases, the hosts can communicate via both TCP/IP and the other protocols used. Some of the combinations could be:

■ *TCP/IP and Novell SPX/IPX*   The DOS client could load a Sequenced Protocol Exchange/Internetwork Protocol Exchange (SPX/IPX) with TCP/IP. The Novell server could add its optional TCP/IP and NFS packages, allowing the Novell server to serve NFS traffic. There are Novell packages for a few flavors of the UNIX operating system. Keep in mind that there are some speed problems involved with adding TCP/IP support to a Novell server, and with adding NetWare support to a UNIX system. Fortunately, Destiny, Novell's version of UNIX, offers the best alternative for the Novell and TCP/IP server.

■ *TCP/IP and NetBIOS*   NetBIOS is used by LAN Manager and Windows NT. Microsoft's concurrent use of LAN Manager and Xenix on the same networks has spawned several vendor's implementations of dual-protocol stacks for DOS, OS/2, and Windows NT systems. Windows NT systems appear to have some difficulty in handling a dual-protocol stack. Microsoft and other vendors are reworking the drivers to deal with this intermittent problem. The only thing left out in the cold here is the UNIX TCP/IP systems that can't decode and use NetBIOS protocols. A NetBIOS implementation on a UNIX system is rarely found.

CP/IP on the Macintosh

The National Center for Supercomputing Activities (NCSA) developed the first TCP/IP product for the Mac. This is also the only shareware version of TCP/IP available for the Mac. In addition, there are two or three commercial vendors of TCP/IP for the Macintosh. TCP/IP server software doesn't really exist for Macintoshes running System 7. The A/UX operating system is what is needed for serving data. One of the more difficult things for Macintosh systems is that the user needs to manually switch between the Ethernet and AppleTalk networks when using both AppleTalk and Ethernet. One work-around for this is to use an AppleTalk-to-Ethernet bridge such as a Gator box.

Macintosh TCP/IP products offer similar features to the DOS products. These include the following:

- *NFS client capabilities*   These are offered by both commercial TCP/IP vendors.
- *FTP and Telnet client capabilities*   All TCP/IP packages offer these.
- *X Window software*   This feature is equally new for the Macintosh- and DOS-based PCs. X Window software allows the Macintosh systems to execute X Window applications. One vendor, Caymen Systems, also offers to execute Macintosh applications and display them on an X Window system.
- *WWW and Gopher software*   This software provides access to much of the data on the Internet in a user-friendly and intuitive interface. It is usually shareware that can be downloaded from the Internet itself.

TCP/IP and the UNIX Operating System

DARPA is primarily responsible for having made TCP/IP synonymous with UNIX. DARPA funded the integration of TCP/IP protocols with BSD (Berkeley Software Distribution). BSD was the low-cost version of UNIX that was common on most university platforms. In 1983, The Office of the Defense also required that all DARPA systems, which at that point included all of the ARPANET, use TCP/IP. With these two events, UNIX and TCP/IP became the preeminent combination on the Internet. It would be difficult to find a UNIX vendor that doesn't support TCP/IP.

Connecting to the Internet

Connecting to the Internet itself is a time-consuming process best attempted by detail-oriented individuals. IP addresses need to be assigned. If there are previously unassigned IP addresses, they need to be removed or placed behind a router that doesn't broadcast out. A domain name needs to be registered. A service provider needs to be selected. Connectivity hardware must be selected and installed.

Connecting to the Internet can give your organization more visibility, allow e-mail exchange with around 25 million people, and give access to the vast data resources of the Internet itself. Despite the complexity of the process itself, there is a lot to be gained from connecting.

Service providers are companies that will provide access to the Internet. This access can range from a simple dial-in connection, to a full T1 connection with domain name service listing, and a Net News feed. ISDN is becoming a popular and cost-effective method of connecting to the Internet in places where your local phone company's ISDN equipment is compatible with the phone company ISDN equipment near the service provider. The disparity in equipment is decreasing. However, it currently isn't possible for someone who lives in certain parts of Mountain View, California, to connect via ISDN to an office in Palo Alto ten miles away.

IP addresses actually come from the NIC (Network Information Center). By sending them an e-mail or snail mail request, you can get a range of addresses reserved for your company's use. The NIC manages IP addresses because each IP address on the Internet must be unique. If your company may get an actual connection to the Internet, it is vital that addresses be reserved for your use. If you choose not to request specific IP addresses and use whatever range you make up, you'll probably need to change addresses if an Internet connection is ever made. Domain name registration is also handled by the NIC.

The Future of TCP/IP and the Internet

There are some people who argue that the Internet is the basis for the National Information Infrastructure (NII) that the U.S. government is sponsoring. In many ways this is true. The Internet is the most widespread electronic communications web currently available. However, the Internet cannot fill the bill for the NII plan, which requires the capacity to handle millions more users than the Internet currently can handle. The Internet is going to be hard pressed just to keep up with current expansion. When the real information superhighway is finally established, it will be able to migrate the best technology straight from its use on the Internet.

TCP/IP was not originally designed to be a high-speed network. Currently, Novell's IPX protocol out-performs TCP/IP in sheer speed. There are many vendors developing products that will increase the speed of TCP/IP, but TCP/IP will not become the premier network for LANs in the near future. Its assets lie in the area of internetworking—bringing together networks of networks. It has the installed base of the Internet itself, and a wide range of applications and application protocols.

TCP/IP will need to address nomadic computing issues. People aren't willing to sit in an office to have access to a computer, its network, or even the Internet itself. There is a company called RadioMail Inc. which provides Internet e-mail exchange over radio waves. This new service is becoming extremely popular for the laptop and HP palmtop users. As mobile as people may be today, they will be infinitely more so later. TCP/IP now maintains a host at a base station, thus providing an interface between the wandering user and the Internet connection. TCP/IP will need to evolve to directly connect these nomadic people instead of providing a static way station.

TCP/IP will need to develop a method for address expansion to accommodate the need for additional addresses. The TCP/IP address space may seem unlimited. After all, one billion hosts does tend to make a fairly large network. However, the Class B section of the address space is quickly being used up. It is estimated that the Class B addresses will be exhausted by 1995 or 1996. Measures are in place to borrow addresses from other classes, but the long-term solution is to expand the address space by using still longer addresses.

```
Network Working Group                           V. Cerf
Request for Comments: 968                          MCI
                                          December 1985


        'Twas the Night Before Start-up'

STATUS OF THIS MEMO
This memo discusses problems that arise and debugging techniques used in
bringing a new network into operation. Distribution of this memo is unlimited.
```

DISCUSSION

'Twas the night before start-up and all through the net,
    not a packet was moving; no bit nor octet.
The engineers rattled their cards in despair,
    hoping a bad chip would blow with a flare.
The salesmen were nestled all snug in their beds,
    while visions of data nets danced in their heads.
And I with my datascope tracings and dumps
    prepared for some pretty bad bruises and lumps.
When out in the hall there arose such a clatter,
    I sprang from my desk to see what was the matter.

There stood at the threshold with PC in tow,
    An ARPANET hacker, all ready to go.
I could see from the creases that covered his brow,
    he'd conquer the crisis confronting him now.
More rapid than eagles, he checked each alarm
    and scrutinized each for its potential harm.

On LAPB, on OSI, X.25!
    TCP, SNA, V.35!

His eyes were afire with the strength of his gaze;
    no bug could hide long; not for hours or days.
A wink of his eye and a twitch of his head,
    soon gave me to know I had little to dread.
He spoke not a word, but went straight to his work,
    fixing a net that had gone plumb berserk;
And laying a finger on one suspect line,
    he entered a patch and the net came up fine!

The packets flowed neatly and protocols matched;
    the hosts interfaced and shift-registers latched.
He tested the system from Gateway to PAD;
    not one bit was dropped; no checksum was bad.
At last he was finished and wearily sighed
    and turned to explain why the system had died.
I twisted my fingers and counted to ten;
    an off-by-one index had done it again...

                                —Vint Cerf
                                December, 1985

Chapter Eight

Novell's IPX/SPX

by Ken Neff, Novell, Inc.

This chapter describes the various network communication and transport protocols supported by Novell's NetWare operating system products. It begins with a basic introduction to NetWare's native communication protocols—Internetwork Packet Exchange (IPX), Sequenced Packet Exchange (SPX), and companion protocols—explaining the advantages and disadvantages of each. It then discusses how NetWare 3.*x* and 4.*x* support other transport protocols, including TCP/IP, AppleTalk, SNA, and OSI, as well as various types of clients (DOS, Windows, OS/2, Macintosh, and UNIX). It concludes with a discussion of the enhancements Novell has made to accommodate the increased demands of global, wide area network environments.

NetWare's Communication Protocols

In the early 1980s, Novell developed a suite of network communication and transport protocols patterned after the Xerox Network System (XNS) protocols. Novell's Internetwork Packet Exchange and Sequenced Packet Exchange (IPX/SPX) communication protocols serve as an interface between the NetWare operating system and the various types of network media (Ethernet, ARCNET, and token ring). The IPX/SPX protocol stack is closely linked with other programs and routines that together are responsible for forming, sending, receiving, and processing the data packets transmitted on the network.

Figure 8-1 shows the communication protocols used in a native NetWare environment consisting of DOS, Windows, and OS/2 clients. Since NetWare was originally designed at about the same time the OSI model was being finalized, there is a close but not exact correlation between NetWare's communication functions and the OSI model layers.

Internetwork Packet Exchange (IPX)

IPX is a simple, but fast, Network-layer protocol optimized for use on LANs. Adapted from the XNS Internet Datagram Protocol, IPX transmits information in *datagrams*—self-contained packets that travel independently from source to destination in a connectionless mode. IPX datagrams provide what is sometimes called a "best effort" service, in which there is no guarantee that packets will arrive at the destination or that they will arrive in proper sequence. Removing such overhead improves performance in transmission.

IPX doesn't wait for an acknowledgment that a packet has been received. Rather, it assumes that the packet arrived intact when the response is received from the destination. This request-response mechanism works well for two reasons. First, every IPX packet contains Cyclic Redundancy Check (CRC) codes, which ensure 99-percent accuracy. With that kind of success rate, waiting for a "packet received intact" acknowledgment is not necessary. Second, IPX automatically resends the packet if the receiver does not respond within a certain amount of time. This covers the rare case when a packet does arrive damaged.

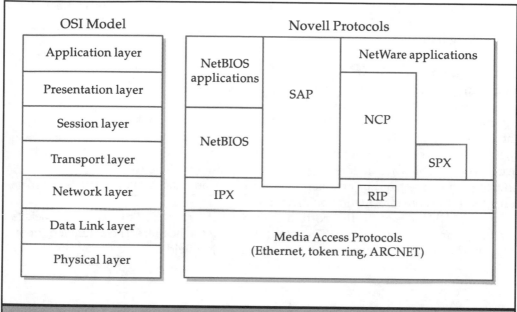

Figure 8-1. *The native NetWare protocols used by DOS, Windows, and OS/2*

IPX's speed is also attributable to the minimal amount of overhead involved in packet transmission. As a connectionless protocol, IPX doesn't have to establish and maintain a session connection between sender and receiver, nor is it concerned with sending and receiving packets in any particular order. If it is necessary to establish a connection and provide packet sequencing (e.g., for long, continuous transmissions between the same source and destination), an application can use the higher-level SPX protocol, as explained later.

To achieve networking-hardware independence, IPX neither defines nor makes any protocol-specific assumptions about the physical network over which it sends data. Instead, it uses a well-defined interface to communicate with various media access protocols such as that used by Ethernet networks or by token ring networks. To send or receive a packet, IPX interacts with a *LAN driver* that is custom-written for each type of network. It is the LAN driver that actually places the packet information into "frames" of data and sends them out over the wire. You can think of a frame as a block of data bits that is transmitted serially over the wire. Each frame is a separate entity that may contain an entire datagram or a fragment of a datagram. Each type of network (Ethernet, token ring, etc.) defines its own frame type. As packets of information are passed down from upper-layer network protocols to the physical layer, they are either fully or partially placed in frames. Some types of networks have larger frame types than others, or allow variable frame lengths. The LAN driver is also responsible for receiving packets and checking them for internal consistency. Because all the peculiarities of a specific type of network adapter or topology are abstracted by driver software, IPX doesn't have to make any distinctions among types of networking hardware.

Structure of an IPX Packet

By building packets according to the structure specified by the IPX protocol, networked PCs can send packets to, and receive packets from, any node on an internetwork. Figure 8-2 shows the basic structure of an IPX packet. In this example, the IPX information is encapsulated within an IEEE 802.3/802.2 Ethernet frame. Note that the frame contains information added by an Ethernet driver, such as the media access control (MAC) header and service access point (SAP) fields that define the source of the packet and its destination (Source SAP and Destination SAP). See Chapter 4 for more information on this topic.

The first 30 bytes of the IPX portion of the packet form the *IPX Header*. IPX packets can be of varying lengths, up to 576 bytes (including the header). The actual length of a given IPX packet is contained in the header's Length field.

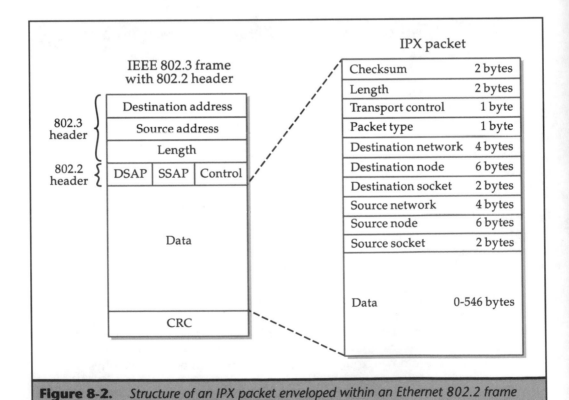

Figure 8-2. *Structure of an IPX packet enveloped within an Ethernet 802.2 frame*

The IPX header also contains the network address, node address, and socket number for both the sender (source) and the receiver (destination). These items are explained below.

- **Network address**   This is a 4-byte number assigned to a network cable segment. For example, a server containing two Ethernet cards identifies the network attached to each card by using a distinct network address for each one. Network addresses are also used by routers to forward packets to their final destination segment.

- **Node address**   This identifies a single network adapter attached to the network. Every station must contain at least one network adapter, with a unique node number to distinguish it from all other nodes on the network. Ethernet network adapters have factory-set node addresses; node addresses for ARCNET and token ring adapters are set via jumpers or switches.

- **Socket numbers**   These are used for determining what to do with a packet once it has arrived at a particular node. An IPX socket plays two roles. First, the socket number can signify what type of information is contained in that IPX packet's data field. Novell has defined several well-known sockets for specific purposes, including 451h for file service packets, 453h for routing information packets, 456h for diagnostic packets, and many others. Second, applications can use sockets for their own purposes. For example, two applications wishing to communicate with each other over the network can negotiate for sockets. NetWare also uses sockets to filter and route packets internally.

On a NetWare network, the successful delivery of packets relies on proper addressing in the IPX address fields and in the MAC header.

The remainder of the packet contains the packet's data, if any. An IPX packet doesn't necessarily have to contain data, but it must have the 30-byte header. Since Ethernet frames must be at least 64 bytes long, the data portion is sometimes padded with bytes to achieve the 64-byte minimum frame size.

equenced Packet Exchange (SPX)

The Sequenced Packet Exchange (SPX) protocol is a higher-level, connection-oriented extension to IPX. SPX uses IPX to send and receive packets, but it adds a functional interface to establish and maintain a virtual circuit, or session, between the sender and receiver. Unlike IPX, which assumes that a packet arrived intact when it receives the response, SPX provides for an explicit acknowledgment when packets are received. It also performs rigorous verification to ensure that packets are not corrupted during transmission.

As its name implies, SPX also provides a sequencing mechanism to exchange messages in a sequenced packet stream. On an internetwork, it isn't uncommon for IPX packets sent from the same host to take different routes to their destination, therefore arriving out of sequence. SPX not only arranges packets in the proper order, but it also resends packets that are missing or out of sequence.

SPX packets have the same basic structure and fields used in IPX packets, with 12 extra bytes added to the header for connection control and sequencing information. SPX also includes a flow-control mechanism to reduce packet congestion during peak network loads.

Because of the additional overhead required to maintain sessions between nodes and to sequence packets, SPX suffers a slight performance loss as compared to its underlying IPX datagram service. For this reason, the NetWare operating system itself avoids using SPX for many of its internal functions. Instead, the operating system uses session maintenance and sequence control mechanisms built-in to the NetWare Core Protocols (explained next). However, certain applications require the extra reliability that SPX provides. For example, Novell's Remote Console facility and Print Server application use SPX. Third-party developers can design applications to use SPX if they require guaranteed packet delivery.

NetWare Core Protocols (NCPs)

Novell's NetWare Core Protocols (NCPs) are a proprietary set of well-defined messages that control server execution. The NCPs define procedures that NetWare follows to accept and respond to client requests. Novell invented NCPs because there were no standard service protocols available that supported PC client operating systems. NCP service protocols exist for every service a client might request from a NetWare server, such as enabling and disabling a service connection, manipulating directories and files, opening semaphores, altering drive mappings and security, printing, and so on.

NCPs are the key to accessing NetWare services. A client node may have a perfectly good IPX/SPX stack and an active physical connection to a server; yet, without knowledge of NCPs, that client won't be able to coax any services out of the server. Novell keeps the NCPs proprietary for several reasons. First, it is critical that both the client and the server be in complete agreement as to what each NCP means. If even one bit of one NCP is out of synch between a server and a client, NetWare won't work correctly. Second, as the capabilities of the NetWare OS are augmented or modified, the NCPs must change correspondingly. In fact, NCPs undergo continual change, which simply reflects the successful evolution of NetWare.

It is the tight integration of IPX and NCPs that enables NetWare to be equally efficient at servicing client requests *and* at handling the system calls of server-based applications. The NCP provides its own session-control and sequencing mechanisms rather than relying on SPX. NCP running on IPX is a very streamlined protocol stack because it avoids the overhead of the Transport, Session, and Presentation layers of the OSI model.

The current method for passing NCPs to the server is through specially flagged IPX packets. However, there is no technical barrier to transmitting NCPs by using other datagram protocols such as the User Datagram Protocol (UDP) in TCP/IP-based networks.

outing Information Protocol (RIP)

To get packets where they need to go on an internetwork, NetWare incorporates a *routing process* within the NetWare operating system. Each server tracks the other servers and routers on the internetwork and retains their location and distance in a Routing Information Table. The routing process then uses this information to forward packets along the shortest route to their final destination.

To exchange route information, NetWare servers use a special type of IPX protocol called the Routing Information Protocol (RIP). With RIP, a server broadcasts its routing table to every other server on each local network segment at regular intervals (the default interval is one minute). Thus NetWare servers periodically receive updated routing tables from other servers. Each server checks the information received against its own internally maintained routing table. If a server detects inconsistency between RIP information and its own routing table, it will generate alerts declaring some type of routing problem.

NetWare's adaptive routing mechanism is designed to react quickly and automatically to changes in the internetwork configuration. When a new router comes up, it requests routing information from all other routers and builds its routing table from the responses it receives. When an existing router is shut down, it notifies all other routers so they can update their tables. If a router fails, the other routers ascertain that it is gone and search for alternate routes that bypass the nonfunctional router.

In addition to the internal routing capability of NetWare servers, external routers are often used to build large or complex internetworks. Novell provided a crude router-generation utility with NetWare 2.x and 3.x so customers could create their own external routers. The resulting ROUTER.EXE program had the same (limited) IPX routing capabilities as NetWare 2.x and could run as either a dedicated or nondedicated process in a networked PC. Because of the single-protocol focus and other limitations of this routing method, many organizations turned to third-party routers to interconnect their NetWare networks.

ervice Advertising Protocol (SAP)

The Service Advertising Protocol (SAP) is a mechanism by which information about available services is distributed throughout the internetwork. SAP requires a server to advertise three pieces of information to the network every 60 seconds: the server's name, the type of server it is (for example, file server or print server), and its network address. Servers use IPX to send SAP packets. Other servers pick up this information and store it in their Server Information Table.

In the NetWare 3.x environment, keeping track of server addresses is important because a potential client must know where a server is located before it can establish a connection with the server and use the server's services. To facilitate server address queries from potential clients, each server copies all the server names it knows about, along with their types and addresses, to a database called the *bindery*. A client desiring a particular service can query any bindery on the internetwork and find out the physical address of a server that can provide that service. Once the address is known, the client can establish a connection to the server via IPX.

SAP provides an efficient way of keeping track of the services available in a dynamic network. When a server knows it is going down, it tells the SAP, and all binderies are updated to indicate that the server is unavailable. If a server stops advertising without advance notice, the SAP assumes after a time that the server is no longer available. Word of the server's assumed unavailability is spread throughout the internetwork by the SAP.

In NetWare 4.*x*, Novell replaced the server-centric bindery with a globally distributed database called NetWare Directory Services (NDS). NDS represents entities such as file servers, print servers, volumes, and users in an X.500-derivative directory. Because NDS stores information about services available within a specific context, clients can locate the services they seek by consulting an NDS server. This significantly reduces the amount of SAP broadcasts on the network.

Even with NDS, NetWare 4.*x* networks still use RIP and SAP. SAP is used to advertise the existence of NDS servers and to facilitate time synchronization between servers. Most NetWare 4.*x* installations use the bindery emulation feature to maintain compatibility with NetWare 3.*x* servers and with existing third-party devices that haven't yet been updated to support NDS.

NetBIOS Emulation

NetWare also provides emulation software to support applications that have been written to IBM's Network Basic Input Output System (NetBIOS) interface for peer-to-peer communications on IBM Token Ring and IBM PC networks. Novell's NetBIOS emulator is a translation mechanism that offers complete compatibility for NetBIOS applications.

Multiple Protocol Support in NetWare

Originally, the pathway for communication between the physical network and Novell's IPX/SPX protocol stack was strictly monolithic. Novell-compatible LAN drivers could recognize and transmit only one type of packet using a single protocol stack. Beginning with the release of NetWare 3.*x* and continuing in NetWare 4.*x*, this one-lane communication pathway has been expanded into a multilane highway capable of passing traffic over a number of different protocol stacks.

Figure 8-3 illustrates NetWare's sophisticated new protocol engine capable of supporting a variety of network communication protocols. It is this protocol engine that allows NetWare 3.*x* and 4.*x* servers to provide services to DOS, Windows, OS/2, Macintosh, and UNIX clients. It also facilitates interoperability between NetWare and other network systems in larger enterprise networks.

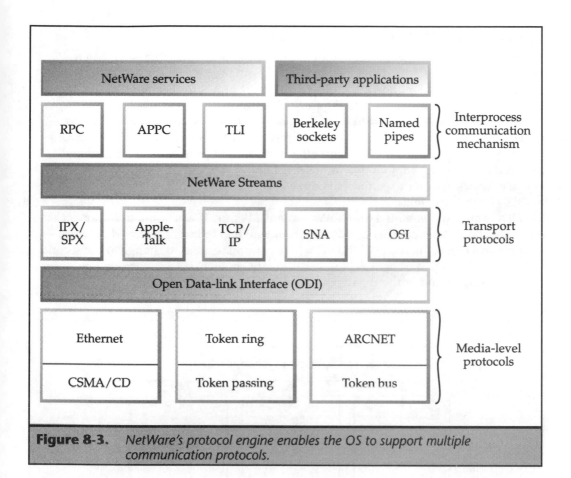

Figure 8-3.   *NetWare's protocol engine enables the OS to support multiple communication protocols.*

Novell pioneered the concept of LAN media independence. By encouraging network hardware vendors to write specialized drivers for NetWare, Novell has been able to support a wide assortment of network adapters and cabling. At the media level, NetWare supports the CSMA/CD (IEEE 802.3), token passing (IEEE 802.5), and token bus media access protocols used by Ethernet, token ring, and ARCNET hardware, respectively.

NetWare 3.*x* and 4.*x* support the various frame-encapsulation techniques (or *frame types*) that have emerged from groups involved in the development of Ethernet. These include Ethernet II, IEEE 802.3 "raw," IEEE 802.3 with 802.2 (LLC) header, and IEEE 802.3 with 802.2 and the SNAP extension. NetWare also supports both IBM Token Ring and Token Ring SNAP frame types. The key to supporting these different frame types is the FRAME parameter that can be specified when binding a protocol stack to a driver.

Open Data-link Interface (ODI)

The main technology that makes multiple protocol support possible is the Open Data-link Interface (ODI), developed by Novell with the help of Apple. ODI provides a standard interface for allowing multiple transport protocols to share a single network adapter without conflict. Figure 8-4 illustrates how ODI works.

By using LAN drivers written to ODI specifications, a network adapter can handle packets from more than one protocol at a time. In effect, ODI creates logical network interfaces through which packets formatted for different protocols can be sent and received on the same adapter over a single cabling system. In this way, you can use a single network adapter to connect to both NetWare and non-NetWare networks (such as TCP/IP or AppleTalk).

ODI is also implemented for NetWare clients. Before, if you wanted to connect a NetWare client PC to another network system, you had to install a second network adapter and driver, then reboot the PC whenever you wanted to change to the second protocol. With ODI, the client PC can use different protocol stacks with just one network adapter and without having to be rebooted.

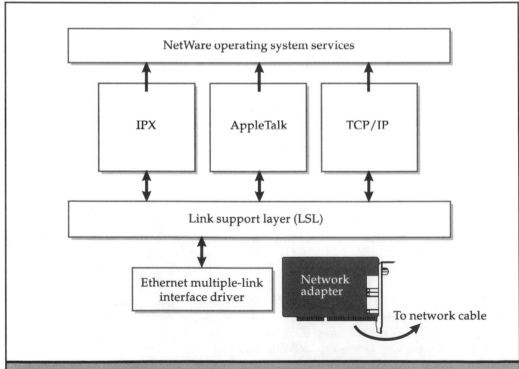

Figure 8-4.   *Through the Open Data-link Interface, a network adapter can communicate over more than one protocol stack.*

NetWare Streams

NetWare Streams is a general-purpose data exchange protocol based on AT&T's STREAMS technology for establishing Transport layer-independent communication between varying network protocols. The Streams interface forms a two-way data transfer path that can be manipulated through simple operations such as open, read, write, and close. The interface can also be multiplexed so that a single upper stream can provide access to multiple lower streams, each leading to a different protocol stack with a different API (application programming interface). This allows network requests to travel over a variety of transports (IPX/SPX, TCP/IP, or OSI) using a variety of interprocess communication mechanisms (APPC, NetBIOS, or Named Pipes). Novell implements Streams as a set of NetWare loadable modules (NLMs).

Other Protocols Supported by NetWare

In addition to the native IPX/SPX protocols described previously, NetWare 3.*x* and 4.*x* currently support a number of other transport protocols. These protocol stacks are either built into the operating system itself, or are available as add-on NetWare loadable modules from Novell or third parties.

UNIX Environment Protocols

NetWare 3.*x* and 4.*x* servers can participate in the standard UNIX computing environment through built-in support for the TCP/IP transport protocols and the optional NetWare NFS product. NetWare TCP/IP is Novell's own implementation of the Transmission Control Protocol/Internet Protocol. Once the exclusive domain of universities and government agencies, TCP/IP is rapidly gaining acceptance in mainstream, multivendor business environments.

Through its TCP/IP transport stack, NetWare has the ability to route TCP/IP packets as well as IPX/SPX packets between any connected Ethernet, token ring, or ARCNET cabling systems. In addition, you can attach a NetWare server to an existing TCP/IP wide area network and tunnel IPX packets across the WAN. *Tunneling* simply means encapsulating the IPX/SPX packet within a TCP/IP datagram and sending it via TCP/IP links.

NetWare's TCP/IP stack provides two other important capabilities:

- A Simple Network Management Protocol (SNMP) agent that can supply information to an SNMP-based TCP/IP console application. The NetWare server can then receive SNMP alerts and remote configuration information.

- Support for commonly used UNIX APIs such as AT&T STREAMS/TLI (Transport Layer Interface) and Berkeley Sockets v4.3. Thus, developers can write NLMs that use familiar TCP/IP interfaces.

An optional Novell product called NetWare NFS lets UNIX clients see the NetWare file system as an extension of Sun Microsystems' Network File System (NFS) and access NetWare volumes using the standard UNIX mount command. NetWare NFS also allows UNIX clients to access NetWare's printing services to submit documents to NetWare print queues.

Another option for integrating NetWare and UNIX environments is known as NetWare for UNIX (previously Portable NetWare). It is essentially a port of the NetWare operating system that runs as a set of application programs on a UNIX host. With NetWare for UNIX, the host can provide file and print services to NetWare clients.

Novell recently introduced NetWare/IP, a set of protocol-conversion NLMs that lets NetWare users access native TCP/IP resources without going through IPX. It can also be configured as a gateway to interconnect IPX and IP networks.

> **NOTE:** *In 1993, Novell acquired UNIX System Laboratories (USL) and has since owned the source code to UNIX System V Release 4.2. Novell is currently offering its own UNIX variant, called UnixWare. The product is divided into the UnixWare Application Server for running applications and the UnixWare Personal Edition for operation as a client. Both UnixWare products offer seamless integration with the NetWare operating system.*

IBM SNA Environment Protocols

Novell has maintained a long-standing relationship with IBM to support the Systems Network Architecture (SNA) protocols for communicating with IBM mainframe and minicomputer hosts. NetWare 3.*x* and 4.*x* include an SNA transport stack that can be used to communicate network management information to IBM hosts. These alerts help NetWare fit into enterprise-wide SNA management systems (such as IBM's host-based NetView).

An optional Novell product called NetWare for SAA provides LAN-to-host connectivity. This product enables NetWare clients to establish full communication sessions with IBM hosts. The NetWare HostPrint NLM routes host print jobs directly to NetWare print queues.

Macintosh Environment Protocols

NetWare 3.*x* and 4.*x* support AppleTalk clients through a set of NetWare loadable modules known as NetWare for Macintosh. NetWare for Macintosh allows Macintosh files to be stored on a NetWare server and accessed by both Macintoshes and non-Apple systems. It also provides support for the entire AppleTalk protocol suite, including AppleTalk Filing Protocol (AFP), AppleTalk Data Stream Protocol (ADSP), Printer Access Protocol (PAP), and others. NetWare for Macintosh supports both AppleTalk Phase I and Phase II routing methods.

)SI Standard Protocols

Another optional product, NetWare FTAM (File Transfer Access and Management), implements major protocols from all seven layers of the OSI Reference Model. These protocols include FTAM, ACSE, Presentation, ASN.1, Session, Transport Class 4, and CLNP. By adding support for these OSI protocols, NetWare 3.x and 4.x systems fulfill the basic requirements of the U.S. GOSIP 1.0 specification. Once the NetWare FTAM modules are loaded on the server, FTAM clients can transfer files between NetWare and any other OSI-compliant system. Novell recently transferred the NetWare FTAM product to Firefox Inc. in Kirkland, Washington.

Support for Multiple File Systems

Another important element that enables NetWare to support multiple protocols is the multiple name space capability of the NetWare file system. The original NetWare file system was patterned after the hierarchical system used by UNIX, with some ideas incorporated from the CP/M and DOS file systems as well. Even though the NetWare file system was not the same as that used by DOS, DOS workstations could read and write files on the server by making the appropriate NCP requests.

As the need arose to store other types of files (such as OS/2 and Macintosh files) on the server, Novell enhanced the file system to accommodate *multiple name spaces*. Multiple name spaces allow more than just DOS conventions to be used for naming and storing files. By loading the appropriate name space NLM, NetWare's "universal" file system can support name spaces for files created on the following types of computers:

- DOS/Windows workstations using DOS's File Allocation Table (FAT) system
- OS/2 machines using the High Performance File System (HPFS)
- Macintosh computers using AppleTalk Filing Protocol (AFP)

Through other products, NetWare servers can store files created on the following:

- UNIX workstations using the Network File System (requires NetWare NFS)
- OSI clients using the File Transfer, Access and Management (FTAM) file naming conventions (requires NetWare FTAM)

With name spaces, NetWare assigns each file and directory a DOS-compatible name by default. Files created on other types of workstations can use their own naming conventions. For example, the AppleTalk Filing Protocol used by Macintosh computers allows filenames up to 32 characters long. With the Macintosh name space loaded on a NetWare server, a file created on a Macintosh workstation retains its full Macintosh filename and attributes when stored on that server. If the file is accessed by a DOS workstation, it sees the DOS-compatible filename. The Macintosh name space also accommodates both the data fork and resource fork inherent to all files created on a Macintosh. A fork is a division of a file that holds a particular type of information.

Client Environments

One of the greatest benefits of NetWare is its ability to support a variety of client environments, including DOS, Windows, OS/2, Macintosh, and UNIX. The name space capability discussed previously is one way in which NetWare accommodates the varying needs of these different client types. In most cases, Novell has taken the approach of letting each type of client access NetWare services through their native operating system interfaces. Following are brief descriptions of how various clients interact with NetWare.

DOS/Windows Clients

Before the release of NetWare 4.0 in April 1993, PCs running DOS and Windows communicated with NetWare servers through TSR software known as the NetWare shell. The shell (NETX.COM) sat on top of DOS and intercepted all application requests. If the request could be handled locally (such as a read request for a file on a local hard drive), the shell handed the request to DOS. If it was a network request, the shell formulated it into an IPX/NCP packet and sent it through the network adapter out onto the wire.

With NetWare 4.x and 3.12, Novell introduced a new network interface for DOS/Windows clients: the NetWare DOS Requester. This new software meshes more closely with DOS and is implemented as a set of Virtual Loadable Modules (VLMs). The DOS Requester lets DOS determine which requests can be handled locally and which should be passed on to the network, based on DOS's drive tables and other internal information. Novell calls the DOS Requester its "universal" DOS client software because it allows a PC to interface with NetWare 4.x, 3.x, and 2.x servers, and with servers in Novell's Personal NetWare peer-to-peer networks.

OS/2 Clients

PCs running OS/2 communicate with NetWare servers through the NetWare Requester for OS/2 software. The OS/2 Requester uses IPX/SPX as its transport protocol and NCP as its service protocol. It also provides support for the Named Pipes interprocess communication mechanism that is often used by OS/2 applications through a TSR (terminate-and-stay-resident) program supplied with the Requester.

NetWare 3.x and 4.x support the long filenames that are possible with OS/2's High Performance File System (HPFS). Available since OS/2 1.2, HPFS lets OS/2 users store files under names that exceed the eight-character length limitation imposed by DOS. When OS/2 users store such files on a NetWare server with the OS/2 name space loaded, NetWare automatically assigns them a DOS-compatible name in addition to the long name.

Macintosh Clients

As discussed earlier, Novell supports AppleTalk clients through the NetWare for Macintosh NLMs loaded at the server. When the AppleTalk modules are loaded, they intercept AppleTalk messages from Macintosh clients, translate them into equivalent

IPX messages, and forward the translated messages to the NetWare server. Responses from the NetWare server follow the same path in reverse.

Macintosh clients simply run a NetWare Control Center utility that allows NetWare servers to appear in the Chooser when AppleShare is selected. No changes are necessary to Apple's System 7 operating system already running in the Macintosh. NetWare for Macintosh also provides AppleTalk with an interface to NetWare print queues and other network services.

UNIX Clients

Novell offers several add-on products to facilitate interoperability between UNIX and NetWare. In addition to the products mentioned previously, Novell offers a LAN Workplace product line that provides a TCP/IP protocol stack for DOS, Windows, OS/2, and Macintosh clients on a NetWare network so they can perform Telnet and FTP file transfers from UNIX hosts. A number of third-party vendors also provide TCP/IP-to-NetWare communication products.

Enhancements for WAN Environments

As networks have grown from small, departmental LANs into large, enterprise-wide computing systems, the capabilities of Novell's IPX/SPX and companion protocols have been stretched in ways the original designers had not entirely foreseen. Over the past several years, Novell has provided numerous enhancements to NetWare and other products to better accommodate the requirements of wide area networking environments.

Novell's Multiprotocol Router (MPR)

In 1992, Novell introduced its Multiprotocol Router product to provide more sophisticated routing capabilities. NetWare MPR software is an NLM that runs either on a NetWare server or on a separate computer running NetWare Runtime (a single-connection version of NetWare). In addition to IPX routing, MPR performs routing for TCP/IP, AppleTalk, NetBIOS, and OSI protocols. It also provides more efficient routing over wide area links and supports Point-to-Point Protocol (PPP), Telnet, X-Window, and SNMP for easier remote management. MPR can be managed under Novell's NetWare Management System (NMS) or through a third-party network management console such as Hewlett Packard's OpenView, IBM's NetView, or Sun Microsystems' SunNet Manager.

SAP Filtering

As networks started to be connected over wide area links with limited bandwidth, concern arose that the IPX RIP and SAP traffic between NetWare servers and routers was taking up too much of the available bandwidth. Novell came up with a SAP filter NLM that could be used to limit how much SAP traffic was passed across WAN links. (This filtering mechanism has since been incorporated into the NetWare Multiprotocol Router.)

In addition to reducing the amount of routing and service information being propagated throughout the network, RIP and SAP filtering can be used for security reasons. For example, it can restrict access to accounting servers containing sensitive data.

Large Internet Packet (LIP)

In early versions of NetWare, when a client initially connected to a server, the client would negotiate with the server to determine an acceptable packet size. If the server detected the presence of a router between it and the client, the server limited the maximum packet size to 576 bytes (512 bytes for data plus 30 bytes for the IPX header and 34 bytes for the NCP or SPX header). This occurred regardless of what size packet the network topology and hardware would allow. Since both Ethernet and token ring allow larger packets, this 576-byte packet limitation had an adverse effect on network throughput across routers and bridges.

Novell's Large Internet Packet (LIP) enhances packet throughput over bridges and routers in a NetWare network by allowing the packet size to be increased. With LIP, the client still initiates the packet size negotiation process. However, the server doesn't default to 576 bytes when an intermediate router is detected. Instead, the client checks the maximum packet size supported by the router. LIP functionality is implemented for DOS clients through the NET.CFG file.

Packet Burst Protocol

Novell's Packet Burst protocol is built on top of IPX to speed the transfer of multiple-packet NCP file reads and writes. It does so by eliminating the need to sequence and acknowledge each packet, which often created a "ping-pong" effect over wide area communication links. With Packet Burst, the server or client can send a burst of packets before an acknowledgment is required. Packet Burst monitors dropped packets and retransmits only the missing packets. By adjusting the number of packets in a burst to minimize dropped packets, Packet Burst provides a sliding window-like capability for IPX/NCP communications.

The IPX Registry

To set the stage for the eventual creation of an IPX-based version of TCP/IP's Internet, Novell has established an IPX Network Registry. Through this registry, NetWare users can register their IPX addresses with Novell to ensure that the addresses are unique. Besides facilitating remote network access for mobile NetWare users, having unique IPX addresses will allow NetWare nodes to participate in public networks through services provided by carriers such as AT&T and Sprint.

NetWare Link Services Protocol (NLSP)

Novell's original RIP and SAP protocols were designed when networks were relatively small and usually confined to a single geographic area. As discussed earlier in this chapter, RIP-based routers exchange information about the network's topology through periodic broadcasts with their immediate neighbors. Each node then consolidates the information it has received and passes the summarized data along to other routers, servers, and end nodes (such as printers and workstations). RIP is an example of a *distance-vector* routing protocol.

Some of the characteristics of RIP and SAP are not ideal for large internetworks, especially on a global level. For example, a large amount of routing and service advertising activity can burden the network with frequent broadcast packets. Servers using SAP periodically broadcast their entire services database, taking up substantial LAN bandwidth and saturating low-speed WAN links. If a faulty connection or bad network adapter causes a server to come up and go down frequently, internetwork performance may become sluggish because the servers must continually update their routing tables.

To overcome the limitations of RIP and SAP, Novell has developed the NetWare Link Services Protocol (NLSP). NLSP is a link-state routing protocol that replaces RIP and SAP. *Link-state* protocols scale more readily than distance-vector protocols to handle large, complex internetworks, and they can adapt more quickly to network topology changes.

With RIP-based routers, the Routing Information Tables contain only information about immediately adjacent routers. NLSP-based routers store a complete map of the network. This map includes information about the network's routers and servers, the links connecting them, and the operational status of the routers and links. Clients can find out about available network services through the map maintained by their nearest router. Because they have a clear picture of the entire network, NLSP routers can send packets along the most efficient route to their destination.

With RIP, broadcasts are made even when the routing information has not changed since the previous broadcast. In contrast, NLSP only transmits routing information when something has changed or every two hours, whichever comes first. As a result, NLSP uses less bandwidth over both local and remote connections.

NLSP periodically checks links for connectivity and for the data integrity of the routing information. If a link fails, NLSP switches to an alternate link. It also updates the network topology databases stored in each node when there are connectivity changes anywhere in the routing area. This ensures that all routers can continue to select the optimum routing paths. As with any link-state protocol, NLSP takes longer than distance-vector protocols to calculate the best routes for packets. However, this extra overhead is small in the overall scheme of things. The reduction in bandwidth usage often more than makes up for NLSP's slower convergence speed after a network failure.

NLSP has a standardized management interface so that any SNMP-based management console on a Novell network can monitor and control the operation of an NLSP router. A map of the entire internetwork can be derived from a single NLSP router. The Management Information Base (MIB) implementation for NLSP allows network topology changes to be observed in real time, enabling trouble spots to be isolated and problems solved before they affect the entire network.

NLSP is compatible with existing NetWare routers, enabling servers and routers to be upgraded to NLSP one at a time if necessary. NLSP can automatically detect the presence of non-NLSP routers and servers, and generate the periodic RIP and SAP broadcasts they expect to see. Such broadcasts are restricted to the network segments containing those nodes, so that the rest of the internetwork is not flooded with the high traffic load typical of RIP and SAP communications.

Novell is implementing NLSP as a NetWare loadable module that will run on NetWare 3.11 and later. It will also be included in future releases of NetWare Multiprotocol Router software. RIP and SAP will still be included with NetWare for compatibility with Novell and third-party network devices that have not been upgraded to NLSP, and for communications between routers and workstations.

Novell is also making the NLSP specification available to router vendors and other third-party developers so that they can implement it in their products for compatibility with NetWare networks. Because NLSP is based on the OSI Intermediate System-to-Intermediate System (IS-IS) protocol, vendors who already offer an IS-IS protocol stack can easily adapt it to support NLSP.

Chapter Nine

Connecting
Disparate Systems

by James Pringle,
CompuCom Systems

Until the late 1980s, mission-critical data was mostly housed on mainframes and minicomputers. Computer manufacturers such as Hewlett Packard, IBM, Sun, DEC, Honeywell, and Prime provided the hardware platforms. Each platform used proprietary software and was usually unique in its connectivity requirements. Dumb terminals were connected to their data via asynchronous, twin axial, and coaxial cabling schemes. Access to remote computers usually hinged on the remote computer being the same platform, and remote access was provided either through a host computer or through a concentrator. Each host computer had its own unique operating system. Incompatibilities existed not only between vendors, but also between platforms from the same vendor.

Around 1987, short-haul modems, 3270 gateways, terminal emulation programs, and terminal emulation cards empowered the personal computer to take the place of dumb terminals. Although programs and data still remained centralized on the minicomputer and mainframe platform, users became more productive by gaining the ability to toggle from the mini/mainframe connections while still in their applications. Throughout the 1980s, substantial software and hardware advancements allowed the large platforms to maintain hardware performance and operating system advantages. However, the performance margins between microcomputers and the larger platforms were decreasing rapidly. At this time, PCs were too slow, lacked functionality, memory, and storage, and were too unreliable to be entrusted with critical data.

This began to change starting in 1990. PC technology breakthroughs were occurring at an ever faster pace, quickly lessening the gap between minicomputers and microcomputers. Today, personal computers are able to replace many of the functions that only mainframes and minicomputers were previously capable of. Private and public organizations are starting to *right-size,* moving applications and data to the best-suited platform. Mainframes, minicomputers, and other legacy systems are not outmoded. They are merely being utilized more efficiently. Although many applications are being migrated from the larger computer systems' PC-based networks, the transition will take many years, and in some cases data will remain on these larger platforms for a variety of reasons.

Beginning in the mid-1980s, a connectivity revolution began to form. The demand for information grew. Multiple hosts were needed, and PCs needed to connect to them. Networks were beginning to be implemented. The age of PC network connectivity began. Although the Internet was widely used by the U.S. government and educational community at this time, large PC networks and interconnectivity solutions were not common to the commercial world. Mainframe and minicomputer gateway and terminal solutions began to appear. To support the growing requirements, the movement towards IEEE standard LAN topologies (802.3 and 802.5) gained momentum. Proprietary network topologies such as ARCNET and various nonstandard networking implementations lost their popularity. Certain network protocols had entrenched themselves and became the industry standard, including:

■ Novell's hybrid of XNS (Xerox Network Systems) protocols IPX, SPX, and XNS

■ IBM/Microsoft NetBIOS, SNA LAN DLC

■ Apple's AppleTalk (LocalTalk, EtherTalk, and TokenTalk)

■ XNS and the Xerox protocol family

■ TCP/IP

IS organizations have invested a great deal of money and time to build complex and integrated systems. These systems are productive today and would require years to redevelop and export wholesale to the PC platform. Because of hardware and software specialization, today's enterprise network usually is a multivendor network, with each computer system filling a special need. Computer networks consist of disparate, seemingly unrelated computer equipment unable to share information. These perceived islands of information can be integrated into a true enterprise network from a client workstation perspective. This chapter is structured to expose the reader to the options available to develop a true integrated network from the user's viewpoint. These solutions make it possible to access any network resource from a given client. The network resources we will be targeting in this chapter are PC file servers, IBM hosts, DEC VAXes, HP 3000, and UNIX hosts. On the client side, we are addressing the PC DOS, Microsoft NT, IBM OS/2, and Apple Macintosh workstations.

Intercommunications

Before addressing specific connectivity solutions, we need to establish a general understanding of how connections are made across the network. All interaction on a network takes place through protocols. A *protocol* is a set of rules, defined by mutually agreed upon syntax and meaning, that enables communication between systems. Under a given protocol, a computer can initiate a conversation with another computer by using a redefined vocabulary. Every part of the vocabulary has a specific meaning. By adhering to the protocol implementation, disparate systems can communicate.

The CCITT (Consultative Committee for International Telephony and Telegraphy) and the ISO (International Organization for Standardization) developed guidelines for layered networks and protocols. Known as the OSI (Open Systems Interconnection) model, it was designed to provide standardized design and methodologies for connections between systems. In February 1980, the IEEE (Institute of Electronic and Electrical Engineers) began Project 802. Although the 802 model adheres to the OSI Physical layer, the IEEE committee further subdivided the Data Link layer into two separate layers. These are known as the MAC (Media Access Control) and LLC (Logical Link Control) layers.

The MAC layer defines the access method to the transmission medium. The MAC layer is comprised of further standards, each defining a specific frame format. These frames are:

- 802.3 CSMA/CD (Carrier Sense Multiple Access/Collision Detection)
- 802.4 Token Passing Bus
- 802.5 Token Passing Ring
- 802.6 Packet Switching in a Metropolitan Area Network

The LLC layer is defined by the IEEE 802.2 standard (see Figure 9-1). The LLC layer is responsible for reliable transmission of the data packets across the Physical layer. The MAC layer handles the addressing of the data packet to be sent across the Physical layer. One responsibility of the MAC layer is to provide the source and destination address of the packet. This address is known as the MAC address and is either provided on the ROM of the NIC (Network Interface Card) or is software configured. The major difference between the OSI Data Link layer and the IEEE LLC layer are SAPs (Service Access Points). SAPs allow communication access to multiple higher-layer processes. Simply put, SAPs are a means by which multiple conversations can be held from one layer of the OSI model to another.

We will be limiting our discussion in this chapter to four of the seven layers of the OSI model: the Data Link layer, the Network layer, the Transport layer, and the Session layer. We will not be discussing the details of the Presentation and Application layers, as we are not concerned with the format of the message or the data. Additionally, no discussion will be made about the Physical layer. The assumption is that the transmission endpoints are accessible through a network conforming to the IEEE 802 standard.

Under the OSI model, each layer can only communicate to a peer layer. Figure 9-2 depicts a data packet being sent from one computer to another. The data packet (consisting of Application and Presentation layer information) has additional control information appended to it as it cascades through the various layers. Each layer sandwiches the packet information (called a *protocol data unit*, or *PDU*) from the previous level with header and trailer information. The total packet is formed by the time it reaches the Data Link layer. There it is placed in a frame and transported across the network using Physical layer protocols. A large data packet may be segmented and placed in more than one frame for delivery. When frames arrive at the destination, the data packet rises up through each layer. As it is passed off to each layer, the protocol information that belongs to each layer is stripped off until the raw data arrives at the Application layer of the destination system. Each layer uses the information passed to it from the peer layer of the sending system to coordinate and control its particular function in the communication process with its peer layer.

The Data Link Layer

The Data Link layer reduces the data frames to be transmitted into a format that corresponds to the Physical layer. The Physical layer could be fiber-optic, unshielded twisted pair, coaxial cable, and so on. Additionally, the structure of the frame will vary by topology such as token ring or Ethernet. So, for example, the Data Link layer could

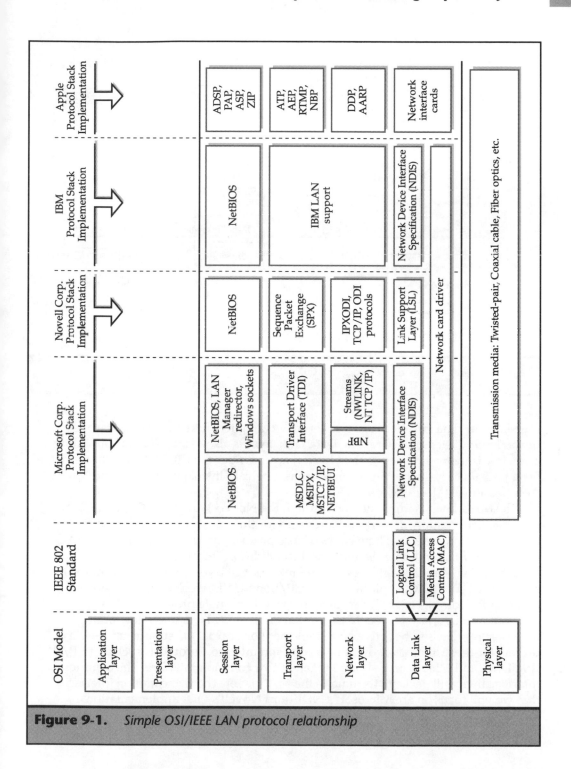

Figure 9-1.   *Simple OSI/IEEE LAN protocol relationship*

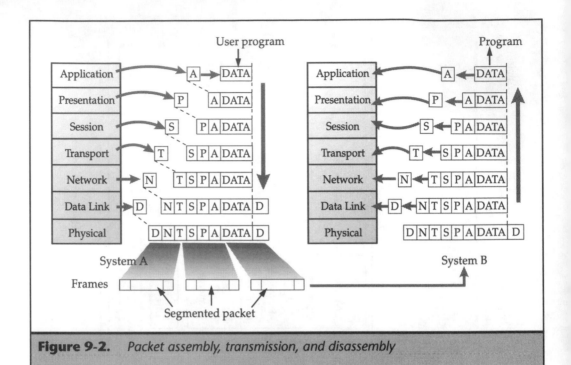

Figure 9-2. *Packet assembly, transmission, and disassembly*

translate our data into electrical signals conforming to a token ring format across unshielded twisted-pair wire. The Data Link layer is also responsible for providing error-free transmission across the Physical layer. Under the IEEE 802 specification, the Data Link layer is divided into two sections: Logical Link Control (LLC) and Media Access Control (MAC) layers.

The MAC layer is implemented through the Network Interface Card (NIC). NIC manufacturers supply drivers and interfaces for their cards to be used on different operating environments. There are two basic protocol types that address the MAC layer's *monolithic* and *common* interface. Monolithic protocols address the MAC layer directly rather than through the Logical Link Control layer. Some monolithic examples are Novell's IPX/SPX, AppleTalk, and TCP/IP on UNIX workstations. Users of monolithic protocols typically are able to use only a single protocol per NIC.

Common interface protocols are located on the LLC layer and allow multiple transport protocols to be active on a single network card. NIC suppliers provide drivers for these interfaces. By using a common interface, protocols such as TCP/IP, IPX, DLC, and others can be bound together to a common interface. The common interface then will package the data to the MAC layer. The two common interfaces that we will focus on are Microsoft's NDIS and Novell's ODI implementations.

In 1989, Microsoft and 3Com jointly developed an interface to allow transport protocol drivers (IEEE layers 3 and 4) to communicate with the MAC layer. This interface was published as the Network Device Interface Specifications (NDIS). NDIS supports up to four NDIS-compliant transport protocol drivers to be bound to any single NIC. The NDIS interface is not only used by Microsoft in all of its networking products, but also by IBM, DEC Pathworks, and LAN Manager for UNIX. Most NDIS implementations use a protocol manager as the interface overseer. Microsoft NT's implementation is known as an NDIS wrapper.

Also around 1989, Novell and Apple jointly developed the Open Data-link Interface (ODI). Founded upon similar concepts as NDIS, ODI supports up to four ODI-compliant transport protocol drivers. ODI is managed by the Link Support Layer (LSL). Although announced at around the same time as NDIS, the ODI developer's specifications and toolkits were not readily available until a year later. Additionally, as Microsoft continues to dominate the workstation interface through its Windows products, its networking methodology will, as well. Due to the different implementations, NDIS and ODI are not compatible. To use ODI with NDIS, Novell has released a patch program called ODINSUP. ODINSUP operates as a translator between NDIS and ODI.

The Network Layer

The Network layer is responsible for establishing the route from the source node to the destination node on the communications subnet. The Network layer also supplies the destination address to the frame, performs the route calculation, packet disassembly, and reassembly in the proper order, determines the link to dispatch the packet, and performs congestion control. The protocols from Figure 9-1, and their uses, are discussed next.

Microsoft

- *MSDLC*   Provides IBM SNA connectivity (IBM AS/400, remote printer support) in Microsoft networks.

- *MSIPX*   Provides Novell IPX connectivity to NetWare servers.

- *NetBEUI*   Codeveloped by IBM and Microsoft, NetBEUI is a transport protocol that integrates with NetBIOS to provide a communication system for workgroup LANs. It is not intended for wide area networking.

- *MSTCP/IP*   Microsoft protocol for connecting to IP (Internet Protocol).

Novell

- *IPX*   Provides the standard connectivity protocols in the NetWare environment.
- *IP*   Provides Internet protocol for connecting to IP hosts in the NetWare environment.

IBM

- *LAN Support*   Provides the same connectivity as NetBEUI and NetBIOS in the Microsoft protocol stack.

Apple

- *DDP (Datagram Delivery Protocol)*   Packages data in 568-byte datagrams for delivery over AppleTalk networks.

NOTE: Networks are usually classified by Network layer protocols. It is common practice (though not necessarily technically correct) to classify a workstation connected to another station by its Transport and/or Network layer protocols. Examples would include an IPX or a TCP/IP connection.

The Transport Layer

The Transport layer builds upon the services of the Network layer and provides the uppermost layers with reliable transport service between systems. Other responsibilities are error recognition and recovery, transmit rates, addressing of application processes, and congestion control. Each of the transport protocols in Figure 9-1 provides the control process for a reliable transmission. For example, Sequenced Packet Exchange (SPX), as discussed in Chapter 8, provides reliable transport services in the Novell NetWare protocol environment, and TCP provides reliable services in the Internet's TCP/IP protocol stack.

The Session Layer

The Session layer manages the dialogue between systems. The Session layer determines whether the conversation will be full duplex (two-way simultaneous), half duplex (two-way, one at a time), or simplex (send or receive only). Timing and synchronization with interrupt points are also assumed.

As illustrated in Figure 9-1, NetBIOS is commonly used at this layer, although it is falling into disuse due to its lack of support for wide area networking. NetBIOS (Network Basic Input Output System) is responsible for establishing logical names on the network, establishing connections (sessions) between two logical names, and reliable data transfer between two sessions. The NetBIOS Session layer interface was originally developed by Sytek Inc. for IBM's broadband computer network. To support the emerging standard, Microsoft developed a compatible NetBIOS interface. Some earlier implementations of Novell protocols were also based on NetBIOS.

Novell's Session layer protocol centers around NCP (NetWare Core Protocol). NCP provides file services, print services, name management services, synchronization, and NDS (NetWare Directory Services). NCP is implemented on both the client and NetWare file server. On the client, it is implemented in the NetWare shell, and access is limited to an NCP server. NCP uses the IPX protocol directly and provides session control, error detection, and retransmission.

Gateways

In considering connectivity solutions, the gateway is often overlooked and underestimated. Gateways are generally workstations or servers, combined with software to perform protocol conversion. An example would be NetWare for LAT (Local Area Transport). A workstation can connect to a LAT gateway using the IPX protocol. The gateway converts conversations based on IPX to LAT in order to connect to DEC VAX systems. The VAX, likewise, communicates back to the workstation through the LAT gateway. Gateways play an important role in providing connectivity to different operating environments and protocols. Gateways can augment a single protocol network by allowing connectivity to hosts, which may not support the protocols employed by the network environment. Following the trend of standardizing on a single network protocol, gateways can provide 3270, AS/400, DEC, Hewlett Packard, TCP/IP, and AppleTalk connectivity solutions by using a single protocol such as IPX, NetBIOS, or TCP/IP.

Figure 9-3 illustrates a few gateway combinations. Gateways are generally used for dynamic connections, protocol integrity, sharing of resources, and meeting special connectivity needs not available directly on the network.

Dynamic connectivity leverages resources. By availing a set of connections between users, more users than connections can be supported. For example, assume that we have 500 users in the company. Some of these users seldom need connectivity to an IBM mainframe, some frequently use the mainframe, and others always require mainframe connections. A gateway need only be configured once for the mainframe connection, and from then on supports all users (see Figure 9-3, segment A). In addition, should new users be added to the network, or should existing users relocate, the interface remains the same without any need for reconfiguring the host. With this method, a many-to-one relationship can be implemented by providing one connection for every two or three users, according to necessity.

Segment B in Figure 9-3 shows that IPX/SPX clients and NetBEUI clients can connect with the UNIX system through the gateway using TCP/IP protocols. Segment C shows IPX/SPX clients communicating through the gateway to an IBM

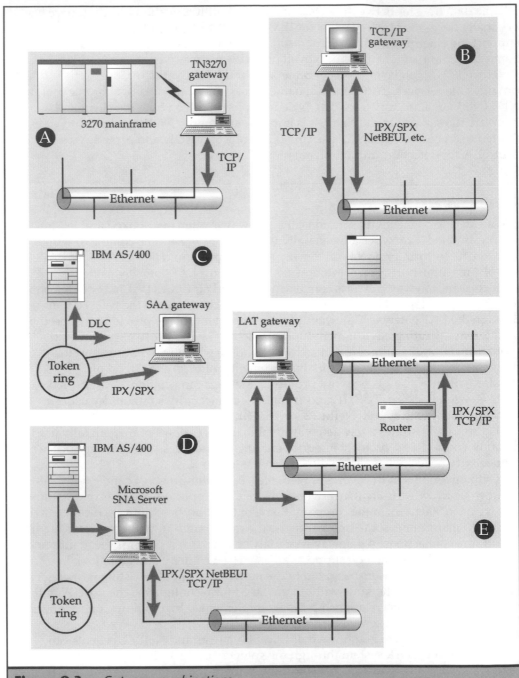

Figure 9-3. *Gateway combinations*

minicomputer system. Segment D shows a variety of protocols supported by the Microsoft SNA Server, thus allowing access to the IBM minicomputer system.

Gateways allow the network engineer to maintain protocol integrity across the enterprise network. Implementing a gateway solution can eliminate the need to maintain a variety of protocols. Under most routed environments, only routable protocols such as TCP/IP or IPX are supported between network segments. Any other protocols are prevented from passing from one segment to another. Segment E in Figure 9-3 illustrates a gateway solution. In this example, we want to connect to the DEC VAX located on the segment shown. The VAX can only understand LAT (Local Area Transport) or DECnet in our example. Our workstation can only speak IPX/SPX and TCP/IP. The gateway becomes an intermediary. We converse with the gateway, which translates our requests to LAT and sends the information back across the Ethernet segment to the DEC VAX. The gateway provides access to the VAX when we would not otherwise be able to converse.

Gateways leverage limited resources both on the workstation and on the host. Directly connecting to a given host usually requires additional protocols to be added to the workstation. Resources on the workstation may be scarce. For instance, connecting to an AS/400 could require one or more protocol stacks to be run in conjunction with the LAN protocol stack. By using a gateway, users can connect to the desired host using their current LAN protocol, thus eliminating additional configuration and protocol support on various computers. Figure 9-3 demonstrates a few possible combinations. On the host side, a gateway permits a user community with a simple managed client interface, while only requiring a single interface to the host. For example, Segment A is a gateway connected to an IBM mainframe using a telecommunications line. In this example we can utilize an existing V.35, X.25, or other interface without purchasing additional host equipment or software, which tends to cost significantly more than a gateway solution.

There are a plethora of gateway products available for just about every need. The hardest part of a gateway solution is locating the providers and discerning the gateway best suited for your environment. In addition to third-party solutions, most large computer manufacturers have their own gateway products. Although gateways are often a viable solution, there are some drawbacks to using them, as listed next, rather than setting up direct connections with clients.

- Some gateways only provide simple terminal emulation to the desired host.
- You may be limited to certain file transfer options.
- Gateways usually do not support a full suite of functions versus installing the full protocol implementation on the workstation.
- There are limited connections to a host for each gateway, such as 32, 64, 128, or 255.

Although not suited for every environment, gateways will usually meet the general user community requirements. Before you decide on a gateway solution, be sure to investigate the capabilities and limitations of the product. Most customer dissatisfaction arises from user's unmet expectations of service.

Table 9-1 lists a few common gateway solutions to get you started. This is far from being a comprehensive list; consult with gateway vendors for other possible solutions.

NOS and Host Interconnectivity

A few Network Operating Systems (NOSs) have proven to be so popular that they have implementations on platforms other than PC file servers. The two major ones are Novell NetWare and Microsoft LAN Manager (and more recently Microsoft NT Advanced Server). Although not identical in services, the various implementations range from basic client connectivity to peer-to-peer file access and printing services.

Microsoft LAN Manager has been around since the mid-1980s in various forms. IBM LAN Server and 3Com 3Share were based on Microsoft LAN Manager. The Microsoft LAN Manager NOS has been implemented on the DEC as Pathworks, and under a UNIX variant on UNIX as LAN Manager for UNIX (LMU). Microsoft NT Advanced Server itself is slated to be a portable operating system, supporting the DEC ALPHA, MIPS, and various other RISC platforms at this time. In these environments, the client workstation can use a single connectivity solution.

True to Novell's stated direction of NetWare becoming a portable NOS, NetWare's base services have been exported to two other platforms. These two implementations are NetWare for VMS (DEC VAX) and NetWare for UNIX. Although supported at one time by Novell, NetWare for VMS was released back to the original developers, Interconnections. Novell pressed ahead with its own vision by purchasing USL (UNIX System Laboratories) from AT&T.

NetWare for UNIX servers is UNIX V, Release 4.2, with NetWare features added in. Under UnixWare for UNIX, both UNIX and PC client workstations can share

3270 (IBM Mainframe)	5250 (AS/400, SYS/38)	DEC LAT	TCP/IP to UNIX Host
Novell NetWare SAA gateway	Novell NetWare SAA	Novell NetWare for LAT	Novix for NetWare (Firefox)
Microsoft SNA Server	Microsoft SNA Server		Catipult (Ipswitch)
EICON gateway (Eicon Technologies)	EICON gateway		
TN3270 (various manufacturers)			

Table 9-1.   *Gateway Solutions for Some Common Computing Environments*

files and print services between the two operating systems. Novell supports NFS (Network File System), which allows the UNIX clients to view the server as a UNIX host. Look to the late 1990s for true seamless connectivity between NetWare and UNIX. With UnixWare, Novell is on the road to true seamless integration of NetWare and UNIX. It has even gone so far as to submit SPX/IPX as a standard UNIX protocol to the standards committee.

Printing

Printing services play an important part in interoperability support. In designing a heterogeneous solution, print services are a necessity. Most printing done by hosts is performed by printers connected to the host only. Terminal emulation products have been the only exception to that in supporting local workstation printing.

Until 1993, most printers were connected directly into PC file servers, shared through a hardware spooling device, or serviced by a single protocol print server. Excepting terminal emulation packages, most printing from hosts was performed by host-connected printers. In 1993, a surge of multiprotocol NIC printer cards and print servers emerged.

Now, printers made by Hewlett Packard and Lexmark, can be configured as through on-board NICs, print servers for TCP/IP hosts, MS LAN Manager, IBM LAN Server, DECnet, and NetWare servers simultaneously. Not to be outdone, external print servers such as those from IBM, Lantronix, and others now also support multiprotocol connections. Not all host systems are able to use print servers; many still use gateways to service printers. Be prepared to see this change over the next year or so.

Interoperability

The previous sections of this chapter have described how client workstations communicate across the network and the internal steps that are required to establish a session with another system. The communications section explained the mysteries of the network connection. The gateway section discussed connection method alternatives to burdening the client with servicing connections between hosts. The NOS interoperability section will detail the status of current interconnectivity of local area networks. Lastly, the printing section will restate the importance of printing to a heterogeneous system.

The message of this chapter is to reveal the current methods and solutions for providing user access to the various resources across the network. This includes supporting multiple PC LAN servers simultaneously as well as mini/mainframe computer system connections. As explained earlier in this chapter, our host systems discussion will be directed toward the IBM mainframe, IBM AS/400, DEC VAX, HP 3000, and UNIX hosts. The connectivity solutions will revolve around the client workstation connecting to some or all of these computer systems. The client workstations that we will be working with are the Apple Macintosh and the IBM PC compatible running DOS, OS/2, or NT. The PC network server configurations will be the IBM LAN Server, Microsoft LAN Manager, and Novell NetWare.

Every network environment is different. Some support a single protocol, others support a suite of protocols, and still others do not attempt to control protocol traffic at all. We can generally divide these network configurations into three categories, discussed next.

Large Networks (10,000+ nodes)

These are routed networks with collapsed backbones supporting one or two protocols on a global scale, but allowing other protocols on local segments. Large networks tend to have a broad range of hosts (mini/mainframe computers) and various file servers connected in a complex to extremely complex configuration.

Medium Networks (1000 to 10,000 nodes)

These networks support combinations of bridging and routing. Usually these networks have recognized a need to migrate to fewer network protocols, but still support special cases on a global scale. The medium networks normally contain 40 to 50 host systems. Local network segments tend to use a larger suite of network protocols. Networks this size are attempting to limit bridging and multiprotocol support, trying to consolidate to three or fewer. Network configurations vary from above average to very complex.

Small Networks (10 to 1000 nodes)

These networks tend to support a broad suite of protocols. Resource connectivity is the driving source of support of what is implemented. The network usually contains one to three host (mini/mainframe computers) systems.

We are going to model each of these networks and the connectivity solutions. In providing solutions, we will be referring to the tables—called solution matrixes—at the end of this chapter. They are used to supply choices given certain operating environments. The products mentioned are solutions familiar to the author. There may exist other comparable products.

Large Network Configurations

Figure 9-4 shows an example of a large network. Most large network solutions implement routing to minimize traffic and use bandwidth efficiently. These networks typically support IPX and TCP/IP as the only routed protocols. Rapidly gaining popularity, though, is IBM's APPN (Advanced Peer-to-Peer Networking). APPN is IBM's method of routing SNA traffic. Due to the large installed base of IBM equipment, a grassroots movement is the driving force of APPN implementation rather than any standards committee. Many routers and hubs are beginning to support APPN.

Although only one network segment is shown per building, it is actually made up of many routed or bridged segments. Peer-to-peer services such as Windows for

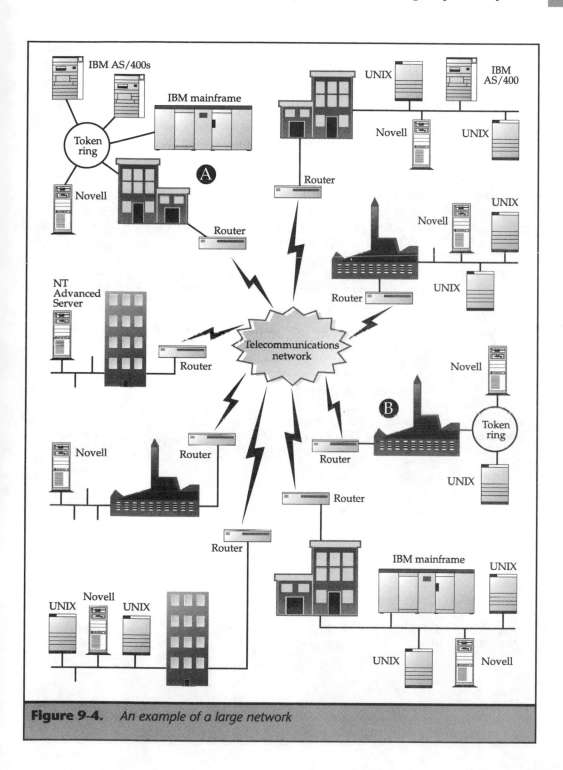

Figure 9-4. *An example of a large network*

Workgroups, using protocols such as NetBEUI, are typically supported only on local segments due to their broadcasting nature. The workstations in our example are DOS/Novell, DOS/Windows for Workgroups/Novell, AppleTalk/Novell, and DOS/Windows for Workgroups. Although only one icon for each type of hardware is shown, there are actually many servers and hosts.

On segment A, we have IBM mainframes and AS/400s. The workstations can connect to the mainframe and AS/400 directly, using only TCP/IP. IBM does not have a terminal emulator that uses TCP/IP connections in DOS. The WSF (Work Station Function) program in IBM's PC Support program supports only the DLC connection, which is not routed on our network. However, local users that are bridged could use the DLC protocol. This would pertain to segments A and B. Users using the TCP/IP protocol would have to use a product such as Attachmate's EXTRA! for their terminal emulation. See Table 9-2 for other solutions.

Operating System	3270	5250	DEC	HP 3000	UNIX-Based
DOS	Reflections EXTRA! DCA IBM\various	Reflections EXTRA! DCA IBM\various	Reflections DEC Interconnect	Reflections HP	Reflections Novell DEC
Microsoft Windows	Reflections EXTRA! Rumba IBM* Novell*	Reflections EXTRA! Rumba IBM* Novell*	Rumba DEC* Novell		Rumba Novell Attachmate
OS/2	IBM Rumba	IBM Rumba			IBM Rumba
Windows NT	Microsoft* Rumba EXTRA!	Microsoft* Rumba EXTRA!	Microsoft* Rumba Reflections Extra		Microsoft Rumba Reflections Extra
Apple Macintosh	EXTRA! Apple*	EXTRA! Apple*	Reflections		Reflections Apple Extra

*Solution provided by third party

Table 9-2.   *Terminal Emulation*

If you are directly connecting to all hosts via TCP/IP and using IPX for NetWare, the startup files should look similar to those shown here:

CONFIG.SYS
device=himem.sys
device=emm386.exe
dos=high,umb
other.. .. ...

AUTOEXEC.BAT
path.. ...
.. .. ..
lh LSL
<NIC Card Driver,ex. 3c509.com>
IPXODI
VLM

Under Novell, the TCP/IP address and configuration parameters are maintained under a text file called NET.CFG.

Shown next is the same configuration, but with IBM LAN support:

CONFIG.SYS
device=himem.sys
device=emm386.exe
dos=high,umb
device=protman.dos
device=NIC Driver,ex. ELNKIII.DOS>
device=DXMAOMOD.sys
device=DXMCOMOD.sys *(token ring)*
OR
device=DXMEOMOD.sys *(ethernet)*
device=DMXTOMOD.sys *(token ring)*

AUTOEXEC.BAT
path.. ...
.. .. ..
NETBIND
lh LSL
<NIC Card Driver,ex. 3c509.com>
IPXODI
VLM
ODINSUP

The LAN support program supplies the DLC drivers to direct-connect to an IBM mainframe and/or AS/400.

When using Windows for Workgroups, install the Microsoft TCP/IP stack and use NetWare IPX. In Windows for Workgroups, the TCP/IP information is under a file called PROTOCOL.INI in the Windows directory. Microsoft also has a DLC driver that will give us the equivalent functionality of the IBM LAN Support. The best recommendation, if all servers are Novell, is to use Novell's LAN Workplace with Windows, not Microsoft's Windows for Workgroups. If there is a Microsoft LAN Manager or NT Advanced Server, then use the Microsoft protocols for those users connecting to the NT server (see Table 9-3). NetWare performs best with LAN Workplace. Microsoft products are optimized for Microsoft networking products. Refer back to Table 9-2 for a list of some terminal emulators available under Windows.

OS/2 and Macintosh PCs can use LAN Workplace for the TCP/IP services. These services will give them access to all of the host systems via TCP/IP and IPX. NetWare,

Operating Environment	TCP/IP Stack	NetBIOS	DLC	SPX/IPX
DOS/Windows	MSTCPIP	NetBEUI	MSDLC	MSIPX
Microsoft NDIS	LAN Work group	ODINSUP*	ODINSUP*	IPXODI
Novell ODI	FTP	LAN Support	LAN Support	
IBM NDIS	WRQ			
Other	Wollongong			
Microsoft NT	MSTCPIP	NetBEUI	MSDLC	MSIPX
Microsoft NDIS				NT Client
Novell ODI				
OS/2	OS/2 Client	OS/2 Client	OS/2 Client	Novell
IBM		LAN Man		Client
Microsoft		Client		
Novell				
**Apple	WRQ IP			
WRQ				

*ODINSUP allows ODI and NDIS to work together.
**AppleTalk is supported by Novell and MS LAN Manager and NT Advanced Server.

Table 9-3.   *Protocol Stacks*

NT Advanced Server, and Microsoft LAN Manager all support OS/2 client software and AppleTalk connectivity for local PC file server access.

The most popular method to connect to the AS/400 and IBM mainframe across a network, exhibited in Figure 9-5, is to use a TN3270, Novell SAA, or Microsoft SNA gateway. The gateway would be located on the segment of the IBM host to support true SNA traffic on that segment. We connect to the gateways using either IPX or TCP/IP. Direct connections require constant maintenance and support—such as VTAM--from the host side. A gateway only has to be configured once, and users can share the connection without conflicting with other users. The gateway will dynamically allocate its resources to connecting users.

The one caveat of using a gateway versus a direct connect is that they usually do not support all of the SNA functionality. Most gateways only support printer and terminal emulation services. IBM's direction is APPC (Advanced Program-to-Program Communications). Although not globally supported at this time, expect gateways to support true LU6.2 in the near future. LU6.2 support is needed to support the client/server applications using Microsoft's ODBC (Open Database Connectivity) and IBM's DRDA (Distributed Relational Database Architecture), APIs (application

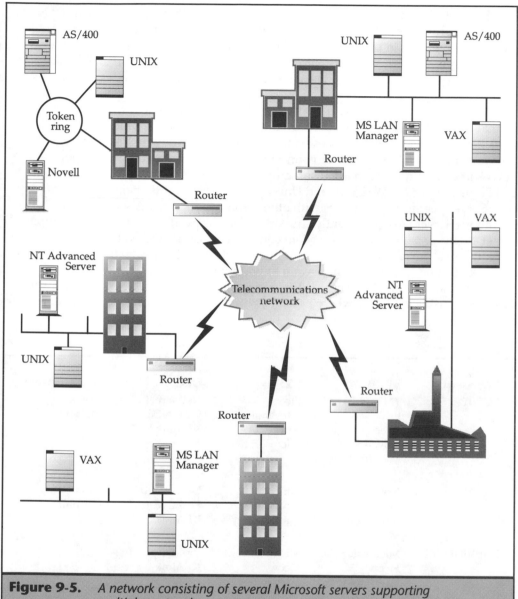

Figure 9-5.   *A network consisting of several Microsoft servers supporting multiple protocols*

programming interfaces) for client/server database access. Where possible, use gateways to provide the IBM connectivity, and you will find your network much easier to support.

The UNIX host's connectivity is solved by using the Microsoft TCP/IP or LAN Workplace protocol stacks as mentioned before. The VAXes support two types of connection methods in our model. The first is TCP/IP and the second is LAT (Local Area Transport). Users can connect to the LAT gateway using TCP/IP or IPX (see Table 9-4 for gateway matrices). The gateway is located on the same segment as the VAX to resolve routing problems.

Until recently, most VAX and UNIX users have been content to run terminal emulation and file transfer functions. Another solution exists in which the client workstation can have peer services on these machines. Under the VAX umbrella, NetWare for VAX allows NetWare connectivity and DEC Pathworks to support Microsoft connectivity. Both Microsoft and Novell support UNIX peer services with LAN Manager for UNIX (LMU) and UnixWare. LMU supports client connectivity only. Server peer-to-peer services with other products such as LAN Manager or NT Advanced Server are not currently supported. UnixWare, on the other hand, supports server-to-server peer services and client connectivity. UNIX and NetWare servers actually can share resources in addition to supporting each other's clients. Although it may take awhile, UnixWare will play an important part in future connectivity.

In summary, for the large network, we can communicate to all of our hosts using TCP/IP. By using gateways where possible, we eliminate the need for nonroutable

Protocol	3270	5250	DEC	UNIX-Based
TCP/IP	TN3270 Eicon Technology Novell SAA Microsoft SNA	Eicon Technology Novell SAA Microsoft SNA	NetWare LAT ProLINC LAT KEAlink LAT	Novix Catipult
PSX/IPX	Novell SAA Eicon Technology	Reflections Eicon Technology	NetWare LAT ProLINC LAT KEAlink LAT	Novix Catipult
NetBEUI	Microsoft SNA Eicon Technology	Microsoft SNA Eicon Technology	ProLINC LAT KEAlink	

Table 9-4.   *Gateways*

protocols across the network and minimize administrative support on the IBM hosts. Gateways exist for both the LAT and SNA architectures should it be decided not to support direct connectivity to the hosts. Both Microsoft and Novell supply TCP/IP solutions.

1edium Network Configurations

The major difference between a large and medium network is that in a medium network, we are likely to see bridging used more often than routing to interconnect network segments. More protocol suites can be used under a bridged network than a routed one. However, routed solutions do apply in the medium network as well as in the large.

With bridged environment, a large community of AppleTalk clients, for example, can function as a single network. As we pointed out in the discussion of large networks, NT Advanced Server, LAN Manager, and NetWare all support the AppleTalk protocols. Figure 9-5 illustrates a network consisting of several Microsoft servers that support multiple protocols. In this environment, NetBIOS is an important

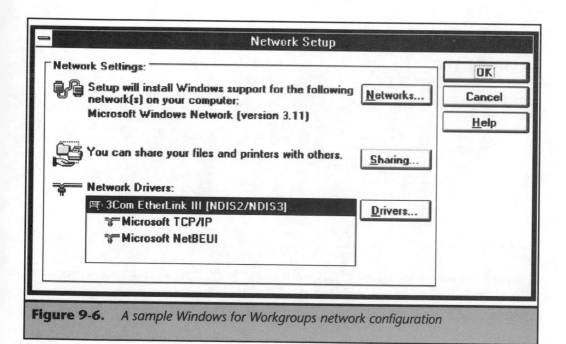

Figure 9-6. *A sample Windows for Workgroups network configuration*

protocol. We can choose to connect to our servers and hosts with either NetBIOS (Microsoft NetBEUI) or TCP/IP. Figure 9-6 illustrates a configuration dialog box in the Windows for Workgroups environment. Note in the lower box under Network Drivers that both Microsoft TCP/IP and Microsoft NetBEUI are installed and operating over the 3Com EtherLink III device driver. For DOS connections, under a Microsoft solution, we can use the Microsoft LAN Manager or IBM LAN Support solution. (These configurations also work with Microsoft Windows.)

Here are sample startup files for a Windows for Workgroup configuration:

CONFIG.SYS	**AUTOEXEC.BAT**
device=himem.sys	path.. ...
device=emm386.exe	.. ...
dos=high,umb	umb
other.......	tcptsr
device=ifshelp.sys	tinyrfc
	nmtsr.exe
	emsbfr.exe
	net start

And shown next are sample startup files for an IBM LAN Support configuration:

CONFIG.SYS	**AUTOEXEC.BAT**
device=himem.sys	path.....
device=emm386.exe	.....
dos=high,umb	netbind
other.......	
device=protman.dos	
device=<NIC driver,ex. ELNKIII.DOS>	
device=DXMAOMOD.sys	
device=DXMCOMOD.sys (token ring)	
OR	
device=DXMEOMOD.SYS (ethernet)	
device=DXMTOMOD.SYS (token ring)	

This configuration does not supply TCP/IP. For TCP/IP support, third-party products such as the FTP, Wollongong, or Novell TCP/IP could be used.

Here are sample startup files for the Microsoft LAN Manager DOS client supporting TCP/IP, NetBEUI, and Microsoft DLC:

CONFIG.SYS	**AUTOEXEC.BAT**
device=himem.sys	path...
device=emm386.exe	.....
dos=high,umb	umb.exe
device=protman.dos	net start work station
device=<NIC card driver,ex. ELNKIII.DOS>	load netbeui
device=tcpip.drv	load tcpip
device=nemm.exe	load DLC

These drivers are part of the Microsoft LAN Manager package. The DLC drivers equate to the IBM LAN Support drivers. With DLC, we can establish LU6.2 connections with IBM hosts.

In summary, the connectivity solutions for the large network hold true for the medium network as well. The difference is usually that more bridging occurs, which allows increased use of nonroutable protocols such as DLC and NetBIOS in specific workgroup areas.

mall Network Configurations

A small network configuration (see Figure 9-7) can have all the properties of a large and medium configuration, but in many cases, the networks operate in a peer-to-peer configuration. There are a number of peer-to-peer solutions, including those listed here:

- Microsoft Windows for Workgroups
- Macintoshes running AppleTalk
- DOS systems running Artisoft's LANtastic
- DOS systems running Novell's NetWare Lite

Larger networks usually use Microsoft NT Advanced Server, Microsoft LAN Manager, or Novell NetWare with peer-to-peer services available. These larger networks are usually bridged or actually contained on one segment or on multiple segments that are interconnected with bridges. Because routing is typically not used, all of the protocol configurations mentioned in the large and medium networks can be used.

It is not necessary to use gateways unless wide area connections are utilized. If wide area connections are being used, it is recommended that a more suitable protocol (less broadcast and not easily given to time-outs) be used. Protocols such as TCP/IP and IPX are recommended.

In summary, small networks do not usually have the same constraints as the larger networks. Since they tend to be locally connected and use less bandwidth, routing is

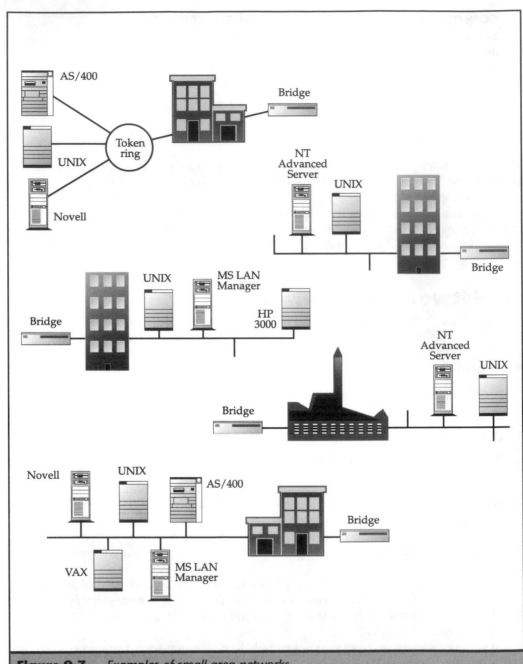

Figure 9-7.   *Examples of small area networks*

not necessary. Administrators have a larger choice of connectivity options. Although more solutions are available, you should consider the growth and goal of the network. If it has potential to grow into a larger network, the network engineer should build a connectivity foundation for future expansion that implements network protocols more suited to wide area connectivity, such as the TCP/IP protocol suite.

PART THREE

Application-Level Technologies and Services

Chapter 10

Enabling Technologies for Distributed Enterprise Environments

by J.D. Marymee, Novell, Inc.

As the networking industry has progressed, the technologies used to create enterprise networks have expanded significantly. No longer can a single vendor provide all the interoperability needed to implement a functional, efficient enterprise network. Much like building blocks, these technologies leverage today's off-the-shelf hardware into low-cost, flexible computing systems.

In the 1980s, the early days of PC computing, it was enough simply to be able to share data among multiple users, initially just to make efficient use of expensive hard disks and printers. While still true today, the LAN industry is moving more toward *cooperative* processing instead of just simple file sharing. This has resulted in other technologies being created to further the sharing and utilization of data.

Several of these new technologies include:

- Client/server strategies
- Remote procedure-based data exchange
- Information organization through directory services
- Protection of data through security
- Coordination of global networks through time synchronization
- Easing file management through distributed file services
- Exchanging information through messaging systems
- Simplifying the use of systems through user interfaces
- Coordinating shared work through document interchange
- Coordination of data within applications using DDE (Dynamic Data Exchange) and OpenDoc

Using these technologies in a cooperative manner will enable the computing systems of today to interoperate at a much higher level of efficiency, both for the data being processed and for the user.

With a variety of technologies to choose from, it can be confusing for an IS (Information Systems) manager to design a workable system that interoperates with emerging technologies while still utilizing the old. There's not necessarily only one "right" system. Different integrated systems yield different levels of results based on hardware and software selections.

With this in mind, this chapter is designed to help people choose systems that can best provide the results required for a particular organization.

Client/Server Architecture

Though client/server is a very hot topic, very few applications take full advantage of a networked environment and today's technology. A good example is the way most monthly statements are still processed today—in a monolithic, centralized processing environment. The past decade advanced how users perceive an application (via the user interface), and the applications are easier to use and they do more. Yet they don't distribute the workload around the network efficiently. In fact, the predominant applications are single-user in nature, but behave adequately in a networked environment.

In a client/server environment, logic or data is shared across several platforms (whether the same or different CPU types), thus executing the parts of the application in the most effective location. Depending on the sophistication of the application, the processing may be distributed among two or more locations, allowing the application to scale based on user requirements.

A good example for client/server processing is a database. When a user runs a single-user database, the application is downloaded from the file server and loaded in its entirety at the workstation. Data still usually resides on the server. When a record is retrieved, the database requests the data as if it were located locally. Therefore, if a search is occurring, the database must make multiple requests to the server while searching for the record. This monopolizes significant bandwidth, especially if the database is large and the record is located deep within the database.

In a client/server application, processing and databases can be split up. Therefore, the code can be executed in the most efficient place, decreasing network load and actually improving response time. Using this model, the lookup engine of the database could be stored on a server of some type. This could be a file server based on OS/2, NetWare, UNIX, or some other operating system robust enough to handle many requests. The engine's only responsibility would be to take multiple requests, process them locally, and then return results. The front-end application would merely be the user interface, presenting a clear and user-helpful navigation screen, while also providing pleasing formatted data returned to the workstation.

For instance, a pilot (user) needs to look up statistics for a certain airplane before flying it. In this case, let's say the plane is a Bellanca Citabria. The flow of the lookup would be something like this:

1. The pilot, looking for Bellanca, requests a record from the database of airplanes.
2. The user interface formats the request for the send and hands it to the transport mechanism.
3. The transport (consisting of IPX/SPX, NetBIOS, TCP/IP, and so on) sends the request to the server (database engine).
4. The engine receives the request and begins the query. The query takes place at the server so that *none* of the requests for Search Next takes place across the wire.
5. The record is found and readied for reply.
6. The reply is sent to the pilot.
7. The user interface formats the data for display.
8. The pilot goes flying.

As you can see, several benefits are gleaned:

■ From a code standpoint, the user interface doesn't need to be very large. This means better applications in a smaller code space. The redundant part of the database is kept at the server.

■ There is less traffic on the wire (for Search Nexts).

■ The server code is faster because lookups take place inside the server across the server's data bus, instead of across the network cable.

■ You can support different front-end user interfaces as long as they interact with the back-end in similar fashions.

■ If the back-end (server) supports it, you can also support multiple transports (TCP/IP, IPX/SPX, and so on).

Where Does Client/Server Make Sense?

Obviously, client/server implementations can take many different forms. In certain cases, it may not be feasible to utilize a client/server scenario simply because of equipment, user requirements, and software availability. There aren't many applications today that truly utilize client/server effectively. The main platforms that support it are database platforms such as Oracle, Informix, Sybase, Gupta, and so on. As the networking industry pushes on, tools and systems will make it easier to implement solutions utilizing a distributed approach.

In essence, whenever you have a group of networked machines and a shared process such as a database or shared message process such as Lotus Notes, there lies an opportunity for a client/server design.

Remote Procedure Calls—Why and How?

To implement several architectures we have described here, it is necessary to have some sort of a mechanism for getting data (in the form of application logic) from point A to point B. Many networks have their own way of transporting data but not remotely executing code on another machine. Some application vendors have created their own styles, but ultimately, distributed applications need to rely on a more flexible approach for distributing code. In addition, such technologies as Distributed Object technology also need to rely on a common logic transport. This is where the Remote Procedure Calls (RPCs) approach comes in.

In a client/server application, one of the first things the developer has to do is decide how the user interface tells the server to do a remote lookup. Does the sending station (user interface) send a packet of data with a request inside? Or should a special set of libraries be written to provide this function? The dilemma is that although distributed applications are growing in number, the significant part of the market is still stand-alone. Therefore, should the application be written twice, thereby necessitating revision management between the two versions? Here's where the RPC mechanism is most useful.

When an application is written, the developer chooses the flow of the logic to open a database, read a record, and so on. Perhaps the logic flow goes something like this:

1. Prepare variables and memory for data lookup.

2. Ask user for input.

3. Open the database.

4. Read a record.

5. Check for errors.

6. Close the database.

7. Format the data for output.

8. Display the data.

This is an example of a common stand-alone application. In a stand-alone database, during the Open Database, Read Record, and Close Database functions, if the file containing the database were contained on a remote server, the program would still treat it as if it were local. The Open, Read, and Close functions would be sent to the server. This isn't so bad, in and of itself, but if we need to make an intensive search, each read would go on the wire.

The common elements for this example—Open, Read, and Close—can take advantage of an RPC to distribute code cleanly and effectively without affecting the source code itself. At the point where Open, Read, and Close are executed, a stub* could be placed in the client so that if the application were compiled for client/server with a stub kept locally, then the actual code that was executed before is no longer here. It now would reside at the server end. The server end could have the same code as before, just compiled (along with a server stub) in the native platform's environment such as OS/2, NetWare, or UNIX. The flow would be something like this:

1. The client stub receives the information that the calling routine provides (that is, Open Database AIRINFO.DBF).

2. The stub formats the data required for the call into a packet and sends it to the server.

3. The server receives data for the call (via the server stub) and executes normally.

4. A return code (error or success) is returned to the stub and transmitted back to the client.

5. The client receives code as if the call were executed normally.

As you can see, with merely the flip of a software switch, the application can be either stand-alone or client/server. There is a small amount of additional coding

---

*A stub is a small routine that calls a progam.

required to split the server and client pieces as well as some RPC housekeeping routines that need to be created, but the return makes it well worth the effort.

Multiple Transport Support

Another major benefit of using an RPC is that the stub does not need to be transport-dependent. Depending on the vendor, the stub can be made to support multiple protocols by changing the type of stub that is used during compilation. Since the code that is remotely called has almost no idea that it's being morphed into a client/server piece of code, it really doesn't matter whether it's TCP/IP or IPX/SPX. All that matters is that the right code gets to the server side with the proper parameters. This feature is dependent on the manufacturer of the RPC technology. Since RPCs tend to be proprietary, this may or may not be possible.

Common RPC Mechanisms

One of the most common RPC mechanisms available today for development is the TI-RPC technology originally developed by Sun, now part of OSF's DCE architecture. It was chosen because it can use TCP/IP as a standard transport, yet is flexible enough to support other protocols.

Directory Services

A lot of networks today operate in a stand-alone environment. That is, they are single server in nature even though they communicate through a common backbone in order to pass routing information about each other and other available services. Instead of acting as a concerted network, however, each server maintains its own security database and rights assignments. Therefore, for an administrator to properly manage a network of many servers, he or she must log in to each server separately. This means that the administrator has a separate account for each system. The same holds true for users. If user Chuck Yeager needs to use server Glennie and server Apollo, he must be a defined user on each system. That also means that both he and the supervisor must maintain at least two passwords, one for each system. Even though they may be the same password, each is treated as a separate entity and stored separately at each server. The solution to this is to provide a means by which all services and users can be part of a single collection of resources. This is where directory services come in.

A good example of a common everyday directory service is the yellow pages. If you're looking up a phone number for a service, you don't want to drive around each city block looking. Instead, it's more efficient to simply look at a common repository of information. The scope of the information provided is limited only by the size of the book. Searches can be accomplished through an alphabetical organization of the information.

Architecture of a Directory Service

A directory service can appear in a number of formats, but they all have things in common. The basic architecture usually is taken from the X.500 specification originally created to handle large amounts of information such as the public phone system. Most vendors don't implement all the aspects simply because of the amount of items X.500 specifies. Most simply aren't needed for common networks. As a result, there really is no X.500 fully compliant directory service for computer networks. Instead, the features that make sense are designed into a system adhering to the specifications put forth in the X.500 specification. This makes for a more common-sense approach.

Naming is a standard characteristic of a directory. Rather than refer to network services as individual items, they are related to the user and the administrator as a hierarchy. Typically, this could be the company's name at the highest level, although it could be a country name (such as USA, Germany, Canada, and so on). Next comes one or more organization components such as regional locations, office names, departments, or anything that resembles the company's infrastructure. These are called *containers*. Within a container, there can be end nodes such as users, servers (file servers, database servers, application servers), groups, and so on. These are sometimes referred to as *leaf nodes*. Leaf nodes do not contain other objects. They are the objects that users will look for and use. Containers are used principally for the organization of the tree.

A user such as CRogers would have a full name that uniquely identifies him in the tree, such as:

> CRogers.San Diego.Training.Training International

The user can also be identified by a full distinguished name identifying his name, container, and organization, such as:

> CN=CRogers.OU=San Diego.OU=Training.O=Training International

This is an example of the directory service created by Novell. CN stands for Common Name, OU stands for Organizational Unit, and O stands for Organization.

What Can a Directory Service Be Used For?

The traditional problem with server-centric systems has mostly been a problem of administration. Users must maintain several passwords as well as establish multiple log-ins each time they need to get on the system. Even if this is automated via scripting, it still means someone has to create and maintain the scripts. That someone is usually the administrator. If not, it's not uncommon for users to maintain their own scripts.

With a directory service, the user must only be created once in the system and maintained as a single user, even though he or she may access multiple systems. One utility can be used to change rights assignments or passwords. One of the more effective advantages is deletion of a user. Since users in large systems tend to exist on many servers, it's difficult to erase them (kind of like a virus!). In a directory-based system, the user need only be erased once.

During log-in, the user only supplies a single systemwide (secure) password that is used for authentication on all servers in the directory. This can really enhance security, since users with multiple passwords tend to write them down, forget them, and so on. A single log-in eases the everyday life of users, especially if they are casual users.

Other systems that may benefit from a common directory include electronic mail (e-mail) systems. Since network-based systems almost always include e-mail, the two systems can be integrated through the common directory. E-mail users need a name, a mailbox, and a method of looking up other users (something the directory is designed for). With the two tied together, the whole system benefits for several reasons:

- Only a single directory must be maintained, instead of two.
- The users need learn only one method of user lookup.
- The systems tied together require less system resources.
- Security for e-mail can be tied into the directory.

Other benefits include synchronization of a directory to other databases such as an employee database. A company can implement the system so that when a new user is created in the system, he or she is automatically added to the external employee database. In addition, when changes are made to an employee's record (such as home address), the change can automatically be synchronized in the background.

Future LAN technologies such as Distributed File Systems can also benefit from a directory. Traditionally, files systems are seen as static devices such as volumes. As such, rights are assigned based on location of the volume. The rights assignment to the files and directory are based on the location of the volume instead of a logical assignment. A distributed file system abstracts the location of the files. To do this, though, there has to be a central authoritative repository of where the actual files are, in relation to their logical names.

Examples of Directory Service Systems

Directory service systems are starting to emerge on major network operating system platforms. The most important of these services are discussed next.

UNIX Systems   In UNIX systems, a common information base used for just such a thing was called Yellow Pages, now called Network Information Services (NIS). It's usually included in most implementations of UNIX in order to provide a method of resource lookup.

Banyan VINES   Banyan has provided a three-level directory service called StreetTalk that provides most benefits of a directory service. Although limited to only three levels, it provides sufficient structure for most systems. All resources such as e-mail, volumes, users, and servers are created as objects within the context of the three levels: Organization, Group, and Object.

Novell Directory Service   Novell traditionally has been based on a server-centric approach, and only within the last two years has a directory service been developed for NetWare. This feature appeared in NetWare version 4.0 as the NetWare Directory Services, or NDS. Novell based NDS on X.500 recommendations. It provides any number of levels in the directory including country designations as well as organization and organizational unit containers. This allows administrators to create tree structured directories in which different organizations of the company are placed at the top of the tree (in organization containers) and departments are placed within those containers. So, for example, an organization might group its networking resources into two main branches, say Los Angeles and New York, and then create subbranches that represent each department at those locations. Of course, users and resources on the network would be organized under these main branches of the tree.

Security in an Internetwork

The need for security, especially in large networks, is obvious. The more sensitive the information, the more you need to protect it. What is needed is a system that can logically provide adequate security, yet be simple to use and administer. Usually, systems provide levels of security for the user system or directory service, as well as levels to support access to the file system and directories.

These can be categorized in the following levels:

- Authentication—the log-in process
- Rights to the directory structure or volume
- Rights to the files themselves
- Attribute rights on resources

ʺthentication

Authentication usually includes several levels associated with user access to the system. The main controls are:

- User log-in
- Requiring passwords
- Requiring password changes
- Minimum password lengths

- Allowed log-in times
- Account disabling (expiration of accounts)

Directory/File System Rights

Once users are in the system, access usually isn't (and shouldn't be) universal. Therefore, some method of controlling user access to files and directories usually is implemented. These consist of several abilities granted to users:

- Reading a file
- Writing to a file
- Opening a file
- Copying a file
- Erasing a file
- Viewing a file or directory
- Executing a file

File and Directory Attributes

At the lowest levels, attributes can be defined on the system, providing a means by which certain access can be available to users on a global scale. That is, they usually apply to all users if the given attribute has been placed on a file or attribute. Examples include:

- Read-only access to a file
- Read/write access
- System attribute (usually file and directory)
- Hidden attribute (also usually file and directory)

Today many of these security measures are applied to varying degrees to PC LAN systems.

Security Encryption Methods

As important as the security measures themselves is the method of security implementation. Security doesn't provide many benefits if the security is easily overcome by creative hackers. Although there are many ways of securing a system, several standards have been developed and utilized to secure today's network systems.

One of the more popular methods is called a public key cryptosystem. Using this technology, the concept of a software key is used to guarantee that people logging on to a system are who they say they are. In essence, the user has a key and the system has a key. When the authentication is requested, the user utilizes a key to encrypt the string to prove identity. The host system also contains a key to verify the encrypted request. Using the key pair, authenticity can be verified, provided the security of the key itself has not been compromised.

Other methods provide encryption methods that use uncommon values such as log-in times, dates, physical addresses, and such to provide a secure log-in.

Some of the better-known encryption methods are:

- RSA (Rivest Shamir Adleman) encryption
- DES (Data Encryption Standard)
- Kerberos
- MD (Message Digest) algorithm

Different software would be used depending on the implementation of the system. Whichever system is used, the level of security is usually adequate for most systems.

Distributed Time Services

In any collection of systems, proper time management can either be a nuisance or a real problem. Many LAN operating systems haven't had a comprehensive method for managing time between servers. Usually in a server-centric environment, it's not a very critical issue. When an enterprise network is created, time becomes much more important, not simply because of mismatched time stamps, but more for the underlying services.

One major service that relies on time synchronization is a directory service. Updates made to the directory need to occur on the system in the proper order based on when the event occurred. For example, if a user is updated and then deleted, the update must occur first, then the delete. To do the reverse would not be possible and could result in a system error.

The architecture of a time synchronized system can take several forms. It may be monolithic (requiring a single time source) or hierarchical (utilizing a voting scheme). Regardless, the system needs a way of determining and using an ultimate reference for time.

In the case of NetWare Directory Services, a hierarchical system is used that consists of three sources:

- Reference or Single-reference servers
- Primary servers
- Secondary servers

Reference servers and Single-reference servers provide an ultimate time resource. No matter what the other servers say, the Reference server will always override the others. Usually, the Reference server has two characteristics: it has ties to an accurate time source such as the atomic clock at the National Institute of Standards and

Technology (NIST), and there is usually only one per directory system. This way, servers don't compete for ultimate time sources. Access to accurate time sources such as NIST can be obtained from the Internet using one of several utilities.

Primary servers are utilized as secondary time references in the network. They are the source of time for Secondary servers in the event that a Reference is not immediately available. If there are multiple primaries, they will continually vote among each other, arbitrating the proper time. If present, a Reference server always wins, thereby making it the ultimate time reference. If the Reference server fails, the primaries will keep perfectly synchronized until the Reference server comes back on line. The major contributing factor to time-desynchronization is the PC's onboard clock.

Secondaries only receive time from a time source whether it's the nearest Primary or a Reference. They do not participate in the voting process (like the primaries). Instead they merely trust the nearest time source.

Messaging Systems

Originally, when LAN systems were installed, the main purpose as stated before, was for file and print sharing. Today, one of a LAN system's main functions is electronic mail. E-mail is just one part of the overall messaging architecture. Messaging can also be used for a variety of things:

- Fax servers
- Group scheduling
- Workflow applications
- Library systems

A common messaging infrastructure provides the foundation for many kinds of store-and-forward-based systems in the network. If properly designed, it can also interoperate with several other messaging systems to provide interoperability to other nonnative systems.

Some examples of messaging architectures include:

- Message Handling Service (MHS), Novell
- Simple Mail Transfer Protocol (SMTP), the Internet
- Vendor Independent Messaging (VIM), Lotus and others
- Messaging Application Programming Interface (MAPI), Microsoft

There are other types of messaging systems used in legacy systems (such as SNADS—SNA Distributed Services) that can interoperate with the PC LAN enterprise as well. Typically this is done in an existing mainframe environment where traditional legacy e-mail systems need to share messages with the PC LAN system.

All the preceding systems allow message transfer in one form or another (usually through gateways) to one or more of the other systems. Usually the base platform is chosen based on the primary LAN itself. UNIX systems usually use SMTP, NetWare systems use MHS, and LAN Manager systems use MAPI. In addition, MAPI is used with Microsoft Office (a popular productivity application set). VIM and Lotus can be found in many multivendor systems that have standardized on an e-mail package called cc:MAIL. The main thing to look for in these systems is if they integrate with your existing architecture.

User Interfaces

Presentation of the data is what every user sees regardless of the infrastructure. How good the system appears is largely dependent on the effectiveness of the user interface. As a result, systems like Microsoft Windows enjoy wide popularity because of their ease of use and simple user interfaces. In addition, they can make a traditionally difficult operating system interface (such as UNIX) easier to navigate and use.

The main user interfaces available today for the enterprise include:

- Microsoft Windows
- OS/2 Workplace Shell
- Motif
- OPEN LOOK
- NeXTStep
- Macintosh

Microsoft Windows

Windows owes much of its popularity to the overwhelming number of DOS machines in use today. DOS has enjoyed a life span of over ten years in the computing environment but, being character-based, hasn't had a great user interface. Windows adds a layer to DOS that provides an easier method for working in the network with significantly less training.

Although Windows supports a DOS environment, various add-ons allow it to work in other environments such as TCP/IP (UNIX) and IPX/SPX (NetWare).

OS/2 LAN Workplace Shell

IBM and Microsoft worked together on the OS/2 operating system to provide a new generation of desktop operating system. When OS/2 did not initially meet its marketing expectations, IBM took over OS/2 entirely and redesigned the interface, calling it Workplace Shell. Workplace Shell places an easy-to-use graphical system on a powerful, true 32-bit system. It's easy to use, but still lacks applications specifically written for Workplace Shell.

One major advantage to Workplace Shell is its ability to run applications for Windows and DOS, giving it three levels of application support. For many people, this makes OS/2 and Workplace Shell a great choice for enterprise networks.

Motif/OPEN LOOK

Many people who use UNIX and have learned it well, vouch for the power and flexibility of the UNIX operating system. Traditionally, UNIX has had a nasty reputation of difficulty in use because it consisted of a large collection of obscure command-line utilities. With the addition of Motif and OPEN LOOK, UNIX enjoys a user interface similar to Windows. In the recent past, there were two standards for UNIX interfaces: Motif (for example, on System V release 4.*x*) and OPEN LOOK (on Sun Systems). Recently, most UNIX vendors have chosen to provide Motif as the common standard.

NeXTStep

NeXTStep is a reasonably new interface designed on a UNIX kernel and devised by NeXT. Although its interface is similar to other UNIX Windows environments, it has features that are tailored specifically to the NeXTStep operating system.

Macintosh

Macintosh has had one of the most imitated user interfaces since its inception on the Apple LISA, circa 1984. With its folder and file design for designating the disk organization, it's still one of the easiest-to-use interfaces available. The Macintosh interface runs 100 percent of the time on a high-performance operating system, shielding the user from all aspects of the lower layers.

Document Interchange

Imagine the common office today, where there are many different machines used for different functions. Typically, the main uses are word processing, spreadsheet, electronic mail, and database services. Often, different users in different departments need to share created data between dissimilar systems.

With the diverse platforms, there needs to be a way to interconnect all the different systems such as AppleTalk, NetWare, NFS, and NetBIOS. More than that, to exchange information, the document types need to be interchangeable. Before that can be accomplished, the underlying structure must be available in order to allow utilities such as AppleTalk Filing Protocol (AFP), and Network File System (NFS) to store and retrieve files on a NetWare file system. To then get document interchangeability, the application vendor must provide similar file formats between platform versions of the application (such as the UNIX, Windows, and Mac versions).

WordPerfect, for example, lets you create a document on WordPerfect for Windows that a WordPerfect for UNIX user can then open and manipulate. Because the file format is similar between platform versions, document interchangeability can be achieved once the lower layer infrastructure is in place. Another good example of this is Lotus 1-2-3 and AmiPro. Both provide common formats (vendor-specific) for this level of application integration.

Dynamic Data Exchange and OLE

When a user begins to use several applications, it often becomes necessary to share data among them. For example, suppose you are using a spreadsheet and word processor at the same time. The information used in the spreadsheet may be used in the word processed document and may need to be occasionally updated. Another example might be an application that can provide real-time data to another application. How can both these actions be performed in today's environment?

Dynamic Data Exchange (DDE)

In today's PC environment, there has been very little need to share data among applications. However, this is changing as users realize that data used in one application can be utilized by another. Take an example of a management platform that receives data and forwards it to a database. Without the ability to interact between applications, the management application would have to know how to write and update information in the database. This could be hazardous if the management platform were poorly written and corrupted the database. It would make more sense to give the data to the database code and let *it* do the update. The challenge is providing the transport and mechanism to accomplish such an event. This is the function of DDE.

DDE Servers and Clients

An application has to be written to support DDE either as a client, a server, or both. As a server, it can communicate with a client and provide data to it as well as receive updates. A client itself cannot be updated unless it's also a server.

Object Linking and Embedding (OLE)

Applications originally didn't need to interact and share data, especially of different types, among themselves. For example, a spreadsheet application created data uniquely for the spreadsheet. There was no way to export that data to another application such as a word processor.

Another example is sending e-mail with an embedded file such as a sound file. To play the sound file, the e-mail system has to know what type of object the sound file is. Once the sound file is associated with an application, the sound file can be played when it's received. The same holds true for the spreadsheet/word processor combination. When the document is displayed, the spreadsheet automatically updates (based on the spreadsheet object in the document) and displays.

Embedding an object means taking a particular type of data and placing it within another application as in the example of the spreadsheet/document combination. The spreadsheet file/data would be embedded in the document file. Then when the document is brought up, the spreadsheet automatically displays.

Linking allows the embedded object to automatically update to an external data source. This means the same spreadsheet could look up the existing data in the original spreadsheet file before it displays in the document. In this way, the spreadsheet information remains as current as the source file. Without this linking capability, data must be updated manually between the document and the spreadsheet.

Currently OLE2 has been implemented in a number of applications. However, Microsoft is not the only vendor working on document interchangeability. A consortium of vendors headed by Apple is working on a new standard called OpenDoc. OpenDoc, when delivered, will offer the advantages described earlier for OLE and more. There is currently a lot of debate over which standard will finally win this battle, and the stakes are high.

Summary

The issues addressed in this chapter will be dealt with in greater detail in the remaining chapters in this part of the book. Most of the technologies are in flux, and the options available to users are changing quickly. Standards are still being shaped, and the battles like the one between OLE and OpenDoc may last for years. However, being aware of these options can help you make the best decision to suit your needs.

Chapter Eleven

Building a Common Infrastructure

by Mary Hubley,
Datapro Information Services Group

Infrastracture technologies are the glue that holds together an organization's disparate computing hardware platforms, operating systems, and application software. Infrastructures are environments that consist of many of the elements discussed in Chapter 12, but are available as encompassing, all-in-one products.

With infrastructure technologies, end-user organizations have been successful in building interoperable environments. Through client/server-based LANs and distributed computing solutions, these users have paved the way for all of us to achieve interoperability. Recently, full-blown distributed computing environments have emerged as the most powerful infrastructures on which to build enterprise-wide interoperability.

Two technologies exist that provide extensive distributed computing infrastructures. The Open Software Foundation's (OSF) Distributed Computing Environment (DCE) and SunSoft's ONC (Open Network Computing) are the only two standard technologies on the market. Network Operating Systems (NOSs) such as Novell NetWare, Banyan VINES, and Microsoft LAN Manager can also be considered infrastructures, but address more limited client/server, rather than distributed, architectures. In addition, some operating systems (which are also considered infrastructures in older host-based computing environments) either are being modernized and expanded to hook into LANs or are being bundled with distributed computing facilities. These operating systems include Microsoft Windows NT, Novell UnixWare, the Santa Cruz Operation Open Desktop/Open Server, and SunSoft Solaris.

Distributed Environments

Most large organizations are faced with a severe problem: they must find a way to get their disparate computing environments consisting of, for instance, Windows-based LANs, UNIX workstations and servers, and legacy IBM mainframes, to work together. However, end users have found that although they may have pieces of enabling technologies, achieving enterprise-wide interoperability is too massive a puzzle to piece together. Thus, the vast majority of end users have made do with homegrown environments that are barely sufficient.

Distributed computing environments have emerged over the past couple of years to solve the problem. These environments provide an enterprise-wide structure that connects an entire organization's computing power—mainframes, workgroup environments, and LANs—into one huge, heterogeneous environment.

Distributed computing is a step up from client/server architectures. While client/server computing generally provides information and services only between servers and their clients, distributed computing extends the sharing of services, so that servers can share with other servers, and clients can share with servers other than their own. Thus, data is not centrally located as in client/server configurations, but is shared among many servers that may be geographically dispersed and connected with wide area networks. Figure 11-1 shows how distributed computing differs from client/server and older centralized computing models.

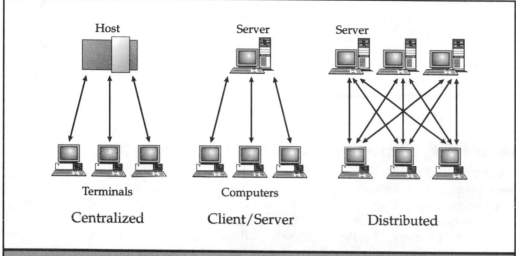

Figure 11-1. *Distributed computing has evolved from centralized and client/server computing.*

But even with commercially available products, distributed computing is still difficult to achieve, especially since standards have been slow to develop, and application development software and management tools are still in their infancy. In addition, end user organizations must deal with migration difficulties and a host of unknown technology factors. Information systems managers are also faced with the massive task of redefining the basics: how they approach their applications as well as their infrastructure.

Nevertheless, even with the difficulties, distributed computing is the only real choice in building enterprise-wide interoperable environments. While it may be difficult, migrating an enterprise to distributed computing is not impossible; many leading-edge end-user organizations have made successful transitions.

OSF DCE

The Open Software Foundation's (OSF) Distributed Computing Environment (DCE) enables open systems interoperability and distributed computing between networks, on heterogeneous platforms, and on different operating systems. DCE allows users to take advantage of a wide range of systems resources without having to understand the specifics of how various systems and peripherals communicate over a network.

DCE-enabled software can run on PCs, workstations, servers, and mainframes and is independent of the underlying operating system, architecture, or network software. DCE's core services run in the background on each network platform, providing the platforms with common services such as file sharing, security, and application sharing.

Multiple network file systems and directories appear to the DCE network as a single system. In fact, DCE's appeal is that it takes a group of loosely connected systems and makes them appear as a single, tightly coupled system. The key to making multiple CPUs function as one is the Remote Procedure Call (RPC). In DCE, RPCs let multiple computers work as one by executing applications, or parts of applications, on the computer best suited for the task. A major benefit of this function is that DCE can split work between multiple network computers to reduce computing time and improve performance.

Where DCE Stands and Where It Is Going

Vendor neutrality is DCE's greatest asset. While several proprietary distributed computing solutions were developed before DCE by such vendors as IBM, Digital Equipment Corporation, and Computer Associates International, these solutions are proprietary, and most are limited to specific vendor hardware.

Because DCE supports heterogeneous platforms and was built through an industry consortium with input from many computer-vendor and end-user organizations, DCE is widely accepted. Standards proposed by companies offering alternative, but proprietary, distributed computing solutions—IBM's System Application Architecture (SAA), Digital's Network Applications System (NAS), and Computer Associates' CA90s—now support DCE.

However, DCE is not without competition. SunSoft's* ONC has been around longer than DCE and has been implemented in many more end-user sites. DCE's biggest limitation is that it is still new; it has not been fully implemented in as many end-user sites as ONC. In addition, most end-user organizations take several years to build a full distributed computing environment. Thus, ONC, which has been available for several years, has a lead over DCE in installed base. However, SunSoft recognizes DCE's growing importance and has therefore built into ONC+ the capability to coexist with DCE.

DCE Components

DCE services are grouped into two categories: the Fundamental Distributed Services provide development tools to build end-user applications and services, and Data-Sharing Services provide information access. DCE Architecture is shown in Figure 11-2.

The Fundamental Distributed Services consist of five basic tools required by software developers to create the end-user services under DCE. These tools are:

- Remote Procedure Call

- Distributed Directory Service

*SunSoft is a division of Sun Microsystems.

- Time Service

- Threads Service

- Security Service

The Data Sharing Services build upon the Fundamental Distributed Services. These tools are:

- Distributed File System (DFS)

- Diskless Support

DCE also provides support for the MS-DOS file system and support printer services.

Remote Procedure Call (RPC)

The remote procedure call is the primary building block of DCE. The RPC allows applications or portions of applications to run on remote computers located anywhere

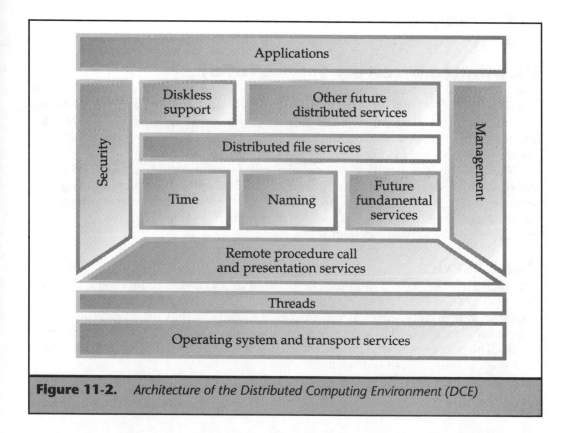

Figure 11-2.   *Architecture of the Distributed Computing Environment (DCE)*

in the DCE network. Through RPCs, DCE can spread the computing load across the network for better overall network performance and more effective use of CPU capabilities. RPC masks the differences between data representations on different machines, allowing programs to work across heterogeneous systems. The goal of the RPC is to make remote data application access as easy as accessing your local hard disk drive.

There are two parts to the DCE RPC Service: the RPC facility itself, and a compiler that converts high-level descriptions of remote procedures (the actual instructions from users to the remote application) into portable C code that is passed along the network.

The RPC enables application capabilities that were previously either impossible or extremely difficult to implement through traditional programming. These capabilities include the following:

■ Allowing multiple clients in a client/server network to interact with multiple servers, and multiple servers to handle multiple clients simultaneously

■ Allowing clients to identify and locate network servers by name

■ Enabling protocol independence across the network to any platform

■ Enabling secure communications across the network

■ Supporting large applications by permitting unlimited argument size

Distributed Directory Service (DDS)

The DDS provides a single naming model throughout a distributed environment built upon the DCE. The DDS provides access to network services such as printers, servers, and other network platforms without the necessity of knowing where the resource is located within the network. This lets users access a network resource even if the resource has been moved to a different physical network address.

The DDS incorporates the X.500 global naming system, including full X.500 application development support through a published application programming interface (API). The Directory Service also lets users replicate data across multiple network platforms, using the RPC, so that data remains available despite communication and hardware failures.

Time Service

The DCE Time Service lets multiple platforms work together without timing problems that tend to affect event scheduling and duration. The distributed time service regulates system clocks on each network computer so that they match each other. Clocks are synchronized to a single standard, and the service ignores faulty system clocks. This service supports the Network Time Protocol Standard for network sites that wish to use time values from outside sources.

Threads Service

The Threads Service allows all DCE-enabled applications to execute multiple actions concurrently so they may perform more than one operation at a time. The threads service enables multithreading to accept simultaneous actions from users, execute RPCs, and access databases at the same time.

Security Service

The DCE Security Service provides authentication, authorization, and user account management. DCE facilitates these services through the RPC, which maintains the integrity of information passed across the network.

- The authentication scheme is based on MIT's Project Athena's Kerberos, which validates users by protecting the identity of the user from the network, where it could be intercepted and duplicated. This facility maintains the user identity in encrypted files.

- The authorization mechanism grants authorized users access to resources and rejects requests from unauthorized users.

- The user registry service permits users access to multiple network resources through a single password and single log-in. This registry is a database of user information that is replicated around the network. User passwords are centrally stored, secure, and universally available.

Distributed File System (DFS)

The DFS is DCE's foundation for information sharing. It makes global file access possible over the network. DFS replicates files and directories on multiple systems to protect against communication and network hardware failure. It also caches copies of currently used files on user workstations to minimize network traffic and provide fast data access.

Diskless Support

Through the DFS, DCE supports diskless workstations. Diskless workstation support allows users to install files on networks and use server-based storage instead of expensive local disk storage.

tandards Support

DCE supports many Open System Interconnect (OSI) standards for global interconnectivity. DCE also uses the International Standards Organization (ISO) directory system, known as CCITT X.500. Other ISO standards, such as the Remote Operations Service Element (ROSE), the Association Control Service Element (ACSE), and the ISO session and presentation standards are supported. DCE also supports Internet standards, such as TCP/IP protocols, the Domain Name System, and the Network Time Protocols. The Open Software Foundation is a member of X/Open, and supports the X/Open Transport Interface (XTI).

SunSoft ONC and ONC+

SunSoft's Open Network Computing (ONC) and its latest ONC+, released in 1993, are network computing architectures consisting of networking protocols and distributed services that provide access to computing resources across a heterogeneous network. ONC is independent of computer architecture, operating systems, and network transport protocols.

Sun was the first company to develop and widely market a distributed computing architecture. ONC is licensed by leading system vendors and is available to support most major operating systems.

ONC includes value-added services such as Sun's Network File Service (NFS), Sun's Remote Procedure Call (RPC), and Sun's External Data Representation (XDR). These services and protocols have gained wide acceptance because Sun has made them freely available in the public domain. Source code for them can also be licensed from several vendors.

Where ONC Stands and Where It Is Going

OSF DCE is emerging as a powerful contender for SunSoft. The biggest reason for DCE's popularity is that it was developed from the ground up with input from many organizations; thus, it is perceived as a more standard product than ONC, which was built by and is controlled by one vendor, Sun. In addition, DCE is being placed in very large, WAN-based enterprise-wide environments, while ONC has traditionally been implemented in somewhat smaller environments (although ONC+ has increased its scope to include the global enterprise). SunSoft recognizes the importance of DCE and other environments, and has thus included the capability to have ONC+ coexist with other environments including DCE, NetWare, and the Open Systems Interconnection (OSI).

Actually, Sun does not compete directly with the OSF, but instead with IBM, Digital Equipment, and Hewlett Packard, who offer their own proprietary distributed computing environments, as well as end-user implementations of DCE that run on these vendors' platforms.

While ONC may lose ground to DCE, SunSoft continues to support it and enhance it. Because ONC+ is bundled as a central component of SunSoft's Solaris operating system, ONC's continued use is guaranteed. ONC+ and Federated Naming Services have strengthened the product so that it can coexist with other environments, and new features include multithreading, a better naming service, and security.

ONC Components

ONC provides three basic tools for distributing applications across a network. These are:

Network File System (NFS), for the distribution of data

REX (Remote EXecution), for the distribution of CPU usage

ONC RPC/XDR (Remote Procedure Call/eXternal Data Representation), for the distribution of programs

Other components built on top of these ONC tools are:

Network Information System (NIS—formerly called Yellow Pages)

Automounter

Lock Manager

ONC+ is the next phase of ONC. ONC+ includes the following:

■ Updated NFS features

NIS+ Naming Server

TI-RPC

■ Security

Figure 11-3 shows the ONC core protocols.

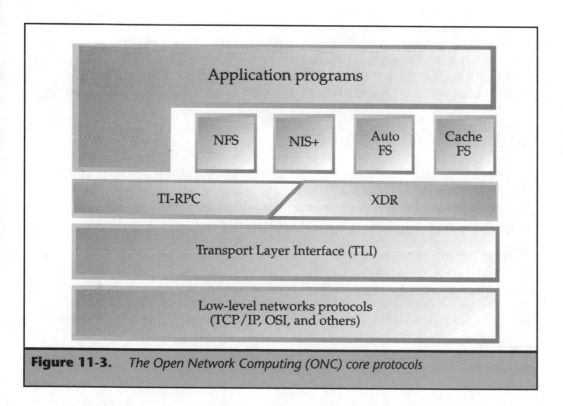

Figure 11-3. *The Open Network Computing (ONC) core protocols*

ONC Remote Procedure Call (RPC)

Sun's RPC is a set of operations that execute procedures on remote systems. It standardizes how programs running under the control of different operating systems request services of each other without having to adhere to the different systems' unique call processing.

ONC+ includes an enhanced version of the RPC called the Transport Independent RPC (TI RPC). TI RPC is implemented on top of the Transport Layer Interface and provides run-time transport independence. Allowing the RPC to determine the transport mechanism at application run-time eliminates the problem of specifying all permutations of hardware, software, and network protocols.

External Data Representation (XDR)

XDR provides an architecture-independent method of representing data across different platforms. XDR resolves differences in data byte ordering, data type size, representation, and alignment. XDR routines are extensible and recursive, and can build complex data types from primitive routines. These complex data structures are described with a C-like declaration language and are generated using the RPCGEN compiler.

Network File System (NFS)

NFS enables file sharing among network devices. With NFS, network-attached devices are identified as either a client or a server by the user issuing appropriate commands or system calls. NFS retains knowledge of the locations of all mounted file systems and all the clients that have access to mounted file systems. Thus, clients can issue UNIX I/O commands to files in these file systems without having to know where the file system physically resides. With ONC+, NFS includes multithreading and the Kerberos authentication services.

Automounter

Automounter automatically mounts and unmounts remote directories on an as-needed basis, thus providing increased transparency and availability of NFS file systems. Automounter mounts a file system as soon as it is accessed by a client. Automounter then periodically tries to unmount the file system following a period of inactivity, thereby freeing up resources that otherwise would be wasted.

PC-NFS

PC-NFS is an NFS implementation that allows PCs to access files on NFS servers. It provides authentication and print spooling services to PCs running a DOS implementation of ONC. PC-NFS also provides TELNET and FTP for terminal emulation and file transfer, respectively.

NETdisk

The NETdisk module provides support for diskless workstations.

Remote Execution (REX) Service

REX executes user commands or programs on remote systems. It provides access to computer capabilities not available on the local machine. The network administrator must explicitly enable REX on the server. Furthermore, the user must be known to both client and server, and the server uses the RPC's authentication to establish identity.

Network Information Service (NIS and NIS+)

Formerly known as Yellow Pages, Network Information Service provides network data management. NIS stores system information such as host names, network addresses, user names, and networks within an extensive database. With ONC+, NIS+ replaces NIS to provide a hierarchical enterprise naming service for large networks. It is more scalable and secure than NIS, and easier to administer.

Lock Manager (LM)

Lock Manager provides file and record locking for files accessed through NFS. It prevents users from destroying data by simultaneously modifying the same file or record. In addition, LM assists in rebuilding after a server crash by working with Status Monitor, which detects system reboots following a crash. Once the server crash is detected, clients reestablish their locks during a grace period provided by the LM. During the grace period, no other locks may be established. Should a lock be lost, the LM sends a signal to the process holding that lock. When the server detects the reboot of the client, it discards the locks held by that client.

Authentication

Authentication mechanisms for ONC include Secure RPC; ONC+ includes Kerberos. ONC+ licensees can also obtain rights from SunSoft to use the RSA (Rivest, Shamir, and Adleman) data encryption technology for network authentication, under agreement with RSA Data Security Inc.

Time/Synchronization Services

ONC includes the Internet Network Time Protocol, which provides a standard time throughout the network to synchronize events.

tandards Support

ONC supports most major networking standards, such as the TCP/IP protocol suite from DARPA, all seven layers of the Open Systems Interconnect (OSI) protocol stack, and the IEEE 802.3 hardware standards. SunSoft does not offer token ring support, although some licensing vendors offer implementations of ONC that run over token ring. It also supports Ethernet and the FDDI standard for connectivity over fiber-optic cable.

Network Operating Systems (NOSs)

Network Operating Systems (NOSs) are extremely popular infrastructure technologies. NOSs are much more widely used than distributed environments, although they are not as flexible or as scalable. In addition, NOSs are more often considered the domain of Intel-based client/server LANs rather than large heterogeneous environments typically marking distributed environments. In addition, resource sharing is not as flexible as in distributed environments. There are two dominant products in the NOS market: Novell NetWare and Banyan VINES. Microsoft LAN Manager continues to be a player, but is no longer actively marketed by its manufacturer.

Novell NetWare

NetWare consists of a product line, ranging from simple and inexpensive NetWare Lite to large-scale enterprise NetWare 4.*x*. NetWare is not based on any one operating system, as VINES is based on UNIX and LAN Manager on OS/2; instead, NetWare was built from the ground up to be a network operating system.

NetWare supports workstations running DOS, Windows, OS/2, and UNIX. Support for Macintosh, NFS, and OSI FTAM (File Transfer Access and Management) can be added as options. NetWare is also hardware-independent. This allows network managers to integrate heterogeneous hardware within a single network. NetWare supports the largest variety of hardware of any NOS on the market. The basic product line includes the following:

NetWare Lite   This is a peer-to-peer NOS for two to 25 users. It runs on top of DOS and is compatible with Windows. Users can set up a network for sharing files, applications, and printers with little networking knowledge.

NetWare 2.*x*   This is for small- to medium-sized businesses and workgroups. NetWare 2.*x* runs in dedicated or nondedicated mode in Intel-based systems. It provides local and remote internetworking support as well as tools for network administrators.

NetWare 3.*x*   This is for hundreds of users on a single, dedicated server. It is a full 32-bit operating system that uses a single address space with no segmentation. NetWare 3.*x* is modular and expandable, with the capability to integrate diverse systems, including minicomputers.

NetWare 4.*x*   This is for a large enterprise. It includes NetWare 3.*x* capabilities as well as new features that enable administrators to create a distributed multiserver environment with directory services and enterprise network support.

Where NetWare Stands and Where It Is Going

NetWare is the most mature NOS and dominates the market with 60 to 70 percent of the market share. NetWare products are consistent; they install and run smoothly compared to other NOSs, which frequently experience annoying problems. In fact, no other NOS has ever really come close to NetWare's market share. Even Microsoft, which dominates in other areas of the microcomputer market, has experienced disappointing results with its LAN Manager product.

NetWare is acknowledged as the best performer by many independent testers. It is a mature technology and is hardware independent. NetWare's consistent dominance in its market, and Novell's aggressiveness in adding more value to NetWare, guarantee this NOS's continued success.

NetWare Services

NetWare typically resides in an Intel-based server. It supports a client/server architecture, allowing the desktop systems to handle much of the processing load, freeing the server to perform other tasks.

The NetWare client's core service is the redirection software, which is typically loaded when the client boots. The redirector intercepts commands for NetWare servers and sends them across the network. Non-network commands are sent to the local operating system. The NetWare server's core services include file system management, memory management, and processing task scheduling.

NetWare Loadable Module (NLM)

The NLM can be added to NetWare 3.x and 4.x, effectively expanding NetWare to provide the following services:

- Support for non-DOS file storage
- Communication services
- Database services
- Messaging services
- Archive and backup services
- Network management services

The NLM modules can be loaded or unloaded at any time from the server. They reside along with NetWare in the server, and are tightly coupled with NetWare, allowing instant access to services.

Open Data-link Interface (ODI)

The ODI provides simultaneous support for different network protocols and interface cards. The drivers of these cards attach themselves to the Open Data-link Interface layer. Packets are directed to the appropriate protocol stack above the ODI layer. Near the top, service protocols provide file and system support for the operating systems on the NetWare server.

Name Space Support

NetWare supports the file naming conventions of different operating systems at the server console. The name space facility supports files with different name lengths, legal characters, and case sensitivity.

Security

Security features include log-in/password security, account restrictions, object and file security, and internetwork security. Reliability features include read-after-write specification, duplicate directories, duplicate file allocation table, system fault tolerance, a transaction tracking system, and UPS monitoring.

Miscellaneous Services

Other NetWare services include:

Internetwork Routing   Internetwork routing services allow connection to as many network segments as the server will hold network cards.

Communication Services   NetWare 3.11 and 4 products provide LAN-to-host, LAN-to-LAN, and remote-to-LAN connectivity.

Print Services   The NetWare 4.*x* print services package allows 256 printers to be shared over the network.

Distributed Directory Services   The NetWare 4.*x* NetWare Directory Services (NDS) keep track of all network users, servers, and resources across an internetwork.

Management Features   NetWare 4.*x* includes the NetWare Administrator that manages NDS users, resources, directories, and files. MONITOR is an NLM that lets the network administrator perform management tasks at the console. The NetWare Remote Management Facility (RMF) provides NetWare maintenance facilities. SERVMAN is included with NetWare 4.*x*, and allows supervisors to view and change the server configuration.

Banyan VINES

Virtual Networking System, or VINES, is a UNIX-based network operating system primarily known for multiserver networking features. It can support a large number of nodes and geographically separated servers. With VINES, information system managers can replace their wide area terminal systems with PCs that are both locally networked and connected across a wide area. It supports DOS, OS/2, Windows, UNIX, and Macintosh systems, allowing them to share information and resources with each other and host computing systems.

VINES has a small installed base, although many of its features are superior to its competitors. For instance, VINES is easier to install than LAN Manager or NetWare, as the setup process is almost completely self-contained and requires little use of instruction manuals. Likewise, VINES is easy to maintain; a network administrator can manage a VINES network of 25 servers and 1000 users with little difficulty. VINES is not a graphical system—its management facilities are based on traditional command-line- and menu-based UNIX systems. UNIX also provides it with full NFS support and TCP/IP.

VINES is targeted to large, enterprise-wide environments, and, includes such enterprise services as security, messaging, administration, host connectivity, and wide area network communication. In addition, its StreetTalk directory services allow managers to keep track of users and resources on the network.

StreetTalk Directory Service

StreetTalk, the VINES global directory service, translates logical names into physical addresses. StreetTalk is the core of the VINES product; it is the structure around which all network resources and user accounts are organized. This service integrates and manages heterogeneous environments including Banyan networks, UNIX, and NetWare. VINES automatically replicates any changes across the network, making it easier for system administrators to move resources between servers to relieve network load. The StreetTalk Directory Assistance (STDA) package provides distributed directory services. It allows users to substitute actual names when they do not know the network address.

VINES Operating System Services

The VINES operating system services include the following:

Security Services   These include multilevel access privileges, workstation authentication, and DES password encryption. Services provide log-in restrictions, password control, directory access controls, and internetwork security for all items in all groups maintained on a particular server.

Network Management Services   Management services provide a way for central staff or administrators to control or monitor all critical network connectivity or performance-related data and events in real time from any location on the network.

System Administration Services   These services manage users on the network with such tasks as moving or adding services, managing lists, and allocating resources.

Messaging Services   VINES messaging services provide electronic mail to every user on the network. Messaging is integrated with StreetTalk so users can locate other users' contact information.

Where VINES Stands and Where It Is Going

StreetTalk is a major strength. Novell has not yet introduced a global naming service as advanced, easy to use, and comprehensive. Another advantage is VINES' support for mainframes and minicomputers. Network design also is easier than with the others, even with thousands of users linked by integrated gateway, bridge, and router software.

However, VINES is plagued by a small market share (approximately 7.5 percent of the NOS market). In addition, over the past couple of years, Novell has been blowing away its smaller competitors; 3Com, the largest LAN Manager OEM, withdrew from the market, and Microsoft is no longer actively marketing LAN Manager. Novell's dominance has increased concerns that Novell may soon eliminate all competition from this market. However, Banyan continues to be a serious, albeit smaller, competitor. Banyan has made strategic moves to pursue markets in which it does not encounter as many loyal Novell customers. The most important move has been Banyan's repositioning of VINES to address the enterprise level, in which it claims 25 percent of the market.

Microsoft LAN Manager

Microsoft designed LAN Manager for the small- and medium-sized network environment. Key features include managing multiple servers and fast file copying.

LAN Manager has never been able to win a significant market share from Novell. In addition, small but bothersome technical problems have kept most IS managers from taking it seriously. Thus, Microsoft has replaced LAN Manager with NT Advanced Server. While Microsoft and its OEMs (Original Equipment Manufacturers) continue to support current LAN Manager installations and provide bug fixes, the company encourages new sales of NT.

LAN Manager includes the following features:

Security Features   These include password encryption, file protection, and delegation of some administrative functions to different users.

Network Maintenance   This is performed through a single menu-driven program.

Naming Service   Domain Naming, LAN Manager's global naming service, allows administrators to group multiple servers into a domain. The group of servers can then be managed as a single entity. All servers in a domain share user IDs, groups, and resources.

Server Operating Systems

The distributed processing and client/server architecture trends have made an impact on operating systems. Traditionally, the operating system was the central computing infrastructure in the old host-based computing model. Now, however, as host-based, master/slave processing has practically become extinct, manufacturers of operating systems are responding to the need for work to be divided among several servers and many clients on a networked infrastructure.

The new operating system infrastructures include several systems that have network-ready capabilities and are available in a client and in a server version. These operating systems include Microsoft NT, Novell UnixWare, SunSoft Solaris, and the Santa Cruz Operation Open Desktop and Open Server. These operating systems have facilities that can either act as the foundation for, or have hooks into, a heterogeneous computing environment.

Microsoft Windows NT Advanced Server

Microsoft Windows NT Advanced Server (NTAS) is a set of networking services that effectively replaces Microsoft's LAN Manager as the company's strategic networking infrastructure technology.

Windows NT represents Microsoft's move toward a new generation of advanced operating systems that include Cairo, being developed by Microsoft, and the Pink system, being jointly developed by IBM and Apple.

NT runs 32-bit applications for Windows NT as well as supporting applications for MS-DOS, Windows 3.1, POSIX, and OS/2 1.*x*. It can be integrated with mainframes, minicomputers, and networking and communications software, including Windows networks, Novell NetWare, Banyan VINES, LAN Manager for OS/2, UNIX, VMS (Virtual Memory System), and SNA networks. It can access data and resources in multivendor environments using TCP/IP, RPCs compatible with OSF DCE, Windows Sockets, Named Pipes, and Data-link Control.

NT File System (NTFS)   Windows NT's NT File System (NTFS) features 64-bit addressing, allowing a single system to access up to 4 gigabytes (Gb) of RAM. Up to 408 billion gigabytes (408 million terabytes) of hard disk storage are supported as well. With such large storage space available, single applications can access up to 2Gb of virtual memory.

Network Management Features   Administration of all servers in a domain is facilitated through domain management as if they were a single server. Alerts can signal disk and printer failures and security violations. NTAS also tracks selected network statistics and logs errors. Network tasks such as file backup or other program execution can be scheduled to occur automatically. SNMP agents are provided with NTAS; optional management functionality using IBM's mainframe-based NetView system is achieved via SNA Server for Windows NT.

Administration of any server is possible from any client workstation, but DOS clients provide only command-line interaction with management utilities. Management services include a file manager, print manager, control panel, user manager disk administrator, and event viewer.

Where NT Advanced Server Stands and Where It Is Going

Microsoft has tried before to compete with Novell in this market, but previous attempts have failed miserably. Further, there is no indication that NT is as wildly successful as Microsoft claims. End users are not entirely convinced that NT can provide them with anything they do not already have. A big factor in the equation are Novell NetWare and Banyan VINES, which have a large base of happy customers. These NOSs have held strong against Microsoft for many years now, and are well regarded by users and developers. Their users are unlikely to switch. Another limiting factor is that NT is a new player on the scene. It is difficult to predict whether it will mature to a stable production environment, or be quickly replaced as Microsoft's newer operating systems are delivered.

However, for now, Microsoft is trying to compete by means of low pricing and bundled features such as Macintosh support and remote access capability that were formerly offered as options to LAN Manager. In addition, Windows NT has some advanced features that are not offered by the NOS competitors, such as support for symmetric multiprocessing (SMP) platforms, large amounts of RAM, and large hard disk storage devices.

UNIX

Several UNIX implementations are available in client/server versions, the foremost being Santa Cruz Operation Open Desktop/Open Server, Novell UnixWare, and SunSoft Solaris. These operating systems are designed to interoperate with many different computers and operating systems, as well as other networks.

SunSoft Solaris

All versions of Solaris, including the desktop version, include ONC+, which, as mentioned earlier in this chapter, is SunSoft's distributed computing service, used to build a heterogeneous distributed computing environment. Thus, when you purchase a Solaris-based platform, you essentially have the building blocks necessary to begin implementing distributed computing.

Another advantage is that Solaris directly supports two of the most high-yielding hardware architectures on the market today—SPARC and Intel. Applications are source-code-compatible between the two platforms, allowing developers to create one application for two architectures.

SunSoft provides three implementations of its Solaris operating environment—all are bundled with ONC+:

Solaris Desktop   This system is designed to meet the needs of the client desktop. It includes SunOS 5, ONC+, networking, multiprocessing, and system and network administration, both for SPARC and for X86 platforms.

Solaris Workgroup Server   This environment is for the small to midrange departmental server. It includes all the features of Solaris Desktop, plus server networking, naming services, and remote system administration.

Solaris Enterprise Server   Designed for the enterprise-wide server, this system includes all the features of Solaris Workgroup Server, plus advanced system administration, I/O, and installation features.

Novell UnixWare

UnixWare provides users with seamless access to the dominant networking environment—Novell NetWare. NetWare protocols are built into the operating system, making network setup and configuration unnecessary, since users can access the NetWare network immediately upon installation.

Novell is working toward moving UnixWare to a microkernel environment over the next few years, and the current version of UnixWare provides an evolutionary path toward this microkernel. A microkernel is a stripped down operating system that provides only core-level services, such as access to devices and interfacing, to a particular processor. Users can add an operating system component of choice over the microkernel, such as UnixWare, OSF/1, OS/2, and MS-DOS simultaneously. Any application that is native to these operating systems will run on the microkernel platform. In addition, a microkernel will expand the operating system's scope to deliver more advanced distributed configurations and integration of multiple application environments.

One problem is that UnixWare is available only on Intel-based systems, although its base operating system, System V 4.2, continues to be available for other processors. However, when using UnixWare as a server on the NetWare LAN, its hardware architecture should be considered a minor limitation, because its instant NetWare access allows connection to all other network servers, regardless of their hardware architecture.

Connectivity to NetWare services is accomplished over standard IPX/SPX protocols, the Novell C interface for the UNIX API, automounting, autoauthentication, MHS mail, and the Packet Burst Protocol enhancements for transfer of large files. It includes both Ethernet and token ring drivers.

There are two UnixWare operating system products:

Personal Edition   This is a single-user client UNIX system designed for seamless integration into NetWare.

Application Server   This is a distributed server UNIX system providing multiuser access to UNIX applications. It incorporates TCP/IP and IPX/SPX networking and provides seamless integration with NetWare.

The Santa Cruz Operation (SCO) Open Desktop and Open Server

SCO is another UNIX developer that concentrates on the client/server network market. Its Open Desktop and Open Server products are networked graphical UNIX environments for Intel platforms and multiprocessor systems. It is intended to provide a foundation for distributed workgroup applications.

Interoperability is fostered through a suite of networking services, which include TCP/IP, Network Information Services (NIS), NFS, and the client portion of Microsoft LAN Manager. It supports IBM Token Ring, 3Com, Western Digital, and other networks.

SCO's most notable strength is that its products support more computer systems and applications than those of any other UNIX vendor. Their built-in networking facilities make them capable of being used with diverse, distributed, and heterogeneous environments. Open Server's protocols can act as gateways between networks such as NetWare and LAN Manager.

Like UnixWare, SCO's operating environments are limited to Intel-based architectures, although this should not be considered a limitation in a LAN-based environment, because it is interoperable with other non-Intel-based systems. One possible detriment is SCO's choice of LAN Manager as its basis for interoperable networking. LAN Manager has been dropped by Microsoft, which is only providing support to the product.

The SCO operating system product line includes the following:

Open Desktop   This is a desktop version, which includes SCO UNIX, DOS/Windows/UNIX integration, Motif graphical user interface, networking services, and personal productivity and groupware accessories.

Open Desktop Lite   This is a smaller desktop version including SCO UNIX, Motif, and TCP/IP, but it does not offer NFS, NIS, LAN Manager client, or MS-DOS/Windows support.

Open Server Network System   This is an integrated server system designed for Novell and TCP/IP networks. It is designed for use with database engines, multiple communications protocols, text-based software, and client/server environments. It includes SCO UNIX, TCP/IP, NFS, and IPX/SPX protocols.

Open Server Enterprise System   This is a server system with a high-performance server for company-wide networks of PCs, workstations, and centralized business systems. It includes SCO UNIX, DOS/Windows support, Motif, and networking services. It also includes IPX/SPX protocols and the client section of Microsoft LAN Manager.

Summary

Depending on the level of interoperability required, the selections for an infrastructure vary. Distributed computing environments provide the most powerful, most flexible environments, but they are difficult and complex to develop and manage. In addition, the end-user development cycle is lengthy. However, distributed computing environments promise the best interoperability in a large-scale heterogeneous environment.

NOSs may also reach the large-scale audience, but they are much less flexible and provide client/server relationships rather than true distributed services. Likewise, traditional server-based operating systems generally provide client/server facilities, not distributed environments, except for SunSoft Solaris, which is bundled with the ONC+ distributed environment.

Nonetheless, infrastructure technologies are unavoidable. Making the right decision could mean the difference between spending millions of dollars and several years on something that works, or on something that doesn't.

Chapter Twelve

Client/Server Technologies

By Joe Salemi

W hen you think of how pervasive the Client/Server architecture is today, it's sometimes hard to believe that the term *client/server* didn't even exist a decade ago. The computer world first heard the term in late 1987, with the release of a report from Forrester Research, Inc., one of the many companies that specialize in analyzing trends in the computer industry. The title of the report was "The New Client/Server Paradigm," and the term Client/Server was adapted by Microsoft and SYBASE to describe the technology behind their SQL Server. Client/Server (C/S) usually refers to the architecture underlying a number of database products. However, the C/S architecture is also used by other applications that bear little resemblance to traditional databases.

This chapter will cover the terms and technology behind the C/S architecture, and the ways in which it differs from traditional LAN applications. I'll then cover some of the popular C/S database products, including database servers and front-end applications. And finally, I'll finish up the chapter with a discussion of some of the other types of C/S applications available.

The Client/Server Architecture

Before you can decide whether the C/S architecture is right for your organization's needs, you must have an understanding of what it is, how it works, and the benefits it can and can't provide. This section will cover the technology and terms used in the Client/Server architecture, the hardware and software platforms it runs on, and the network capabilities needed to run C/S applications.

I'll be using database applications to describe the Client/Server architecture, since databases are currently the most common C/S applications. However, keep in mind that the architecture can be (and has been) applied to other applications as well. The applications may differ, but the underlying concepts remain the same.

The Technology Behind Client/Server Systems

Traditional PC-based Database Management Systems (DBMSs) range from the low-end non-programmable databases to the high-end systems where little can be done without programming. Their data handling capabilities range from accessing a single data file to those that provide semirelational capabilities, such as looking up data from other files and joining the data from two or more files into a single query result or report.

Single-user databases have the advantage of speed, as both the application and the data reside on the same PC. The speed advantage, though, is offset by two other factors that make a single-user database less than the ideal solution for an organization. The first factor is that because it *is* single-user, the data can't easily be shared with others who need it. Second, and perhaps most important, is the lack of security provided by a single-user PC—anyone with access to the PC can usually access the data in the database.

Moving to the LAN

The majority of LAN-based databases start out on a single-user system, running one of the traditional PC-based database applications, such as FoxPro or dBASE. The database application then gets moved to the LAN so that more users can access the data. Most PC-based databases come with either a built-in LAN option, or have a LAN-ready version available. Putting the database on the LAN is as simple as moving the data files and application software to the file server, and establishing the necessary number of users, up to the maximum supported by the LAN version. The database users can then load the database application off the server, and share the same data files. The type of LAN operating system, protocol, and cabling used doesn't matter. Anything from a peer-to-peer network to the top-end networks, such as NetWare and VINES, can support a multiuser database.

But there's more to it than just moving the data and giving the users access to it. Data sharing leads to a number of complications that the DBMS has to address. The most important is concurrency control, or data locking, which determines how the DBMS handles two or more users accessing the same file or record to make changes to the data. *Concurrency control* determines which changes take effect, and in what order, by preventing other users from changing the file or record until the first user's changes are applied.

There are many ways to implement concurrency control, and different applications use one or more of the common methods. In traditional PC-based DBMSs, concurrency control is usually left entirely to the DBMS. In some cases, though, the high-end applications provide the user or programmer with a choice of concurrency control based on the action being taken on the data.

The simplest method is to give the first user who opens the data file, for data entry or updating, exclusive read/write access, locking all other users out. This method pretty much defeats the purpose of having a multiuser database, so it's not commonly used except in some limited situations, such as a batch update, or a sorting or packing operation.

Some DBMSs provide a file locking mechanism where the first user to open the file for entry or updates is given read/write access, and all other users are given read-only or browse access. With this method, other database users can still do lookups and reports on the data. Some DBMSs can also notify those with read-only access that the file has changed and can even automatically show the change on their screen.

Sophisticated multiuser DBMSs can use record-level locking, where only the record being added or changed is locked. Other users can still make changes to other records in the same file, without causing a conflict. A few DBMSs even provide field-level locking, where only the field being changed gets locked. This method represents one of the highest levels of concurrency control for a traditional DBMS, though it's usually not necessary.

The maximum amount of concurrency control is provided by *transaction processing*. This method differs from the others in that any data entries or updates are entered in a separate file called a transaction log, instead of directly in the data file. The data updates are written to the data file when the user or application specifically commits them. Transaction processing was originally developed and implemented on multiuser host-based databases running on a minicomputer or mainframe, and has become a feature of Client/Server DBMSs as well. Few traditional PC databases implement it, and the ones that do (such as dBASE IV and FoxPro) only apply it to a single record. Transaction processing will be covered in greater detail later in this chapter.

The biggest disadvantage of using a traditional database on a LAN is the increase in network traffic. When a user wants to access the database, the first thing that usually happens is that the file server sends the application code to the workstation, where the actual processing happens. In some cases, the entire data file and any related files such as the indexes are sent across the network cable to the user's PC. This happens even if the user is only browsing or editing a single record. As the number of database users increases, the amount of data passing back and forth on the network also increases, which can lead to a general performance slowdown. Figure 12-1 shows how this process works.

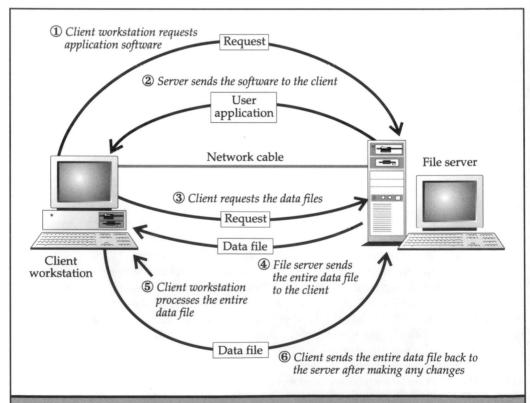

Figure 12-1. *Using a traditional database on a LAN results in significant network traffic.*

There are a number of actions that take place when a user accesses a traditional PC-based DBMS across a LAN.

The performance of the database itself is another issue. As was mentioned previously, with some LAN-based database applications, all processing actually takes place on the user's workstation. The file server acts as nothing more than a remote shared hard disk. As the size of the database increases, the workstation's performance can decrease, especially if it's not a high-powered system.

Last but not least, there are security issues involved when using a traditional PC-based DBMS. Most PC DBMS file formats are well-known, and can be accessed by a number of different applications. This is especially true with the common XBASE data file format. While some DBM provide data encryption or password access features, it's still possible for a user to circumvent the security programmed into the DBMS that created the data file, by accessing the file with a different DBMS or application. It's also possible for an external application to make changes to the data file that cause the data to become corrupted, or to become inaccessible from the primary DBMS.

The Client/Server architecture represents a solution to these problems.

Client/Server Databases

The first Client/Server DBMS was announced in 1988, when Microsoft and Ashton-Tate licensed the SYBASE SQL Server DBMS for use on PC-based LANs, with the database server running on OS/2. Up to this time, Relational Database Management Systems (RDBMSs) that usually ran on minicomputers and mainframes were only available as single-user applications for PCs; the ORACLE RDBMS was a prime example. The combination of the high-powered Intel 80386 CPU and a multitasking operating system for PCs finally provided the power to run resource-intensive RDBMSs on the desktop.

Though Ashton-Tate soon dropped out of the project, other RDBMS vendors were quick to follow Microsoft's lead. Oracle, IBM, Informix, and Gupta soon provided C/S versions of their RDBMSs that ran under OS/2. Novell entered the C/S market with the release of NetWare 3.0, which provided the ability to run sophisticated applications on the file server. Today, the major Client/Server RDBMSs are available for OS/2, NetWare, VINES, and Windows NT Advanced Server, as well as a number of UNIX versions, giving LAN and database administrators the ability to use the C/S architecture regardless of which network operating system they use.

The first step toward understanding the difference between traditional and C/S DBMSs is an examination of the relational database model. The relational model was developed in the late 1960s by E.F. Codd, a scientist with IBM. The relational model introduced the idea of data independence and mathematical set concepts as the foundation for a database architecture. Up to that point, database applications directly accessed the data files to manipulate them; in addition, the data was stored in records consisting of fields of individual data items.

The relational model makes the DBMS itself responsible for accessing and managing the data. The user database application asks the DBMS for the data or passes the data along to the DBMS for storage, and the DBMS then accesses its own files to do the appropriate processing. The details of how the data is stored on the server's disk are hidden from the user's application.

The relational model also introduced the concept of *data tables,* where the data is presented to the user as a series of rows in one or more columns. The columns and rows are respectively equivalent to fields and records used by other databases. This concept gives the RDBMS more flexibility in sorting and presenting the data to the user, while hiding the actual details of how the data is stored and manipulated. Thus, the relational model both increases database flexibility and provides greater data security and integrity protection.

The relational model remained a paper concept until the late 1970s, when minicomputers and mainframes began to have enough processing power for experimental relational databases to be developed. IBM performed the initial experiments, and eventually brought its own RDBMS to market. At the same time, IBM released the Structured Query Language (SQL), which eventually became the standard programming language for relational databases. Oracle Corp. was actually the first to release a commercial RDBMS that used SQL. Other companies such as Ingres, Informix, and SYBASE soon followed with their own RDBMSs.

In addition to the relational capabilities, the host-based RDBMSs provided better support for concurrency control through transaction processing (TP). In a TP system, all the data updates, deletions, and data entries are treated as a group of actions called a *transaction,* and kept in a transaction log. They're not written to the actual database until the database application issues the command to commit the data. The RDBMS then processes the transactions and makes the appropriate changes to the database itself. It notifies the users if the changes are unsuccessful, or if there's a conflict between one user's changes and another's.

The transaction log is also stored with the database for an administrator-determined amount of time, to provide an extra level of data integrity protection. If the DBMS should crash, the database administrator (and sometimes the DBMS itself) can use the transaction log to restore the database to its last known consistent state.

Host-based relational databases used the features of the minicomputer's or mainframe's multitasking operating system to separate the user applications from the RDBMS. Users on a terminal ran the database application on the host as one task, and the application passed the data queries and updates to the RDBMS, running as a separate task, through the operating system's interprocess communications facilities. The RDBMS would then process the query or update, and send the result back to the user application.

Pros and Cons of the Client/Server Architecture

The beauty of the Client/Server architecture is that it takes this concept one step further—the user application is moved to the user's workstation, and the RDBMS runs on its own computer. The user workstation is commonly referred to as the *client,* and the user application as the *front-end*. The back-end system that the RDBMS runs on is called the *database server*. The C/S architecture splits the data processing load between two or more computers, spreading the load around the network, instead of relying entirely on the processing power of the client system.

The advantages of the C/S architecture are immediately obvious. First and foremost, the performance of the database application is no longer dependent on the power of the client system—the client only has to have enough power to run the front-end application. The client system just formulates the query or update, and passes it along to the server for processing. The server does all the actual database processing, and only has to send the portion of the data that fits the query criteria, or the results of the update, back to the client, as Figure 12-2 shows. The only high-

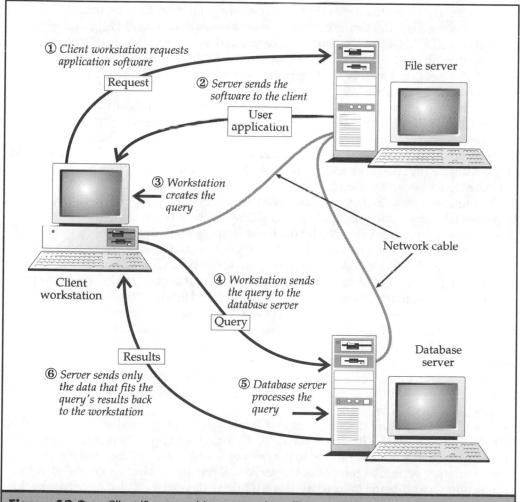

Figure 12-2.   *Client/Server architecture makes efficient use of computer power and network transactions.*

powered machine necessary is the server that runs the database, and it's also the only machine that needs to be upgraded as the database gets larger, or as more users are added.

The Client/Server architecture splits the processing between the client system (the user's workstation) and the server. Note that only the necessary data travels across the network cable, significantly reducing network traffic.

Though it's generally not a good idea to do so, small C/S databases, or those with only a few users, can be run on the LAN file server. As the number of users or size of the database increases, the RDBMS can be moved to its own dedicated system, without any change in how the clients access it.

The C/S architecture also provides increased data security, as the users no longer have to directly access the data files for queries or updates. In fact, the users generally can't access the data files or the database server at all; all data access is provided through the RDBMS. Data security is also enhanced by the RDBMS's ability to grant user security on multiple levels, right down to the column level in most cases. Users can even be restricted to only reading certain portions of the data, based on database rules enforced by the RDBMS.

Another big advantage of the C/S architecture is that it can significantly reduce network traffic. As you can see in Figure 12-2, the only traffic going from the client to the database server is the query or update. The database server only has to send back the result set that satisfies the query or update. Unlike a traditional LAN database, the entire data file isn't passed back and forth across the cable, leading to a corresponding decrease in network traffic loads.

The final advantage of the C/S architecture is front-end independence. In a traditional database, the user applications all have to be written using the programming language provided by the DBMS. Application developers have few choices in what language to use and are limited in how the user interface appears by the DBMS's application development tools. In a C/S system, the application developer can use any front-end application that can talk to the particular DBMS in use. Users who need to update the database can use one front-end application, while those who only need to browse or report on the data can use another, simpler one. Front-end applications are also available for a number of operating systems and environments; DOS, UNIX, OS/2, Macintosh, and Windows users, for example, can all access the same database server.

The next step up from the C/S architecture is distributed databases, which are beyond the scope of this chapter. Distributed database technologies will be covered in greater detail in Chapter 13.

The C/S architecture does have its disadvantages. The biggest disadvantage is the extra level of complexity it adds to the LAN. Using a C/S application at the minimum means adding an additional server to the network, which may or may not run the same operating system as the rest of the servers. If the data it holds is critical to your organization's well-being (and what data isn't these days), you'll also have to take the necessary precautions in case the database server crashes, such as having a dedicated tape system for on-line backups and an uninterruptible power supply (UPS) to keep the server running if the power goes out.

It may also mean having to use an additional network protocol to provide communications between the clients and the servers (protocols are covered later in this section).

As the C/S application grows, the time will come when managing the database server becomes a full-time job, so you'll also have to hire a full-time database administrator. And don't forget the costs of retraining your existing application development staff in the new languages and concepts needed to successfully develop and support a C/S application.

Hardware for Client/Server Systems

The general rule-of-thumb for a network file server is that disk speed is the most important factor in network performance. In a C/S system, disk speed is only one of three factors that determine how well the server performs. Disk speed is important, though, because faster hard disks mean that the database server software can get to the data faster.

Processor speed is also important to the overall performance of the C/S system. Remember that at least half of the application processing takes place on the server itself. Add to that the extra processing required by multiple users making data updates or requests at the same time. The faster the CPU, the better the overall system performs.

The final factor in determining overall system performance is the amount of RAM in the server. Most C/S server applications require at least as much memory as the base operating system just to function. Each user connection also requires additional RAM (the amount needed is different for each application), and the server software can use additional RAM for cache buffers or shared user workspace to increase response time. A perfectly acceptable amount of RAM for a file server usually represents the bare minimum for a C/S application.

So what's the basic hardware required for a C/S server application? Taking all the above factors into account, the basic server platform, when running Intel-based systems, should consist of at least a 80486 CPU, running at 66 MHz, with 16MB RAM and at least a 500MB hard disk. The hard disk should be the fastest you can get, preferably using the RAID architecture to provide an extra level of data protection.

A RISC workstation or server can also be used as the server in a C/S system. However, using a RISC platform usually adds more complexity to the overall system, including the need for expertise in a different operating system (usually a form of UNIX), and a different networking protocol (usually TCP/IP).

No matter what type of hardware you choose for the server, don't forget to include a tape subsystem for real-time backups, and a UPS to keep the server running in case of a power outage. The vast majority of C/S server applications include some form of crash recovery capabilities, but it's better to prevent the crash in the first place.

Operating Systems That Support Client/Server Computing

One of the reasons the C/S architecture was developed was to take advantage of the (at the time) new multitasking operating systems that became available for PCs. Initially, the only choice available was OS/2, but today you have a number of operating systems to choose from. In addition to OS/2 1.3 or better, most C/S server applications are available for NetWare 3.1 or better, Windows NT, and one or more of the many UNIX variants available for PCs or RISC workstations.

Just about all C/S vendors have a PC-based server version that runs under OS/2, and most have been updated to take advantage of the 32-bit capabilities of OS/2 2.x. OS/2 is a viable platform for server applications, as long as you keep in mind the fact that you'll probably have to use an additional networking protocol to communicate with the server if you don't run an OS/2-based LAN.

NetWare is the most popular network operating system around, and most C/S vendors have an NLM (NetWare Loadable Module) version of their software available. Because of this, many NetWare users are tempted to run the C/S application on the same server that the network services (file and print) run on. Don't give in to this temptation, particularly with a database server. Even though it may seem that you have enough capacity on your file server to add the database server software, you'll be much better off in the long run putting the database on its own server right from the start.

Windows NT has the potential to become the best platform for C/S applications, primarily because of its scalability. In addition to the version that runs on Intel-based PCs, there are versions of NT that run on RISC platforms, such as the DEC Alpha systems. This gives you the ability to start your server out on a PC, and move up to a larger system as your database grows, without having to change your server application (other than getting the appropriate version for the new platform, of course). NT is relatively new, though, so only time will tell if this potential pans out.

Finally, there are a number of UNIX variants you can use for your server operating system. Many C/S vendors sell a version of their software that runs on the PC-based UNIX systems. However, if you decide to use UNIX for your server, you should go all the way and use a RISC system for the hardware. It's better to run UNIX on a system that's designed for it from the ground up, instead of on a system that UNIX has been adapted to.

Networking Protocols for Client/Server Systems

The type of network topology you use for a C/S system is immaterial. As long as the client workstations can communicate over the cable with the file server, the same cable can be used to talk to a C/S server.

The network protocol used is another matter. Today's PC LANs are based on technology that was developed before the C/S architecture became available. IPX and other XNS variants were designed more for speed than for application-to-application communications. NetBIOS was designed for communications between applications, but has its limitations on how much data it can carry. Neither is really designed to carry the amount of data that can pass between clients and servers in a C/S system. Running a C/S system on a PC-based LAN requires both compromises and additional protocol support to make up for the lack of C/S capabilities found in the network operating systems.

The C/S vendors have taken a number of different approaches to solving this problem. Microsoft and IBM developed an extended version of OS/2's interprocess communications capabilities called Named Pipes, which are used to provide communications between the clients and servers running on OS/2 and now Windows NT. Named Pipes are built into these companies' network operating systems, so the only additional software needed on the workstations is a small driver that handles the interface between the application and the protocol. However, if you're using another network, such as NetWare, you'll also have to load any Named Pipes support drivers provided by the network vendor.

Other companies, such as Oracle and Gupta, developed their own C/S protocol that has to be loaded on the workstations and the server in addition to the network protocol drivers. These C/S protocol drivers can take up anywhere from about 20K RAM on the client workstation to over 200K, depending on the vendor.

Some C/S vendors have added support for using IPX as their communications protocol. This support comes at a price, though, because IPX wasn't designed to support C/S communications. The native IPX version of the C/S software usually lacks one or more features that are found in the versions that use the vendor's C/S protocol.

TCP/IP can also be used as the communications protocol for some C/S systems, especially those that run on UNIX. TCP/IP isn't used as the native protocol in most PC-based LANs, though, so you'll have to factor in the additional memory requirements needed by the TCP/IP drivers on the client workstations.

The additional RAM requirements on the client workstations can be a big factor in choosing the appropriate C/S software for your organization. One way to solve this problem is to run Windows or OS/2 on the client systems. Both make use of the extended memory found on 80286 and better systems, and also provide virtual memory services, so the amount of RAM used by the C/S drivers is less of a factor than it is on a DOS system. The majority of C/S vendors provide their protocol drivers in Windows DLL (Dynamic Link Library) format, and also have OS/2 drivers available. In any case, be prepared to have to run (and support) an additional protocol when you set up a C/S system.

Client/Server Databases

Database servers are the most common C/S application. The majority of RDBMS vendors have a version of their software that runs on PC-based LAN; the only major exceptions at this time are DEC's RDB/VMS, and Hewlett Packard's ALLBASE. There are even a few C/S DBMSs that are designed from the ground up to run on PCs.

It's impossible to cover all the features of all the C/S DBMSs available in a single chapter; whole books have been written about them (including three by this author). This section covers the three most popular C/S databases, with a brief discussion of some of the others. It also covers some of the many front-end applications available. For more in-depth coverage of these products, check the database section of your local computer bookstore.

Client/Server DBMSs

The top three C/S DBMSs are SQL Server from Microsoft and SYBASE, ORACLE from Oracle Corp., and DB2/2 from IBM. Other popular products include Gupta's SQLBase, and Watcom SQL, as well as products from Ingres and Informix.

SQL Server

The SYBASE SQL Server was the first Client/Server DBMS, though at the time it was developed, the term C/S didn't exist. SQL Server was initially developed and released for UNIX, but the version that caught the attention of the computer industry was the jointly developed version for OS/2 that was announced by Microsoft and SYBASE in early 1988. Under the joint development agreement, Microsoft was responsible for developing versions of SQL Server for its operating systems, and SYBASE would develop versions for UNIX and VAX/VMS.

Microsoft's backing of SQL Server quickly made it the top-selling PC-based C/S DBMS. To this day, the Microsoft SQL Server has had the greatest support among third-party front-end vendors. Slight differences between the Microsoft and SYBASE versions make it difficult, though not impossible, to support both companies' versions from the same front-end application, though this problem has diminished over the years.

Microsoft SQL Server 1.0 was based on SYBASE 3.0 code. When SYBASE released version 4.2, Microsoft jumped to the same version number to reduce confusion between the two companies' products. However, SYBASE continued to add features to their own version (including many developed by Microsoft), so their current version is 4.9. Microsoft continued developing the OS/2 version, as well as a version for Windows NT. SYBASE added a NetWare NLM version to their product line. The current products from both companies are functionally equivalent.

Microsoft's OS/2 version of SQL Server runs under OS/2 1.3. It will also run under OS/2 2.x, but it's still a 16-bit application and doesn't take advantage of 2.x's 32-bit capabilities. Microsoft has promised an OS/2 2.x version, but has yet to release it (probably a result of Microsoft's abandonment of all responsibility for OS/2 to IBM). The 32-bit version of SQL Server was released in mid-1993 for Windows NT. Microsoft SQL Server's primary network protocol is Named Pipes, and it also supports IPX and TCP/IP, though with reduced security features.

SYBASE's NLM version of SQL Server runs on NetWare 3.11 or higher, and uses either IPX or TCP/IP as its protocol. SYBASE SQL Server is also available for over 100 different versions of UNIX, using TCP/IP as the protocol. In early 1993, SYBASE announced System 10, a completely new version of SQL Server that updates its capabilities to provide better support for large databases and distributed database processing. System 10 also updates the native SQL Server language (called Transact-SQL) to support the most recent ANSI SQL standards. System 10 also includes a family of related products that provide additional support for distributed processing. At the time of this writing, SYBASE SQL Server 10.0 is available for a limited number of UNIX systems. SYBASE expects to release 10.0 for all of the operating systems currently supported by 4.9 by the end of 1994.

Microsoft initially announced that it would be updating its versions of SQL Server to the System 10 level. In early April, 1994, Microsoft and SYBASE separated, and Microsoft announced that it would be developing its own database server product. The full ramifications of this announcement are as yet unknown; however, it appears that future versions of Microsoft SQL Server (assuming it continues to use the name) will bear little resemblance to the SYBASE versions. In the long run, SQL Server users will have to decide if they want to continue using the Microsoft products, or to stick with the SYBASE SQL Server technology.

Oracle

Oracle Corp.'s ORACLE RDBMS had the distinction of being the first SQL-based database management system commercially available. ORACLE was originally developed for DEC's VAX/VMS operating system, and VMS remains its primary platform. However, versions are available for everything from the PC to an IBM mainframe, including most UNIX variants. ORACLE has always been the best-selling RDBMS overall, but ranks second in popularity in the C/S market.

Shortly after the initial SQL Server announcement, Oracle adapted its ORACLE 6.0 RDBMS to include C/S capabilities, and released an OS/2 1.x version. ORACLE 6.0 has since become available as a NetWare NLM, and in a 32-bit OS/2 2.x version. ORACLE uses its own communications protocol, called SQL*Net. SQL*Net supports virtually all the networking protocols available, which makes ORACLE one of the most network-independent C/S databases available today. ORACLE also has the advantage of scalability—all versions are identical in features and functions, and front-end applications designed for the PC versions can be used to access any other version of ORACLE through SQL*Net. This means that you can easily move your database to a larger platform without having to change the database itself or the front-ends that access it. The biggest problem with ORACLE 6.0 is that it is a resource hog, using more than twice as much memory per user than other C/S RDBMSs.

ORACLE 7.0 is designed specifically to provide better support for the C/S architecture. It was first released in late 1992 for the VMS operating system; the OS/2 and NetWare versions became available in late 1993. In many ways, version 7.0's new features provide the same level of support for C/S applications as SQL Server, while improving both performance and resource usage over those offered by ORACLE 6.0. ORACLE 7.0 is still too new to have had a significant impact on the C/S market at the time of this writing—however, the split between Microsoft and SYBASE could help Oracle dominate the C/S market in the same way it dominates the overall database market.

DB2/2

When IBM first released OS/2, it sold both the basic operating system, and the Extended Edition. OS/2 Extended Edition included three additional applications, including an OS/2 DBMS called Database Manager (DM). At first, DM was a stand-alone product, but its capabilities were extended to support C/S applications with OS/2 1.2. DM was a stripped-down version of IBM's flagship RDBMS, the mainframe-based DB2. DM used Named Pipes running on NetBIOS as its protocol.

With the release of OS/2 2.0, IBM dropped the Extended Edition and made DM a separate application. In 1993, IBM replaced DM with DB2/2, a complete 32-bit OS/2-based version of DB2. DB2/2 supports the full IBM SQL, as well as all the features and capabilities of its big brother. DB2/2 uses Named Pipes running on NetBIOS as its protocol, and also supports IBM's APPC (Advanced Program-to-Program Communications) application programming interface.

DB2/2 is primarily designed for organizations that are looking for a way to interface their LANs to a mainframe running DB2. IBM's primary business is still large systems, and DB2/2 represents an ideal solution for organizations looking for a way to combine different databases running on IBM hardware into an enterprise-wide database system. DB2/2 also has enough power and capabilities to become a significant player in the PC-based C/S market.

Other Client/Server DBMSs

Gupta's SQLBase was the first C/S DBMS designed specifically for PCs. The current version is available for OS/2 2.x and as a NetWare NLM, and uses its own protocol to provide communications. The driver runs on IPX, TCP/IP, and NetBIOS. Gupta has also released SQLBase for a limited number of RISC workstations, primarily the Sun Microsystems SPARC systems. SQLBase was the first C/S RDBMS to provide full support for relational integrity, one of the key data integrity features in the relational model. It also has the distinction of being the least expensive C/S DBMS available today. However, it hasn't become as popular as the other C/S databases available, primarily because the protocol driver SQLBase uses takes up over 200K RAM on DOS workstations. Gupta is better known for its C/S applications and development tools (covered later in this section).

Watcom is primarily known for its third-generation language compilers, but in 1993 it released Watcom SQL, a full-featured C/S database server that runs under DOS, Windows, and as a NetWare NLM. The Windows version is single-user; the DOS version supports up to six users, and includes a 32-bit DOS extender. The NetWare version supports up to 32 users. Watcom SQL uses either IPX or NetBIOS as its communications protocol. Watcom SQL would probably be a minor player in the C/S market if it weren't for the fact that a copy of the single-user version is included with every copy of Powersoft's PowerBuilder, one of the top Windows-based C/S application development toolkits.

Ingres and Informix are best known for their UNIX-based RDBMSs, though both have OS/2 versions and are working on NLM versions. Neither has had a significant impact on the market for PC-based C/S database servers, but many organizations use the UNIX versions for C/S applications. Both use TCP/IP as their primary protocol.

The newest entry in the C/S marketplace is Borland's InterBase, a UNIX-based RDBMS. Borland has announced, though not yet released, versions for NetWare, OS/2 2.*x*, and Windows NT. At this time, InterBase uses TCP/IP as its protocol, and the only front-end support is provided by Borland's own products.

ront-End Applications for Client/Server Systems

The server is only half the equation in a C/S system—equally important is the client, or front-end, application that your users will use to access the server. You'll find a wide variety of front-end applications available, ranging from development toolkits that let you create custom front-ends, to add-ons that let your existing PC applications access data from a server, to query and reporting tools, and to applications that let you create complex data analysis applications. There are also a large number of vertical market C/S front-ends available, designed to fit the needs of a particular organization or function.

In recent years, various C/S vendors have created Application Programming Interfaces (APIs) that are designed to access different database servers and files from a common front-end. The first, and currently foremost, API is Microsoft's Open Database Connectivity (ODBC). Borland banded together with a number of other application vendors to create the Independent Database Application Programming Interface (IDAPI), though a working version has yet to be released. And Oracle recently entered the fray with ORACLE Glue. Application developers can use these APIs to give their applications access to a number of database servers and file formats, without having to worry about the details behind how the data is accessed.

The products in this section are some of the more common front-end applications available today. The presence or absence of an application in no way implies an endorsement of any particular products.

evelopment Tools for Client/Server Systems

The most complex front-end applications are the development tools that let you create your own custom applications. These development tools give you a lot of power and control over your front-end applications, at the price of having to have your own in-house application programming staff, or having to hire a consultant to develop the applications for you.

Most RDBMS vendors also sell application development toolkits that are designed to work with one or more 3GLs, such as C, Basic, or COBOL. As you can guess, these toolkits are primarily designed for creating front-end applications to the vendors RDBMS. For example, Oracle has Oracle*Tools, a series of development toolkits that help you create user interface screens, menus, and reports that can be integrated into your 3GL programs, or can be run as stand-alone applications with the available run-time modules. Oracle*Tools is available for all the platforms supported by the

ORACLE RDBMS, and applications created for one operating system can easily be ported to another.

SYBASE also sells a series of tools called the APT Workbench, which run on UNIX. APT Workbench consists of a number of modules that make it easy to prototype, edit, and develop front-ends for the SYBASE SQL Server. As part of System 10, SYBASE has announced a new series of application development tools, which it calls the Momentum family. The Momentum toolkits are GUI-based, and will eventually be available for all the platforms supported by SQL Server.

Microsoft's primary application development toolkit is Visual Basic, which runs under Windows. The standard version of Visual Basic doesn't provide support for accessing C/S databases, so you'll also need the Microsoft Programmer's Toolkit for Visual Basic. The Programmer's Toolkit is included in the Visual Basic Professional Edition.

Third-party vendors have created application development toolkits that can access a number of different database servers and files. The most popular of these are Powersoft's PowerBuilder and Gupta's SQLWindows. Both products are based on Windows, and both are roughly equal in features and capabilities. As each vendor releases a new version, the other soon comes out with another version that at least equals and usually surpasses its competitors.

PowerBuilder is currently the more popular of the two. PowerBuilder comes in two versions: the basic PowerBuilder Desktop, a stand-alone development platform that uses the included copy of Watcom SQL as its data engine, and the PowerBuilder Enterprise, which extends Desktop's capabilities to access a number of database servers, including SQL Server, DB2/2, SQLBase, and ORACLE, as well as any others that support ODBC. PowerBuilder is known for its object-oriented interface that uses a number of screen painters to help the developer design, develop, and debug front-end applications. PowerBuilder uses its own PowerScript, a C-like script language, as its native development language.

Gupta's SQLWindows is also object-oriented, though the different modules aren't as tightly integrated as PowerBuilder's. SQLWindows comes with a stand-alone version of SQLBase as its database engine, and also comes in two versions—the basic SQLWindows package and the Corporate Edition. SQLWindows provides direct support for accessing an SQLBase server. Other servers, such as SQL Server, ORACLE, and DB2/2, are supported through add-on routers and gateways that Gupta sells. The basic package includes a copy of Gupta's Quest, an easy-to-use query and reporting tool that's also available separately. The Corporate Edition includes TeamWindows, which contains an application generator and version control capabilities that make it easier for a team of developers to work on the same application.

Existing Products as Front-Ends

Most organizations move up to a C/S database from an existing PC-based application or database. To help maintain this legacy data, and to remain a player in the C/S market, a number of PC application vendors provide add-ons to their products that let them access data from a database server.

For example, Lotus provides a number of their DataLens drivers with the current versions of 1-2-3. DataLens drivers for dBASE, Paradox, SQL Server, Informix, and IBM's DM are included with the base product. A DataLens driver for ORACLE is available from Oracle Corp. Figure 12-3 shows how external data sources can be accessed from within 1-2-3.

Lotus 1-2-3's DataLens drivers hook into the database menu to provide access to external databases.

Borland's Paradox is a popular PC-based database, and its reach can be extended to database servers through the add-on SQL Link modules. Paradox SQL Links are available for SQL Server, ORACLE, IBM's DM, and Borland InterBase, among others.

Access is Microsoft's entry into the grown Windows-based database market. In addition to its own data files, Access 1.1 comes with ODBC drivers that support SQL Server and ORACLE.

The most versatile add-on for Windows and OS/2 users is Pioneer's Q&E Database Editor. Q&E provides both query and update services for a number of

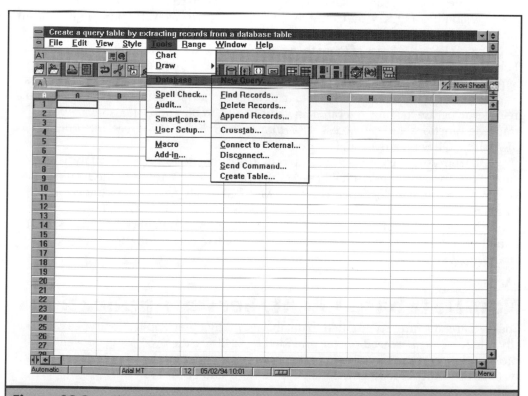

Figure 12-3.   *The 1-2-3 menu sequence for accessing external data sources*

database servers and files. More important, it supports Windows' and OS/2's Dynamic Data Exchange (DDE) capabilities to send the results of a query to other applications that don't have their own direct access to the database. It does its job so well that Microsoft includes a licensed version of Q&E with the Excel spreadsheet application.

Query and Reporting Tools

Many database users don't need anything more than the ability to query and report on the information stored in the database. To fill this need, third-party vendors have created query and reporting tools, which are simple applications that provide end-users an easy way to access the database server. Some of these tools may also provide update capabilities, though that's not a necessary function for this category of front-ends.

One of the more popular query and reporting tools is Gupta's Quest. Quest runs under Windows and uses dialog boxes, drop-down menus, and point-and-shoot capabilities to shield the user from the SQL commands needed to carry out the data request. Quest queries can be saved to disk and can be used for creating reports. The latest version has a Query-by-Example (QBE) interface, as well as a number of built-in charting functions. Quest supports the same databases as SQLWindows.

Trinzic's Forest & Trees is more than just a query and reporting tool, though it does those jobs well. Forest & Trees is also a data analysis tool that provides the ability to combine and examine data from multiple data sources. Forest & Trees uses Windows' graphic capabilities to present the data in a series of views that can be combined into a tree-like structure to show overall data values and combinations. It also provides graphing functions and can access data from over 15 different sources, including ORACLE, SQL Server, dBASE, Paradox, and R:Base.

GQL from Andyne Computing Ltd. provides query, reporting, and analysis capabilities for a number of GUI-based systems, including Windows, the Apple Macintosh, and the UNIX Open Look and Motif GUIs. GQL can access data from a number of database servers, including SYBASE SQL Server, ORACLE, Ingres, and Informix. GQL's strength lies in its point-and-shoot development capabilities, which combine with its dynamic joins of various databases to create complex query, reporting, and data analysis applications.

Non-Database Client/Server Applications

The C/S architecture isn't limited to databases; many other application types can take advantage of the increased power provided by splitting the processing between the client system and the server. Two of the more common examples of non-database C/S systems are many LAN-based e-mail applications and Lotus Notes.

-Mail

Some LAN-based e-mail applications used the Client/Server architecture before the term even existed. Such e-mail systems are split between the client package that's used to create and read messages, and the server package (which may run on the actual file server, or on a dedicated PC attached to the LAN) that takes care of routing the messages to the proper destination. These e-mail servers are usually referred to as store-and-forward systems, but the technology behind them is the same as that used in C/S systems. I sometimes suspect that the early store-and-forward systems were one of the inspirations behind the C/S technology.

The best early example of this type of system is 3Com's 3+Mail, which ran on 3Com's 3+Share and 3+Open network operating systems. 3+Mail users created new messages in the client package. After they saved the new message, the mail software running on the server would examine it and route it to the proper users, or even to another LAN.

A current example is Novell's Message Handling Service (MHS). The standard MHS package uses a dedicated PC attached to the LAN to handle forwarding the mail, which is usually stored on the file server. Standard MHS can be used with virtually any LAN system. Novell's Global MHS is sold as an NLM, and runs on the same server where the mail is stored. One of the advantages to using MHS as the mail transport is that any number of client packages can be used to create and read the mail, as long as they know how to interface with MHS.

otus Notes

Lotus Notes was one of the first of a class of software applications now known as groupware. Notes is actually a type of C/S database system that uses its own proprietary database. The Notes server currently runs on OS/2; Windows and NetWare NLM versions of the server software are scheduled for release in 1994.

The Notes client software runs under OS/2 and Windows. Notes' best feature is its flexibility. Notes databases appear as folders on the client screen and can be used for group discussions, shared data files, shared documents, or virtually any other group application that can be imagined and developed. Notes comes with a number of database templates that can be used to create common groupware applications, such as an e-mail system or a scheduling system. Notes also has built-in replication services, which automatically share databases across multiple servers so that users in various locations can take part in the same group applications.

The biggest disadvantage of Notes is its pricing; each client package costs almost $500 on the current price list. If you have a large number of users, the costs can add up quickly.

Other Applications

The C/S technology is spreading to other types of applications as well. One new class of C/S applications is group conferencing packages, which are primarily designed to provide the same group discussion capabilities found in Notes, at a more reasonable price. Group conferencing packages let LAN users hold meetings without actually having to be present in the same room at the same time; messages are posted in common discussion areas, or forums, and anyone with access to the forum can read and comment on messages left by the other users. Group conferencing packages typically use a store-and-forward e-mail system such as MHS, or their own messaging server to manage the message databases and routing.

Another new class of LAN-based applications are the workflow packages. These applications are designed to replace the paper forms found in most organizations with screen-based equivalents. Workflow applications such as Delrina's FormFlow have built-in form-design capabilities that let developers create exact duplicates of paper forms. The forms are filled-in on the screen, and then manually or automatically routed to the next processing point. Most workflow applications interface with either a standard e-mail package or their own e-mail store-and-forward engine to handle the routing, so these applications can be classified as C/S systems. Workflow applications are still in their infancy, but have the potential to become a major class of LAN-based C/S applications in the future.

Chapter Thirteen

Distributed Information Access Technologies

by Irving Robinson, AT&T

D uring the past decade or so enterprises have invested staggering sums into the creation and maintenance of numerous databases. The trends toward decentralization, open systems, and flexibility have also encouraged totally heterogeneous computing environments. Enterprise databases are being used to increase access capabilities across the enterprise, to provide decision support, and to increase efficiency through integration and automation. These initiatives are driving demands for distributed information access technologies.

At a very high level, the technical requirements for accessing distributed information seem simple:

- Understand the structure of the target databases.
- Understand the semantics of the data in the databases.
- Understand the usage of the access language or methods for the databases.
- Understand how to establish connections to the databases.

Of course, actual implementation can be much more complicated. The level of complexity will depend on how many "high hurdles" are in the execution path. For example, if the target databases are all well-designed and normalized relational databases on open UNIX computer systems supporting standard interfaces and open networking, it's entirely possible that the distributed access implementation will be straightforward. On the other hand, if you complicate matters a little by including navigational legacy databases, vendor-proprietary networking, nonstandard clients, or non-mainstream computing platforms (normal complicating factors found in many large enterprises), the implementation can become a very serious and risky project.

The perceived success of an implementation will depend on the enterprise's requirements and expectations for the distributed information access system. Stringent performance or response time requirements, expectations for completely seamless functional characteristics in a heterogeneous environment, or support for very large environments (for example, thousands of networked systems) are difficult goals to achieve with current technology. Grand-scale results should be expected to have grand-scale costs.

Database Models and Structures

Over the years, a number of models have been developed for storing data in computer systems. These models and structures are described in the following sections, starting with the simplest, and moving up to advanced data storage techniques that support the distribution of data in an enterprise environment.

File Systems

The structure of the target databases is the fundamental determinant for achieving distributed access. Commercial databases generally fall into three categories, or data models. The first and simplest are *file systems*, primary data structures generally accessed through some variation on read and write commands. File systems seldom have formal *metadata* (information about how the database is structured and defined), and especially lack metadata regarding the usage of fields in records. Field-level information is normally only available in the source code of the application programs that use the files, and there are no guarantees that any two applications will use a given file in a consistent manner. Seemingly the best thing to do with files is to ignore them, because they present so many problems for distributed access. But as we all know, there's an enormous amount of enterprise data still resident in file systems such as VSAM and UFS. It's also very unlikely that most of these files are going to be replaced anytime soon, because the same problems that make them difficult to access in a distributed environment make their associated applications difficult to reengineer.

Perhaps the best conclusions to draw about file systems is that, if you must provide distributed access to them, your job has become much more complex. As we'll discuss later, there are potential strategies for integrating file systems into distributed access environments, but a red flag should go up in your mind if file systems are in your distributed access plans.

Network and Hierarchical Databases

The second database category in most commercial environments is network and hierarchical databases. Some of these products are called CODASYL (Conference On Data Systems Languages) databases, after a committee that defined a standard for them. We'll group inverted list databases into this category, even though they have different attributes and behaviors than the network and hierarchical types. These products are more formalized than file systems, which is to say they generally have independently accessible metadata and the means to enforce data independence. Some of these products, like some modern file systems, are relatively sophisticated and can provide features like the tracking of transactions and, if necessary, rollback of transactions, concurrent access by multiple users, authorization, recovery, and so forth. Because these products typically require special application programming to navigate the physical structures of the databases (they lack a generalized query language), and because information is embedded in the storage structures (for example, the physical ordering of records in a file), they have limited use in an enterprise system where applications and data must be distributed to many locations.

Data stored in file systems and hierarchical or network databases is often called *legacy data*. Legacy data is usually stored on proprietary mainframe computers that often lack open systems connectivity. These systems also typically require programming and development skills that are viewed as arcane by IS (Information Systems) professionals trained in open systems and client/server networked environments. For many large enterprises, legacy data can be some of the most important information in the organization. For these enterprises, distributed access that doesn't include legacy data is unacceptably limited. There are strategies for enterprise-wide legacy data access, but having the proper expectations is the key to success. As you will see from the alternatives to be discussed later, if legacy data is involved, you might have to expect some combination of higher access costs, less flexibility, lower performance, loss of data freshness, or all of the above, as compared to a purely relational database environment.

Relational Databases

Relational databases have become the clear leader for commercial environments. There have been all sorts of books and articles written over the years detailing the advantages of the relational model, and they won't all be reiterated here. There are, however, certain characteristics that make relational databases especially amenable to distributed access environments, and it's probably best that we discuss them so that you will avoid choosing designs that might negate these advantages. First, and probably foremost, the relational model specifies that all relational databases consist only of two-dimensional tables with rows. The rows are not allowed to be in any inherent order, and a single dimension of columns is common to every row in the table. Rows are supposed to have a unique primary key that defines a sort order or other criteria. The model doesn't specify exactly how tables are physically represented; they could be in indexed files, hash files, chains, or what-have-you, but the key point is that this structure is supposed to be invisible to users of the database. All you see are tables and rows and columns.

Structured Query Language (SQL)

In almost every relational database product there is one other universal attribute, Structured Query Language (SQL). SQL, invented by IBM, but now standardized by an ANSI committee, is a combination of data definition language and data manipulation language that nominally consists of a few simple verbs (for example, CREATE, GRANT, SELECT, UPDATE, INSERT, DELETE) that can be used to develop very complicated database accesses involving multiple tables and selection criteria. SQL, at least implemented as the standard intends, specifies the targeted values of the queries or updates, but allows nothing to be specified about how the data is to be accessed. (However, SQL does include the concept of cursors that technically allows you to navigate a table row by row.) You can't choose indices, propose a query plan, save a pointer, or any of that performance-oriented nonsense that made legacy data such a frustrating legacy. Relational databases are expected to have efficient optimizers that make all of these decisions either at compilation time or at execution time. Depending on the distributed access strategy you select, the quality of a distributed optimizer can be a critical success factor. We'll discuss this further when we examine distributed schemas and distributed SQL accesses.

istributed Relational Databases

Relational databases make distribution easier because the access software can know reasonably what to expect from each local database. It will see a collection of two-dimensional tables that can always be accessed with SQL. This commonality means that it's far easier to associate information stored in one database with information stored in another, especially if the database administrators have taken care to normalize the data properly. (Normalization is the process of properly choosing keys, arranging the proper columns into rows in the proper tables, and eliminating duplicates.)

Contrast the distributed relational environment with that for legacy databases. Each site would likely have a different set of programs required to navigate the target databases. One site might have databases organized as a collection of flat files, while another might have databases with complex hierarchies, or perhaps pointer chains to be followed, complete with coded records.

It's probably worth mentioning that all of these positive characteristics of relational databases for distributed access, the semantic orientation of SQL, the simplicity and commonality of data structures, and the lack of navigational and low-level programming capabilities, are often pointed to as being responsible for a certain lack of flexibility and loss of performance. In theory, this simply isn't true; in reality (with real-world products) it probably is. The proper perspective is that distributed access is complicated and difficult enough that any factors which can be simplified should be simplified, and relational databases are the best compromise for most environments.

Database Semantics

A key problem with using and interpreting distributed data, is that the semantics of the information (the meaning and interpretation) is often encrypted, or perhaps is only meaningful in the context of a local application. Common examples of semantic problems include:

- Columns that have names like "usage_code," where the field can have an integer value that is normally interpreted by an application.

- Multiple databases that refer to the same data by multiple names. Classic examples are "customer number" also being called "account number," and "department codes" also being called "organization codes."

- Databases that appear to have common information, but in which applications have added prefix or suffix values to the supposedly common fields.

These are just a few and perhaps the easiest to comprehend of a large universe of potential problems. More subtle are the differences inherent in the design of the databases themselves, such as table design and normalization. If all the databases to be accessed are relational, and have been rigorously designed in the same form, then connectivity might not be a problem; however, this ideal kind of uniformity is seldom the case. Local databases are often purposely denormalized for better performance with a specific database product, or for the sheer convenience of a particular application. These are only two reasons that can make denormalization seem legitimate at implementation time. The problems caused by denormalization are usually manageable when only one or two local databases are involved; however, understanding the idiosyncrasies of tens or hundreds of databases can present an overwhelming challenge.

Database Connectivity

Database connectivity is a much more solvable problem than it was even a few years ago. The rapid implementation of open networks, TCP/IP, open computer systems, and the availability of networking and connectivity software from database companies means there are potential off-the-shelf choices for accessing databases throughout the enterprise. This trend has even extended, though not with nearly the same success, to legacy data. There are several products emerging under the guise of database middleware that provide some level of access to legacy data through SQL commands. From the client/server perspective, there are many gateways available that act as protocol and language translators from various client environments to various server environments (for example, gateways are available that allow Ingres database clients to connect to Oracle database servers). Also in the client/server area is Microsoft's Open Database Connectivity (ODBC) specification, which has the goal of allowing any ODBC-compliant client application to interoperate with any ODBC-compliant server database manager. From a functional standpoint, there's been impressive progress in connectivity product availability.

The key challenges for database connectivity are performance and flexibility. Often the impressive connectivity and functionality has been achieved by adding several layers of generalized software to the execution path, but in many instances those layers have not been optimized for best performance. Caution (in other words, expert investigation) is probably necessary if response-time-sensitive applications are going to perform many database functions, or if large numbers (thousands) of rows or records must be returned to clients. It's almost impossible to predict whether performance requirements can be met without knowing the specifics of a particular application and environment combination; a good rule of thumb is that the more likely an application is to exercise the interfaces and gateways required, the less likely it is you will be satisfied by the performance of the application. The solution to these performance problems often means using the databases' native client/server protocols and implementing the most direct connectivity path available. The result of a high-performance strategy is often a restricted application environment, especially for database tool sets and query tools, or perhaps separate versions of each application for every database. There's a trade-off to be made between generalized connectivity and high efficiency and performance.

The flexibility aspect of connectivity is complicated by the continuing efforts of most DBMS vendors to differentiate their products through proprietary extensions to SQL, and through special database procedural languages. It can be a frustrating problem; the strategy to provide open database connectivity and heterogeneous applications often means you must sacrifice the use of the very differentiators that drove your organization to select a particular database product! This dilemma has been made especially clear with ODBC, as it's entire goal is vendor independence, and many users and industry pundits have complained about ODBC being a "lowest common denominator" standard. A reasonable person would have to wonder how it could be any other way. That same reasonable person would have to conclude that if portability and heterogeneity are one of your organization's goals, lowest common denominator functionality is likely to be a factor you will have to live with in your system designs.

Perhaps a more esoteric factor in the database connectivity issue is that SQL statements composed for optimal efficiency with one database manager might be significantly less than optimal for use with another database, even if you've composed in lowest common dominator SQL. In theory, the optimizers and internal "query rewriters" of the database managers should compensate for the differences, but the reality of optimizer quality is that the compensation probably can't be counted on to mask the differences. It's also a matter of the range of compensation available to even a perfect optimizer. While SQL is becoming standardized, the underlying database processing in file systems, data structures, and memory management is not. Databases using different storage structures and indexing techniques can be expected to have different performance characteristics. There's also the matter of sensitivity to the physical schema design. While it's not a practice that's really in step with the intentions of SQL or the relational model to be independent from physical structures, database schemas are often designed to be efficient with a known workload, even to the extent of denormalizing the data. It is probably reasonable to expect that in a truly heterogeneous environment with real-world database products, some SQL functions composed for one database will execute poorly on others.

Challenges of Distributed Access

Administrators of distributed systems face many challenges. Users should be able to access data wherever it is located without getting bogged down in specifying the location of that data or worrying about whether it is properly synchronized with data in other locations. This section defines some of the challenges that face administrators.

Transparency

Transparency describes the effect of keeping the complexities of the information distribution hidden from the applications and tools that will use the information.

Two of the most important kinds of transparency are location transparency and operational transparency.

Location transparency is easy to understand; the goal is to allow applications to access necessary information without having to know where it's located. The primary advantages of location transparency are that the enterprise network can evolve without affecting applications, and that users and programs can remain naive about the complexities of data placement. The fundamental technology strategies that support location transparency are logical naming of resources and globally accessible directories. Every mainstream distributed access or distributed database product provides a means to implement location transparency. It's a solved problem and should be a requirement of any distributed system.

Operational transparency is more sublime; the goal is to execute any function in a distributed environment that could be performed in a local environment. For example, many organizations have implemented distributed systems that allow relatively simple functions to include multisite processing, but complex functions (such as decision support queries) are often unavailable and often show unacceptable performance or reliability when they are available. The archetypal challenge for distributed data access is the so-called "intercontinental multiway join," a query that derives information from multiple database tables. It would be considered a common function if all the tables are on a single computer, but becomes a grand challenge simply by introducing distribution. Many distributed access products claim to support distributed SQL processing, especially products that fall in the middleware category, yet they are really unable to execute any arbitrary SQL command. The provided support is often just a rather restricted query language with a syntax much like SQL. *Caveat emptor.*

Synchronization

The relationships between distributed databases tend to fall into two categories: databases that contain information related in use to information in another database, and databases that contain information that is copied or somehow derived from information contained in another database.

Databases that contain different, but related, information are often logically tied together through the applications that update them. When applications update multiple databases, there are choices to make regarding the level of consistency expected between the databases. For gathering statistical information, for example, it might be acceptable to assure that a majority of the updates are actually made. For example, there might be very little penalty for losing an update due to a database malfunction or a computer failure. On the other hand, financial information is expected to be absolutely consistent, without lost updates. The processing costs someone would be willing to pay might be much more for the financial data than for the statistical information.

For applications that update multiple databases, the most popular technique to assure consistency and synchronization between the affected databases is called a *two-phase commit* (sometimes abbreviated as 2PC) process. Two-phase commit processing assumes the use of transaction semantics by the application, and some sort of consistent enforcement by the participating databases during processing, normally in the form of locking. The transaction semantics are used by the application, to define the boundaries for a logical unit of processing, usually called a *transaction,* and the databases use locking to reserve information for use by the transaction during its duration. Depending on the implementation and granularity of the system, locks can occur at the database, table, page (block), or record level. Granularity defines the amount of information that the system will give to each user at one time. For example, record level granularity in a name/address database allows each user to view only one name/address at a time. (More than one user can access the database simultaneously, but none can access more than one name/address record at a time.) The smaller the granularity of the locks, the more users can be currently accommodated, generally speaking. Note, however, that highly granular locking can increase processing requirements, so some vendors claim their products are actually better because they have fewer granular locks—for example, page locks versus record locks.

When the transaction finishes processing and is satisfied that the work is completed properly, a *commit function* is issued to a component typically called a *commit coordinator.* The commit coordinator sends commit request messages to all of the participating database managers, requesting a vote as to whether the transaction should be allowed to complete properly. The participating databases are expected to send their votes, positive or negative, back to the commit coordinator. If all of the votes are positive, the commit coordinator sends commit confirmation messages to every participant signaling that the transaction should be completed and its locks released. In every other instance (negative votes or missing votes) the commit coordinator sends commit-abort messages to the participants.

Transaction semantics, locking, and two-phase commit processing can keep multiple databases synchronized to a very high degree. The problem with two-phase commits is processing cost. If each participating database contains only one record or row to be updated, it's entirely possible that the processing cost of the commit protocol will exceed the cost of actually accessing and updating the database, perhaps by a very large amount. It is also likely that maintaining synchronization at this level will affect response times considerably.

Alternative techniques for synchronization—batched deferred updates, and periodic "catch-up" functions—will likely have much less processing cost than performing a two-phase commit for every transaction, but a price is paid in data freshness. This is probably the main trade-off, data freshness and synchronization versus processing costs.

Strategies for Database Placement and Distribution

One of the most fascinating problems in distributed data management and access is determining the best types of computer systems and places to store the databases. Naturally, there really doesn't seem to be consensus in the industry about the best or recommended distribution strategies. For the purposes of this discussion, let's define three basic distribution strategies: centralization, distributed autonomous schemas, and distributed partitioned schemas.

Centralization

Sometimes the best distribution strategy is to limit distribution of the data. A centralization strategy should not be interpreted as attempting to put all of the enterprise's information on one computer system. Centralization should be viewed as the strategy to place highly shared and consolidated computing and database resources where necessary in the enterprise. A large enterprise, for example, could have several centralized systems acting as regional repositories. Some IS professionals view a distributed data strategy as always specifying that data be placed on relatively small computers near the source of the data creation or usage. That's one view, but as you will see in the upcoming discussion of data warehousing, centralization can be a useful tool even when distribution is a goal.

Distributed Autonomous Schemas

This is the distribution strategy that most enterprises really implement. There are many computer systems, many databases. For the most part, they're independently designed and administered. It's a fortunate situation, indeed, where there are standards for database design, data semantics, and naming, that cross system boundaries.

Distributed Partitioned Schemas

Partitioning a single database schema (a logical set of interrelated tables or files) across multiple computer systems, and having the ability to view the entire schema as if it were local, comprise most professionals' idea of a real distributed database. Most of the academic research in distributed databases falls into this category, and some years back much attention was paid to the technique by the relational database industry and the trade press.

There are three classic partitioning strategies for schemas: placing each table or file as a whole on a selected computer, placing subsets of the rows or records on separate computers, and placing subdivided portions of individual rows or records on separate computers. Distributing subsets of rows is usually called *horizontal partitioning*, and distributing subdivisions of rows is normally called *vertical partitioning*. A popular example of horizontal partitioning is an employee table for an enterprise with multiple locations, where each employee's row resides in the local partition of the table stored in a local computer system. Good examples for vertical partitioning are usually rather contrived, but vertical partitioning has been successfully employed for columns of tables that are best stored on different media than the rest of the columns on a table, such as incorporating a picture of the employee in the employee table. The picture may be stored on optical disk, while the balance of the row is stored on direct access storage devices.

Strategies for Providing Access to Information

The key to a successful information access strategy is understanding the enterprise's workload requirements. There are several potential strategies, none superior in every situation.

Distributed Application Processing

Distributed application processing is relevant to distributed information access because it is one technique for accessing distributed data—distribute the application processing rather than the database processing by executing applications (or portions of them) on the local computer that manages a database. There are currently three popular techniques for distributing applications to local computers, remote procedure calls (RPCs), transaction managers, and database server procedures.

Remote Procedure Calls

RPCs work at the lowest programming level of these techniques. An RPC is essentially a message passing interface that causes the execution of a specific program on the recipient computer. The key advantages of RPCs are performance and flexibility. The primary issues for using RPCs to distribute application processing are the lack of a single RPC standard, and the lack of execution-time support features such as recovery and workflow management. RPCs are probably best left to system software, or perhaps to brute-force custom applications with stringent development requirements.

Transaction Managers

Transaction managers such as Encina, Top End, or Tuxedo provide execution environments and message management services for applications written in standard, open programming languages (for example, C, C++, COBOL). The transaction managers typically comply with X/Open standards for distributed transaction processing, interact with database products by treating them as resource managers, and use the standard XA protocol for access and transaction control activities. Most mainstream database managers either support the XA standard, or plan to do so.

The key advantages of transaction managers is that they insulate applications from communications protocols and interfaces, process management activities, provide message queuing, handle recovery responsibilities (this varies significantly for each transaction manager product), provide authorization and security, and normally include system administration services (another capability that varies greatly by implementation). A good transaction manager allows developers to concentrate on the application functionality and assists in the construction of environment-independent applications.

Transaction managers can also increase performance, by reducing memory and processing requirements through multithreading and dynamic execution techniques. For example, in cases where each user executes applications in a separate UNIX session, which means a separate UNIX process and address space, thousands of processes might be necessary for large application environments. A transaction manager, on the other hand, might need only a few tens of processes shared among the same population of users. This trick is accomplished either by multiplexing user requests through a pool of server processes, or by dynamically creating threads of execution as requests are received. Resources are saved by dramatic reductions in the amount of process switching and the amount of process context required.

Using a transaction manager as a distributed execution environment has the effect of encapsulating local computing environments, because from the applications' perspective the entire network is viewed as a specific set of logical services. The encapsulation effect can have a very positive impact on system maintainability and extensibility, as distributed applications are insulated from changes to the local environment. Another benefit is that the manner in which the local systems and databases are used by remote clients is a known set of functions that can be carefully defined and regulated. In a relatively unstructured environment—a partitioned global schema with full SQL capabilities, for example—there is much more risk that a remote client will accidentally (or intentionally) initiate a function that could compromise the databases or monopolize system resources.

Database Server Procedures

Database managers such as Informix, Oracle, and SYBASE support database server procedures, sometimes called stored procedures, which are simply applications executed by the database server processes. At this time the programming languages for these procedures are not standardized, making applications written using them restricted to the database vendor's proprietary environment. The languages also vary widely in capability. The key advantages to database server procedures are execution efficiency and a high level of integration with the database environment. Database server procedures can also offer a common development environment on heterogeneous hardware and operating systems, because many relational database software products are very widely ported. (Oracle, for example, has been ported to over 70 different platforms.)

Some database vendors are offering their server procedures as alternatives to transaction managers. Since these server procedure languages typically include transaction semantics, and sometimes the ability to send requests between server instances, the database vendors can offer a significant portion of the functionality offered by transaction managers. The decision comes down to a trade-off between performance and portability. The database vendors claim that the performance of server procedures is higher than can be achieved with transaction managers.

Limitations of Distributed Applications

Distributed application processing is normally unsuited to ad hoc query processing or to very complex query processing. The lack of applicability to ad hoc processing is due to the need for specialized coding for each application. For processing complex queries, application programmers would essentially have to mimic the types of processing normally done by databases (joins, merges, sorts, and so on), and this seldom makes sense when general-purpose alternatives are available.

istributed Data Access Middleware

Distributing the database processing is the technique most capable of providing transparency to the application. In the most general sense, distributed access makes all of the data look local. Transparency makes distributed access best for query applications that span several databases or that are predominantly ad hoc. Other cases best suited to distributed access include applications that require multidatabase access but that are not readily partitionable, or multiple application sets that have a very high degree of data sharing.

Choosing between the two distributed access paradigms, distributing a single schema or logically connecting multiple autonomous schemas, means examining your requirements for ease of administration, flexibility, heterogeneity, and performance.

Partitioned schemas imply a centralized design with rigidly imposed standards and interoperation. While the view mechanism of SQL can impart a significant level of independence between the applications, a high level of intersite design coordination is still necessary. Partitioned schemas are also likely to be homogeneous (that is, require use of only one DBMS product) for the foreseeable future. The bottom line is that if your organization requires autonomous local sites or heterogeneous database products (heterogeneous hardware is much less of a concern), partitioned schemas are probably not a realistic consideration.

Distributed access across multiple autonomous schemas is becoming the domain of data access middleware, available from database vendors and independents. The middleware products have two critical differentiators: how well they can logically integrate the databases to be accessed and how much performance they can provide. The integration is usually implemented by providing a logical global schema in the middleware layer, insulating applications from the details of the local schemas from having to establish sessions on every local database. The application view of the integration is often a middleware-specific version of SQL.

Some enterprises, especially those that have multiple DBMS products throughout the enterprise, find that developing their applications using the middleware SQL is an advantage. The middleware has the effect of allowing the enterprise to do application development independent of the DBMS and its particular SQL implementation. This aids portability and flexibility, and in some cases can circumvent the need for separate versions of applications for each DBMS. As we discussed in the Database Connectivity section regarding ODBC, however, this insulation from the DBMS vendor's SQL can prevent you from fully leveraging the vendor's product features and performance. It's probably worth reiterating that there's very likely to be a trade-off between the level of DBMS independence you achieve and maximizing performance or feature availability.

Distributed access middleware is likely to show future performance improvements in the areas of optimizers and parallel processing. Much of the argument for middleware is the ability to execute queries that access many databases, and the efficiency of these queries is largely a factor of optimizers. Optimizers examine factors such as access and communications processing costs, the relative distribution of data involved in a query, the availability of processing resources, and information about data structures (for example, indices). Optimizers also have numerous execution strategies to choose from, and they formulate query execution plans based on the cost factors and clever use of the execution strategies. Since optimizers are invisible to applications and have such a profound effect on the enterprise's satisfaction with the middleware product, optimizers are likely to emerge as key differentiators in this field.

Parallel processing also has the potential to emerge as a key differentiator because of its ability to dramatically improve response times for the queries in distributed access environments. Several database vendors are developing parallel processing capabilities for multiprocessing computers, and it's reasonable to expect that once those implementations mature, it will be tempting to improve the competitive standing of their distributed access offerings.

Data Propagation

Data propagation is the process of placing information on a conveniently accessible computer system and using a mechanism that generates a new instance of the information. The propagation process can be as simple as a data copy, or could be a subset, a derivation, a summary, an aggregation—there are many alternatives.

The key advantages to propagation are scalability and workload isolation. Each new information instance generated by the propagation process theoretically allows the resources of another complete system to be employed using the information in the source database. For decision support and data analysis purposes, this can be the one advantage that makes propagation the strategy of choice. Another important factor is that scalability can be implemented using relatively small workstations and servers, which are normally much more cost-effective than upwardly scaling very large computers. The workload isolation advantages of propagation are intuitive; enterprises have been dedicating separate computer systems to applications for performance and security reasons.

The critical costs of a propagation strategy are increased storage, data communications, and administration. The storage costs are mitigated to a great extent in that many requests for a new data instance are for a summary or subset. The data communications costs are similarly affected, but it is important to remember that data transfers cost processing and storage capabilities on the source and destination computer systems. While the use of summary or aggregated information by the new instance may save storage and transmission costs, the creation of that summary could result in what amounts to a complex query on the source system.

Administration costs are an often overlooked issue for propagation strategies. Maintaining the consistency of the directories, the freshness of the propagated instances, the availability of storage on receptor computers, and the proper aging (and deletion) of propagated information is not a trivial matter. Propagation can also have critical data security implications, both for storage and transmission (encryption may be required), and for some enterprises this may be the most complicated factor.

ata Warehousing

Data warehousing is the notion that the most efficient technique for accessing multiple databases of uncoordinated design is to accumulate copies or extracts of the original databases in one or more warehouse databases. Typically, computers that store data warehouses are large multiprocessor servers. The technique then specifies that access to data originally distributed is made to the warehouse, allowing more efficient access (the data is not distributed) to logically normalized information. Data warehousing also includes the concepts of data cleansing and transformation of the information warehoused, making access easier and results more accurate.

Data warehousing can also include the storage and management of historical information and levels of detail that may be impractical on local systems, or at least impractical to access when they are physically distributed.

The popularity of data warehousing is on the rise—probably because many organizations have successfully implemented data warehouses for large and very large databases, and the expectations for these implementations are largely met or exceeded. It could be that the very architecture of a data warehouse system forces enterprises into solving problems that other alternatives, such as distributed access, attempt to solve with clever software.

The act of transferring information from a local database into the warehouse database forces enterprises to make the transferred information compliant with the warehouse database schema design. While it might be considered impossible to alter the local (existing) schema to comply with a subsequent global design, it's often possible to write a transformation function that acts on the information as it's being imported into the warehouse. This gives a data warehouse an enormous advantage over a distributed access design with autonomous local databases. It makes many applications possible that might not be in a distributed access environment, such as complex decision support queries. Note that the single schema design advantage would hold true even if the warehouse were a virtual one, with the warehouse database itself being physically distributed.

Data warehousing also provides the workload isolation and scalability effects of a data propagation strategy. Very often local computer systems have relatively low capacities for cost reasons, and upgrading what could be hundreds or thousands of local systems can be a much greater task (and risk) than simply adding data warehouses to the enterprise as necessary.

The primary issue for data warehousing is typically cost, and this issue is often driven by the need for the data warehouse database to be resident on very large computers. Large systems generally have higher costs per unit of processing power and storage, and can normally be counted on to incur higher costs for everything from administration to maintenance to electrical power. While it is possible to implement data warehouses on clusters of smaller systems, this is clearly an emerging capability, and most successful warehouses have been implemented on very large servers or mainframes. Perhaps the class of computer best suited to data warehouses are the Massively Parallel Processing (MPP) systems beginning to emerge in the open server marketplace. Microprocessor-based MPP systems offer much more processing power for comparable cost than previous generations of large systems, and relational database implementations are becoming available to leverage these new computing platforms.

Chapter Fourteen

Object Technologies: Key Components of the Interoperable Future

by Larry Joseph,

Virtual Firmware

For most companies, obtaining benefits from object technologies will require changing many business and work practices. There is a direct parallel between the application of new technologies today and in the early days of the industrial age. At that time, simply applying the new technology of steam engines to pour water onto water wheels did little to increase productivity. Only when the *process* was changed, and steam engines were used to turn the wheels directly, did productivity radically increase.

Many of our work processes, such as the management of work with hierarchical organizational structures, are holdovers from the industrial age. Numerous people today are engaged in meaningless work with no connection to modern realities (fill out the form in quadruplicate, file one copy there, another copy there...). Or as business reengineering consultant Jordan Powell often says, "If all you do is automate meaningless processes, all you get is meaningless work done faster!" These processes are analogous to using new technologies to pour water onto water wheels; there must be fundamental changes before we can make the transition from the industrial to the information age. Major areas of change include:

- Turning PCs into enterprise profit tools
- Bridging the communications barrier that separates information technology from business
- Learning new information management tools and methods
- Achieving a more effective division of labor in information management

Object technologies (objects) embody the next generation of information-age tools, materials, and methods we will use to build interoperable applications for single-user PCs, departmental systems (PC LANs), and enterprise systems (networks of PCs, minicomputers, and mainframes).

Almost everyone has an opinion about why objects are important to them. Business is desperate for objects because they seem to offer rich development environments that automatically generate highly interoperable applications. Objects could make it easier for business to downsize (replace mainframes and minicomputers with less expensive cooperative PC LANs) or to upsize (consolidate stand-alone PCs into enterprise networks.) Application developers and software users, their appetites stimulated by tasty morsels thrown their way by vendors, hungrily await more objects.

Even popular columnists (cleverly disguised as visionaries) have climbed onto the object bandwagon, predicting that in only a few years we will live in a global village built from interoperable objects. In this global village, you and I will work in cyberspace at virtual companies, and mundane chores like buying, manufacturing, and shipping will be completely automated.

Meanwhile, back at the software factories, the major vendors have been creating the infrastructure needed to make object-based applications and development environments a reality. In addition, they've been sorting out which vendors will lead which platforms (PC desktops, local area network servers, enterprise servers) and sectors (financial trading, accounting, manufacturing, and so on).

The results of their labors are beginning to have some impact. New products are emerging that will bring highly interconnective operating systems and development environments to market. (Two examples are Cairo and Taligent.) Software vendors have invested huge sums in object technologies hoping to receive tremendous returns on their investments.

Objects appear to have something for everyone: something for business, something for developers and users, something for software vendors. And yet, looking at the object landscape today, we should reflect on the difficulties that were involved in bringing interoperability to its current point. We should remember the tendency of vendors to make zealous presentations of new technology at press conferences when it doesn't quite operate the same way in the real world of mixed environments—as well as their tendency to point fingers when their products don't work in such environments.

Can we accurately decide today which unseen object products we should invest our time and money in, based on vendor claims of interoperability in mixed environments? I guess we could if we were not concerned about preserving our companies, credibility, or sanity. However, those of us who place a priority on self-preservation don't have to stop dead in our tracks, waiting for tangible evidence to support today's promises of future interoperability. There are actions we can take today that will move us toward realizing the benefits of interoperable object technologies while minimizing the risk of unforeseen problems. With this as our objective, we move forward into an overview of the new, largely uncharted world of object technologies.

How Objects Work

Usually, when you ask object programmers to explain object technologies (objects), they will begin by talking about either the benefits of object-oriented languages such as C++ and SmallTalk, or about concepts like inheritance, polymorphism, and encapsulation.

While they may be relevant to some programmers, such explanations are of little value to most of us. What most of us want to know is how objects will help us build stable, interoperable systems (preferably inexpensively and fast).

Objects and object models are systems for converting complex software applications into groups of simpler interoperable components. The main principles behind creating software from objects are the same ones used to create every other mass-produced product in modern industrial society. Complex objects, like PCs, are assembled from prebuilt subassemblies, like motherboards and hard drives. These subassemblies are, in turn, composed of other prebuilt subassemblies, like chips and switches. Mass production techniques allow teams of highly differentiated laborers to more effectively work together, or interoperate. The people at Intel or Motorola make processors, while other people make motherboards, power supplies, and so on. Imagine how many PCs would be built if every business built their PCs from elemental metals, silica, and plastics! Yet this is how the vast majority of business software is created: hand-coded, usually by one person, sometimes by a small team, with few off-the-shelf components to reduce time or costs. To better understand interoperable object applications, an object component analysis is relevant.

Object Component Analysis

Every piece of object business software consists of three major components:

- *User Interface Component(s)*   User interface components or modules are, on their surface, the application windows, menus, buttons, and icons you see on the computer monitor. They are the client or front-end in client/server or distributed systems.

- *Data Management Component(s)*   Data management modules manage the storage and retrieval of application data. In client/server and distributed systems, data management objects are usually stored procedures and triggers on database servers.

- *Business Model Component(s)*   Business model modules (business objects) model the behavior of business entities, such as customers, orders, or products.

By using objects to model the behavior of real-world things, businesses can develop software faster. For example, if I need an object to track the sales staff in a sales application, it should be easy for me to remove an Employee business object from a Human Resource Management application to use in the Sales application.

An important aspect of an object's ability to model the behavior of real-world things is the design of classes and subclasses. *Classes* are the categories that objects naturally *belong* to. For example, if an object consists of salaried employees and management employees, the class is Employee. The more detailed forms of Employee (Salaried Employee and Management Employee) are the *subclasses* of the Employee object. All employees must have a social security number, so the social security number is an attribute of the more general Employee object. But not all employees have an hourly rate of pay, which is an attribute of a Salaried Employee object. In the language of object programmers, we have just described how two subclasses (Salaried Employee and Management Employee) *inherit* an attribute (social security number) from the Employee class.

Business objects are manipulated by methods. An example of two methods for an Employee object are *PayEmployee* and *TerminateEmployee*.

To understand how objects interoperate, think about three objects needed by every business: Customers, Orders, and Products. When a new customer is discovered, the customer is entered into a Customer Form (User Interface) object. When the data on the form is saved, a message (or remote procedure call) is sent to a Customer

Qualification object requesting: "Does this person qualify for some of our valuable attention?" If the answer is "Yes," a message is sent to a Data Management object, instructing it to create a record for this customer. Next, a message is sent to an Order Form object requesting its display on the desktop. As the order is entered, the Order Form object is sending messages to a Product object for data on availability and cost. The Product object may respond by sending messages to a supplier's objects, to confirm shipment status, availability, or cost. The Product object receives messages back, and in turn responds to the Order Form object.

These objects, while acting as if they were one application, could be widely separated from each other: the Customer Form object could be on the laptop of a traveling salesperson, while the Product object could be at a shipping or headquarters terminal. Interoperabilty allows the application to be split into component modules that transparently trigger each other on different computers. As we design widely distributed systems, we gain the flexibility to run each component on a computer best suited to the processing and data storage requirements of each component.

> *NOTE:*   *As the state of the art in object interoperability progresses, objects will be*
> *able to locate idle processors on networks and migrate themselves to those*
> *computers automatically.*

Three of the primary mechanisms used today that allow objects to interoperate and allow us to control groups of objects as if they were one application, are compound document architectures, object request brokers, and transaction managers.

ompound Documents

Compound documents provide a seamless desktop interface for objects, whether they are widely distributed or local. Compound documents allow data (text, graphics, audio, and video) from more than one application and/or location to interoperate in such a way that they appear to the user as one application.

The need for a seamless interface is quickly grasped when you observe software use in businesses. Most people use three to seven applications in their work (spreadsheets, word processors, drawing tools, accounting and bookkeeping applications, and so on) and are constantly frustrated by the inability to easily mix features from different applications ("If I could only get the sales figures from Excel into Word and have them show up as a map in this marketing report!"). In companies that have a mix of computers, you will also see a lot of inefficient data conversions as data is moved from one platform to another.

Problems like getting the sales figures from Excel into Word and having them show up as a map are easily solved with compound documents. Compound documents make interoperability easy for business software users. Today's best compound document architectures support automation, linking, embedding, and visual editing.

■ *Automation* allows applications to programmatically activate and use other applications, like a contact manager that activates a word processor to accept data from a database and print a set of mail-merge letters.

■ *Linking* creates an active connection between data in a compound document and its source, so that as the source is modified, the data displayed in the document is updated. For example, after a linked spreadsheet is embedded into a document, the spreadsheet cells displayed in the document are updated as the source spreadsheet changes.

■ *Embedding* allows one object to be placed within another object, as when a range of spreadsheet cells is copied and pasted into a text document.

■ *Visual editing* allows the user to modify an application embedded in a compound document without leaving the compound document. For example, as the cursor in a compound document moves from word processing text onto the cells of an embedded spreadsheet, the menus and tools of the document automatically change to the menu and tools of the spreadsheet. The user can then edit the cells without switching to the spreadsheet application.

Object Request Brokers

Object request brokers (ORBs) manage interactions between objects—they find objects, deliver messages, return responses, handle delivery problems, enforce security, and so on.

How do they work? When an ORB intercepts a message from an object, it checks its directory (which is like a phone directory) to locate an object that can process the required method. The ORB then forwards the message along with any required parameters to the object that can fulfill the request. If the receiving object responds with a message, the ORB handles its routing. Exception handling tells the ORB what to do if a message can't be delivered. Security makes sure that an object has the required clearance before allowing it to send a message to a controlled object.

The function of an ORB seems simple, and it can be, in a tightly controlled, homogeneous environment like a laboratory. Achieving interoperability between ORBs in the real world is tremendously complicated by the wide variations in platforms, processors, data storage methods, network connections, client applications, server applications, programming languages, and so forth.

That is why most of today's ORBs that control highly distributed interoperable systems exist within tightly controlled and largely homogeneous operating environments. These ORBs have been developed, typically by large companies, at great expense. Most of them exist on UNIX LAN and enterprise servers, and their primary purpose is to route intercompany messages.

During the next two to five years, as object operating systems such as Cairo and Taligent become more widely available and affordable, ORB functions will increasingly become part of the operating systems. They will become much more affordable and will be better able to interoperate in the real world. However, it is highly probable that for quite some time after their widespread availability, their safe use will require operating them within fairly strict conditions (not quite the real world).

One last word on ORBs—sometime in the future, commercially available ORBs will acquire the ability to break up a task into groups of tasks and send them off to execute on different processors simultaneously!

ransaction Managers

Transaction managers serve two functions in interoperable object systems and applications. One is to hold messages until they are processed. For example, suppose a broken network connection or some other technical problem hinders the delivery of a message. A transaction manager would hold the message until it could be delivered. In this capacity, a transaction manager can be part of the ORB.

Database transaction managers can meet another important requirement of interoperable object applications. When a process is composed of an ongoing series of tasks, a database transaction manager will ensure that the tasks are performed at the correct times. For example, an order from a large customer may actually be a number of orders that are to be shipped on different dates. The role of a database transaction manager in this case is to assure that the right order messages are sent at the right times.

The Benefits of Objects

For businesses, personal computers are a major expense category. As personal computing has increased, so has its cost to businesses—including the costs of desktop hardware, networks and servers, software, training, and support. Most businesses do not regard these outlays as generating a measurable return on investment (ROI), because most of the work done with personal computers, while making individuals more productive, is clerical and does not directly generate revenue.

To make personal computers generate a measurable profit, their use must be redirected to enterprise functions. Business Process Reengineering (BPR) is an effective methodology both for planning and for managing the redirection. BPR applies new information technologies, like objects, to redefine the processes that make up organizational operations.

A common technique employed in BPR is the automation of business processes, both within companies and across company boundaries to include suppliers and customers.

Mass merchandisers like WalMart were early in applying new information technologies to reengineered business processes. For large retailers and their suppliers, it is worth a lot of money to know, in real time, which products are selling well and which are not. Mass merchandisers integrated their cash registers (PCs with cash drawers) with their suppliers' computers, allowing suppliers to automatically increase the production and shipping of fast-selling goods and decrease production of slow-moving items.

In this case, BPR yielded a tightly integrated distributed system that meets the needs of customers and suppliers across multiple enterprises. It also frees people from performing tedious clerical tasks like taking inventories and placing orders, which can be done by computers.

Until recently, systems that integrated multiple enterprises required minicomputers or mainframes. Today these systems are easily built with personal computers, so hardware is not a limitation in their implementation.

The primary limitation is software. Traditional software development methods take too long, cost too much, and the risk of failure is too high for most businesses. Interoperable objects address the problems of response time, cost, and risk of failure.

The limited configurability of today's software is another problem that hinders its deployment as a streamlined tool for improving workgroup and enterprise productivity. Shrink-wrapped software tends to contain features for every potential user. However, excess features tend to bewilder new users and impede learning.

Object-based software is highly configurable: every major feature or module is itself an object that can be installed or left uninstalled. This configurability simplifies software use for people who don't want or need a wide range of options or features.

Configurability also benefits power users, who have requirements beyond clerical activities, and domain experts, such as managers, physicists, accountants, lawyers, and so on. Power users and domain experts need specialized applications like calculators and drawing applications. For example, a domain expert who specializes in quantum physics has different needs from a network designer. Yet they both need basic word processing. With object technologies, adding or changing a word processor's drawing program or calculator only requires installing a specialized module.

Additionally, with the increased availability of high-level tools such as Power Builder and Visual Basic for assembling objects into highly customized systems, the number of power users and domain experts building their own information solutions will steadily increase. Their numbers will grow as computer-literate schoolchildren move into the workforce.

Bridging the Communications Barrier That Separates IT from Business

As the use of PCs in business has increased, businesses have seen the competitive pace accelerate and response time shrink. These pressures drive the need to quickly turn strategies into strategic systems—hardware and software that provide unique competitive advantages. A road block in the rapid translation of thought into action is the communication barrier between business and information technologists, that is, the language of information technology (IT) is different from the language of business.

Now that the focus of business is turning to business process reengineering (BPR), and the focus of IT is turning to objects, a common language is emerging. The language of process improvement can be mapped directly into the object analysis language used by IT.

The linking of terminology allows business to describe the real-world behavior (methods, rules, look and feel) they want from their software. IT can readily translate business requirements into the technical language of interoperable hardware and software.

For both business and IT, linking terminology has a profound effect on response: businesses are much more likely to get what they asked for, faster. For IT, faster response addresses the most common reason for criticism—that they can't deliver the right information to the right place at the right time.

etooling Information System Development

The enterprise is changing far faster than information systems can be built or modified, in large measure because software is mostly hand-built in monolithic structures. The applications backlog, or inability of software developers to keep up with the demands of their customers, is well documented. The increasing emphasis of business on fast response is placing inhuman demands on information technologists. They find themselves in the impossible situation of maintaining existing systems based on outdated technologies while supporting a growing number of nontechnical computer users. At the same time, they are pressured to quickly develop interoperable systems in response to rapidly changing business needs (this is known as "programming at a moving target"), while keeping up with rapid advances in software development tools and techniques.

Objects, with their emphasis on reusable modules, facilitate the assembly of new applications from prebuilt parts. Building software from prebuilt parts allows software to be developed much faster and more cheaply than through conventional methods.

Companies now have a number of options for acquiring prebuilt components, including the ability to buy industry class libraries, which they begin modifying to reflect their unique characteristics.

When prebuilt components cannot be purchased, information technologists can create software in components instead of monolithic structures Then large projects can be more easily divided into smaller projects, with each subproject being performed by specialists.

Beyond components are tools; rapid system development requires rapid development tools. Today's object development tools (for example, FoxPro, Enfin, Visual Basic, and PowerBuilder) have moved state-of-the-art in interoperable object applications Far beyond yesterday's object-oriented programming languages, like SmallTalk and C++. These new object-oriented power tools make the development of applications from objects considerably less procedural, time-consuming, and problematic.

The ability to model business processes in software is another powerful feature of objects. Objects allow the construction of a working model of operations as operation processes are modeled and increasingly enhanced, in effect becoming evolutionary systems that grow and develop into larger, more valuable systems. A number of vendors are working on developing animated object model diagramming tools. These tools allow you to interconnect objects with workflow lines and watch their interaction in real time as work products move through the processes that make up the value chain—the movement of sellable products from suppliers to customers.

Object development promotes the standardized use of rapid development methodologies, which provide a streamlined process for creating applications and systems. Good rapid development methodologies describe the overall development process and the major steps or tasks within the overall process. They also specify what techniques should be used to perform the tasks. Good methodologies also include warnings of potential problems and techniques to avoid. As highly qualified developers work with a methodology, they tend to improve it. In this way the methodology becomes a record of expertise that can then be utilized by others.

And finally, objects promote wrapping. *Wrapping* refers to the ability to use objects to "wrap" non-object applications, so that the non-object applications can communicate through standardized object messages. Wrapping can be very valuable in interoperating object-based applications and systems with legacy applications and systems.

Why Is It Taking Us So Long to Get There?

Why is it taking so long to achieve the benefits of interoperable objects? It is helpful to think of interoperability at three layers in the organization: at the desktop, on a LAN server, and at an enterprise server.

Desktop application interoperability has been achieved to some extent by Microsoft with its OLE 2.0 compound document architecture and COM model. Microsoft has demonstrated interoperability between desktop applications and LANs with Distributed OLE. IBM, Sun, and others have achieved interoperability at LAN server and enterprise levels with their object models.

Microsoft's desktop application results have been duplicated by a number of its competitors who want to advertise OLE compatibility for their products. However, LAN and enterprise demonstrations have only been done in strictly controlled, homogeneous hardware and software environments. As most of us are painfully aware, when you start mixing hardware, using incorrectly configured software, and bridging servers in heterogeneous environments, the world takes on a much meaner face. There are tremendous technical obstacles to achieving interoperable distributed object Nirvana in the real world.

Most businesses (those concerned with self-preservation) are unwilling to risk adopting object technologies until there is greater assurance that the major vendors have achieved a larger critical mass of interoperability in their products and have agreed among themselves on standards that provide for interoperability between their products.

The major vendors, obviously aware of our concerns, have been working on this problem. While building implementations of their object technologies, they have been both competing and aligning themselves to reduce the number of variables in object standards, object models, and compound document architectures. As things stand today, the two front-runners in object standards are Microsoft's OLE specification and The Object Management Group's Common Object Request Broker Architecture (CORBA). The two front-runners in object models are Microsoft's COM (Common Object Model) and IBM's SOM/DSOM. The leaders in compound document architecture are Microsoft OLE and the OpenDoc Consortia's OpenDoc, while the expected leaders of tomorrow's object operating systems/development tools race are

Microsoft's Cairo, Taligent Partner's Taligent, and the Sun/NeXT implementation of NeXT's NeXTStep. While it is interesting to speculate about Taligent and Cairo, both products are at least a year away from release and have been shown only to a few people under strict NDAs (nondisclosure agreements). So, while we have no concrete evidence, it is a given assumption that vendors will extend the interoperability envelope far beyond today's boundaries.

The Object Management Group and the CORBA Standard

The Object Management Group (OMG) was formed in 1987 by a group of software and hardware vendors, both to explore and publish general information about objects, and to develop standards for networked object interoperability. Today, the OMG has more than 300 members including Hewlett-Packard, IBM, Novell, and Sun. The main standard for OMG is the Object Management Architecture (OMA). The purpose of OMA is to facilitate the interoperability of distributed object applications. The OMA consists of four parts: Object Services, Common Facilities, Application Objects, and Common Object Request Broker Architecture (CORBA).

CORBA is the core of OMA; it is the OMA's specification for an object request broker. As described earlier, CORBA provides a mechanism for finding objects, delivering messages, returning responses, handling delivery problems, enforcing security, and so on.

OMG's progress in creating a detailed CORBA specification has been slowed for several reasons. To have standards, you need some commercial, market-proven implementations to compare. The difficulty that vendors have experienced in developing and marketing CORBA implementations has hampered progress. Another obstacle is the difficulty in getting members to agree on standards that can successfully integrate the wide variations in platforms, data storage methods, network connections, applications, development systems, and programming languages that are represented among the OMG membership. Even the UNIX vendors, with much to gain from a standard language implementation, have found standards impossible to agree on. And, as with all standard-setting bodies, vendors tend to favor the ways that make their work easiest or that provide them a competitive advantage to be the standard everyone else adopts.

Consequently, the OMA and CORBA leave broad areas unaddressed, and are relying on the vendors to define standards and negotiate agreements for interoperability between themselves as they move forward with their individual object implementations. Digital, Expersoft, Hewlett Packard, Novell, IBM, NCR, Sun, and Texas Instruments have all developed CORBA-compliant implementations. CORBA-compliant applications have also been created at a number of large corporations. Most of the CORBA-compliant applications are on UNIX servers with TCP/IP networks and on PC LANs running on Novell NetWare.

The vendor agreements are moving forward (as you are reading in the popular press every week), and in the next two years we should see an increasing degree of ORB interoperability between different OMG members' implementations of CORBA.

Microsoft and the OLE Standard

Microsoft, although a member of the Object Management Group, was one of the major vendors that never supported the CORBA standard and instead moved forward, largely on its own, developing its Object Linking and Embedding (OLE) standard and the Common Object Model (COM).

The reason Microsoft moved on its own is traceable to their market-share leadership. Microsoft DOS and Windows are the most widely sold and used operating systems for Intel-based PCs. Windows is currently selling at a rate of over a million copies a month. Because of their leadership position, the folks at Microsoft believe that they, and not the Object Management Group, are best suited to develop standards for Microsoft products.

By moving forward on their own, without the constraints of having to build consensus among a wide variety of factions and interests, Microsoft has established itself as the leader in the wide-scale commercialization of objects. Running OLE 2.0 applications on Windows has been the primary experience with component objects for most software users. Microsoft's VBX and now OCX custom controls has also been the first experience of component software for most software developers. (For more information on Microsoft's recognized leadership in commercializing component software, see *BYTE* magazine: "ComponentWare," May, 1994.) Microsoft is further extending its reusable component strategy by adding LOBjects (Line of Business Objects) to its custom control architecture.

Until recently, Microsoft has used object technologies primarily for creating interoperable desktop applications designed to capture the hearts and minds of PC users. Their latest strategy, however, involves moving into the midrange server market with Windows NT Advanced Server and extending OLE 2.0 from a single-machine technology to a distributed object architecture. The major OMG vendors (IBM, Sun, and Novell) have focused on achieving object interoperability on their servers, largely ignoring the desktop, and now find themselves threatened by Microsoft's advances into their traditional strongholds. This conflict has impeded the achievement of interoperability between the two camps. Recently, however, Microsoft formed an alliance with Digital Equipment (DEC) to map DEC's CORBA-based ObjectBroker to OLE—with the objective of achieving transparent interoperability between the two object systems. Microsoft and DEC are creating a new Common Object Model that will generate objects that work across OLE and DEC's object technology, which should lead the way for other OMG members to map their CORBA implementations to OLE.

IBM SOM/DSOM

IBM SOM (System Object Model) and DSOM (Distributed System Object Model) form the basis for IBM's model for developing objects for single desktops and network objects. SOM/DSOM define how objects communicate with each other as described earlier in "Object Request Brokers." SOM defines object communications for single-machine use, while DSOM defines communications for network objects. DSOM currently supports IPX/SPX, NetBIOS, and TCP/IP networks.

SOM/DSOM are advertised as language neutral (not tied to C++ compiler) and CORBA- compliant object models. SOM/DSOM have been implemented on OS/2, and IBM is extending their implementation to IBM's other platforms. IBM is also working to influence other OMG members to adopt SOM/DSOM. Currently, the SOM/DSOM models have been adopted by OpenDoc's OpenDoc and Novell's AppWare. In addition, SunSoft (the software subsidiary of Sun Microsystems Corporation) is working to make their DOE (Distributed Objects Everywhere) architecture interoperate with SOM, giving ORB interoperability between their products.

Component Integration Laboratories and OpenDoc

In an attempt to counter the expanding influence of Microsoft's OLE, Apple, IBM, Novell, Oracle, Taligent, WordPerfect, and Xerox have formed Component Integration Laboratories (CIL) to develop a compound document architecture they call OpenDoc.

OpenDoc is widely viewed as being behind OLE in functionality, but OpenDoc is reported to support the ability to store and track multiple document versions, an important groupware feature not currently available in OLE. OpenDoc is built on top of IBM's SOM. It will have cross-platform support for DOS, Windows, OS/2, and System 7, and for Windows 3.1 (16-bit) applications. At this time it is unclear, however, whether Windows 32-bit applications such as Chicago and Cairo will interoperate with OpenDoc applications.

OpenDoc is currently in alpha testing and is expected to be released into production by the end of 1994.

NeXTStep

NeXT's NeXTStep was the first cross-platform, object-oriented development environment and has been in use for about five years. NeXTStep offers an excellent rapid development environment and supports network distributed objects. Unfortunately for NeXT, NeXTStep has been slow to gain a critical mass of customers.

Recently, NeXT and Sun announced a joint licensing agreement that will port NeXTStep to the Solaris and HP-UX versions of UNIX. This will make NeXTStep accessible to the majority of UNIX workstations. In making the agreement, Sun's objectives are to provide a more robust development environment its UNIX operating system and to counter Microsoft NT's moves into the UNIX market currently dominated by Sun.

Making the Jump

Making the transition to a fully distributed, object-oriented environment will not be as easy as the vendors and the popular press are projecting. The vast majority of people who are seriously considering making the jump to distributed objects will be in for a lot of unexpected traps and problems.

You can expect to see increasing interoperability between desktop applications and local servers, but you can also expect to see major problems between local desktops and bridged servers in heterogeneous environments. Therefore, don't expect to see seamless interoperability between widely distributed objects in heterogeneous environments for quite some time. However, vendor agreements are addressing this issue, and you may find that the required agreements have been negotiated between your vendors and that for you, object interoperability is readily possible.

Other Recommendations

Now for some more specific recommendations. Start projects with a clearly formulated problem and a targeted set of results you want to achieve. If you are building an environment from scratch, figure out the exact level of interoperability you need: a local machine, a server, a local area network, widely distributed. After you have identified the degree of interoperability required, then try to find one vendor who can supply all the software you need. The ability to create an environment with one vendor's products will definitely reduce problems. After you have successfully implemented your environment and are comfortable that you have proof of concept, then you can get creative with making the environment more heterogeneous.

Other things to remember include the standard list: choose the first applications carefully, plan to invest in reeducation and build experience, standardize hardware and software as much as possible, and ignore much of what you read in the popular press.

Beyond the standard list is the difficult-to-accept advice. For most companies, receiving benefits from object technologies is going to require significant change to many comfortable business practices. As pointed out at the beginning of this chapter, there is a direct parallel between where we are today and the beginning of the industrial age. Much of our behavior (such as hierarchical organizational structures and congregating in places to work) is a holdover from the industrial age. Many people today are engaged in meaningless work with no connection to modern realities.

Many of our current work practices are analogous to using new technologies to pour water onto water wheels and must be reengineered. Major areas of change include:

- Turning PCs into enterprise profit tools

- Bridging the communications barrier that separates information technology from business

- Learning new information management tools and methods

- Achieving a more effective division of labor in information management

To successfully change will require leadership at all levels of the organization, from the top down, throughout the ranks. CEOs and executives must make the commitment to change. Management commitment is a critical variable. If management does not make the commitment to changing work practices as well as adopting new technologies, there is a high probability of failure. Software developers and software users must also be leaders to help guide change. For software developers, using small teams of motivated developers to act as pathfinders is a proven strategy for success.

Things to Watch Out For

Neither the adoption of object technologies, nor the conversion from using PCs as personal productivity tools to using them as enterprise profit tools, will be easy. Potential problems include the following:

- Distributed objects are an immature technology. Self-preservation tells us not to risk too much on immature technologies.

- Skills are in high demand—watch out for charlatans, especially in design. Poor designs have ongoing costs that, once implemented, are difficult and expensive to repair.

- Recognize that some people are not going to be able to adapt to all of the required changes and will not easily find productive new roles.

Summary

Finally, concerning timing, it has taken about three years to move client/server from the bleeding edge to the leading edge to an architecture with a critical mass of successful implementations. It has taken about two years to get stable interoperable applications running on stand-alone desktops. Widely available and affordable distributed object computing, like the impossible, is going to take a little longer.

Chapter Fifteen

Electronic Mail and Mail Backbones

by Barbara R. Hume,

Network Technical Services

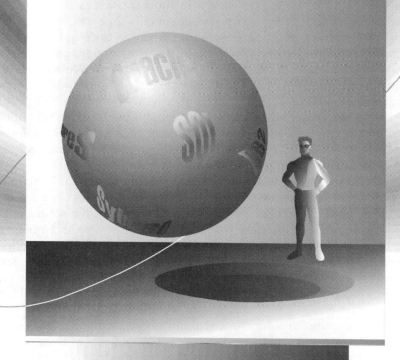

E lectronic mail (e-mail) refers simply to the use of electronic messaging technologies that allow computer users to communicate with each other. An electronic message can consist of anything from a single-line message on the screen's 25th line to a multimedia document encompassing text, video, and sound. E-mail consists of messaging and file transfer, plus such data transmittal features as file storage, file copying and forwarding, return receipts, and the ability to attach additional files. Some applications, such as groupware and workflow products, use electronic mail to service their data-sharing needs. People use e-mail at work for many reasons. It enables users to communicate quickly, avoid telephone tag, transfer complex documents simply, and craft a communication before dispatching it. Because it's an efficient, cost-effective, and convenient form of communication, e-mail has become a primary means of communication within corporations as well as among individual users. An e-mail user can send a message or document to the computer in the next cubicle—or to a computer on the other side of the world.

Today, electronic mail is probably the most common application used on networks. Most electronic mail software uses a store-and-forward method that lets users pick up mail at their convenience. Most packages provide a simple text editor. An e-mail user might find a desired feature, such as the ability to attach multiple documents, in one e-mail package (for example, cc:Mail) and another preferred feature, such as the ability to link messages into a chronological stream, in another (such as The Coordinator II).

E-mail systems on the enterprise must often function in a cobbled-together or widely disparate environment. E-mail systems were initially designed for workgroup or departmental use, but the need to connect all departmental mail systems led to inevitable difficulties. Many departmental LANs grew up as mavericks, with product selection and control handled by department managers. There was little connection with an organization's central MIS department or with systems in other departments. As enterprise network requirements grew, IS managers began to face the difficult challenge of connecting legacy WAN e-mail systems, such as PROFS (Professional Office System) and Digital Equipment's ALL-IN-1, with LAN systems. Connectivity was found to be (and remains) problematical.

As LANs became more and more prevalent in the corporate environment, LAN-based mail systems became popular—and necessary. LANs have become more robust, and LAN mail systems have become better suited to large-scale use. During the past few years, corporations have replaced many mainframe and midrange systems' e-mail products with LAN-based systems. Large firms have installed microcomputer LAN e-mail packages with thousands of users. But the legacy systems are still an important part of the enterprise network, and a communication method that works in a department or between LANs still might not function well for the enterprise environment.

These days, computer-to-computer communications facilitate many—perhaps most—business transactions. Not only does e-mail allow users to share data in a usable electronic form, but it also helps people to collaborate on projects and coordinate their work even if they're in different departments—or different countries.

The chief difficulty, of course, is obvious: different e-mail packages don't often communicate well with each other. Network administrators still struggle with the issue of enabling electronic communication between any two users on an enterprise network. Many vendors continue striving to set the standard, protecting their own territory rather than providing connectivity. The result is a plethora of solutions, most of them only partial solutions. If you're really determined, you can enable enterprise-wide messaging. But you probably won't enjoy it.

Issues to Consider Before Establishing E-Mail

Users and managers planning to implement a new e-mail system or expand their existing systems must weigh a number of factors. For example, consider these questions:

- What are the platform(s) that the e-mail system will run on?

- Does the proposed e-mail system support messaging standards such as X.400 and MHS (Message Handling System) to ensure connectivity?

- Which e-mail systems are already in use on the network?

- Is a corporate-wide e-mail standard in place, or do various workgroups and departments use a variety of e-mail products? If the latter, how can you enable communication among these groups?

- What kinds of documents does the corporation need to send from user to user or from department to department? Are these document transfers best supported by workflow software? (See Chapter 16.)

- What key features must your e-mail system provide to meet the needs of its users? Does the proposed e-mail system support multiple attachments, carbon copies, return receipts, and other useful features?

- How extensive are the training and support requirements for the proposed e-mail system?

- Does the e-mail system offer a user interface that fits into your current networking environment?

- How stringent are the security needs of your organization? Must your e-mail system provide security measures, such as password protection or encryption?

- What effect will the physical components of the existing network have on your choice of e-mail products?

- What messaging infrastructure is necessary to support a particular e-mail system? Can your network architecture successfully implement current and future strategic messaging applications?

■ Does the proposed e-mail system support gateways to enable connections to other networks?

■ How well can your preferred e-mail system handle future internetwork growth?

Another factor you may need to consider, especially when weighing costs, is the matter of commercial versus corporate e-mail systems. A corporate e-mail system that you build and maintain yourself requires the purchase and maintenance of hardware and software to support e-mail functions. For a business with widely scattered sites, the cost of installing and maintaining a private network can be prohibitively expensive. Commercial-service e-mail, on the other hand, lets an outside organization, usually a telecommunications carrier, provide mail services for a fee. Even considering the expenditures involved, outsourcing your e-mail service to a commercial entity can provide cost-effective e-mail service. Some corporations connect corporate and commercial services via a gateway, thereby broadening access to other e-mail systems and users. Commercial-service products include AT&T's EasyLink and Mail, Sprint's Sprint Mail, and MCI's MCI Mail.

Hardware and software issues aren't the only matters you need to consider. Human issues come into play as well. Users can exhibit strong preferences for one e-mail system over another (preferences frequently based on interface rather than technical superiority), and at times internal politics exert a strong influence on the choice of a corporate application standard. Even such issues as on-line indiscretion, management-imposed censorship, and the right to privacy can affect the way a business uses its e-mail system.

Yet another consideration is the current trend toward integrated software suites. This integration often results from corporate mergers, such as the 1994 merger of Novell and WordPerfect, or the 1994 purchase of Beyond Inc., manufacturer of the BeyondMail e-mail system, by Banyan. Small providers of single-function products, such as pure and simple e-mail, are sometimes forced out of the marketplace by this trend to integration. At present, enterprise network administrators are encountering a shrinking range of product choices in terms of stand-alone e-mail functionality, while groupware products and even operating systems offer more and more e-mail services. For example, Microsoft Windows for Workgroups is a network operating system add-on that provides electronic mail and groupware applications in the form of scheduling software.

Because today's e-mail environment includes LANs, WANs, and hosts, each and every computing environment on an internet might conceivably have its own e-mail system; each e-mail system might be fundamentally incompatible with the others. Current e-mail products, therefore, need to incorporate sophisticated means of translating from one message format to another and transporting data across dissimilar networks. Not only must an enterprise e-mail system be able to deal with disparate environments, but it must also be able to handle a greater volume of increasingly complex documents.

In short, a network administrator planning e-mail implementation on an enterprise network needs to thoroughly understand the technological and personnel needs of the organization to avoid committing to a solution that may prove inadequate.

How Does E-Mail Work?

How do users create and send electronic messages?

When an e-mail user sends a message, the program has the user add identification information (including the names of the sender and the receiver, the date, and the subject) to the message. The user may append an attachment, such as a data file. Some e-mail programs, such as Lotus' cc:Mail and Lantec's XPost, allow multiple attachments with a single message. This capability can prove critical in a business environment where information must usually be transferred in the traditional corporate time frame— ASAP.

When the user is finished creating the message, he or she sends it to the recipient's *mailbox*, located in a message store or *post office*. A mail message may go through several post offices before reaching its target mailbox. This method of message transmittal is called *store-and-forward*.

When the message arrives at the recipient's mailbox, the e-mail program notifies the recipient that mail is waiting. The message remains in the recipient's mailbox until the recipient opens it. After reading the message, the recipient has several choices: to answer the message, discard it, forward it, save it, or delete it.

To support all of these processes, the architecture of e-mail software incorporates three types of services. *User services*, which act as clients on the user's computer, provide the user interface to the e-mail system. As such, user services control which e-mail functions a user can actually perform. *Transport services*, which move messages between users, and *directory services*, which perform administrative tasks, such as maintaining user lists, reside on network servers.

User Agents

User services, or *user agents*, let users interact with the e-mail system. As clients for network e-mail servers, user agents reside on users' desktop computers and provide user access to the features and functions of the e-mail system. (In X.400 e-mail systems, the user agent packages the data, creates headers, and addresses and forwards messages.)

Transport Services (MTAs)

Transport services move messages from one user to another, even across multiple dissimilar networks and e-mail systems. These services are also known as *Message Transfer Agents* (*MTAs*).

To move messages, an MTA must have certain information available to it. It must know:

- The names and locations of all users, both local and remote.

- Which applications will use the transport services. (This group may include the e-mail program itself, mail-enabled applications, and workgroup applications that provide messaging. All three are discussed in this chapter.)

- Which networks are on the enterprise net and how to reach them.

Of course, it's easiest for an MTA to establish a connection between two identical LANs using the same e-mail program, since the MTA on one system can talk directly with the MTA on the other system. When the MTAs are different, however, a translation is necessary.

It would seem a logical step to establish a standard MTA that wouldn't be tied to one specific network OS. The MTA specified by the X.400 e-mail standard was intended as such a standard, but X.400 has been slow to gain acceptance. (We'll look at why later on in this chapter.) Several proprietary MTAs, which have been available for business use for some time, are now firmly entrenched in the user base. The three most popular proprietary MTAs at this time are Novell's Message Handling Service (MHS), Lotus Corporation's Vendor Independent Messaging (VIM), and Microsoft's Messaging Application Programming Interface (MAPI).

Novell's Message-Handling Services

MHS is the message transport protocol supported by Novell's NetWare. Since Novell's LAN market share is close to 65 percent, its MHS has become the *de facto* MTA standard. Since MHS is actually a back-end system, it can operate with a variety of front-end applications, making it suitable for heterogeneous e-mail environments. Although MHS is proprietary, Novell has documented it to encourage third-party developers to write to it. Some e-mail software, such as that from Da Vinci Systems, requires NetWare and MHS.

Lotus Corporation's Vendor-Independent Messaging

Lotus, whose cc:Mail e-mail package is a market leader, has joined with IBM, Borland, and Apple to specify the VIM (Vendor-Independent Messaging) message transport protocols, based on transport services used in cc:Mail and Lotus' Notes groupware product. Developers writing to the VIM interface can connect any e-mail application into a VIM-enabled operating system without having to write format translation software.

Microsoft's Messaging Application Programming Interface

The third well-established proprietary MTA is MAPI from Microsoft. By including MAPI in Windows and in Windows NT, Microsoft is adding front-end capabilities to its operating systems.

The Internet Simple Mail Transfer Protocol

Simple Mail Transfer Protocol (SMTP) is the most commonly supported standard among UNIX users. Most corporate e-mail systems can connect to an SMTP environment, thereby giving users access to UNIX-based mail services and to networks such as the Internet.

IBM SNADS

In the IBM market, the most important MTA standards are *System Network Architecture Distribution Service (SNADS)* and X.400. LAN systems that connect to a mainframe host must be able to communicate with SNADS. The IBM mainframe environment also uses Professional Office System (PROFS).

The Apple Open Collaborative Environment

Message transport in the Apple Macintosh environment is handled by the Apple Open Collaborative Environment (AOCE) as well as by the VIM and MAPI MTAs. Working with Apple's System 7 operating system, AOCE serves as an open messaging architecture that allows developers to plug-in their favorite MTAs and other mail services. AOCE services include message exchange between applications, e-mail-enabled applications, directory naming services, authentication services, and digital signatures. AOCE lets users send e-mail from within applications without regard to addressing, document format, or network topology. AOCE does not let you send a Lotus spreadsheet to an Excel user, but it will let you send the spreadsheet as an e-mail message while working in Lotus rather than having to exit to a separate e-mail application.

irectory Services

Directory services manage the files and directories the e-mail system uses. They maintain information about users and user post offices. An e-mail address, for example, usually begins with the user name and the e-mail server name. Directory services keep all this information straight. Directory services can also save system support time and costs by automatically performing some administrative tasks.

Although user mailboxes are easy to manage on a small network using only one directory, a larger network can have multiple post offices, each with its own list of users. By maintaining and updating user locations, directory services help to preserve an e-mail system's efficiency and reliability.

Making sure that all directories contain the same information is called *directory synchronization*. The actual updating of the directories is called *directory propagation*. Directory propagation is an important task performed by an e-mail system's directory services.

Directory services represent a difficult challenge to e-mail vendors. Although enabling users to read directory information is fairly simple, enabling users to update directories is more problematic. The problem is that a change to one directory must be transmitted to all other directories on a network. In an ideal world, vendors would work together to ensure that changes occur throughout the corporation, but vendors aren't always willing to work with competitors.

At first, many LAN e-mail systems used only one server for directory information. To access the information, the user needed to know only the name of the server with the recipient's address. But a global directory stores information on different servers; users have to acquire information from a variety of directory servers. The most basic implementation provides one central directory with the information users need to find addresses. In most cases, however, vendors store address subsets on different servers.

Directory services store information about other network items as well. For instance, they can identify network resources, such as printers.

Today's computing environment makes demands on directory services that didn't exist when LAN e-mail products were being developed. For instance, many directories were designed to support only eight-character user names or were designed to run on a single server. Many initial e-mail products were based on simple flat-file systems rather than on DBMS (Database Management System) products, making it difficult for vendors to build directories with sophisticated global features.

If you've ever implemented a NetWare 4.*x* enterprise network from scratch, you understand how complex—and frustrating—directory service issues can be. Because of all these issues, and because of the rapid growth of enterprise networks, "directory services" is currently a major discussion topic in the industry. With the recent interest in enterprise mail systems, vendors like Novell and even directory service veterans such as Banyan have been implementing improvements as quickly as possible. In general, a company can use LAN e-mail directories on large networks with thousands of users—but these abilities are usually limited to the vendor's products only. Easy interoperability between competing e-mail systems does not as yet exist.

Vendor Solutions to Directory Services Issues

Different vendors have come up with different ways to address the issue. Lotus' cc:Mail offers a sophisticated directory system designed for enterprise networks. The product features a global addressing feature to link directories running on different LAN servers and was designed to conform with emerging directory services standards.

Microsoft Mail version 3.0, a widely popular LAN e-mail system, automatically updates electronic mail systems, gateways, and personal directories. It includes serialization and error-checking facilities to ensure that changes are made to all directories, as well as a feature for synchronizing other vendors' directories. The system is set up to collect changes made to various directories at specified times and change all associated directories. The synchronization works with any gateway that supports encapsulation.

Banyan Systems was one of the first LAN vendors to provide directory services. StreetTalk, the global directory system for the VINES network operating system, offers many advanced directory features. StreetTalk provides the most mature LAN e-mail directory service, although Novell is now providing its own directory services in NetWare 4.*x*, aimed at the enterprise market.

Novell's MHS, designed for small workgroups, doesn't work well with large networks. But Novell's NetWare Global Message Handling Service (GMHS) includes global directory services and supports large numbers of distributed directories. Not an e-mail system itself, MHS allows applications to communicate with each other.

Vendors of larger systems have also developed directory systems. For example, IBM's OfficeVision can provide the addresses of users on different systems. Digital's Distributed Directory Services (DDS) lets companies build products that work with directory information from other electronic mail packages. The product requires constant updating, however.

Soft*Switch stores directory information in a product called Names Directory. Soft*Switch offers the ability to work with cc:Mail directories, Banyan VINES, and some mainframe e-mail systems.

In addition to user, transport, and directory services, an e-mail system also contains message storage facilities and one or more gateways that connect the local network to other networks and external services.

essage Stores

The message storage component of an e-mail system acts like a central post office box, holding messages until a receiver picks them up. The message store holds both incoming and outgoing messages, as well as previous messages the user may want to refer to in the future. Unlike other forms of communications, e-mail doesn't require a sender to establish an endpoint connection before sending a message.

The message store can be on the user's own hard disk, on the server's hard disk, or both. You can more easily back up and secure messages stored on the server, but users of portable computers and users who need access to past messages may need a local message store.

Mail Gateways

As already mentioned, when microcomputer LANs began to proliferate in the corporate arena, they often developed as islands of connectivity, such as departmental or workgroup networks. As these disparate networks connected into larger internetworks, the need arose for messaging between differing e-mail systems.

One solution, developed in part because no single messaging protocol was accepted as a standard, has been the e-mail gateway, which translates between one e-mail system and another: for example, between Lotus' cc:Mail and Novell's MHS. You should be able to find at least one gateway product to connect any two differing mail systems. (The problem on the enterprise, of course, is that more than two systems are likely to need connectivity.) Most e-mail gateways use X.400 as a common denominator, since most e-mail systems can read and interpret X.400 messages.

Gateways may be necessary at this stage of enterprise e-mail connectivity, but they're no one's favorite solution. They're difficult to install and administer, and different gateways have different capabilities. Gateways create additional points of failure, require extra hardware, and sometimes lead to delayed transmissions. Some industry participants believe that application programming interfaces (APIs) common to backbones could eliminate the need for gateways, but none are available at this time, so gateways are still necessary.

A gateway understands the transport protocols, message structure, and data formats supported by each system it connects. It receives messages from the source system, translates those messages to a format that the local system can process, and then forwards them to their destination on the network.

Some gateway products are more sophisticated than others. A gateway product may support only the least common denominator between systems. For example, you may be able to send a simple text message from one system to another, but may be unable to transmit attached files.

Encapsulation, a translation system that puts envelopes around messages without stripping any information, lets all the data reach its destination—but the receiving system may not be able to deal with it. For instance, you may be able to transmit an image, but the recipient may not be able to read or alter the image. Encapsulation also creates larger messages and uses up more bandwidth than other techniques.

On any gateway platform, including a WAN, gateway connections can be point-to-point, hub-based, or backbone gateways.

A *point-to-point* gateway is designed to make two specific e-mail products work as if they were a single system, providing the user with the features of both. A *hub-based* gateway consolidates files coming from multiple mail products at a single point, making the translation and the conversion as transparent to the user as possible. Hub-based gateways are primarily protocol converters. Most *backbone* gateways, such as SNADS, Digital's Message Router, and X.400, use a database to provide the directory synchronization and format conversion.

If you have to choose an e-mail gateway for your enterprise network, keep in mind the critical nature of the applications that will use the gateway. How many messages can pass through in a given period of time? How important is transmission speed from one node to another? How flexible will the system be?

Gateways, while enabling necessary communication to enterprise users, are still far from transparent. Seamless connectivity remains a distant goal.

Vendor Solutions to E-Mail Gateway Issues

Clearly, there are problems involved in the use of e-mail gateways. If you're working in a large corporation with several e-mail systems, you may have to deal with several gateways, a situation that can hamper you in tracking the source of a problem. The products themselves are not always optimized; in general, network e-mail suppliers have concentrated more on enhancing their basic systems than on creating e-mail gateways. And the fact that the market for gateway software is relatively small discourages gateway development.

Then, of course, there's the familiar industry problem of vendors who, in fear of legitimizing their rivals, resist establishing connectivity with competing products. Protection of turf, however, is a factor that works against industry growth *and* against giving the customer what he or she really wants and needs. In order to remain viable in a multivendor environment, rival vendors have had to develop gateways to one another's systems.

The main gateway suppliers have in the past concentrated on connecting larger systems, such as IBM's OfficeVision and Digital's ALL-IN-1, because they represent the largest installed base. Recently, however, gateway suppliers have begun delivering products to connect the most popular LAN e-mail systems.

Most e-mail packages support Novell's MHS; some, such as Da Vinci Mail, rely on MHS for MTA services. But other LAN e-mail vendors, who don't offer native MHS support, have developed gateways from their proprietary MTAs to other electronic mail systems.

Multipurpose Internet Mail Extensions (MIME) provides Internet e-mail support for messages containing formatted text, sound, images, video, and attachments. Now that corporate sites are attaching to the Internet in record numbers, MIME will become more significant. Proponents emphasize that MIME is easier to implement than X.400. MIME may well become the *de facto* mail gateway between proprietary mail systems. MIME is backwards-compatible with earlier messaging specs and is easier to implement than X.400. MIME is free, and it's transparent to X.400 and SMTP.

Too many gateway products are on the market to discuss here; as always, you'll have to conduct your own research. I'll mention a few that I've seen used on the enterprise, but consider them representative rather than inclusive.

CE Software's QuickMail is a popular cross-platform messaging package for Macintosh messaging users. It needs no gateway between PC and Macintosh users, but it includes point-to-point gateways to public services like CompuServe.

HP OpenMail from Hewlett Packard supports X.400, X.500, SendMail, and X-Open standards. It operates on a variety of servers, including non-Hewlett Packard UNIX platforms. HP OpenView connects a wide range of disparate workstations and terminals as well as fax, public communications service gateways, and HP DeskManager, which provides an HP OpenMail gateway to proprietary electronic mail systems such as PROFS, DISSOS, and ALL-IN-1. HP OpenMail offers a choice between OSI and TCP/IP transports.

Both PC and Macintosh versions of Microsoft Mail offer wide-ranging gateway alternatives. Microsoft Mail itself uses a store-and-forward architecture; a directory feature of Microsoft Mail makes it possible to set up mailboxes on other LANs, wide area networks, and public services. Microsoft itself markets gateways for connection to remote servers, and users or third-party software developers can configure multiple gateways on a single server or spread them across multiple servers to balance loads. Gateway management is integrated with Microsoft Mail network management.

CompuServe Inc. lets cc:Mail users exchange messages and files with other users through a gateway device located on CompuServe's international value-added network. The device, called the CompuServe Mail Hub, lets cc:Mail users who have cc:Mail Router or Mobile exchange messages with users on several e-mail services and systems, including AT&T Mail and AT&T EasyLink, MCI Mail, Sprint Mail, CompuServe Mail, and the Internet, among others.

cc:Mail Gateways   Lotus' cc:Mail, the leading LAN e-mail package, runs on a variety of microcomputer operating systems, including Macintoshes, MS-DOS and Windows, and OS/2. Lotus has developed gateways for cc:Mail to Novell's MHS, IBM's PROFS and SNADS, and the TCP/IP SMTP mail systems. Lotus also sells packages enabling users to better access electronic mail telephone network services, such as AT&T Mail, MCI Mail, and Sprint Mail.

Microsoft Mail Gateways   Microsoft offers gateways to Novell's MHS, IBM's PROFS and SNADS, fax servers, X.400, and TCP/IP SMTP. Microsoft also offers products designed for e-mail systems on Macintoshes, on AppleTalk networks, and on IBM microcomputers and LAN protocols.

Soft*Switch Gateways   Soft*Switch Inc. is the leading supplier of e-mail gateways. Its Enterprise Mail Exchange accommodates a wide variety of computing platforms and e-mail systems. Soft*Switch's product line has been used primarily in mainframe environments, but in recent years Soft*Switch has moved into the LAN gateway market. The company's Soft*Switch MHS Gateway was designed to work with MHS-compliant systems.

In addition to supplying gateways, Soft*Switch sells tools to manage gateway connections. Retix, another gateway supplier, offers Open Server 400, an X.400-compliant gateway that features a Windows-based front-end for adding users, transport agents, and information about gateway connections.

Network operating system vendors also provide e-mail gateways. Novell's Global Messaging Service is a set of NetWare Loadable Modules supporting Novell's proprietary MHS transport protocols, X.400, SMTP, SNADS, and other LAN-based e-mail transport agents.

E-Mail Management

Because e-mail is becoming more prevalent and more necessary to corporate-wide communications, users are starting to feel the need for more sophisticated mail management tools. Users want to be able to do more than send and receive documents; they want to be able to store, organize, manipulate, and search the data they've gathered in the form of e-mail messages, just as they do with documents they create on their own systems.

For example, Oracle Mail is a relational database that tracks e-mail messages. BeyondMail, from Beyond Inc., is an e-mail system that includes a tool kit for creating customized e-mail applications capable of automatically prioritizing messages according to their content. The Folio Corporation also provides a mail management tool. Known as MailBag, this utility provides storage, sorting, and search capabilities for e-mail messages.

The ability to manage e-mail also comes in the AlertView cc:Mail Router Agent and in AlertVIEW for Lotus Notes, from Shany Inc. These products add application-specific management features to the company's existing network application management system. The agents find and report all cc:Mail router problems or Notes application errors and allow the network manager to define automatic correction procedures.

Mail management products represent a growing segment of the e-mail marketplace. If users on your enterprise network receive a great deal of their important data in the form of e-mail messages, you should be aware that products are available to let your users access this information quickly and efficiently.

Mail Within Applications

E-mail doesn't exist only as a separate product category. More and more applications developers are creating "mail-enabled" applications, thereby allowing users to send files and messages from within their other applications. Mail-enabled applications save users from the annoying hassle of exiting an application, invoking the e-mail program, sending a message, exiting e-mail, and then bringing the original application back up.

Mail-enabled applications employ e-mail functionality to send messages, data, and documents. By including these capabilities within applications, developers enable users to send and receive e-mail from within word processors, databases, and spreadsheets. This ability is important to the enterprise environment, since it reduces the number of processes users must deal with in order to transfer mission-critical information in a timely manner.

Several vendors now market products to enable developers to add this kind of functionality. Raindrop Software, for example, offers a Windows development tool kit to help software developers e-mail-enable their applications. Open Mail System (OMS), a library of source code, lets programmers develop applications compliant with VIM, MHS, and MAPI protocols.

What About Groupware?

Groupware products, used properly, can eliminate the yellow-sticky-note-on-the-computer-screen form of office communication. With groupware, applications run on top of the messaging system. Products supporting groupware applications, such as Lotus' Notes, are becoming significant in the LAN/WAN environment. Notes applications bring functions such as e-mail to every application. All applications use the same conventions when communicating with the user, and the system automatically handles management details. Lotus Notes, a unique product when first released, actually pioneered the groupware category of software products.

Mail-enabled groupware lets users perform such tasks as scheduling meetings, circulating documents for electronic annotations from several individuals, and screening out unwanted e-mail. For example, a scheduling function can choose a meeting time that fits everyone's indicated schedules.

Groupware products use e-mail as the main method of exchanging information. Five leading groupware applications are BeyondMail, The Coordinator II, Higgins, Lotus Notes, and WordPerfect Office. All these products include basic point-to-point e-mail support, support for address lists, carbon copies, built-in text editors, import and export of text files, attachment of files to messages, and other e-mail features.

Microsoft Mail and WordPerfect Office provide e-mail as an integrated part of the whole system. These groupware products also include calendaring, scheduling, reminders, phone messages, group notices, and to-do lists.

At the high end of the groupware/e-mail line are products such as Digital Equipment's *TeamLinks*, an office-automation product that combines many groupware products into a single package. TeamLinks still depends on server software running on minicomputers, but it works with multiple clients, including OpenVMS, Ultrix (Digital's version of UNIX), and OSF/1 terminal and workstation users, as well as with Macintosh and Microsoft Windows users.

To help their products find a more definable market niche, some vendors have positioned their products as enhanced e-mail. Beyond Inc., Da Vinci Systems, and Enable Software position their groupware products as e-mail products first and groupware second.

Backbone Services Provided by E-Mail

In addition to gateways, another means of integrating diverse e-mail systems involves the use of *backbone switching*. This approach routes all messages to a single computer or to a group of interconnected computers that act as a backbone. Such a backbone system handles messages from e-mail packages, gateways, and applications. One reason to implement backbone strategy is to minimize the number of gateways. A mail backbone also helps to centralize management.

An important backbone-switching system is the Enterprise Mail Exchange (EMX) from Soft*Switch. EMX provides full interoperability with e-mail systems using such protocols as SNADS, SMTP, and MHS.

Several vendors offer X.400 backbone connectivity, either via a gateway or direct connection. For example, the WorldTalk Corporation offers a family of gateways and servers that support Microsoft Mail, AppleTalk, cc:Mail, Novell MHS, and SMTP for UNIX mail.

The Wollongong Group's Pathway Messaging product integrates X.400 message handling and X.500 directory services. It consists of a UNIX-based, multiprotocol backbone mail switch (server) and a desktop messaging application (stand-alone e-mail client) for PCs, Macintoshes, and UNIX workstations.

Although backbones aren't standardized as yet, there's an inevitable trend in that direction.

Standards Used on the Backbone

Three emerging backbone standards currently receive a great deal of industry support. X.400 and the Internet's Simple Mail Transport Protocol (SMTP), are public, while Novell's Message Handling Service (MHS) is proprietary. While X.400 is enormously popular internationally and is being pushed as a standard by the international market, the SMTP-based Multipurpose Internet Mail Extensions (MIME) e-mail standard seems to enjoy wider favor, especially where Internet use is common—for example, in universities and corporate engineering departments. And even though MHS is a Novell proprietary standard, it's quickly becoming a *de facto* standard, making it almost mandatory that certain developers write to it.

UNIX has become synonymous with the Internet—that vast internetwork of computer networks. The TCP/IP network protocols adopted for the Internet are native to most UNIX implementations. Several vendors offer products that add the NetWare IPX/SPX protocols to UNIX alongside TCP/IP.

The trend toward splitting the user-agent side from the infrastructure may assist the move toward a backbone standard. But even if backbones do come into extensive use, administrators still must deal with the need for directory synchronization to handle all the post offices on the enterprise.

SMTP (Simple Mail Transfer Protocol)   As I've mentioned, SMTP is a standard mail protocol based in UNIX and employed by the Internet. As a native UNIX MTA, it's available for free. E-mail developers can use SMTP to enable them to employ any user interface as a front end. Even on a PC, an SMTP-based mail system lets users exchange communication with UNIX users or with the Internet without having to use a gateway.

SMTP, fast becoming a *de facto* standard for integrated network management systems, was designed as a standard for moving mail messages. The standard currently supports only text documents, but it's scheduled to be made compatible with other types of messages, such as Electronic Data Interchange information. The fact that SMTP doesn't support encryption, however, is a mark against it for the enterprise environment, where data security is often a significant concern.

Despite its shortcomings, SMTP is gaining acceptance. Like many TCP/IP standards, SMTP support has been incorporated into vendors' UNIX operating systems.

TCP/IP   The original goal for the Transmission Control Protocol/Internet Protocol (TCP/IP) suite was to enable the kinds of connectivity this chapter deals with: communication among a variety of independent, mulitvendor systems. Interest in support for TCP/IP has consistently grown. For example, in 1983 TCP/IP became the official transport protocol for the Internet. It offers strong internetworking capabilities, and the protocols are well tested and documented. Since the TCP/IP standards are published and available, developers have been able to maintain consistency and thereby enable reliable communication.

Emerging Techniques for Integrating Enterprise Mail Systems

Today every major vendor from Microsoft to Novell is encouraging the marketplace to accept its own products as the integration solution for the 1990s. But the challenge of integrating these isolated networks of DOS, Macintosh, and UNIX machines—even minicomputers and mainframes—into a coherent whole is a daunting one, and providing e-mail connectivity is a major aspect of that challenge.

Da Vinci, for example, exemplifies e-mail/network operating system integration through its tight integration of eMail's administration and directory structure with NetWare's. In NetWare 2.*x* and 3.*x* networks, eMail uses the bindery to provide this integration. In NetWare 4.*x*, it uses NetWare Directory Services, and eMail 2.5 uses the Novell Message Handling Service (MHS) product line, including MHS 1.5, Basic MHS, and Global MHS.

One way that Lotus' Vendor Independent Messaging (VIM) and Microsoft's Messaging Application Programming Interface (MAPI) provide cross-platform messaging is by supporting *common mail calls* (CMCs), a standard that makes seamless message exchange possible. A consortium of e-mail vendors and end-user organizations have developed the CMC specification to let programs using VIM and MAPI, as well as other proprietary API-based programs, communicate with each other. CMCs allow e-mail to move between applications running on different platforms, across distinct mail systems, and in diverse network environments. They replace proprietary API calls, letting developers come up with one program that can be ported across platforms easily.

CMC provides a basic set of services, including send, receive, and address look-up capabilities. Currently the CMC specification doesn't support advanced features like group calendaring and scheduling, but the specification is widely accepted. For example, Novell's Global MHS and Microsoft Windows include CMC support.

X.400

An important step toward facilitating the daunting task of forcing dissimilar e-mail systems to exchange messages is the X.400 global messaging standard, which establishes an internationally accepted set of rules for exchanging messages among store-and-forward mail systems running on a variety of platforms. Developed by the Consultive Committee on International Telegraph and Telephone (CCITT), X.400 comprises a set of network-level protocols within the Open Systems Interconnection (OSI) model. The purpose of the X.400 specification is to provide compatibility among multivendor products and interfaces as well as among messaging services.

X.400 is a specification, not a technology or service. X.400 outlines the protocols, procedures, components, terminology, and testing methods necessary to build interoperable e-mail systems. E-mail products don't *include* X.400; rather, they *comply* with it.

The X.400 standard describes a communications model that includes user services, transport services, message stores, private domains (a mail service operated by a private organization), and administrative domains (a public mail service operated by an authorized telecommunications provider).

The first version of X.400, completed in 1984, included a user agent and message transfer agent. This version was designed to help users send messages to public electronic mail systems. But the 1984 version wasn't well-suited for enterprise systems, lacking as it did security features such as encryption, digital signatures, and authentication. The 1988 version of X.400 was better suited for corporate networks; this version includes a message storage facility and security features. Unfortunately, connecting 1988 and 1984 X.400 products requires gateways, but the 1992 standard is backward-compatible with the 1988 standard.

Many users claim that even the most recent version of X.400 is costly, complex, and difficult to use and administer. Some complain about the additional hardware and resources required. Nor does it offer integrated directory services specification. Even so, all major commercial service e-mail suppliers have signed X.400 interconnection agreements, and large suppliers such as IBM and Digital Equipment have made substantial commitments to X.400. Gateway companies like Soft*Switch have already added X.400 capabilities to their products. The fact is that users are demanding standardization of their computing environments; e-mail providers have to provide X.400 compatibility. Despite its shortcomings, industry observers predict eventual widespread acceptance of X.400. To date, X.400 hasn't been widely used for LAN e-mail systems, but the X.400 API Association (XAPIA) is involved in defining standard APIs for X.400 messaging systems.

.500

Since one shortcoming of the X.400 messaging standard has been the lack of a specification for directory services, we now have X.500, a CCITT companion standard to X.400 that does contain a directory services standard. X.500, adopted as an international standard, defines the way an organization can share names and the objects associated with those names over a global enterprise. The X.500 directory is actually a distributed database of name and address mappings for people, addresses, and peripherals.

Unlike other areas of electronic mail implementation, directories require that different systems support identical information. X.500 directory services are designed to allow companies to divide networks into domains, each with its own set of users. Information then passes between domain servers, using addresses containing country, company, organizational unit, and locality to find the proper recipient.

Alternatives to X.400 and X.500

Until X.500 is more widely implemented, some e-mail users continue to develop their own custom directory services solutions in-house. Among vendor-supplied directory services are Soft*Switch's Directory Synchronization Enterprise Address Book, Lotus'

Automatic Directory Exchange product, and Digital Equipment's Directory Synchronizer, a set of utilities to help users administer DECmail networks.

Another type of vendor solution comes from Firefox Inc., which offers products designed to help enterprise users build messaging and directory backbones based on the X.400 and X.500 standards, including an X.400 Message Transfer Agent (MTA) NetWare Loadable Module (NLM) for NetWare and an X.400 MTA for UnixWare. For directory services, Firefox offers an X.500 directory that runs on top of UnixWare and NetWare and a gateway on NetWare that bridges X.500 and Novell's NetWare Directory Services (NDS).

Several third-party gateways link e-mail packages or directories to the X.400 and X.500 standards.

How the Internet Fits In

The Internet connects more than 5000 networks in 33 countries. Most Internet-connected computers run UNIX and related protocols such as TCP/IP. Traditionally, most Internet users have belonged to universities, government offices, and research institutions, but commercial and corporate e-mail users are establishing more and more Internet links. Most corporate sites now install gateways to the Internet because of its low cost to use and its worldwide communications capabilities.

The major problem with e-mail on the Internet is that you can send ASCII text only. You can't send images or digitized voice; you can't get confirmation that your intended recipient has received or looked at your message; you can't get a guarantee of timely delivery. (X.400 does perform these functions.) Most corporations depend on these capabilities; therefore, the Internet serves certain e-mail functions, such as wide-ranging message-sending, but such functions as guaranteed delivery or graphics transmission are also needed. MIME will solve some of these problems.

The Internet offers an incredible depth of information. However, since the Internet isn't a service per se, having evolved from a casual grass-roots connectivity solution, there's no guarantee you'll be able to find what you're looking for. Although Internet use is becoming easier, the plethora of books written to help users maneuver around the system is a good indication that the Internet still isn't completely user-friendly.

Other on-line services such as CompuServe offer e-mail capabilities as well. Since the major on-line services charge for connect time in addition to monthly fees, corporations often restrict the use of company accounts to those who use the services to add value to corporate resources. For example, a corporate librarian can access on-line services to perform valuable research tasks on behalf of the company.

On-line services use two general methods for organizing the flood of replies that often appear to messages in their forums. With *chaining*, each posting follows in sequence from the posting before it. Some services, including CompuServe and ZiffNet, use a *thread* system, which allows discussions to branch off in several directions, with separate simultaneous conversations resulting from the various replies.

Specific E-Mail Products

In addition to traditional e-mail and mail-enabled programs, other programs exist to help people get messages from one place to another on the network. The field changes rapidly, especially as smaller vendors are forced out of business. But network administrators need to be aware of different kinds of choices.

In the Macintosh world, for example, General Magic's Telescript is a communications language that enables e-mail. Not only does Telescript encompass a standard for addressing messages, but every message is also a piece of software. Like today's e-mail, the simplest Telescript agent carries a message to its recipient. A more advanced agent can even hunt down the recipient via pager or wireless network connection if the message is urgent enough.

Safe-tcl, being developed as an adjunct to the Internet-based MIME e-mail standard, is designed to allow scripts written in tcl (a general scripting language for applications) to be part of e-mail messages and to execute when they arrive. The "safe" part of safe-tcl means that a tcl script embedded in mail is limited in what it can do so it can't harm a receiving system. No commercial products yet exist, however.

Apple's System 7 Pro for the Macintosh microcomputer contains PowerTalk, an integrated e-mail system.

Jensen-Jones Inc. has added e-mail enabling to Commence, its personal information manager. Commence 2.1 lets users store, organize, view, and share information.

PowerRules for System 7 Pro from Beyond Inc. lets you build rules-based e-mail-handling systems that filter messages, automatically create replies, and perform other functions based on your mail's contents. PowerRules uses System 7 Pro's PowerTalk and Apple's scripting language, AppleScript, to file and forward e-mail messages. PowerRules works with any PowerTalk- or PowerShare-compatible e-mail front-end or transport gateway.

Some e-mail packages, although not sophisticated enough to be labeled as groupware, provide much more than basic e-mail functions. Microsoft, for example, integrates Schedule+, its scheduling and calendaring package, with e-mail.

The Future of E-Mail on the Enterprise

Future growth seems necessary and inevitable in the area of electronic mail on the enterprise. In addition to the growth of e-mail as an application, new groupware products will enable electronic messaging systems that support workgroup computing models. Industry observers also expect to see more new network servers dedicated to communications.

Other significant issues that will affect the e-mail industry include widespread adoption of the X.400 and X.500 standards and the division of user, directory, and transport services into separate components.

Multimedia e-mail also seems to be a future trend. InterActive Inc., for example, recently released a communications package called M-Message, actually a multimedia upgrade for e-mail and other voice-enabled or OLE-compatible Windows 3.1 applications. The product supports cc:Mail, Lotus, Microsoft Mail, and WordPerfect Office. According to InterActive, M-Message's audio features let you record your own message or use a previously recorded sound file. You can add scanned images, paste text from the Clipboard, or compose messages within M-Message itself.

As messaging applications become more common and as the e-mail community moves toward standardization, the e-mail back-end will meld into other components of a LAN environment, such as the network operating systems themselves. This incorporation will focus the competition in the e-mail market on the front end of the system—that is, the interface. The interface will inevitably become the user's clearest means of differentiating between a number of e-mail products that all deliver messages reliably and seamlessly.

Chapter Sixteen

Groupware and Workflow Software

by Barbara Bochenski,
The Bolden Group

This chapter describes groupware and workflow software, and explains their similarities and differences. The chapter also discusses the interoperability aspects of these products, and provides examples of how they are used. The strategy of major vendors—such as IBM, Microsoft, and Novell—in regard to these technologies is described. The chapter ends with some speculation on the future role of groupware and workflow software as an integral part of business procedures.

Workgroup Computing

Early in the 1980s, serious research was under way in the area of computer-supported cooperative work (CSCW) that focused on the use of the computer in group work. Many of today's workflow and groupware concepts developed in those early research efforts. Early supporters of CSCW said their goal was to study the relationship between people and information resources as mediated by the computer. The growing use of networking in industry interested many vendors and developers in this kind of technology, too. The term "computer-supported cooperative work" was never widely used by vendors. There are still CSCW conferences being held, but they are usually somewhat academic in nature and often study the more esoteric qualities of cooperative software. Conferences that deal with tools that are being used in most corporations today are more likely to be labeled "workgroup conferences" and "workflow conferences."

One of the earliest packages to gain wide acceptance in the groupware area was Lotus Corporation's Notes. In fact, Notes was probably responsible for defining what groupware is. It permitted a group of dispersed people to share information—to access data, to make changes to some data, and to add their own data. Workflow software came later. Its primary goal was to automate routine business procedures, though some products are now providing tools to help reengineer, or improve, overall business procedures. Both groupware and workflow software are evolving at a fast pace.

Comparison of Groupware and Workflow Software

Groupware and workflow technologies have a number of similarities. Both types of products connect a number of people to permit cooperative work on tasks or business objectives. The primary enablers of both technologies are the widespread use of personal computers, workstations, and networking capabilities, as well as advances in messaging and other communication techniques. Messaging and e-mail are often the basis for various workgroup computing packages. Combining desktop computers and networking is changing the way business is done. A prime example is Electronic Data Interchange (EDI), where e-mail is being combined with transaction processing, offering valuable advantages to companies.

The most common way to distinguish between groupware and workflow software is that groupware is generally passive, while workflow software is active. Groupware packages facilitate document sharing and make it easy for users to access data from a common database, but it does not usually route data to specific individuals for processing. Workflow software, on the other hand, tracks who gets specific information, when they get it, and what is done with that information. Workflow software is usually very procedure-oriented, designed to perform specific business procedures such as completing travel request forms or processing expense reports, while groupware is more oriented toward a group objective or project.

Groupware makes it easy for the *overall* work objective—such as having all knowledge workers in a group keep up with an advanced technology. An employee's workplace no longer has to be an individual, isolated desk where he or she works alone to accomplish a business objective. The employee's workplace can now be an electronic, networked desk where the work objective is shared by co-workers.

Corporations that benefit from groupware often have the following needs:

- To enable employees to work on the same project from locations that are physically dispersed
- To share information in a timely manner with employees and/or clients
- To quickly react to changing market conditions
- To share knowledge about various aspects of the business among a variety of employees

Corporations that benefit from workflow technology may have many of the preceding needs with the addition of the following:

- To complete important procedures that require the work of multiple employees
- To automate business procedures throughout the organization
- To manage the flow of documents in the organization

Workgroup Computing and Other Categories

There is often confusion about terminology in the early stages of evolving technologies. Some people have different names for what is basically the same technology; others use the same name for technologies that are quite different. Some vendors group both workflow and groupware products together under one banner; others insist that there is a clear line between these two terms. One of the problems is that new capabilities are constantly being added to tools, and these new features are sometimes difficult to categorize. In this chapter we will use the term "workgroup technology" to refer to the whole area of collaborative tools known as workflow, groupware, and related tools.

Networking, e-mail, and messaging capabilities form the foundation for both groupware and workflow tools. Intercommunication and interoperability are key components in all of these tools. To qualify as either groupware or workflow, a product must be able to provide a way for people residing in different locations to share information through the networking of their individual desktop or portable computers. Standards for incorporating e-mail into applications and moving messages across a network will further encourage the interoperability and integration of e-mail and messaging within a wide variety of applications.

Software packages that go beyond what is normally expected in e-mail products are sometimes referred to as *smart e-mail*. Encoding of rules and intelligent routing are two examples of extending e-mail, making it smarter. Encoded rules in Banyan Systems' StreetTalk perform such functions as instructing the system to send a copy of the e-mail message to a recipient *and* to the recipient's immediate supervisor. The ability to trigger events is another example of a smart e-mail capability. For example, a message might start a process when it arrives, or be automatically redirected to the recipient at another location. Vendor e-mail software that provides triggers include BeyondMail, Lotus Notes, Digital's TeamLinks for Pathworks, and Microsoft Mail.

Application software—such as word processing packages and spreadsheets—that have had e-mail capabilities added to them are often called *mail-enabled* software. Sometimes this technique is referred to as *hiding* the e-mail capabilities within an application to make sharing work or information with other employees easier. A good example of a mail-enabled application would be a spreadsheet program that has a Mail option in the File menu right along with Print, Save, and other options. The Mail option permits the user to create a message to accompany the spreadsheet on its journey. Once users select Mail, they are presented with a dialog box that provides assistance with creating and sending the message.

If the sender and the recipient both have the same vendor's spreadsheet software, the transmitted spreadsheet can automatically launch the spreadsheet program on the recipient's PC. The recipient can make changes to the transmitted spreadsheet and return it to the sender. If the sender and recipient have different spreadsheet software, many e-mail packages permit the recipient to at least view the spreadsheet. However, the recipient cannot alter the spreadsheet.

In addition to smart e-mail and mail-enabled applications, there are some situations where *applications* send e-mail to each other. Such applications are sometimes labeled *virtual e-mail users.*

Scripting

Scripting is a feature that many workgroup computing tools—especially groupware and workflow software—have in common. It is probably used more widely in workflow tools. Sometimes scripting is the way that an end user or developer describes processing steps to the workflow tool. Scripting is basically a set of instructions to an application, telling it to perform a series of steps. Since it is a set of instructions, a script is quite similar to a program. The difference, which is subtle, is that a program constitutes all or part of an application, while a script is a set of instructions *for* an application. For example, one or more programs comprise a word processing application, while a script can tell that word processing application to behave in a particular manner. A script is similar to a macro (a series of steps that are recorded and stored using a combination of keys, referred to as a short key code) in the PC environment.

Writing a script often requires the expertise of a programmer, though many end users can write their own scripts. Vendors are interested in making it easier for end users to create their own scripts. Some vendors have both a high-level and a low-level scripting language. The end user creates the script in the high-level language. Then, a program generator uses this high-level scripting language to create the low-level scripting language. Some tools offer graphical user interfaces (GUIs) that assist the user in building scripts. After the user utilizes the GUI capabilities, the program generator converts the GUI specifications into the actual scripting language. The low-level scripting language can be modified. Some users are adept enough to modify the low-level language themselves, though often a programmer performs this job. End users also have the option of returning to the high-level scripting language where they can make the changes and process them through the program generator again.

WorkMan from Reach Technology offers *handlers,* which are sections of script language that can define such things as what action should be taken when the user presses a specific button or selects a particular option on a menu. A user can also view or modify scripts by using these handlers. A number of modifiable default handlers are usually provided when handlers are present in scripting languages.

eengineering with Workflow Software

Workflow software usually does more than just digitize data and automate existing business procedures. Workflow tools are often used as part of reengineering efforts aimed at improving and automating business procedures.

Some analysts say that the architecture of a server-based workflow product is particularly valuable for this type of reengineering. They explain that a server-based tool encourages examination of the entire procedure that is the basis of the workflow process. Instead of simply automating the existing steps of an old, and possibly ineffective, process, more thought is given to evaluating the overall business procedure and its objectives.

Other analysts disagree. They say that workflow tools do not encourage developers or users to think through an existing procedure to improve it and eliminate unnecessary steps. However, workflow tools are constantly being improved, and capabilities that assist with the evaluation of business procedures are increasingly available.

roblems That May Arise

Even more severe than the learning curve that comes with new software is learning to work in new ways. Change can be extremely troublesome for some people. Many people are accustomed to working alone. They may object to leaving familiar ways of working, and resist adapting to new procedures. However, once most users have an opportunity to work with groupware and workflow tools, they like them and want even more capabilities from this type of software. Changing work habits is most successful when the employees who are doing the work come up with the idea of changing the procedures they follow.

Another potential problem is directly related to one of the benefits of these technologies—access to more information. If groupware and workgroup tools are not managed properly, they can result in information overload and cause frustration. Exposing workers to information and procedures they do not need to know can waste their time, detracting from their ability to accomplish their work objectives.

Another issue related to workgroup technologies is unrealistic expectations. There has been so much excitement and enthusiasm for these technologies that some people might expect more from these tools than they can deliver at present. Users must carefully study the capabilities of all the tools they are considering implementing to make sure that the tool can meet the specific needs they are trying to address.

Interoperability Facets of These Technologies

Groupware and workflow tools contribute to enterprise interoperability in a number of ways. Primarily, they allow people to communicate and share information with each other. Electronic communication is becoming easier and more efficient as an increasing number of software vendors adhere to uniform standards for workflow products. In addition, vendors are developing interoperability features for existing tools and applications.

People Sharing Information

Groupware is basically software that is designed to facilitate the work of a group of people who are connected by a network. Groupware software, such as Lotus' Notes, coordinates the activities of the group. Workflow software, such as the ActionWorkflow system from Action Technologies, is designed to facilitate work processes. Examples of workflow software are the electronic organization of business procedures that involve routing forms or other types of information among multiple employees. The information on the forms or other papers is digitized and routed to all the people who need to process it—even if they are working on different platforms.

Interoperability Through Adherence to Standards

Increasingly, vendors of groupware and workflow tools are adapting their products to meet various standards that exist or are emerging in the marketplace, thus adding to interoperability capabilities. Some standards are *de jure*—formal national or international standards such as X.400, which ensures that e-mail systems can communicate with each other. Other standards are *de facto* standards—such as Vendor-Independent Messaging (VIM), the Messaging Application Programming Interface (MAPI), and Object Linking and Embedding (OLE), sponsored by Microsoft.

Adding Interoperability to Existing Tools and Applications

The interoperability opportunities offered by groupware and workflow tools will continue to grow as more and more vendors add capabilities to their existing suites of products. Customers are demanding the ability to communicate across different applications, and vendors are responding. Lotus Corporation, for example, has added VIM implementations to Lotus Notes that allow for communication between Windows and OS/2 client applications.

Creating New Combinations of Software

Beyond adding interoperability features to existing tools and applications, vendors are developing entirely new applications by combining different types of software. Electronic Data Exchange (EDI) provides an example of how an entirely new application area becomes possible by combining messaging and application software. EDI helps expedite ordering and delivery of products, among other business objectives. Many EDI applications combine transaction processing activities with messaging features. Creating new, more efficient methods for accomplishing business objectives is expected to be a major contribution of workgroup technologies.

Groupware

As mentioned earlier, groupware permits people in diverse locations to share and modify information in which they have a common interest. There are far too many groupware products for us to discuss—or even list—all of them. We will use Lotus Notes as an example of groupware because, though it was one of the first groupware products, it still exemplifies the primary characteristics of groupware technology.

Lotus Notes

Though Lotus was a leader in offering the first robust groupware package, Notes did not immediately become a best-seller in the marketplace. It took a few years for enterprises to fully understand how Notes could be used. Large accounting consulting firms such as Andersen Consulting, part of Arthur Andersen, and financial firms such as J.P. Morgan were among the earliest companies to install large numbers of Notes. After the initial groupware pioneers showed how helpful this kind of product was, others installed it as well.

When groupware was still relatively new, Notes incorporated important features like high-security e-mail services and database capabilities. Many analysts say that

Notes' early database features are what made the product particularly valuable. These features let users share, organize, and archive ideas with other users in a workgroup. The database capabilities were not in the initial version of Notes, which featured basic routing capabilities, but were added to the product in version 3.0. Combined with e-mail, the database capabilities permitted users to build message databases for transmission over enterprise-wide networks. Many groupware products now either have their own separate database or use an existing relational one.

In addition to database features, version 3.0 also provided forms-based action buttons, centralized forms templates, additional signature control features, and macros that permitted periodic updates. Version 3.0 also automatically sent updates in the form of messages to users based on their profiles or activities. The earlier versions had required that users continually query the product for updates. Also, with version 3.0, Notes could be used on Macintosh and UNIX platforms, rather than on just OS/2 and Microsoft Windows' platforms. Lotus plans to continually update Notes.

How Various Enterprises Use Lotus Notes

Arthur Andersen, one of the largest early users of Notes, has benefited in a number of ways from this groupware product. Andersen Consulting, a $2.3 billion management and information processing consulting firm with 25,000 employees worldwide, and its parent organization, Arthur Andersen, purchased 20,000 copies of Notes to be used throughout the enterprise. The number of Notes installations within Andersen could be larger now.

Andersen Consulting's interest in Notes involved how it could facilitate timely information sharing and enable knowledge sharing. Consultants at Andersen can query Notes for information regarding projects they are working on. This information could be general items such as start date, end date, projected worker hours, or it could be competitive in nature. A basic software infrastructure evolved to further benefit from the product. A database directory that helps locate information is part of this infrastructure.

J.P. Morgan uses Notes to give analysts immediate on-line access to market research. Before Notes, research reports were manually circulated by means of a circulation list. Analysts had to wait their turn to receive the reports. With Notes, the research information is now available on-line to any analyst as soon as it is entered. This large financial firm also uses Notes to file status reports about projects. As a result, information that was previously available only to managers became available to peers as well. Other ways that financial firms benefit from Notes are related to its real-time news feeds from financial wire services and its ability to replicate databases. Financial services firms can pass trading information from an office in Frankfurt, Germany, that is closing for the day, to an office in New York City, where the trading day is still in progress.

Market research firms, such as the Patricia Seybold Group, use Notes not only for research, but also to create and deliver their information products to their clients. Patricia Seybold consultants insert information related to upcoming newsletters in a Notes database. Colleagues, many of whom are frequently on the road, often add comments to the database. Finished information products are available to Seybold subscribers through the Notes database.

To save on paper costs, a large defense contractor uses Notes to distribute documents to 12 offices throughout the United States. Notes also lets the contractor's frequently traveling employees keep up-to-date no matter where they are. In fact, some frequent business travelers have reported that when they tap into the Notes database from afar, they feel they are in the familiar surrounding of their home office.

As an additional interoperability feature, Lotus provides a program called Document Manager, which permits users to access Notes through desktop applications such as word processors. Document Manager has a file-lock feature that can be used across an entire wide area network (WAN). Most file-lock features in document managers only operate across local area networks (LANs). Other features in Notes include a version control capability that tracks changes in a document and a capability that automatically creates a new version of a document whenever a change is made. The older version is saved for reference.

ther Groupware Products

Competition for Notes has come from many sources and will continue to grow. While no two products have all the same features, groupware software is expected to grow in sophistication and functionality. Currently, some products that offer capabilities that are similar to Lotus' Notes include Digital Equipment Corporation's TeamLinks, NCR's Cooperation, Novell's WordPerfect Office, and Oracle's Oracle Office. While new vendors appear all the time, vendors with existing groupware products continue to improve them.

WordPerfect Office, version 3.1, was file-based, but version 4.0 offers an underlying database that integrated the product's messaging and calendaring capabilities. That was an important way of competing with Lotus' Notes. Another important feature of WordPerfect Office's version 4.0 is its rule-based message handling services. Using acknowledgment procedures, the recipient of a message can let the sender know when and how a message was handled. Some ways that recipients can handle messages is to delete, file, forward for informational purposes, or delegate them. Version 4.0 also includes important status tracking and task management features. Using these features, a manager is able to create a task and send it to the appropriate employee. When a task is completed, the employee lets the manager know by placing the work in a "completed" box.

UNIX systems have many features built into them that provide some of the rudimentary capabilities provided by groupware packages. For one thing, UNIX is equipped with a built-in e-mail system. For another, access to the many research facilities and databases that the UNIX-oriented Internet offers is able to satisfy many research needs of UNIX users. However, there are many other capabilities offered by groupware that are needed by UNIX users, and vendors have started to offer products to meet those needs. We've mentioned that Digital provided a UNIX version of

TeamWorks. Lotus and WordPerfect were other early vendors to provide UNIX versions of their groupware products.

Workflow Software

The quality of workflow software that is usually used to distinguish it from groupware is that it is very procedure-oriented. Workflow software is concerned with what the next procedure is in a given task, and who can perform it. It also ensures that the procedure, and subsequent ones, can be accomplished in a timely manner. Workflow software is often used to automate such procedures as processing insurance claims and expense reports.

In spite of the differences between groupware and workflow software, many people use these two terms with a great deal of flexibility. In addition, new software that combines networking and e-mail messaging with applications might not fit precisely into either category. Some vendors refer to extensions to their e-mail packages as groupware or workflow technology. If you ask some vendors whether a particular software package of theirs is groupware or workflow technology, often the answer is "yes."

Workflow Architectures

Different workflow tools emphasize different features. The architecture of a workflow product often determines how the tool can best be used. According to its architecture, a tool may emphasize the ability of end users to manipulate it, or may concentrate on providing centralized control by an organization. There are three distinct architectures for workflow tools. While many workflow tools have aspects of each of these groupings, the architectural classifications are helpful to highlight differences among tools.

The three primary architectures for workflow software are:

- User-based or client-based tools
- Object-based or agent-based tools
- Server-based tools

User- or Client-Based Systems

User-based or client-based tools emphasize the ability of end users to manipulate the tool themselves without the help of professional IS (information systems) personnel. An example is provided by BeyondMail, by the Beyond Corporation, which has a rule-based engine for filtering and sorting mail. Beyond spokespersons explain that users can establish rules for tasks ranging from relatively easy personal mail management to complicated forms routing procedures. New rules can be added incrementally. Beyond Inc. says that BeyondMail utilizes a bottom-up approach to automation. Beyond's FormsDesigner package, along with Beyond's incremental scripting capabilities, facilitates the bottom-up approach. A top-down approach, on the other hand, starts with specific procedures that are chosen as automation candidates, and then an overall automation plan is developed. With the bottom-up approach, end users can apply user-based tools to their own specific tasks.

Object- or Agent-Based Systems

Object-based or agent-based tools have intelligence built into them by the user or developer to process forms involved in a particular procedure. This category of tools treats data on the forms as objects. Using various forms, the end user can view the contents of these objects. Forms also have active fields, which can automatically initiate other activities such as calling a database. The location and functionality of active fields are built into the form when it is designed. The fact that a workflow tool works with forms does not necessarily mean it is automatically classified as an object-based architecture. As mentioned earlier, many tools have several of these architectural characteristics. The major emphasis of a tool determines how it will be classified architecturally.

Server-Based Systems

Server-based tools usually contain a single logical center that an administrator can use to monitor the status of tasks. This facilitates the administrator's responsibility of tracking work flow. Server-based tools often use the capabilities of an existing relational database. An example of a server-based tool is ActionWorkflow from Action Technologies, which monitors and controls task status and work flow using a central database. Knowledge of how to monitor and control tasks is coded into the database by a developer. Having routing information and other knowledge in a central place facilitates replication of this information and permits the functions to be used elsewhere. In addition, this approach offers more control than client-based tools. ActionWorkflow also uses forms. However, the strong amount of central control offered to the administrator puts it in the server-based category.

ers and Applications of Workflow Software

In many enterprises it is the end user who initiates use of workflow software, rather than the information systems (IS) department. Local area networks and e-mail are being installed by networking groups; however, once the systems are installed, end users learn more about the various ways that messaging technology can be used to aid in their work procedures. As a result, end users are often the ones taking the initiative to analyze various packages and implement them. End users are the experts in the business procedures they habitually perform, and often they are the best ones to redesign and automate these procedures. Vendors say that this is one area where end users, rather than IS departments, are pushing the vendors for additional capabilities to assist with their work.

A wide variety of applications is appropriate for workflow automation. The most common applications are ones that involve forms and require the attention of people in diverse departments. For example, many companies have been using e-mail and e-mail extensions for some time to automate the paperwork involved in employee business trips. Now, many companies have added the expense portion of the trip. Typically, employees fill out a standard company expense form indicating their specific expenses. Some companies have even installed scanners for employees to enter expense information by scanning in receipts from the trip. The scanned receipts are then electronically attached to the expense form. After reviewing the data, managers can either send the expense form back to the employee for additional information or affix their electronic signature and forward the document to accounting. Furthering the automation, the accounting department may automatically prepare a check to be sent to the employee. When employees use their company credit card and go over the limit, the accounting department may automatically create a bill to be sent to the employee or, if so indicated on the expense form by the employee, deduct the appropriate amount from the employee's paycheck.

Some workflow software provides protection of business procedures with security features aimed at discouraging inappropriate individuals from tampering with the flow of work. WorkMan from Reach Software, for example, prepares an audit trail of where the form or document has been. This information is stored in Reach's Status Tracker database. WorkMan provides other administrative functions as well.

An innovative example of a money-saving application of workgroup technology is provided by the Texaco Corporation, based in Tulsa, Oklahoma. Texaco uses the technology to prevent seaport overtime charges if a tanker stays in a dock longer than scheduled. There are numerous activities involving many people that take place when a tanker pulls into port. Texaco orchestrates all this with workflow procedures. Assignments are electronically sent to oil terminal workers and automatically updated as the work progresses. All work is carefully monitored to make sure everything is performed in a timely manner. If a task lags, more attention is quickly given to the sluggish area. The goal is to get the tanker in and out as expeditiously as possible and avoid even a small portion of the $10,000 an hour overtime dock rate.

Products and Development Strategies of Major Vendors

The following sections describe groupware and workgroup products, and the strategies of several vendors. Companies like IBM, Novell, and Microsoft have implemented strategies that encompass a wide range of hardware and software products, including operating system enhancements. Other companies are developing products specifically designed to offer exceptional groupware and workflow capabilities.

IBM's Statement of Direction and Products

IBM is one of the proponents of workgroup computing. Dick Sullivan, director of workgroup solutions for IBM, says that IBM workgroups could consist of any of the following:

- A small group of users
- A small business with a group of individuals devoted to similar tasks
- Everyone within the enterprise who has related needs or expertise to share

Sullivan says there are a number of enterprise-wide services for workgroup technology. These are:

- Address book or directory functions
- System administration functions
- Calendaring capabilities
- Library capabilities

The address book function is similar to a directory. System administration functions would tell, for example, what resources are available for LAN administration and/or for mainframe administration. In the category with calendaring capabilities would be the ability to schedule meetings among different people within a group. There is a need for library-type capabilities, because users want to be able to go to only one location to find out where anything is in the enterprise.

Sullivan explains that workflow is the overriding structure in IBM's workgroup strategy. He indicates that *strategically*, IBM looks at workflow technology as consisting of the three areas discussed next: production workflow, ad hoc workflow, and administrative workflow.

Production Workflow

There are two types of production workflow. The first relates to automating existing procedures as they are. The second relates to reengineering. For example, IBM's FlowMark has specific characteristics to aid in the process of reengineering. The product's features help identify bottlenecks in existing, modified, or planned procedures. IBM's workflow products also permit procedures with the ability to link into legacy systems data, which of course includes IMS data.

Ad Hoc Workflow

This area covers workflow procedures that might be used just once. It also includes the process of bringing together a group of knowledge workers or other professionals within an organization to improve awkward or inefficient existing procedures. A manager might say to them, "We have a problem in this line of claims processing. How can we solve it?" Often contributing to the solution are such tools as e-mail (the ability to share information across company lines) messaging, and project management.

Administrative Workflow

This area revolves around forms: the ability to create forms and to route them. IBM's FormTalk is in this category.

Messaging is important across all three of these areas. Sullivan also adds that the strategy must be heterogeneous, recognizing that there are multiple vendors involved in today's work processes: different databases, diverse productivity tools and applications, and a wide variety of e-mail systems.

Figure 16-1 provides an overview of IBM's current overall product offerings and the different categories that the company uses to classify its current workgroup packages.

The diagram shows that IBM currently divides their workgroup solutions into four categories:

■ Enterprise communications

■ Document management

■ Workflow management

■ Decision support

IBM adds another dimension of interoperability to this overall technology: interoperability with mainframe software and data. There is a tremendous amount of legacy data in most corporations' databases; IBM provides ways to access that data using workstation tools. IBM also says these tools will help provide a transition for users migrating to the LAN environment. The software that is directly responsible for the interoperation of LAN-based and host-based components are the following gateway products:

■ Time and Place Connectivity/2

■ Address Book Synchronization/2

■ IBM Mail LAN Gateway/2

Time and Place Connectivity/2 is the interoperability product for Time and Place/2, which is a LAN-based calendar and group scheduling application. Time and

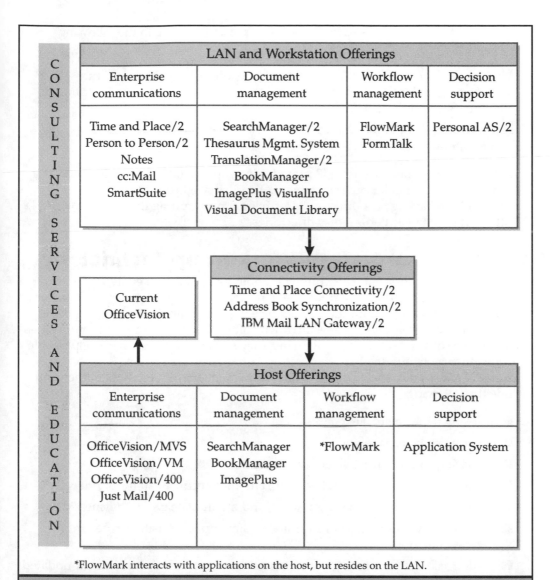

Figure 16-1. *IBM workgroup solutions*

Place Connectivity/2 permits users to connect Time and Place/2 to the following IBM products:

- ■ *OfficeVision/MVS (OV/MVS)*   A mainframe office automation product operating under the MVS operating system that incorporates the Distributed Office Support System (DISOSS).

- ■ *Professional Office System (PROFS)*   The office automation product for IBM's VM operating system. It is used on many 4341 and 4381 systems.

Address Book Synchronization/2 provides interoperability between host and LAN users. Address Book Synchronization/2 handles synchronization issues by automatically extracting host directory information, transmitting the data to the LAN, and updating cc:Mail or Lotus Notes directories.

Microsoft's Approach to Workgroup Technology

Microsoft says that workgroup computing is about extending and evolving tools that people *already* have in order to support the ways they work. The vendor adds that any definition of workgroup computing should be based on an understanding of people and how they work together. As a result, Microsoft describes workgroup computing as open, flexible software solutions built on industry standard technology to help people work together more effectively.

Some of the solutions that people could work together on, according to Microsoft, include the following:

- ■ Tracking departmental expenses
- ■ Creating an enterprise-wide budget
- ■ Preparing a report in a collaborative manner
- ■ Enabling project planning, scheduling, and monitoring of status of projects
- ■ Permitting co-workers to access, share, and manipulate critical business data
- ■ Electronically routing loan or insurance claim applications for processing, review, and approval
- ■ Letting sales and marketing personnel access data from, and/or submit updated sales data to a corporate management information system

Microsoft provides this diverse list to illustrate that there cannot be a one-size-fits-all workgroup tool. That is why the vendor emphasizes the ability to combine many software products from diverse vendors within an open architecture. Microsoft says the three fundamental objectives of their strategy are to provide:

- ■ A solution-based focus that permits users to define solutions according to real-world workgroup activities. This part of the strategy also means that Microsoft will provide products that are easy to use.

- An open architecture that does not restrict an organization to the products of one vendor.

- An evolutionary approach that adds capabilities to existing tools, letting sites leverage their existing investments in technology. This includes Microsoft's operating environment, Windows.

Under the evolutionary strategy, Microsoft Windows is being extended to provide interoperability with tools from other vendors. Reportedly, the software nicknamed Cairo will add to these extensions as well as extend them into the realm of object-oriented capabilities. Fundamental workgroup services that have already been added, or are being added, to Microsoft's operating system include such features as information sharing, a common messaging system, standard directory services, a common data access model, and improved security.

Another major interoperability thrust is Microsoft's Windows Open Services Architecture (WOSA), which assists enterprises whose workgroup solutions must run on multiple electronic messaging systems or must access data in a wide variety of heterogeneous databases. WOSA is a set of open Windows APIs that permits any desktop application, such as word processing, spreadsheet, PC-based database tools, to work seamlessly with a variety of back-end products and services from different vendors, for example, host-based, LAN-based, and public electronic messaging systems. WOSA uses Microsoft's Messaging API (MAPI) and Open Database Connectivity (ODBC) to provide these capabilities.

To use WOSA, developers or system administrators load the appropriate MAPI drivers from a Windows desktop. MAPI drivers are written as Windows dynamic link library (DLL) files. There are separate MAPI drivers for different products—some are written by Microsoft, but most are written by individual vendors for their own products, to provide interoperability with other products. Microsoft defined MAPI using input from many industry vendors. A few of the over 50 vendors who support MAPI include Aldus, Asymmetric Corporation, AT&T, Banyan Systems, Digital Equipment Corporation, Dun & Bradstreet Software, Hewlett Packard, Intel, Novell, Oracle, and WordPerfect.

ODBC is a Microsoft-sponsored data access API that aids with the heterogeneous database problem. This call-level interface (CLI) was developed by over 40 vendors, including the SQL Access Group. It is intended as a vendor-neutral, *de facto* standard that provides developers with a common set of APIs and with drivers that are written for specific databases. These drivers are in the form of Windows DLLs. There are drivers for over 50 databases and for tools like Information Builder's EDA/Server and similar server/database products.

The most prominent of Microsoft's current workgroup technology tools are:

- *Schedule+* Helps schedule meetings among people in diverse locations
- *Electronic Forms Designer* Assists with the job of designing forms
- *Workgroup Templates* Provides ready-to-use examples of commonly used forms

Microsoft also emphasizes the importance of its Microsoft Mail for PC Networks as being the foundation for many of its current and planned workgroup technology products.

Action Technology

Action Technology is one of the most important providers of workflow products. Action offers a workflow designer and an applications builder through its Workflow Management System software. This product can assist with the process of connecting workflow procedures with external packages such as databases or e-mail. Reporting tools permit users to inspect what is happening and alter the flow of work. Action Technology products have traditionally been available on an OEM (original equipment manufacturer) basis; however, the vendor is in the process of changing that.

Action's current marketplace offerings consist of a powerful suite of products collectively referred to as the ActionWorkflow System. The individual products and their utility are discussed next.

- *ActionWorkflow Analyst*   This is a powerful tool to help end users (or application developers) model their business activities. The Analyst permits users to perform what-if modeling by making alternatives using on-screen graphical tools. The what-if model is compared to the original model by the Analyst, providing a comparison of time and value analyses for each.

- *ActionWorkflow Builder*   This takes the model or picture created in the Analyst step and compiles it into an automated workflow application. The Builder phase creates the entries for the Definitions Database and the Transaction Database in which the Workflow Management System stores and maintains information related to the business process.

- *ActionWorkflow Manager*   This manages the workflow process. It makes sure that the system provides the right people with the appropriate information on the correct forms. It also makes sure that all of this is accomplished in the right sequence.

Action Technologies also provides a methodology along with training courses and consulting services to teach users how to use the methodology. The methodology is based on research on how people communicate and make commitments. Within the methodology there is always someone who is doing the work (the performer) and someone else for whom the work is being done (the customer—who may be either internal or external). In modeling the process, the modeler must provide time estimates for each step in the process. In addition, the modeler must consider the successful completion of the process.

The ActionWorkflow methodology reduces every action in a modeled business process to four steps:

1. *Preparation*   The customer either makes a request for service or receives an offer of services.

2. *Negotiation*   The result of negotiation is a clear definition of the condition of satisfaction—exactly what must be done to complete the job.

3. *Performance*   The performer performs the work required and, upon completion, notifies the customer. This is almost always the most time-consuming step in the process.

4. *Acceptance*   A job is not considered completed until the customer is satisfied with the work accomplished and tells the performer the work is acceptable.

An important tool in ActionWorkflow modeling is the *action loop*. Graphically, it appears as an oval on the business procedure model, or map. The action loop, or graphic oval, represents one action in the business procedure being modeled. Each of the above steps is identified for each action loop as shown in Figure 16-2.

Multiple loops are connected together to indicate the overall flow of activities within a business procedure. The finished model of the business process may consist of many loops connected together sequentially as a result of IF statements and other conditions.

racle Office

Oracle Corporation's Oracle Office integrates enterprise-wide messaging, scheduling, calendar, and directory services. It also provides an advanced proofreading service. Oracle Office is built on top of the Oracle7 server database, as are other products in Oracle's family of Cooperative Server Technology.

Oracle Office consists of the following components:

- *Oracle Office Client*   As the user interface, it manages communication between the user and the Oracle Server.

- *Oracle Office Server*   The server provides services such as message delivery and the distribution of directory information.

- *SQL*Net*   This is the networking technology that provides communication between the client and the Office database, and between Oracle Office nodes.

- *Gateways*   Gateways are processes that enable Oracle Office to exchange messages with other e-mail systems such as Unix Mail, MHS-based systems, and X.400-based messaging systems.

- *Application Programming Interface (API)*   The API is a set of procedures providing a programming interface to Oracle Office so developers can create applications that communicate proactively.

- *Oracle7*   Oracle Office uses the Oracle7 database to store and manage all Oracle Office data; users can benefit from the security built into Oracle7, though the database operations are transparent to them.

- *Oracle Office Manager*   Manager software provides administrative features for configuring and maintaining various aspects of the Oracle Office System.

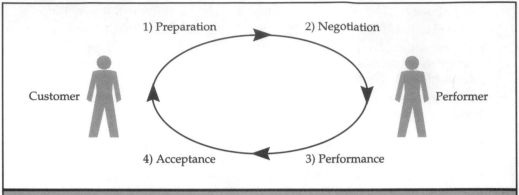

Figure 16-2. *Action loops in Action Technology's ActionWorkflow model*

Oracle's Commitment to Interoperability

The Oracle Office Server is capable of being scaled and will support large parallel processing machines. The ability to support parallel processing is a feature that is increasingly found in workgroup computing products.

Oracle says it is committed to supporting X.400 and X.500 standards. In fact, the Oracle Office directory service was modeled largely after the X.500 specification. When the X.500 standard is completed, Oracle will ensure that Oracle Office fully complies. Oracle Office supports a variety of network protocols, such as TCP/IP, DECnet, SPX/IPX, APPC/LU6.2 and Async. Oracle Office also supports MAPI and VIM. Since the company places such a high value on interoperability—their Oracle7 database can operate on over 40 platforms from diverse vendors—it is likely Oracle will be willing to support other standards as they become established.

WordPerfect and Novell

When Novell completed its acquisition of WordPerfect in the early part of 1994, it went from having no related products to being completely immersed in the office automation and workflow products arena. WordPerfect Office, which was developed by WordPerfect before the acquisition, provides workgroup calendar, mail, and scheduling capabilities. Novell will combine its own tools with WordPerfect tools. For example, the combination of WordPerfect In-Forms, a forms-based workflow tool, with NetWare's MHS mail system and Directory Service will provide an enterprise-wide workflow product. In addition, Novell will offer new capabilities to take advantage of the strength of the acquisition. An example is that new AppWare programming tools will be developed for creating workflow applications.

To take advantage of WordPerfect products and maximize their strengths with its various networking capabilities and existing tools, Novell said it will create a new business unit called GroupWare. This new business unit will integrate document management, workflow, and messaging-based applications. The vendor says it plans to be as much a competitor in workgroups and application areas as it is in networking. Novell plans to continually offer new generations of network applications that will follow published standards and offer open interfaces.

Novell has incorporated WordPerfect tools into its overall networking strategy, which includes combining the best of NetWare and UnixWare into one product. Novell's overall strategy is to pursue a four-layer architecture as follows:

- The first layer (the lowest) consists of the operating system, which provides the foundation of the architecture.

- The second layer is made up of services that integrate separate computing platforms so they can be networked together.

- The third layer is composed of tools that permit developers to leverage services and operating system capabilities into applications.

- Applications constitute the fourth (the highest) layer in the architecture. These applications permit users to use the network in order to collaborate on work projects. WordPerfect tools will make up the application layer for the immediate future.

Evolution of Existing Workgroup Technology

As mentioned earlier, there is an increasing trend to combine various computing technologies and to add new interoperability features to existing products. Digital Equipment added a C language interface to its TeamRoute workflow package so that programmers could add to it specific operations that are better performed with C code. NCR's ProcessIt provides many of the same features as TeamRoute, but claims to offer even more interoperability. It can be modified not only by C, but also by C++ and many widely used 4GLs. It can also interoperate with word processors, spreadsheets, and graphics packages.

One of Borland's objectives for interoperability is to let users send electronic messages without having to exit from the specific package they are working in. To do so, Borland is working on ways to combine applications not only with e-mail, but also with object-oriented technology, using their Object Component Architecture—a structure for object-oriented components—and their overall object-oriented architecture called Object Exchange (OBEX).

Interoperability between old and new systems is an important issue. How can the old and new systems interface or integrate with each other to facilitate migration to the new way of doing business? FileNet Corporation provides some solutions with emulation capabilities and common interfaces. Their WorkFlo package provides support for 3279 and 5250 terminal emulation. Programmers at Pacific Mutual Life

Insurance Company used the 3270 or 327X emulation to connect the FileNet system with the company's 3270-based policy issuing system. FileNet's forms and scripting language were used to build common interfaces to integrate the old and the new systems. Users built forms using either WorkFlo's scripting language or FileNet's AutoForm, which is a Visual Basic type of toolbox with drag-and-drop capabilities.

The Future

Many analysts, and this author agrees with them, believe that collaborative techniques like workflow and groupware will be more widely used in the future—maybe in some ways that we cannot conceive just now. It is clear that more applications will become e-mail enabled or network aware. In fact, it is not difficult to imagine a time when workgroup technology will be an integral part of business procedures. After a technology exists for a while, people become more used to it and find new ways to integrate it into their existing procedures.

A good example is the telephone. Before telephones, companies sent messages to other companies manually. The procedure was for the secretary to type the message and bring it to the company's message center, usually on the ground floor. Messengers—either riding bicycles or driving cars—carried the written message to the message center of the receiving company and left it there. Someone in that company's messaging center would deliver it to the participant.

When telephones were first installed, a secretary would still bring the message to the company's messaging center. Someone in that company's messaging center would place a phone call to the recipient company's messaging center's telephone. The person answering the phone would write down the message and take it to the actual recipient. Of course, at that time, this was a substantial time savings. No messenger had to travel between buildings. Actually this was not a bad way to implement the use of phones since, initially, they were not in widespread use. If a telephone was installed in an executive's office, the executive would only have been able to talk to messaging centers in other companies until a significant number of other executives also installed telephones.

It is amusing for us to think of how the early phones were used because today they are an intrinsic part of how we do business. Someday, the ability to share information and easily communicate electronically with other business associates will similarly permeate every area of how we do business. Workgroup technologies—like the telephone—will likely become intrinsic parts of how we perform business procedures in the future.

The ideas for specific new groupware and workflow products and applications are coming primarily from people like yourself—individuals who become knowledgeable about the capabilities of such software and are aware of the unique needs of their specific corporations. Might some of your transaction processing or decision support systems benefit from the addition of an electronic mail capability? Should an e-mail message be sent to someone if a transaction detects a particular condition in the production database? Asking questions like these and analyzing the needs of your enterprise may reveal valuable new ideas. Any system that involves more than one person is a potential candidate for the effective application of workgroup technology—and the business world has an abundant supply of such systems.

PART FOUR

Management Protocols

Chapter Seventeen

Network Management Protocols

by Raymond C. Williams, IBM

Management protocols are used to gather information about devices attached to a network, and to make that information available to network administrators via a management interface. The network management community is currently using two management protocols: Simple Network Management Protocol (SNMP) and Common Management Information Protocol (CMIP). CMIP, the older and more general of the two, was developed as part of the OSI standardization effort. It has been adopted by the ISO (International Organization for Standardization), ITU (International Telecommunications Union), and others. SNMP was developed later by the Internet community for use in the TCP/IP environment. SNMP and CMIP took a somewhat different approach than most of the existing proprietary management systems. One of the objectives of standardization efforts such as SNMP and CMIP is to achieve interoperability of network management tools and products.

Before SNMP and CMIP, many vendors developed proprietary management protocols for specific devices in their product lines. The protocols tended to have a wide variety of message types used to manage the devices. To accommodate new devices or new features required adding functionality to existing message types and, in most cases, adding new message types to the protocol. This meant that adding new devices or new functionality not only required additional management applications, but it also required modification of the existing management protocol. This greatly complicated quality assurance and version control, since enhancements to the protocol affected all products using the protocol, not just those that utilized the enhancements. This approach was an expensive and time-consuming effort. Further, this continual accretion of functionality did not have a positive effect on the quality of the products, management or otherwise.

The new "standard" protocols, SNMP and CMIP, took a different approach in order to allow extendibility without requiring that all users of the protocol understand everything. The two protocols are based on the same fundamental data storage concepts in which management information is gathered and stored for later retrieval by a management application. Operations are performed on attributes of managed resources that represent the elements of the system. Messages are also defined for delivering information about spontaneous occurrences or conditions in the network equipment.

The use of a data storage model rather than a functional model greatly simplifies management. By expressing all operations in terms of a very small number of operators on objects and their attributes, it is possible to make the implementation essentially table driven. Adding new devices or new features merely requires adding definitions of new objects or attributes to the table. The protocol itself does not change or need to be updated every time enhancements are made. The protocol itself does not understand anything about the objects or the attributes. It merely carries the necessary information. As long as the managed resources know their object and attribute definitions, and an application knows what to do with them, the application can cause the management protocol to carry the necessary information to perform the operations.

- The Internet's SNMP management protocols have been widely implemented. Within the last year there has been a major proliferation of SNMP management products and agents on the market.

- The ITU-T/OSI standard has been adopted by the Internet Network Working Group as Common Management Information Protocol over TCP/IP or Open Internet Management (OIM), and as Common Management over Link Layer (CMOL) by the IEEE.

The ITU-T/OSI standard provides the basis on which the Network Management Forum OMNI*point* and the X/Open network and system management are being built. OMNI*point* is designed to provide a path that vendors can follow to develop management systems that interoperate with other vendor's management systems. The ITU-T/OSI management protocol has been slower in getting established in the marketplace. With the publication of OMNI*point*, ITU-T/OSI-based management will begin to establish a presence in the market. For example, the Service Providers Integrated Requirement for Information Technology (SPIRIT) has selected both SNMP and CMIP for their management protocols. Both SNMP and ITU-T/OSI are included in the Open Software Foundation's Distributed Management Environment (DME). Meanwhile, there will be a large number of customers who will have made a substantial investment in SNMP-based management products.

Internet Management (SNMP)

Simple Network Management Protocol is currently the most commonly implemented management environment protocol. It operates over the Internet User Datagram Protocol (UDP), which is part of the TCP/IP protocol suite. The latest version of SNMP supports other environments as well. SNMP is prolific. Almost every vendor of management software or hardware supports it, which accounts for its popularity, although, as discussed later, SNMP is not as robust as the ITU-T/OSI offerings.

Historical Perspective

Network management for Transmission Control Protocol/Internet Protocol (TCP/IP) was traditionally done with a small set of tools. Commands such as *ping* were, and still are, used extensively to determine whether a specific device can be reached via the network. Some of the tools and commands used in the pre-SNMP environment are discussed next.

ping   Uses a loop-back test to verify the network's ability to communicate with another system on the IP network. Also reports response time.

netstat   Checks networking status information and answers the following questions:

- Are packets leaving or arriving on this machine?
- Are packets thrown away at the link level?
- Are packets thrown away at IP or TCP levels?
- What does the routing table look like?

ifconfig   Checks the network address, network mask, and operational status.

traceroute   Determines where IP is failing on the network.

> *NOTE: In many cases, a logon to a remote machine is required before the commands discussed here can be executed.*

In 1987, Simple Gateway Monitoring Protocol (SGMP) was introduced as an interim protocol for TCP/IP network management. One of the objectives of the interim protocol was to seek reactions from the user community. It included not only the protocol for communication between network management entities—network management protocols—but also defined which variables were to be monitored. Several groups experimented with this protocol and the National Science Foundation Network (NSFnet) backbone used it in 1988.

From 1988 to 1990, many vendors implemented the successor to SGMP: Simple Network Management Protocol (SNMP). This widespread implementation resulted in the SNMP being named an Internet Standard for TCP/IP network management. Document number RFC1157 defines the protocol for managers (clients) to communicate with agents (servers)*. The protocol defines neither how, nor which, network management information is kept, obtained, and handled by agents. It also does not define how network management information is collected, distributed, and presented by managers. RFC1158 MIB II (Management Information Base) defines a base set of variables that represent a managed resource or device. This separation is consistent with the use of a data-oriented model.

In 1989, the Open Systems Interconnection (OSI) network management discussions received widespread attention within the Internet community. A working committee attempted to define an architecture that would allow the use of Common Management Information Services and Protocols over TCP/IP (CMOT). The premise considered was that migration to OSI would be easier in the future if OSI-style network management was used. CMOT uses the same MIB II to define the managed objects. Although CMOT initially received a good deal of attention, it rarely has been implemented. It is still a Draft Standard and largely discounted today. More recent work has been focused on OSI Internet Management (RFC1214).

Client/Server Model

SNMP network management is implemented using a client/server model. *Servers* are defined as entities that own the resource. *Clients* are elements that require services

---

*RFCs (request for comments) are documents that contain ideas, specifications, notes, or other information about proposed or working Internet standards.

from the resource. In the SNMP context, servers are called *agents,* because they "own" the management information base (MIB). Clients are called *managers* because they require services from the agent to monitor and control the network. The agent interfaces directly to the operating system and/or the networking layers to obtain and manipulate the network management information. Since this interface into the operating system and network layers is very implementation dependent, there is no standard for it. At the other side, the agent exposes that information in the form of MIB II objects to clients via the SNMP protocol.

An agent (server) should be running at each network entity that will be managed or monitored. Typically you have SNMP agents running on gateways and routers, as well as on important servers like file servers or mail gateways. This allows the monitoring of the network connections to the servers. Dedicated SNMP agents can also monitor specific hardware or applications. There is no widely accepted mechanism for integrating agents on a single system.

The manager or managing station (client) is the application software that runs at the Network Operations Center. It communicates with the SNMP agents to collect or distribute network management information in the form of MIB variables. There is no mechanism for communications between management stations.

SNMP models all agent functions as alterations or inspections of variables. Variables are either retrieved (Get) or altered (Set). The monitoring of the state of the network is primarily accomplished by polling. Systems are checked in an orderly and periodic manner for information. However, a limited number of unsolicited messages (Traps) guide the timing of the polling.

SNMP is a request/reply protocol that reflects a simple fetch/store paradigm. A manager is restricted to the operations of Set and Get on data items in the agent's MIB. More complex operations on an agent system are accomplished by the side effects of the Set operation. A GetNext command is included to allow traversal of the MIB.

An SNMP agent must implement support for all five SNMP PDUs (Protocol Data Units). These PDUs are listed in Table 17-1.

In general, PDUs are utilized by SNMP manager/agents in the following manner:

1. Get, GetNext, and Set are generated by an SNMP manager.

2. Get_Response and Trap are generated by an SNMP agent.

3. An agent interacts with the UDP/IP layers and operating system to obtain and manipulate the actual network management information.

4. The SNMP manager runs as a standard TCP/IP application.

5. An agent can send a trap to the manager if something important (like a link failure) occurs. This is the exception rather than the rule.

6. The manager sends some SNMP requests to the agent to obtain more information (Get, GetNext) and/or change (Set) the value of some variables. A trap may be used by the manager to change the timing and focus of SNMP requests.

7. To each of these requests, the agent responds with the Get_Response packet.

PDU	Function
Get_Request	This is a request to Get MIB variable(s).
GetNext_Request	This is a request used to interrogate a table for which you do not know the entry names and/or how many entries are in the table.
Get_Response	This is a response to a Get, GetNext, or Set request.
Set_Request	This is a request to change (Set) the value of the supplied MIB variable(s) to the supplied value(s).
Trap	This is notification of a certain event. A trap is a hint that something has happened. A trap only contains limited data to describe a problem. There is no guarantee that a trap will be delivered.

Table 17-1. *SNMP Protocol Data Units (PDUs)*

Normally an SNMP manager will be polling the SNMP agents for information, so the agent generally takes a passive role. Polling is fundamental to the operation of SNMP. Only in a few cases will an agent take the initiative and send a trap (hint) to the manager to inform of the state change. If the manager receives the trap, it can take appropriate action to obtain more information. The specification discourages the use of additional traps, but places no restrictions on their use. This is where vendor extensions are permitted in the trap mechanism.

Management Information Base II (MIB II)

SNMP does not specify which data, objects, or variables are used for network management, or how network management information is represented. Instead, SNMP uses the Internet MIB II as the definition of network management information. The MIB II is defined separately from the SNMP, which allows other protocols (for example, CMOT) to use the same MIB II to provide network management.

Originally, the Internet Advisory Board (IAB) mandated that the SNMP was to use a MIB II that is compatible with the MIB for OSI-based network management protocols. That is no longer the case.

Summary

Internet Management was designed as a rapid solution to an urgent and tractable problem—managing bridges, routers, and the like in TCP/IP networks. The protocol is deliberately simple, and the initial MIB was tailored explicitly to accommodate only Internet-addressable equipment. The quest for simplicity and the specific scope of the problem have introduced limitations in addressing, in requirements for event reporting, in scalability to large networks, and so on.

There are three design criteria for SNMP:

■ Minimized number and complexity of management functions realized by the management agent. This implies lower development costs and easier implementation of SNMP agents for developers of network management tools.

■ Easily expandable functionality for monitor and control to accommodate additional, unanticipated aspects of network operations and management.

■ Independence of the architecture from particular hosts or gateways.

SNMP defines the protocol used to manage the objects defined in the MIB. The objects in the MIB are defined according to the rules set forth in the Structure of Management Information (SMI) protocol. The separation of the definition of network management information (managed objects) and the protocol used to monitor or manage that information has the following advantages:

■ New objects can be added without changing the protocol to manage these objects.

■ Multiple protocols can manage the same objects.

The separation also limits the management protocol to only managed resources defined in the MIB. For instance, if there is no variable in the MIB that represents the status of the physical Ethernet cable, then there is no way to manage or monitor the cable via SNMP. The MIB allows for enterprise-specific extensions, so users can add new variables to the MIB. The new variables can then be managed via SNMP. Implementation of a specific MIB by a vendor does not require that all of the variables for that MIB are present or fully implemented.

The specific features and functions implemented by SNMP agents and managers are left to the developer's choice. There is no adequate standard for specifying the minimum implementation. Therefore, it is difficult to gauge functionality without assessing a vendor's product in depth.

ture Developments

SNMP management seems well entrenched as the method to manage TCP/IP networks. But its future extension to accommodate other types of networks seems questionable. It is very unlikely that SNMP itself will be enhanced. Future developments are likely to come in the form of new standard MIBs. Each new MIB will require changes and additions to the existing MIB-specific applications in order to support these new functions.

SI Internet Management (OIM)

There is continued interest in providing Common Management Information Protocol (CMIP) over TCP/IP as well as over OSI. There was an unsuccessful effort to force the CMIP network management protocols into SNMP. Recent efforts have focused on mapping the reverse, that is, mapping SNMP (MIB II) into CMIP. This will work over OSI service on top of TCP/IP. It would seem inevitable, at least at the functional level, that an application be aware of the differences between OSI managed systems and Internet agent systems.

The primary problem in accommodating the Internet management standard within an OSI environment is reconciling the information modeling paradigms. The OSI paradigm of a managed object is at a higher level of abstraction (and thus a higher level of intrinsic functionality) than that of the Internet MIB.

Simple Network Management Protocol II (SNMP II)

Currently, work is going on to advance the Internet SNMP management standard in the form of Simple Network Management Protocol II (SNMP II). As of today there has been no large-scale movement to adopt SNMP II, primarily because of the lack of a migration path for existing SNMP products. These are some highlights of the proposed standard:

- Security enhancements
- Bulk data transfer capabilities
- Manager-to-manager interaction
- Expanded protocol support (that is, transport)
- Improved definitions for managed objects
- Improved error handling
- Configurable exception reporting (that is, discriminators)
- Less memory

The protocol operations for SNMP II include:

- GetRequest
- GetNextRequest
- GetBulkRequest
- Response
- SetRequest
- InformRequest
- SNMP II-Trap

Dialog between SNMP and SNMP II will require proxy gateways. Therefore SNMP II is not backward-compatible with SNMP.

ITU-T/OSI Network Management

The ITU-T/OSI has created standards that define services and protocols for network management in open environments. Services are defined in the Common Management Information Service (CMIS) standard, and protocols are defined in the Common Management Information Protocol (CMIP) standard.

Historical Perspective

System Management was considered part of ISO standards from the beginning. ITU-T/OSI System Management is an object-oriented request/multiple-reply management protocol. ITU-T/OSI provides a much larger set of capabilities and provides some mechanisms to allow the optimization of the amount of traffic generated by management. In addition, CMIP distinguishes between operations on objects and operations on attributes of objects.

U-T/OSI System Management Specifications

ITU-T/OSI System Management is defined by a set of ITU-T Specifications and Recommendations paralleling the series of ISO standards. The ITU-T Specifications and Recommendations are in the X.700 series.

U-T/OSI Model

ITU-T/OSI uses a client/server paradigm, where the client is known as the *managing system* and the server is known as the *managed system*. The managed system takes the agent role, which involves receiving management notifications, operations, and forwarding notifications to and from the resources being managed. The managing system takes the manager role, invoking management operations and receiving notifications. The X.701 Systems Management Overview further defines how the management model is divided into layers:

- Management communications protocol and service are defined for carrying management operations and notifications.

- Management information is defined to represent the resources that can be managed.

- A series of system management functions is defined to model common tasks related to many resources or applications.

- Five System Management Functional Areas are defined to summarize the requirements for the management of: Fault, Configuration, Accounting, Performance, and Security.

Common Management Information Service (CMIS) defines the services used. Common Management Information Protocol (CMIP) defines the protocols that carry the services. This structure allows the use of different protocols to support the same services.

CMIP Protocol Data Units

Common Management Information Protocol (CMIP) provides two types of service:

- The transmission of event notifications autonomously emitted by managed objects
- The transmission of operations directed toward managed objects

The notification protocol provides fields for identifying:

- The managed object
- The event type
- The time of the event
- An extensible parameter to carry object-specific or operation-specific information

The operations protocol provides fields for:

- Identifying the target managed object or objects
- Identifying the operation
- Controlling access to managed objects
- Correlating the reply with the request
- An extensible parameter to carry object-specific or operation-specific information

The identification of the target managed object can be based on any of the following:

- Its type (class)
- Its name
- Its position in the instance tree
- A predicate referring to its attributes
- A combination of all four

These features allow a managing system to affect a number of objects with a single operation and to select objects for operations depending on their dynamic state (that is, a test-and-set feature).

The syntax of the PDUs and the attributes of the managed object are defined in terms of Abstract Syntax Notation One (ASN.1). The PDUs used in CMIP are listed in Table 17-2.

Scope and Filter

CMIP provides scoping and filtering facilities to allow requests of multiple managed objects in a single request. Filter defines the conditions that must be satisfied for an operation to take place. Scope allows the requester to specify where in the instance tree to start applying the filter. Filter allows the requester to specify the relation

PDU	Function
Event_Report	Invoked by a CMIS services user to report an event about a managed resource to another CMIS services user. The Event_Report in CMIP is an asynchronous indication of some important event in the managed resource. It contains an indication of the event and associated information that may be useful in understanding the event. Event_Reports can be confirmed. CMIP takes an event-driven view of management, so there is wide use of the Event_Report PDU in CMIP.
Get	Invoked by a CMIS services user to request the retrieval of management information from another CMIS services user. The Get operation in CMIP is performed on a list of attribute/value pairs for a managed object. (Modifiers that allow this to apply to multiple managed objects are described later in this chapter.)
Set	Invoked by a CMIS services user to request the modification of management information by another CMIS services user. The Set operation in CMIP is performed on a list of attribute/value pairs for a managed object. The Set operation in CMIP provides four variations of the operator: replacement, add values, remove values, and Set to a default. This reflects the object or database orientation methodology found in CMIP.
Action	Invoked by a CMIS services user to request another CMIS services user to perform an action. An action is provided as an "escape" in case it is determined that there were operations that were too cumbersome to do as a Set or Get.
Create	Invoked by a CMIS services user to request another CMIS services user to create a managed object. Create is an operation on a managed object that creates a new instance of a managed object.
Delete	Invoked by a CMIS services user to request another CMIS services user to delete a managed object. Delete is an operation on a managed object that deletes an instance of a managed object.
CancelGet	Invoked by a CMIS services user to cancel a previously issued Get. Since the Get operation in CMIP can apply to multiple managed objects, this could entail returning a considerable amount of information. CancelGet cancels a Get that is no longer needed (or that is going to return too much information).

Table 17-2. *The Common Management Information Protocol Data Units*

between attributes and values, or several such relationships joined by logical operations (AND, OR, or NOT).

Sets, Gets, Actions, and Deletes may use scope and filter. A filter with a broad scope will apply the filter expression to every object within the scope and perform the operation.

Multiple Replies

A Set, Get, Delete, or Action may apply to multiple managed objects, generate considerable information, or require an indication of interim results. These operations may generate multiple replies to a single request.

Synchronization

CMIP also provides a rudimentary synchronization option that allows each operation to be done as *best-effort* or *atomic*. In a best-effort operation, the receiver will make a best effort to perform the operation on each managed object and attribute selected. In an atomic operation, the receiver will first ascertain that the operation can successfully be performed on the managed object before performing it.

Managed Object Names

Each CMIP operation specifies a managed object class and a managed object instance. A distinguished name is a sequence of (attribute, value) pairs, where the order (the superior/subordinate structure) and attributes (of the pairs) are specified by the Name Binding.

Management Information Model

The key to ITU-T/OSI system management is in object definition. The essence of the object-oriented approach is that all aspects of real-world systems can be described by a single object model. The main features of the object model as described in Recommendation X.720 are that objects are characterized by:

- The operations they accept
- The notifications they emit
- The attributes (data) they make available
- The behavior they exhibit

These properties are expressed in the Guidelines for Definition of Managed Objects (Recommendation X.722). Objects that share identical specifications are grouped into classes. New class specifications are derived from existing class specifications by inheritance. New classes inherit all of the specifications of their ancestors, but also contain additional specifications. (Object architecture is also discussed in Chapter 14).

A key aspect of the object-oriented approach is that objects are characterized by means of an interface specification, not an implementation. The actions, notifications, attributes, and behavior are those observed at the object boundary. How the object is implemented in a real piece of equipment is not defined.

The object-oriented design of the ITU-T/OSI methodology provides for four key functions:

- *Encapsulation* Provides for access to data via methods and hides internal implementation from the user
- *Object Class* Provides the ablility to extend and combine existing interface definations to create new interfaces
- *Class Inheritance* Allows one class to be refined from another class, providing for reuse of specifications
- *Allomorphic Behavior* Provides a mechanism for migration and coexistence between multiple versions of class definitions

andard Management Specifications

The ITU-T/OSI series includes several Systems Management Functions specifications. Systems Management Functions use CMIS services for management communications, and use the ITU-T/OSI management information model for representing managed objects and their attributes. They typically provide a standard representation for a task that is common to a number of management applications. For example, the event control service described previously is relevant to any application that monitors events. These functions provide for generic information and management controls, as discussed next.

Generic Information

Management information common to many managed resources is often specified as a Systems Management Function. This allows the same management information to be manipulated in the same manner, independent of the underlying resource. For example, X.731 defines a generic-state management model which includes common attributes for representing operational, administrative, and usage status, and a common notification for signaling changes in state.

Management Controls

The ability to control management itself is also specified as a Systems Management Function. These functions usually define "management support" managed objects which represent the control capability. This allows the same management protocol and information model to be used to control the management service; no specialized control protocol is required. For example, X.734 defines an Event Forwarding Discriminator "management support" managed object that allows managers to initiate, configure, suspend, resume, or terminate event reporting by the agent.

ummary

ISO has attempted to steer a difficult course by developing a framework that is specific enough to avoid protocol anarchy, but not so restrictive as to stifle management solutions.

Future Developments

Developments of OSI-based standards will take two complementary paths: further development of the framework standards in ISO, and the development of managed-object definitions and implementation agreements by strategic groups. Work has already begun in ISO and will concentrate on extending the single manager/agent architecture, which current standards are based on, to a multiple manager/agent architecture, providing an extended model for managing relationships, and providing tools for schema management.

Comparing SNMP and ITU-T/OSI

This section compares the characteristics of SNMP and ITU-T/OSI within the following end-user criteria:

- Efficiency
- Robustness
- Flexibility and extendibility
- Security
- Application functionality
- Cost of implementation
- Current use

Efficiency

There are several aspects of efficiency that must be balanced in relation to each other. They are:

- Network bandwidth use
- Agent size, complexity, and processor use
- Manager size, complexity, and processor use

The following sections compare the various aspects of the protocols that affect these trade-offs.

Polling Versus Event-Driven Environments

One of the major differences between SNMP and CMIP is the reliance of SNMP on polling. In an SNMP environment, managed devices are polled for information of interest. Managed devices then return the requested information synchronously. The manager is responsible for requesting the appropriate information and filtering of unwanted data. This approach uses a great deal of network traffic and processing power to present useful information. The polling philosophy of SNMP becomes a significant problem in large networks. As the number of managed devices grows, polling cycles become long and unresponsive. In addition, polling generates considerably more than twice as much management traffic as an event-driven approach. Studies have shown the practical limit of networks to be somewhat less than 750 managed resources.

CMIP adopts an event-driven view of the world. Event reports are generated to report any spontaneous events deemed important by the managed resources. Event reports are also used for periodic reporting of performance information. The overhead on the network is considerably less than that of SNMP. Consequently, networks of several orders of magnitude larger can be managed for a given set of management resources. The event-driven approach of CMIP is more in keeping with the nature of networks. A potential problem can arise when a resource fails without generating a notification.

Operations on Multiple Objects

While Set and Get provide a good open-ended structure for the management protocol, their use could be very inefficient in any real system, given the number of attributes that need to be accessed to diagnose a problem or to change a configuration. One of the major optimizations that a management protocol needs to be able to support is modifying several attributes with a single PDU. This is more for efficiency in bandwidth and processing than for any sort of implied synchronization.

SNMP allows operations on multiple objects in a single PDU. While this approach decreases the number of PDUs actually sent (saving their associated overhead), the amount of data sent is not reduced significantly. Since a PDU must fit in a single User Datagram Protocol (UDP) message, there is a definite upper limit on the size of the operations. Thus, performing an operation on a large number of related (or unrelated) attributes requires transmission of considerable address information. The Internet solution optimizes for simplicity of implementation in the agent, at the cost of greater complexity in the manager and less efficient use of network bandwidth.

CMIP handles all of these cases (among others) through the use of Scope and Filter. Additionally, since more complex data types can be represented using CMIP, it is often possible to retrieve data through a single attribute that would require requests on multiple attributes in SNMP.

Scope and Filter   Scope and Filter in CMIP allow operations to be performed on a set of related attributes on the same or different objects. The problem of multiple requests in a PDU, described in the previous section, is thus avoided by issuing only a single request. For example, an ITU-T/OSI management application can request port information for all bridges in a network with a single scoped command. This can greatly reduce the amount of traffic on the network (only one request is sent per applicable host or device, and unwanted values are removed, by the agent, before transmission). This is done at a significant cost in manager and agent size and complexity. The SNMP approach would require a series of requests and would result in the transmission of the normal data as well as the abnormal. The manager would then be responsible for filtering out the unwanted data.

Scope and Filter are very powerful constructs for such a low-level management protocol as the role assumed by CMIP. The constructs are almost as powerful as a database query language. Scope and filter are much more suited for manager-manager interactions than manager-agent interactions. In the manager-agent interactions, it is desirable to keep as much of the processing overhead as possible in the manager and minimize the processing in the agent (since the agent has other work to do besides management). However, there is a creative tension between this requirement and demands on network bandwidth. Herein lies the rub: you want to keep agent implementations as simple as possible. Complete implementation of scope and filter greatly increases the complexity of the agent.

Linked Replies   ITU-T/OSI allows a management application to retrieve large amounts of data from multiple managed systems via a single request; the information is sent back in multiple linked replies. SNMP does not support linked replies. This limitation makes it inefficient to retrieve large amounts of data such as addressing tables. Multiple replies require explicit acknowledgments to ensure delivery. They also introduce the possibility of the loss of order.

Multiple Object Selection   SNMP requires that a management application specifically address the actual object instance. ITU-T/OSI provides a full set of conditional commands based on object type, value, and relative location in the instance tree.

Accessing Tables

One of the major uses of any management protocol will be inspecting tables to determine why a network element is behaving as it is. The two protocols take very different approaches to this problem. SNMP provides the GetNext operation as the means to traverse a table. The requester sends a GetNext for a managed object. The Response contains the value of the next item. The requester then changes the Get_Response PDU into a GetNext PDU and sends it again. This process is repeated until the table has been traversed.

In CMIP, the requester specifies the appropriate scope and filter parameters (or the table may be defined as a single, complex attribute) and sends the Get_Request. The responder returns the entire table either as a single Get_Response or as multiple replies (each containing a table entry). CMIP will generate, in the worst case, half as much management traffic.

Atomic Operations

CMIP allows a Set to be either Best-Effort or Atomic. Atomic means that CMIP will first verify that the operation can be performed on each attribute before performing any operations.

SNMP only provides this form of atomic operation and does not support best-effort. SNMP checks to see if it is possible to perform the operation on everything in the list and if it cannot, it abandons the request.

The Creation and Deletion of Objects in SNMP

SNMP, in the concise MIB definition, has defined a means to use Set to provide the effect of the Create and Delete operations in CMIP. It makes it difficult to guard against the requester making a mistake and inadvertently creating objects that were not intended. The agent can only know whether it is legal to create an object, not whether creation was intended. In general, one would like to have access control on Read, Modify, Append, Create, and Delete at the level of the objects. One would like to give some operators/applications append or even modify access, but not create or delete access. This SNMP approach makes that difficult. It would imply that access control must be granted on a per object (attribute in the case of SNMP) basis, which is a lot more overhead. But even this would not be sufficient to protect against unintended creates.

Application Confirmation

Both CMIP and SNMP provide application (end-to-end) confirmation for Get and Set operations. However, CMIP also provides for unconfirmed Set operations and confirmed Event Reports. This allows greater flexibility for the application developer. Further, the inability to confirm SNMP traps affects robustness.

Information Modeling

Network and systems management is concerned with gathering a large amount of diverse and complex data about systems and networks, and about their interconnection and interaction. Object-oriented modeling techniques provide a means to do this in an ordered and structured manner. ITU-T/OSI uses a data model that is more aligned with the Entity Relation and Object-oriented data models. SNMP uses a model that is more aligned with the Relational data model.

Object Model

ITU-T/OSI uses an information model that declares all the attributes, actions, and notifications. As a result of this, a management application knows that an agent will support all those defined entities. Through inheritance, an existing definition may be expanded to encompass additional functionality provided by a new resource. A properly designed management application can manage the new resource as if it had the original class.

Allomorphism provides a mechanism for migration and coexistence between multiple versions of class definitions. It can be used to manage an object as though it were an instance of another compatible class (which may or may not be a superclass). This allows for updates and extensions. However, it does not provide a mechanism for removing or deleting properties that are no longer deemed desirable. With X.700, object class definitions can be designed for the inclusion or exclusion of properties based on various conditions. This specification tool also assigns packages to an object identifier that can then be used in the protocol to control or monitor which packages are present in a given instance of the class.

SNMP consists of MIBs which define a collection of attributes and is extended by defining new MIBs. An agent may not support all of those attributes for a given resource, and different agents may support different combinations of attributes from more than one MIB. This makes the implementation of reliable management applications more difficult and does not promote standardization.

Actions

CMIP provides for the definition and execution of management operations that are specific to a particular resource.

SNMP does not provide for management operations, but rather for implicit operation, initiated by performing a Set operation on an attribute value. Thus the setting of a "reboot" variable might imply the subsequent execution of the "reboot" operation.

Set Function

CMIP has a richer Set function. The fact that the database aspects of management are more completely recognized in CMIP is reflected in the richer semantics of the Set operation. Beyond the simple replacement operation, CMIP allows Set to have the semantics of adding or removing values from an attribute, or setting the attribute to a default value. The ability to add or delete values is especially useful for attributes which are of the data type *list*. In SNMP, there is no mechanism to get the same effect. The data type *list* is not a supported data element. Each list element is modeled as a separate attribute instance with its own managed object ID. The richer semantics of Set, found in CMIP, will be most useful in exchanges between managers, but may also occur in some of the more complex managed resources.

Security

The OSI security infrastructure is based on the Upper Layers Security Model standards. These standards present a model for security applicable to connectionless and connection-oriented distributed application environments. The standards provide common security service specifications to support security information exchange of authentication (verification of the identity of communicating peer entities); access control (communications authorization and system applications access); data confidentiality (protection against unauthorized access); data integrity (protection against unauthorized data alterations); and security key management and distribution.

Current SNMP security is handled via the *community name* mechanism. This is a minimum security mechanism and is not very robust. As a result, control operations are generally performed via Telnet. While this is still not very secure (passwords are transmitted on the wire in clear text), it does provide a greater measure of protection, one that is at least consistent with the security found in most systems in the Internet environment. Some specific Internet MIBs provide additional access control via the community name.

⸱plication Functionality

Both ITU-T/OSI and SNMP provide functionality that can be used as the basis for management application development. However, the different approaches taken by ISO and IETF (Internet Engineering Task Force) affect the way functionality is provided to applications. ISO defines a set of ITU-T/OSI systems management functions which provide functionality common to a number of applications. ITU-T/OSI functions are typically represented as "management support" managed objects. In the SNMP environment, common functions are not defined in this manner. Instead, attributes necessary for these functions are defined on an as-needed basis in specific technology MIBs, without an overall consistent approach.

The following paragraphs briefly describe several areas of functionality that might be offered by management applications. Within each area, relevant ITU-T/OSI and SNMP specifications which assist in providing this application functionality are identified and contrasted.

Configuration Management

Both Internet- and ITU-T/OSI-style object definitions describe configurations that can be manipulated by management protocols. Applications can be developed that use ITU-T/OSI and SNMP to monitor and control the configuration of managed resources.

Both SNMP and CMIP can be used to find and browse new managed device MIBs. CMIP does this via its multiple object selection capabilities, or through the use of Shared Management Knowledge (management support) managed objects. SNMP does this by use of the GetNext command, or through the use of Internet routing and ping protocols. However, retrieving large MIBs with SNMP can be a long and tedious process for the management application, which must navigate the MIB in an orderly fashion, retrieving one object at a time. CMIP allows a management application to perform multiple object selection with a wildcard and thus retrieve the configuration more quickly.

Neither ITU-T/OSI nor SNMP provides facilities to manage the configuration database from a common repository.

Operations Management

There are many cases where a management application would like to activate/start/turn on an object, or deactivate/stop/turn off a protocol entity, test, or such. Often it is useful to create an object, but not activate it. Similarly, it is often useful to deactivate an object without deleting it. Both ITU-T/OSI and SNMP can be used to provide this capability by setting attributes of an object accordingly. In addition, ITU-T/OSI defines a generic state management function that specifies a common (technology-independent) representation for these attributes. Finally, the ITU-T/OSI Generic Management Information MIB defines activate and deactivate actions.

At this point neither CMIP nor SNMP protocols support such operations. Currently, it is necessary to define an attribute of an object that is Set to have the effect of activating or deactivating.

Ultimately, management applications will be expected to provide automated operations. Supporting functions might include simple command scripts and application programming interfaces to allow expert systems to analyze events/traps and automatically initiate operations. This sort of functionality is not currently provided by either ITU-T/OSI or SNMP. For example, managers should have a methodology for automated bypass and recovery from communication failures; without this capability, the availability characteristics of the management system are greatly undermined.

Performance and Accounting Management

Numerous public domain programs are available that measure network response time for TCP/IP networks. None of these tools, however, have been integrated with an SNMP-based network manager. In addition, there are no SNMP protocols that address the performance and accounting aspects of management. However, several technology-specific Internet MIBs include information relevant to performance and accounting. The representation of this information tends to be tailored to the technology being monitored. For example, a MIB often includes a variety of usage counters, and might include tables which store historical or cumulative information.

ITU-T/OSI objects also include this sort of information relevant to performance and accounting management. Often, however, generic counter, threshold, gauge, or tidemark attributes are used to provide a consistent representation across technologies. In addition, several specialized functions are included in ITU-T/OSI which offer more complex capabilities such as workload monitoring, summarization, and account metering. Management applications might use the support-managed objects defined by these ITU-T/OSI functions to offer performance and/or accounting management.

Software Management

SNMP does not address the requirements of a software management system (that is, software distribution, installation, configuration, and so on). Software management solutions for TCP/IP networks are typically supplied by vendors; they are usually implemented on either Network File System (NFS) or File Transfer Protocol (FTP). ITU-T/OSI does not currently address this requirement either, although a new ITU-T/OSI function is under development for this purpose.

Event Management

Most management applications typically include passive and/or active monitoring of managed devices. Passive monitoring is a means of reacting to an event or trap that is received from a monitored component. Active monitoring is a means of issuing commands to resources in predefined time intervals and waiting for a response (usually applied to elements that do not issue an alert when a failure occurs). SNMP supports the passive monitoring process through the use of traps. However, trap messages do not cover every failure scenario possible. The basic idea of SNMP management is that monitoring at any significant level of detail is accomplished primarily by SNMP manager(s) polling for appropriate information. Traps theoretically can guide the timing and focus of the polling, but since SNMP is based on the unreliable UDP, the managers cannot rely on receiving all the traps sent out by the agents. In contrast, ITU-T/OSI tends to be event-driven, with most object definitions including a substantial number of events which may be confirmed at the manager's discretion.

ITU-T/OSI also defines functions which provide selective reporting of events and/or logging of events at the agent system for subsequent retrieval. Applications may use these ITU-T/OSI functions to provide event management.

Problem Management

Most Problem Management applications involve the monitoring of problem-related events (as described in Event Management). SNMP does not monitor and control all physical components of a network. The base span of control is defined by IAB's MIB I and MIB II RFCs, augmented by a number of technology-specific MIBs. It is the responsibility of product developers to extend the functionality of their SNMP agents and to provide information on problem symptoms and probable causes and recommendations for problem resolution.

ITU-T/OSI defines a generic alarm reporting function which specifies a common representation for problem-related events, including codes for problem symptoms and probable causes common to many technologies. These generic alarm reports are designed for inclusion in ITU-T/OSI objects, and may be extended to include additional text or diagnostic information unique to a given product. This facilitates development of generic alarm monitoring applications; these are usually (although not always) passive monitors.

Neither ITU-T/OSI nor SNMP defines a method to track problems and build a knowledge database from user experiences, although ANSI and the Network Management Forum have defined a Trouble Management function, which provides a common format for "trouble tickets" exchanged between management systems. Management systems should allow operators to archive and retrieve historical information, so problems can be tracked and symptoms can be correlated to the respective recovery procedures.

Security Management

Some management applications are responsible for managing the security of the managed network or system resources.

ITU-T/OSI and SNMP can be used to provide this functionality as follows. ITU-T/OSI defines security alarm reporting and audit trail functions which can be used to monitor and record events of interest to the security management application. Similarly, security-related traps can be used with SNMP, although such traps are enterprise-specific and therefore not consistently represented for different products.

The Cost of Implementation

A major concern with Simple Network Management Protocol (SNMP) is the cost of implementation at the management station. SNMP is relatively cheap for an agent. Each new MIB requires unique or altered application code to support. The first application may be cheap, but each additional MIB is added cost. ITU-T/OSI Network Management, with its object-oriented approach, makes the first application relatively expensive. But subsequent additional objects can be added, and level of management provided, to the level supported by the superclass, at a small incremental cost.

Both protocols seem to understand (in somewhat different ways) the role of the management protocol in the overall management architecture. First and foremost, every reasonable attempt should be made to reduce the burden of network management on the agents. The primary task of managed resources is moving user data, not processing network management data. Both the number and complexity of the protocols that the agent must implement should be minimized. Second, it may not be appropriate for all management dialogue to be accomplished by the management protocol. Some aspects of management may be better served by the use of other protocols, especially if it means adding significant complexity to the management protocol to cover the functionality. However, the number of application protocols an agent must implement should be severely limited.

Basically, it is a classic problem of balancing the trade-offs. The management protocol should be simple to implement and use, but sufficiently rich that an agent needs few, if any, other application protocols. Synchronization facilities should be available on an as-needed basis, such that they would not need to be implemented in all agents, or to the same degree in all agents.

Current Use

Since CMIP and SNMP cannot be used to manage without object definitions that represent the resources to be managed, the availability of object definitions gives some indication of the environments in which CMIP and SNMP are currently used. SNMP is used extensively in local area networks, to manage low-level protocol interfaces and devices. CMIP is more popular in the telecommunications industry, as evidenced by the large number of ITU-T/ANSI-defined objects. This interests end users because the reason for using X.700 or SNMP is to manage in a distributed environment. Thus, it is important to understand what protocols tend to be used in that environment today, and what the plans are for coexistence/migration with other protocols. Currently, OSI and Internet-based object definitions are available or under way for a large number of resource technologies.

Conclusions

The SNMP and ITU-T/OSI protocols, and their related technologies and cultures, are both used within the network management community. They each have their place, and it is unlikely that one will eradicate the other. SNMP's strength lies in its simplicity—the low cost of creating management agents. The result of its simplicity is decreased scalability.

CMIP offers more complete functionality, but in doing so has increased the complexity and implementation cost of the management protocol. The protocol has better scalability properties, and its object orientation provides greater flexibility for extending management facilities while creating standards for various aspects of management.

ITU-T/OSI has developed a number of standard interfaces using GDMO. These are in various stages of development, but mark the direction of creating interface standards. Only the simplest of these can be implemented using SNMP, due to its restricted selection of data types and its limited trap facility.

With the proper design, GDMO interfaces may be used to access agents which may transparently communicate with ITU-T/OSI and SNMP resources. Alternatively, application services may access ITU-T/OSI and SNMP resources through somewhat different interfaces, yet hide the differences from the application itself.

With the almost certain coexistence of SNMP and ITU-T/OSI resources, future work should be done to allow applications to be independent of such differences. This is important to create a more uniform management system, where operators need not be aware of irrelevant differences, such as the management protocol used by a particular device.

Chapter Eighteen

Network
Management
Platforms

by Mark Pielocik, BOSE Corporation

ince its inception, network management has grown from managing the physical network, cable, bridges, hubs, and routers to providing a multitude of services such as network administration, diagnostics and control, network performance, trend analysis, configuration management, and security. Installing a low-end network management platform from a network hardware manufacturer could give you reliable management of their hardware (bridges, hubs, and routers) and inform you of the performance of your network. This is done through a proprietary management protocol. The problem with proprietary protocols is that they only manage manufacturer-specific equipment. The integration and management of other manufacturers' networking equipment into these management platforms can be difficult, if not impossible. In some cases this forces the network manager to purchase several platforms in order to manage a heterogeneous networking environment.

The industry push toward an open systems architecture and a network-distributed client/server computing environment has contributed to the evolution of networks. They have become the cornerstone of the corporate computing infrastructure. Enterprise networks, now viewed as a key part of our corporate computing environment, put more of a burden on network managers to control, diagnose, and analyze their networks. The need to see problems as they occur has shifted to a greater aspiration—to identify problems and automatically correct them, and beyond that--to minimize potential problems. Other key goals include the ability to set threshold rates on LAN and WAN segments, to run reports on violations, to view traffic loads at a glance, and to collect and archive data for trend analysis. Also included in this scenario would be the integration of a notification system that would notify the support staff via electronic mail, page, or telephone automatically when problems, excess loads, or other activities occurred that required manager intervention.

This may seem like a lot to ask from a network management platform, but with the constant need for instantaneous information and increasing bandwidth demands, this poses a necessary, if monumental, task for today's network managers.

Management Protocols

Faced with these challenges, the industry has created network management platforms, which are now viewed as *enterprise management solutions*. These management platforms use an open systems architecture and standards-based management protocols to integrate multivendor hardware and systems. Two of these management protocols are Common Management Information Protocol (CMIP) and Simple Network Management Protocol (SNMP). The standardization committee of the International Organization for Standards (ISO) is developing CMIP, and the Internet community is developing SNMP.

There is also a variation of CMIP that runs over TCP/IP, called CMOT (Common Management Protocol Over TCP/IP). Although CMIP has many advantages, there are some drawbacks to this protocol, such as high overhead and the requirement of meeting the approval of the Open Systems Interconnection (OSI) standardization process. Because this process entails comprehensive definition and possible modification prior to approval, CMIP appears to be on the back burner. Despite the hurdles, many manufacturers are putting substantial dollars into the research and development of this protocol, and numerous enterprise network management platforms will support both SNMP and CMIP. With the availability of specifications designed to allow interoperability between management platforms using SNMP and CMIP, it could prove to be a seamless migration path to the management protocol standard for the future CMIP.

SNMP has been widely adopted as a *de facto* industry management standard. The Internet community uses it to manage TCP/IP over both LANs and WANs, probably due to its easy implementation. SNMP uses less memory and CPU resources than CMIP, and has proven itself to be a viable solution for managing multivendor networks. Another advantage SNMP has over CMIP is that it is transmitted using the highly efficient UDP (User Datagram Protocol) in the IP protocol stack.

UDP is a connectionless transport protocol that does not require the pre-establishment of a communication session for the management station to receive information about a device in the network. Using the standards-based protocol approach can be beneficial—one single management platform can perform network administration, performance measurements, diagnoses, control configurations, and can also set security levels. And with the development of SNMP-II, there will be some new features, such as manager-to-manager communication, bulk data transfers, and security capabilities that will prevent unauthorized users from tampering with network devices.

SNMP-II has many skeptics who feel that the increased cost to integrate it into network devices is not justified, and that there could be problems with mismatched security configurations, making it possible to lock yourself out of managing a device. However, many networking vendors are committed to its development. Some management platforms will incorporate a configuration manager to address some of these issues. In fact, several database companies have formed a group to define and develop an SNMP Management Information Base (MIB) that will allow the network management platform to track availability, performance, configuration, and other information using the SNMP-II protocol. SNMP-II's features will allow the sharing of more information between the management platforms and the database, making it easier to integrate.

Another emerging standard is the RMON (Remote Monitoring of Networks) MIB that runs with SNMP. Some of the features of RMON are segment statistics, trend analysis, alarm thresholds, event logging, host statistics, and packet capture. These features are being deployed as stand-alone probes for the network, and some hardware vendors are incorporating them into their products. Keep in mind, however, that these features utilize many CPU cycles; if the hardware vendor does not have a processor that is powerful enough to handle the additional load, network performance may suffer.

Network Management Platforms

Significant strides have been made with network management platforms in the past few years. Although all of the network management specifications have not been defined, users have an immediate need to implement a solution—one that will evolve with the standards as they are defined *and* that can seamlessly migrate to the new standards. To accomplish all these tasks would be a major undertaking for any one vendor. Thus, an entire enterprise management solution may come from a multitude of third-party software vendors that integrate with the core management platform to perform specific functions. These third-party software packages may or may not utilize the standard management protocols. If they do not, the enterprise management platform must find an alternative means to interface with these applications through external protocol gateways or application programming interfaces (API). True enterprise management platforms should be able to accommodate these third-party vendors.

It is important to purchase a solution that will fully integrate into the systems that you choose. For example, if you have a management platform that can identify problems on the network and report on them, you may choose to integrate a trouble-ticketing system that will automatically dispatch a repairperson when a problem has been detected. You also could integrate an asset management database that would include device locations, serial numbers, software revision numbers, network connections, and any other pertinent data. As the trouble ticket is being issued, all this data would be printed automatically.

Other features to look for are system management tools that will allow the management station to monitor systems for memory and disk space usage, processor health on the CPU, available applications, and security violations. These tools will allow thresholds to be set and reported on, and automated actions to be taken. A network management platform encompassing many or all of these features may seem too expensive; however, with the value of information resources increasing, we can't afford *not* to optimize the management of these resources. Average network downtime in a large business environment is estimated to cost from $5000 to $7000 an hour in lost productivity, and can be justification enough to purchase such a platform.

There are many solutions on the market today. We will be looking at some of the leading industry enterprise management platforms: Hewlett Packard's OpenView Network Node Manager, Digital Equipment's Polycenter, Cabletron Systems' Spectrum, IBM's NetView/6000, and SunConnect's SunNet Manager. HP, IBM, and DEC offer solutions along with their enterprise network management platforms as a means to manage their own proprietary equipment, regardless of the management protocol that is running on them. Cabletron appears to be the only hardware vendor that dares venture into the enterprise management solution.

CAUTION: *If you are looking for enterprise management solutions, be sure to choose wisely. These are not management solutions that can be discarded as standards change—they are poised to change with the times and be your solution for years to come. Be sure to identify the strategic direction of the company that you choose, and make sure that it fits in line with the path of your own network.*

ewlett Packard's OpenView Network
ode Manager

At the time of this writing, OpenView boasts the top-of-the-chart rating as far as installed base and third-party vendor partnerships and support. Network Node Manager is based on the industry standard management protocol, SNMP. It supports all leading management interconnection applications, allowing the preservation of existing assets. This allows Network Node Manager to manage thousands of devices in a heterogeneous network from one workstation. It also supports application integration, which allows data to be displayed in a common format, and multiple network applications to coexist in a single environment. Network Node Manager can also manage the HP3000 series minicomputers.

Network Node Manager supports autodiscovery, which automatically locates IP devices on the network and displays them. Dual topology management is also supported so managers can see multiple topology types displayed on the screen. Network Node Manager can incorporate HP's OpenView Probe Manager, which "bolts on" to it, giving it extensive LAN diagnostics and mapping functions to both Ethernet and token ring networks. Diagnostic probes can be placed on various LAN segments, and Probe Manager can trigger alarms on previously set utilization thresholds, perform real-time statistics and measurement, and display information about those thresholds, statistics, and measurements in an easy-to-read format. Data from six probes can be displayed at one time with all Ethernet statistics on one graph and the token ring information displayed on another. Historical statistics can be stored and exported to a tab-separated variable file format to be read into various spreadsheet programs. These reports can be scheduled on a daily, weekly, monthly, quarterly, or semiannual basis. Host statistics can be displayed in graphical formats by user-defined node name or by media access control protocol (MAC) address. Probe Manager can display data packets sent and received, broadcasts, multicasts, and errors, including non-IP nodes that cannot report statistics to Network Node Manager.

Other features include a resource manager that has a real-time display of traffic and errors for the entire enterprise network, in a radar chart format. This feature can guide you to problem segments in your network and warn you of potential problems. The history analyzer collects data for an extended time, allowing traffic studies to be performed for capacity planning or network optimization. Also available is a traffic expert that can scan all the historical network traffic and recommend actions for optimizing traffic.

Network Node Manager supports a multitude of third-party software solutions to assist in the management of UNIX-based operating systems by reporting on disk space memory usage, CPU cycles, and other various systemwide parameters. An agent is placed on the machine to perform the data collection and report back to the Network Node Manager. This integration allows a single management station to know the status of the network and the systems that are using it. HP has partnered with several hardware manufacturers that have ported their MIB information to Network Node Manager, allowing it to manage their equipment. Network Node Manager supports RMON and HP's Netmatrix. (Netmatrix is software that can reside on any local or remote UNIX machine, gather data on the network, and report back to the management station on the condition of the LAN.) Network Node Manager can be run on HP/UNIX and Sun UNIX machines.

Network Node Manager and its numerous third-party vendors make it an attractive solution for an enterprise network management platform.

Digital Equipment Corporation's Polycenter on NetView

Polycenter is a comprehensive network management solution for heterogeneous multivendor devices and open networks requiring SNMP. It includes both user-oriented SNMP applications for fault, configuration, and performance management; and standard application programming interfaces (APIs) that allow third-party software vendors to integrate their applications. This provides Polycenter with a wide range of services including network management, asset/configuration management, problem/fault management, and management of storage, security, accounting/billing, and performance/capacity.

Polycenter incorporates guidelines and definitions that programmers need in order to create SNMP or CMIP applications for end-to-end management. The SNMP API enables applications to access the MIB information. MIB processing includes support for MIB II and many preloaded vendor extensions, as well as the MIB loader to allow any enterprise-specific MIB extension to be added. The MIB Application Builder allows the development of applications without programming. The MIB Browser allows browsing, retrieving, or setting of MIB values.

The Graphical User Interface (GUI) provides features such as single-glance view of network status, a topology view that displays network maps, a control desk display to view network events, a tool palette that provides fast and easy access to frequently used tools, and a navigation tree. The network view can be configured to be viewed by geographical location and physical or logical layouts. It can also display real-time and historical graphs on network statistics.

Polycenter offers automatic network discovery, which continues to find new devices on the network as they are added. It logically places these IP-addressable nodes where they belong on the map. This feature ensures that the network map is up to date. It also allows you to save network map snapshots to compare with future maps, and to print these maps as an aid in problem resolution.

Polycenter has filtering capabilities that help weed out extraneous information and provide greater control. Polycenter automates actions to be taken as a result of SNMP traps. It also provides real-time administrative change capability, allowing changes in operational parameters without interrupting the ongoing data collection. Also provided is a topology manager that allows not only SNMP, but multiple protocols, to be integrated in the topology map and event displays.

One of the more significant bolt-on features of Polycenter is PathDoctor. This is an interactive network management application tool that can diagnose a problem from end to end, across LAN and WAN links. It automatically traces the path through both forward and reverse routes, and visually displays by color code any device that is bad or suspect. This product works best with Digital, Cisco, Wellfleet, IBM, Proteon, or 3Com routers.

Polycenter on NetView is a full-featured enterprise network management solution.

abletron Systems' Spectrum

Spectrum is an enterprise network management platform that uses SNMP, CMIP, and external protocols. Spectrum utilizes object-oriented design and inductive modeling, a form of artificial intelligence, to sort through the alarms and pinpoint the trouble location rapidly, allowing Spectrum to monitor unintelligent devices. This form of artificial intelligence is how Spectrum promotes rapid fault isolation through alarm suppressions on devices that are not the root of the problems. Spectrum's object-oriented programming allows network managers to customize network statistics to display information within a pop-up window. Network parameters can be displayed by a specific object or object type (single router or all routers). This feature allows network managers to view specific detailed information by pointing and clicking. Spectrum also has an MIB browser feature that allows the network manager to display the MIB information contained in a network device.

The latest release of Spectrum is the industry's first distributed enterprise network management system. Multiple servers can be distributed throughout the network gathering data, and single or multiple GUIs can view the data. This true client/server architectural approach to network management allows multiple users at distributed sites to share information on a common network management database. Extensive security features allow Spectrum to highly define the accessibility of the server to clients. The client/server architecture allows a scalable approach to network management and the capability for network management redundancy.

Spectrum supports five platforms with the same GUI, promoting standardized network management. The ease of use of Spectrum's GUI allows even nontechnical personnel the ability to navigate through the network to identify problems. The multiple view within Spectrum's GUI environment allows the modeling of a network with the various views in multiple layers. The location view can define exact locations of devices from maps to a building by integrating building floor plans. The topology view puts devices in a logical representation of the network. The organization view allows the grouping of network devices in an organizational hierarchy. Spectrum also has a repairperson view that can assign a repairperson when a problem has been detected. This is especially effective in a distributed environment that allows multiple management stations to view who is working on what problem.

Spectrum can generate reports on screen and export data for presentations or future analysis. Spectrum employs an open systems gateway and Distributed LAN Monitoring (DLM). The open systems gateway allows Spectrum to report significant events on devices that occur on other network management platforms. This gives Spectrum the ability to integrate existing network management platforms, allowing them to continue to manage their current devices and share the problems with Spectrum. The DLM is a firmware application available on Cabletron's intelligent network hubs. With this approach, Spectrum can configure DLM devices to monitor other devices on remote LANs and only report on them when a threshold or condition change has taken place. This greatly reduces overall network management traffic and leaves the bandwidth available for other purposes.

The latest release of Spectrum extends the scope of enterprise network management to encompass not only LANs and WANs, but also telephony, PBX management, ATM, and connection-oriented systems.

Spectrum, like other network management platforms, employs a third-party partners program to extend its management by integrating other applications to provide an enterprise network management solution. Cabletron will be working with the University of Maryland to develop a PBX management application for Spectrum. Spectrum's artificial intelligence network models could prove to be very useful in managing PBX systems.

Another third-party solution is Calypso Software's Maestrovision, which is integrated with Spectrum for monitoring and management of UNIX machines. The Maestrovision management agent is based on SNMP and resides on a UNIX platform. Thresholds can be configured to include disk space, CPU utilization, memory and swap space usage, and application management. This agent poses very little overhead to the CPU and no network traffic until the thresholds are met or the management station performs a real-time query into the health of the systems. This approach is another means of reducing management-related network traffic. Cabletron has incorporated support of RMON into their hubs and supports other RMON implementation for Spectrum.

Cabletron's Spectrum product is a very versatile, easy-to-use network management platform that pushes the envelope of enterprise network management.

IBM's NetView/6000

IBM and Digital Equipment combined their network management platforms and formed an alliance of third-party vendors to support both platforms. NetView/6000 is an SNMP- and CMIP-based network management platform that runs on IBM's AIX. NetView/6000 is a graphical object-oriented system that supports X-Window and Motif Windows Manager. IBM is developing this software to be ported to other hardware platforms such as DEC's OSF/1 and Sun Microsystems' Solaris.

NetView/6000 supports application programming interfaces. This will allow continued support from third-party vendors that want to port their applications to NetView/6000. The new version of NetView/6000 incorporates a dynamic network discovery feature that updates network topology maps. It supports IBM's RMON agent (RMONster/6000), which allows NetView/6000 to monitor all nine groups of the RMON standard, as well as the token ring LAN extensions. This means that NetView/6000 can monitor local and remote network performance. IBM will provide support for other manufacturers' RMON agents as well.

NetView/6000 features include alarm and event logging, which logs alarms and events as they occur; alert editor, which allows the customization of alarm levels to be sent by devices; and NetView hub manager, which provides extensive management for IBM 8250 multiprotocol intelligent hubs. NetView/6000 is also a threshold-monitoring system, which allows a network manager to predetermine the threshold of error and percent of network usage, along with other parameters, and configure them on an SNMP-compliant device on the network. When the thresholds have been exceeded, NetView/6000 will report on them.

NetView/6000 can gather historical SNMP MIB information via its MIB data collector. This information can be printed in ASCII format or exported into a spreadsheet for data trend analysis.

ınConnect SunNet Manager

SunNet Manager is an object-oriented database that runs under Open Windows and supports X11 protocols for managing SNMP devices in a heterogeneous network. SunNet Manager allows its console and other applications windows to display information on an X-Terminal, providing that they are attached to a server that supports MIT X11 release 4. SunNet Manager also utilizes service through APIs.

SunNet Manager is comprised of multiple processes that together are the management platform. The core of the system is Manager Services, the management database where information regarding the network and its components resides. Information gathered through SNMP agents are stored here, and the information can be accessed by the console.

The console, through Open Windows, provides a GUI into SunNet Manager that enables you to access data or request the collection of data. Event logs can be viewed through the browser, and the results can be displayed in a graphical format. The console can initiate a discovery of devices on the network, display them in a graphical representation, and add them to the database. The console has a set tool that allows value changes to be made to SNMP attributes. You can change the background raster file to allow customized views within the console.

Features of SunNet Manager include alarm report displays, which display the number and priority of events or SNMP traps that may occur in the network; event/trap reports, which display event reports as well as traps that contain the time the event occurred, the name of the device, and the attribute name; error reports; and event summaries. SunNet Manager allows the integration of other tools, such as a trouble-ticketing, configuration management, performance analysis, accounting, sand security management services.

SunNet Manager is a well-rounded set of network management tools for managing devices in a TCP/IP environment.

Summary

An enterprise network management platform is going to be a platform that you can rely on to maintain the integrity of your network. Do your homework—investigate these and other packages that are available. Know your company's strategic direction and identify how an enterprise network management platform will help keep your network up and running. Look at the third-party alliances that make sense for your situation. These solutions may be expensive, but the bolt-on approach allows you the flexibility to implement your solutions in phases—and network downtime is lost revenue. Enterprise network management platforms have been created because network managers require these tools to keep their growing heterogeneous networks up and running. Network management is more than insurance; it is an investment in maintaining the network infrastructure.

Index

NFS (Network File System), ONC and ONC+, 82, 228
NICs (network interface cards), 4, 11-12
NIS and NIS+ (Network Information Service), ONC and ONC+, 229
NLSP (NetWare Link Services Protocol), 173-174
NNTP protocol, 142
Nodes, 11, 99-100, 105-106
Nonrepudiation services, 26
NOSs. *See* Network Operating Systems
Novell
    Message Handling Service (MHS), 259, 298, 301, 307
    and workgroup technologies, 332-333
    See also NetWare
NT File System (NTFS), 235
NTP protocol, 142
NVP-II protocol, 142

O

Object Management Group (OMG) CORBA standard, 287-288
Object names, ITU-T/OSI protocol and, 350
Object technologies, 20, 278-279
    benefits of, 283-286
    challenges posed by, 286-287
    Common Object Request Broker Architecture (CORBA) standard, 287-288
    Component Integration Laboratories (CIL) model, 289
    future of, 290-291
    how objects work, 279-283
    networks and, 20
    NeXTStep interface and, 289-290
    Object Linking and Embedding (OLE), 217-218, 288
    Object Management Group (OMG) standard, 287-288
    object-based workflow software, 323
    OpenDoc compound document architecture, 289
    SOM (System Object Model) and DSOM (Distributed System Object Model), 289
Object-oriented management information model, ITU-T/OSI protocol and, 350-351, 355
Objects, in SNMP versus ITU-T/OSI, 355
ODBC (Open Database Connectivity), 257, 266, 329
OfficeVision/MVS software, 328
OIM (OSI Internet Management), SNMP and, 345-346
OLE (Object Linking and Embedding), 217-218, 288
OMG (Object Management Group) CORBA standard, 287-288
ONC. *See* Open Network Computing (ONC and ONC+)
Online services, e-mail and, 303-304, 310
Open Database Connectivity (ODBC), 257, 266, 329
Open Data-link Interface (ODI), 11, 85, 166, 181
Open Desktop operating system, 238
Open Network Computing (ONC and ONC+), 226-229
Open Server operating systems, 238
Open Shortest Path First (OSPF) protocol, 142, 148
Open Software Foundation (OSF). *See* Distributed Computing Environment (DCE)
Open System Interconnection (OSI) Reference Model, 70-71
    AppleTalk protocol suite and, 86-88
    Application layer, 72
    Data Link layer, 71-72, 75, 178-181

DEC products, 119-121, 126,
end systems (ES), 70-71
IEEE 802 standard and, 177-178, 179, 180
intermediate systems (IS), 70-71
layering and, 115
Microsoft LAN Manager and, 72, 88-90
NetWare support for, 169
Network layer, 72, 181-182
Physical layer, 71, 74, 75
Presentation layer, 72
protocol layer interaction, 73-75, 182
OpenDoc compound document architecture, 289
OpenMail software, 303
OpenView Network Node Manager, 367-368
Operating systems. *See* Infrastructure technologies; LAN Manager; NetWare; Network Operating Systems (NOSs); Server operating systems
Operational transparency, 268
Operations management, in SNMP versus ITU-T/OSI, 357-358
Operations on multiple objects, in SNMP versus ITU-T/OSI, 353-354
Optimizers, for distributed databases, 274
Oracle database software, 251, 253, 255-256
Oracle Mail software, 304
Oracle Office software, 331-332
ORBs (object request brokers), 282-283. *See also* Object technologies
OS/2
    client/server systems and, 250, 251
    LAN Workplace Shell, 215-216
    NetWare support for, 169, 170
OSF (Open Software Foundation). *See* Distributed Computing Environment (DCE)
OSI Internet Management (OIM), SNMP and, 345-346
OSPF (Open Shortest Path First) protocol, 142, 148

P

Pacing algorithms, in SNA, 95
Packet assembler/disassemblers (PADs), 60-61
Packet Burst protocol, NetWare, 172
Packets, in OSI Reference Model, 74-75
Packet-switching, 50, 136-137
PAP (Printer Access Protocol), AppleTalk, 88, 168
Paradox SQL Links, 257
Parallel processing, in distributed databases, 274
Partitioned schemas, for distributed databases, 270-27
    273
Path Control Network software, 77
Pathway Messaging software, 306
PATHWORKS products (DEC), 121-123, 130
PC Anywhere software, 51
PCIs (protocol control information), in OSI Reference Model, 73-74
PC-NFS, ONC and ONC+, 228
PDUs (protocol data units)
    in ITU-T/OSI protocol, 348, 349
    in OSI Reference Model, 73-75, 178
    in SNMP, 343-344
Performance
    asynchronous communications and, 53
    of cabling, 13, 14, 15
    of client/server systems, 249
    in mainframe and minicomputer environment

Q

R

MAKE THE RIGHT Connection

IT'S WHAT YOU KNOW THAT COUNTS.
WITH INNOVATIVE BOOKS FROM LAN TIMES
AND OSBORNE/McGRAW-HILL, YOU'LL BE
THE ONE IN DEMAND.

**LAN TIMES
ENCYCLOPEDIA OF
NETWORKING**
BY TOM SHELDON
AN AUTHORITATIVE
REFERENCE ON ALL
NETWORKING FACETS
AND TRENDS.
$39.95
ISBN: 0-07-881965-2
AVAILABLE NOW

**LAN TIMES
GUIDE TO SQL**
BY JAMES R. GROFF AND
PAUL N. WEINBERG
$29.95
ISBN: 0-07-882026-X
AVAILABLE NOW

**LAN TIMES E-MAIL
RESOURCE GUIDE**
BY RICK DRUMMOND
$29.95
ISBN: 0-07-882052-9
AVAILABLE JUNE

**LAN TIMES GUIDE
TO INTEROPERABILITY**
BY FRANK HAYES
AND RICK STOUT
$29.95
ISBN: 0-07-882043-X
AVAILABLE JULY

Think Fast

PASSING LANE AHEAD

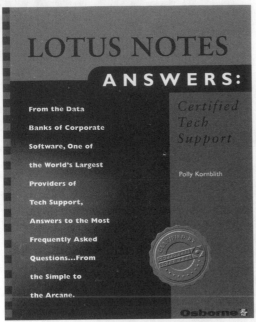

Lotus Notes Answere: Certified Tech Support
by Polly Russell Kornblith
$16.95
ISBN: 0-07-882055-3

What's the quickest route to tech support? Os
new Certified Tech Support series. Develo
conjunction with Corporate Software Inc., one
largest providers of tech support fielding mo
200,000 calls a month, Osborne delivers th
authoritative question & answer books a
anywhere. Speed up your computing and stay in
with answers to the most frequently asked e
questions— from the simple to the arcane. An
for more books int the series.

**The Internet
Yellow Pages**
by Harley Hahn
and Rick Stout
$27.95
ISBN: 0-07-882023-5

**Sound Blaster:
The Official Book,
Second Edition**
by Peter M. Ridge,
David Golden, Ivan Luk,
Scott Sindorf, and
Richard Heimlich.
Includes 3.5-Inch Disk.
$34.95
ISBN: 0-07-8820oo-6

**Osborne Windows
Programming Series**
by Herbert Schildt
Chris H. Pappas, and
William H. Murray, Ill.
**Vol. I - Programming
Fundamentals $39.95**
ISBN: 0-07-881990-3
**Vol. 2 - General
Purpose API
Functions $49.95**
ISBN: 0-07-881991-1
**Vol. 3 - Special
Purpose API
Functions $49.95**

**The Microsoft Access
Handbook**
by Mary Campbell
$27.95
ISBN: 0-07-882014-6

ORDER BOOKS DIRECTLY FROM OSBORNE/MC GRAW-H

For a complete catalog of Osborne's books, call 510-549-6600 or write to us at 2600 Tenth Street, Berkeley, CA

Call Toll-Free: 1-800-822-8158
24 hours a day, 7 days a week
in U.S. and Canada

Mail this order form to:
McGraw-Hill, Inc.
Blue Ridge Summit, PA 17294-0840

Fax this order form to:
717-794-5291

EMAIL
7007.1531@COMPUSERVE.COM
COMPUSERVE GO MH

Ship to:

Name _____

Company _____

Address _____

City / State / Zip _____

Daytime Telephone: _____
(We'll contact you if there's a question about your orde

ISBN #	BOOK TITLE	Quantity	Price	T
0-07-88				
0-07-88				
0-07-88				
0-07-88				
0-07-88				
0-07088				
0-07-88				
0-07-88				
0-07-88				
0-07-88				
0-07-88				
0-07-88				
0-07-88				

Shipping & Handling Charge from Chart Below

Subtotal

Please Add Applicable State & Local Sales Tax

TOTAL

Shipping & Handling Charges

Order Amount	U.S.	Outside U.S.
Less than $15	$3.45	$5.25
$15.00 - $24.99	$3.95	$5.95
$25.00 - $49.99	$4.95	$6.95
$50.00 - and up	$5.95	$7.95

Occasionally we allow other selected companies to use our mailing list. If you would prefer that we not include you in these extra mailings, please check here: ☐

METHOD OF PAYMENT

☐ Check or money order enclosed (payable to Osborne/McGrav

☐ AMERICAN EXPRESS   ☐ DISCOVER   ☐ MasterCard.   ☐ VISA

Account No. ☐☐☐☐☐☐☐☐☐☐☐☐☐☐☐☐

Expiration Date _____

Signature _____

In a hurry? Call 1-800-822-8158 anytime, day or night, or visit your local books

Thank you for your order

Code BC64

AN TIMES Free Subscription Form

es, I want to receive (continue to receive) LAN TIMES free of charge.   ◯ No.

◯ a new subscriber   ◯ renewing my subscription   ◯ changing my address

...re required _____ Date _____	**Free in the United States to qualified subscribers only**
_____	International Prices (Airmail Delivery)
_____ Telephone _____	Canada: $65 Elsewhere: $150
...any _____	◯ Payment enclosed ◯ Bill me later
...ss _____	Charge my: ◯ Visa ◯ Mastercard ◯ Amer. Exp
_____	Card number _____
...County _____ Zip/Postal Code _____	Exp. Date _____

...stions must be completed to qualify for a subscription to LAN TIMES. Publisher reserves the right to serve only those individuals who meet publication criteria.

...h of the following best describe your organization?

...ck only one)
- Agriculture/Mining/Construction/Oil/Petrochemical/Environmental
- Manufacturer (non-computer)
- Government/Military/Public Adm.
- Education
- Research/Development
- Engineering/Architecture
- Finance/Banking/Accounting/Insurance/Real Estate
- Health/Medical/Legal
- VAR/VAD Systems House
- Manufacturer Computer Hardware/Software
- Aerospace
- Retailer/Distributor/Wholesaler (non-computer)
- Computer Retailer/Distributor/Sales
- Transportation
- Media/Marketing/Advertising/Publishing/Broadcasting
- Utilities/Telecommunications/VAN
- Entertainment/Recreation/Hospitality/Non-profit/Trade
- Association
- Consultant
- Systems Integrator
- Computer/LAN Leasing/Training
- Information/Data Services
- Computer/Communications Services: Outsourcing/3rd Party
- All Other Business Services
- Other _____

...ich best describes your title? (Check only one)
- Network/LAN Manager
- MIS/DP/IS Manager
- Owner/President/CEO/Partner
- Data Communications Manager
- Engineer/CNE/Technician
- Consultant/Analyst
- Micro Manager/Specialist/Coordinator
- Vice President
- All other Dept. Heads, Directors and Managers
- Educator
- Programmer/Systems Analyst
- Professional
- Other_____

...hich of the following best describes your job function?

...ck only one)
- Network/LAN Management
- MIS/DP/IS Management
- Systems Engineering/Integration
- Administration/Management
- Technical Services
- Consulting
- Research/Development
- Sales/Marketing
- Accounting/Finance
- Education/Training

- ◯ K. Office Automation
- ◯ L. Manufacturing/Operations/Production
- ◯ M. Personnel
- ◯ N. Technology Assessment
- ◯ O. Other _____

4. How many employees work in your entire ORGANIZATION?

(Check only one)
- ◯ A. Under 25
- ◯ B. 25-100
- ◯ C. 101 500
- ◯ D. 501 1,000
- ◯ E. 1,001-5,000
- ◯ F. 5,001-9,999
- ◯ G. 10,000 and over

5. Which of the following are you or your clients currently using, or planning to purchase in the next 12 months? (1–Own; 2–Plan to purchase in next 12 months) (Check all that apply)

Topologies	1	2
A. Ethernet	◯	◯
B. Token Ring	◯	◯
C. Arcnet	◯	◯
D. LocalTalk	◯	◯
E. FDDI	◯	◯
F. Starlan	◯	◯
G. Other	◯	◯

Network Operating System	1	2
A. Novell Netware	◯	◯
B. Novell Netware Lite	◯	◯
C. Banyan VINES	◯	◯
D. Digital Pathworks	◯	◯
E. IBM LAN Server	◯	◯
F. Microsoft LAN Manager	◯	◯
G. Microsoft Windows for Workgroups	◯	◯
H. Artisoft LANtastic	◯	◯
I. Sitka TOPS	◯	◯
J. 10NET	◯	◯
K. AppleTalk	◯	◯

Client/Workstation Operating Sys.	1	2
A. DOS	◯	◯
B. DR-DOS	◯	◯
C. Windows	◯	◯
D. Windows NT	◯	◯
E. UNIX	◯	◯
F. UnixWare	◯	◯
G. OS/2	◯	◯
H. Mac System 6	◯	◯
I. Mac System 7	◯	◯

Protocols/Standards	1	2
A. IPX	◯	◯
B. TCP/IP	◯	◯
C. X.25	◯	◯
D. XNS	◯	◯
E. OSI	◯	◯
F. SAA/SNA	◯	◯
G. NFS	◯	◯
H. MHS	◯	◯

6. Is your Organization/Clients network... (Check all that apply)

- A. International
- B. National
- C. Regional
- D. Metropolitan
- E. Local
- F. Other _____

7. What hardware does your department/client base own/plan to purchase. (Check all that apply)

	Owns	Plan to purchase in next 12 months
A. Bridges	○	○
B. Diskless Workstations	○	○
C. Cabling System	○	○
D. Printers	○	○
E. Disk Drive	○	○
F. Optical Storage	○	○
G. Tape Backup System	○	○
H. Optical Storage	○	○
I. Application Servers	○	○
J. Communication Servers	○	○
K. Fax Servers	○	○
L. Mainframe	○	○
M. Network Adapter Cards	○	○
N. Wireless Adapters/Bridges	○	○
O. Power Conditioners/UPSs	○	○
P. Hubs/Concentrators	○	○
Q. Minicomputers	○	○
R. Modems	○	○
S. 386-based computers	○	○
T. 486-based computers	○	○
U. Pentium-based computers	○	○
V. Macintosh computers	○	○
W. RISC-based workstations	○	○
X. Routers	○	○
Y. Multimedia Cards	○	○
Z. Network Test/Diagnostic Equipment	○	○
1. Notebooks/Laptops	○	○
2. DSU/CSU	○	○
99. None of the Above	○	○

8. What network software/applications do you/your clients own/plan to purchase in the next 12 months? (Check all that apply)

- A. Network Management
- B. Software Metering
- C. Network Inventory
- D. Virus Protection
- E. Menuing
- F. E-mail
- G. Word Processing
- H. Spreadsheet
- I. Database
- J. Accounting
- K. Document Management
- L. Graphics
- M. Communications
- N. Application Development Tools
- O. Desktop Publishing
- P. Integrated Business Applications
- Q. Multimedia
- R. Document Imaging
- S. Groupware
- Z. None of the above

9. What is the annual revenue of your entire organization or budget if non-profit (Check only one)

- A. Under $10 million
- B. $10-$50 million
- C. $50-$100 million
- D. $100-$500 million
- E. $500 million-$1 billion
- F. Over $1 billion

10. How much does your organization (if reseller, your largest client's company) plan to spend on computer products in the next 12 months? (Check only one)

- A. Under $25,000
- B. $25,000-$99,999
- C. $100,000-$499,999
- D. $500,000-$999,999
- E. $1 billion

11. Where do you purchase computer products? (Check all that apply)

- A. Manufacturer
- B. Distributor
- C. Reseller
- D. VAR
- E. System Integrator
- F. Consultant
- G. Other _____

12. In which ways are you involved in acquiring computer products and services? (Check all that apply)

- A. Determine the need
- B. Define product specifications/features
- C. Select brand
- D. Evaluate the supplier
- E. Select vendor/source
- F. Approve the acquisition
- G. None of the above

ICS1639

---

fold here

LAN TIMES

McGraw–Hill, INC.

P.O. Box 652

Hightstown NJ 08520-0652